VISIONS OF VIRTUE
IN TOKUGAWA JAPAN

堂德懷

The ideographs for the Kaitokudō Merchant Academy of Osaka.

VISIONS OF VIRTUE
IN TOKUGAWA JAPAN
THE KAITOKUDŌ
MERCHANT ACADEMY OF OSAKA

Tetsuo Najita

UNIVERSITY OF HAWAI'I PRESS

HONOLULU

Tetsuo Najita is Robert S. Ingersoll Distinguished Service Professor of
Japanese Studies at the University of Chicago.
He is the author of *Japan: The Intellectual Foundation of Modern Japanese
Politics* and the editor, with Irwin Scheiner, of *Japanese Thought in the
Tokugawa Period (1600–1868)*.

© 1987 The University of Chicago Press
Published by The University of Chicago Press 1987
Published by University of Hawai'i Press 1997

Library of Congress Cataloging-in-Publication Data
Najita, Tetsuo.
Visions of virtue in Tokugawa Japan : the Kaitokudō
Merchant Academy of Osaka / Tetsuo Najita.
p.   cm.
Originally published: Chicago : University of Chicago Press, 1987.
Includes bibliographical references and index.
ISBN 0-8248-1991-8 (pbk.)
1. Japan—Intellectual life—1600-1868.   2. Merchants—
Japan—History.   3.   Social sciences—Japan—History.
4. Kaitokudō—History. I. Title.
DS822.2.N28   1997
650'.071'5—dc21   97–15881
CIP

Cover design by Santos B. Barbasa

In memory of my parents,
Kikuno and Niichi Najita

CONTENTS

ACKNOWLEDGMENTS

A study tends to lose its real "beginning" as it takes on the shape of a book. My study began where the book nears its end, with a curiosity about Yamagata Bantō. That this author of the well-known classic, *In Place of Dreams (Yume no shiro)*, was one and the same person as the financier known throughout the Osaka merchant community as Masuya Kouemon, who was closely observed by the eccentric intellectual Kaiho Seiryō, led me to the Osaka Merchant Academy, the Kaitokudō, where he had studied. Yamagata Bantō emerges at the outer extremity of an intellectual metamorphosis at this academy that spans the eighteenth century.

Drawn to Osaka and especially to Osaka University where the Kaitokudō archive is located, I was given encouragement and support by colleagues there. Shiba Yoshinobu arranged for a seminar in which I could set forth some preliminary ideas that I had. Sakudo Yotaro and Suenaka Tetsuo took me on a most memorable tour of the area in Osaka where the academy once stood. Koyasu Nobukuni, Kobori Kazumasa, and Yamanaka Hiroyuki shared their intimate knowledge of the subject. Wakita Osamu kindly read the completed draft in its entirety and offered thoughtful and detailed comments.

In the course of shaping the study, I benefited greatly from conversations with Akagi Akio, Amino Yoshihiko, Hino Tatsuo, Maeda Ai, Matsumoto Sannosuke, Miyagi Kimiko, Sakai Yukichi, and Wakita Haruko. My colleagues Masao Miyoshi, Irwin Scheiner, and especially Harry Harootunian accompanied me through the study more than once. My wife Elinor commented on substance and style.

I received generous fellowships from the National Endowment for the Humanities and the Guggenheim Foundation. I am also grateful to the Center for East Asian Studies at the University of Chicago for research support. The ideographs for the academy, used for the frontispiece, are from a photoprint, courtesy of the Kaitokudō tomo no kai—Kaitokudō Association of Friends.

O N E

☐ PROLOGUE ☐

ON THE SIDE OF AN IMPOSING MODERN BUILDING IN
THE CENTER OF DOWNTOWN OSAKA—THE HIGASHI-KU OR
EAST DISTRICT—A SMALL, ODD-SHAPED, STONE SLAB INSCRIBED WITH AR-
chaic Chinese ideographs marks the site where the Osaka Merchant
Academy once stood. The Kaitokudō flourished during the eighteenth
century of the Tokugawa era (1600–1868). With the demise of the
Tokugawa Bakufu in 1868, the academy, chartered by that regime, also
closed its gates to further instruction.

In the early 1900s, after Japan's industrial revolution was well under
way, the memory of the Kaitokudō was revived by leading intellectuals
and writers such as Kōda Rohan (1867–1947), Naitō Konan (1866–
1934), and Nishimura Tenshū (1867–1924). Nishimura, an aficionado
of Chinese intellectual history and feature editor of the prestigious newspaper *Asahi*, was especially instrumental in this effort. His public lecture
in 1910 on Goi Ranju's (1697–1762) contribution rekindled the interest of Osaka's intellectual and business communities in the Kaitokudō.
A commemorative association of "friends" was formed to sponsor regular
meetings, and the lectures and proceedings from these meetings were
published in the journal *Kaitoku*. With funds provided by Sumitomo and
other Osaka commercial houses, all seeking no doubt to reclaim an intellectual history out of twentieth century, postindustrial needs, the
academy was renovated to resemble its former dignified self. Tragically
destroyed by the firebombings toward the end of the Pacific War, the
academy has not been rebuilt. Its impressive library, however, which
somehow survived the fires of war, is housed as a research archive at
Osaka University. Although physically destroyed, the academy still re-

mains deeply etched in the cultural memory of Japan and especially of Osaka.[1]

Despite common references to Osaka as the ancient city of Naniwa, it was not of the same order as Kyoto, the early capital of Japan, and only developed into a major metropolis during the warfare of the sixteenth century. Osaka became a castle city undergirding the forces of Toyotomi Hideyoshi (1536–98). After the defeat of Hideyoshi and his descendents and with the unchallenged rise of the Tokugawa house in Edo, Osaka was transformed from a military city into a commercial and banking center which served the needs of the new Tokugawa Baku-han order—especially as a center for converting rice to silver and distributing goods to the rest of the country. Of the population of 450,000, ninety-five percent were merchants. Regional barons and their retinues converted their rice into cash in Osaka but were forbidden to enter the city and take up residence there. A representative of the baron, usually a servitor of lowly samurai status assigned mercantile duties, managed the baron's granary and dealt with merchants to gain a favorable cash income. As a city of merchants, Osaka came to be known as "the kitchen of the nation"— tenka no daidokoro—where merchants greeted each other with the salutation, "How are your earnings today?"—mōkarimakka? The crass "bourgeois" reputation notwithstanding, Osaka was also a culturally diverse and complex city which served as the creative home base for such literary giants of the Tokugawa era as Ihara Saikaku (1642–93), Chikamatsu Monzaemon (1653–1724), and Ueda Akinari (1734–1809). The Kaitokudō occupied an especially distinguished place in a diverse cultural context as a center of scholarly learning.[2]

This intellectual history of the academy will focus especially on the period of the academy's greatest creative achievements that lasted approximately one hundred years following its official founding in 1726. It is a history identified with the founders Miyake Sekian (1665–1730) and Nakai Shūan (1693–1758) and such subsequent scholars and teachers as Tominaga Nakamoto (1715–46), Goi Ranju (1697–1762), Nakai Chikuzan (1730–1804) and his brother Riken (1732–1817), Kusama Naokata (1753–1831), and Yamagata Bantō (1748–1821). Named with classical ideographs that mean a school "to reflect deeply into the meaning of virtue," the Kaitokudō was in those years a proud and thriving educational institution of higher learning that was open to all classes and to the merchants of the Osaka area in particular. As a legally chartered academy— gakumonjo—it came to anchor a good deal of scholarly exchange in all of west central Japan. Although it was referred to in the early years espe-

cially as a school that fostered an "Osaka-type merchant learning"—
Osaka-ryū chōnin gakumon, an epithet not without a grain of truth to it,
during the course of the eighteenth century the Kaitokudō gained the respect of teachers and scholars throughout the country as an academy devoted to the serious study of "virtue."

The Kaitokudō was one among a number of "regional" academies
founded in the Osaka area at about the same time. It is clear from the
case of the Gansuidō of Hirano (where impressive records were kept and
are also housed at the Osaka University), that these regional academies
related to the Osaka Kaitokudō as the scholarly center. Although continuous interactions went on between these academies throughout the eighteenth century, a fundamental difference distinguished the Kaitokudō
from the others. Unlike the other academies, the Kaitokudō's special legal
and public status allowed it to address issues concerning the wider polity,
and it thus provides us with conspicuous evidences as to how commoner
intellectuals conceptualized the political economy of the nation.[3]

Aside from its legal status, the attractiveness of the Kaitokudō as a
center of scholarship was unquestionably reinforced by its being located
near the wealthy establishments of Osaka. It was situated several streets
inland from the principal marketplace that set wholesale prices on all
goods received through the Inland Sea, including import items shipped
to Nagasaki such as valuable medicinal herbs from China and Korea and
scientific books and implements from the West. It was located, moreover, in the shadows of the copper mint—*dōza*—where the distribution
of copper was managed. It was nestled among the leading financial and
trading houses such as Kōnoike, Masuya, Sumitomo, Tennōjiya, and
Hiranoya. A walking tour of the area today still apprizes one of the
powerful convergence of economic and intellectual forces. The former
residence of the great merchant intellectual, Yamagata Bantō of Masuya,
is located only a few minutes away from the site of the academy as well as
the copper mint. His personal library remains in an elementary school
serving the area, the Aijitsu shōgakkō—meaning a school that reveres
the light of day—that Masuya helped to establish in the early 1870s of
the modern Meiji era when Japanese intellectuals first engaged with the
Western ideals of Enlightenment and *Aufklärung*.

The mansion of the banking house of Kōnoike, similarly situated as
Masuya's, readily conveys an impressive sense of financial might and philanthropic capacity. Kusama Naokata, who studied at the Kaitokudō,
served this banking house and was known as Kōnoike Isuke. Aristocratic
exiles such as Kaiho Seiryō (1755–1817), Hirose Kyokusō (1807–63),

younger brother of the influential Tansō (1782–1856), and Asada Goryū (1734–99) sought refuge nearby in order to teach privately among commoners. A colleague of the Kyushu philosopher Miura Baien (1723–89), Asada in particular established his school in scientific study—the Senjikan—with the aid of men at the Kaitokudō. More significant, the influential academy of Dutch Studies in late Tokugawa era, the Tekijuku of Ogata Kōan (1810–63), was located hardly a stone's throw away from the Kaitokudō. Unlike the Kaitokudō, the Tekijuku survived the Pacific War intact, and its location suggests that its reputation in the sciences paralleled the Kaitokudō's reputation in the letters. Some six hundred students, mainly from the samurai aristocracy and "physicians" from regional domains, are known to have come to the Tekijuku to study Dutch language, medicine, and engineering science in this intellectual universe dominated by merchants. Among these students were Fukuzawa Yukichi (1834–1902), Ōmura Masujirō (1824–69), and Hashimoto Sanae (1835–59), important figures during the revolutionary upheavals of the Meiji *Ishin* of the 1860s. In addition, some sixty students from the key western domain of Chōshū alone were known to have studied there.[4]

From its inception, the Kaitokudō attracted leading scholars to it and its immediate environs, sometimes to exchange ideas on poetics and history and to enjoy Osaka hospitality, and on other occasions, to take up residence at the academy for a longer period of study. Traveling scholars often combined their visit to the Kaitokudō with stopovers at other places of intellectual interest in Osaka. At one of these, the Kontonsha, a society that specialized, as its name indicates, in unraveling the mysteries of archaic poetics, the seminars that lasted well into the night offered both serious study and good food and drink. Another favorite place, the residence of Kimura Kenkadō (1736–1802), the eccentric merchant intellectual who devoted much of his life to collecting unusual fauna, herbs, and foreign gadgets, provided visitors with a veritable museum unlike anything known elsewhere in Japan. A perusal of some of the materials at the Kaitokudō archives as well as the general history of the academy by Nishimura Tenshū, *Kaitokudō kō* (1923), quickly reveals the names of scholars of national prominence following a course of travel that invariably included a visit to Osaka and the Kaitokudō. In the 1720s and 1730s, Itō Tōgai (1670–1736) from Kyoto and Miwa Shissai (1669–1744) from Edo frequented the academy to deliver lectures and conduct seminars. In the 1750s and 1760s, Koga Seiri (1750–1817), Shibano Ritsuzan (1736–1807), and Bitō Nishū (1745–1813), academic leaders in Edo, often visited to establish a firm and lasting friendship between them and men at the Kaitokudō. Toward the end of the century, Satō

Issai (1772–1859) studied at the Kaitokudō for the better part of a year before moving on to become the head professor at the Bakufu College in Edo. Similarly, Rai Shunsui (1746–1816) and his famous son, Sanyō (1780–1832), always boarded at the Kaitokudō on their journeys from Hiroshima to Edo and back. Rai Sanyō was read by all of the young radicals of the 1850s who were discontented with the old order. From Kyushu, the disciples of Miura Baien, Waki Guzan (1764–1814), and Hoashi Banri (1778–1852), key scientists in the late Tokugawa period, as well as a dozen of their students, especially Miura's, studied at the academy for lengthy periods. And within Osaka, Ōshio Heihachirō (1794–1837), the philosophical radical who would turn against many of the basic concepts taught at the academy, labored at the Kaitokudō over the methods of decoding classical Chinese grammar. To round out this abbreviated list, the powerful chief councillor of the Bakufu himself, Matsudaira Sadanobu (1758–1829), visited Osaka in 1789 to hear in exhaustive detail the views of Nakai Chikuzan of the Kaitokudō on the state of political economy in the nation—an effort that resulted in Chikuzan's great work, the Sōbō kigen,[5] which is dedicated to Sadanobu.

Mention is made of these examples at the outset simply to suggest the discoursive implication of our subject. Like any "framed" structure of knowledge, the Kaitokudō as an "academy" was not merely an exclusive and enclosed space unto itself. Its intellectual history, therefore, must be understood in terms of a wider set of conceptual relationships that cut across regional and class lines. Indeed, the academy was enmeshed in some of the major intellectual debates of the day which, in brief, centered on the question of epistemology—whether the basis of firm, reliable knowledge was to be located in "history," in recorded human experience, or in "nature," in a universal system that preceded and transcended "language." While seemingly abstract and detached from human actualities, the epistemological alternatives relate to how human "virtue" would be defined and translated, in turn, into action, as in rectifying the faltering conditions of political economy. In small and large doses, these issues were debated in castle towns, cities, and in village councils; they most assuredly flowed into the intellectual life of the Kaitokudō.

The importance of the physical "walls" of the academy must of course be emphasized, for they marked the internal space that was defined as a "legal sanctuary" where merchants as commoners could pursue, with impunity, moral and practical knowledge. No outside authority could forcibly interfere with the inner workings of the academy; here merchants sought universal ideas that confirmed their "virtue" as marketmen and, in turn, made ideological claims about the special knowledge they possessed, especially regarding the economy. As a source of complex treatises and textbooks, the academy was at the same time engaged in broad polemical issues. It served the intellectual and moral needs of merchants by drawing on available concepts, but the Kaitokudō was also the locus of a conceptual *network* that encompassed different regions and social groups. It was in this sense a "center" and not simply an enclosed "sanctuary." The academy's dual identity gave the development of the Kaitokudō as an educational institution a special dynamism.

The relationships that linked the Kaitokudō to a wider universe of thought suggest the need to reassess our understanding of the intellectual history of Tokugawa merchants, especially with regard to their consciousness of politics and political economy more generally. For example, historians have long contended that the merchant class in the Tokugawa era lacked political consciousness and hence remained inert during the upheavals of the Meiji *Ishin* while dissident groups in the samurai aristocracy revolted against and dismantled the *ancien regime*. They therefore concluded that Japan's modern revolution was an aristocratic affair engineered entirely from above, and the merchant class occupies a historical place consistent with that interpretation. Demeaned as an inferior class for over two hundred years, the merchants at the end of the Tokugawa era were manipulated and coerced by various contending political alignments to make, at best grudgingly, monetary contributions to causes of little concern to them.

While not entirely incorrect, this overview probably needs some rethinking. By narrowly defining politics according to who seized power and redistributed it and analyzing the disorderly events of the late Tokugawa era with this framework, the political dimensions of merchant thought and action are obscured. This is particularly true of the economic view of politics formulated by merchant thinkers in the eighteenth century. The diverse involvement of merchants in late Tokugawa and early Meiji is suggestive of a conceptual consciousness grounded in an earlier intellectual development. There is, of course, no problem more elusive to historians than that of "consciousness," especially when causal links between one point and the next can rarely, if ever, be uncovered. Historians and social scientists are, therefore, tenaciously reluctant to engage with a subject that is thought to be too annoyingly imprecise to be researched. Sharp identifiable events and creative geniuses may not delineate the intellectual landscape. Yet historians are constantly reminded in their researches that bits and pieces of thought from previous ideological systems may be reassembled and put to new uses, particularly in the process of shaping ideological visions of the future. In

6

this regard, the Meiji *Ishin* was a crucial "threshold" or revolutionary "moment" for modern Japan.[6] Received concepts from diverse indigenous sources were pieced together in a manner that summarized the past in a radically reductive manner and projected a new future of "national wealth and power"—*fukoku kyōhei*. This ideological formula was recognized by all Japanese citizens as they were mobilized by it, and historians of Japan are well aware of it. Glimpses of merchant involvement can be gleaned by examining this historical process which involved men taking enormous risks without the benefit of a blueprint to chart the course of development.

The merchant Shiraishi Shōichirō (1812–80) worked closely as a supporter and confidant of Takasugi Shinsaku (1839–67), the organizer of the Chōshū rebel army that toppled the Bakufu. Iwasaki Yatarō (1834–85) allied himself with political causes and founded the Mitsubishi combine on behalf of the "public good." Shibuzawa Eiichi (1840–1931) turned his talents as a country merchant to designing the modern banking system. The merchant houses of Mitsui and Sumitomo adapted their investment goals and became powerful modern industrial firms. Regional merchants of obscure backgrounds who remain nameless supported the rebellion of Hirano Kuniomi (1828–64). Godai Tomoatsu (1834–85) devoted his energies to rallying the merchant houses of west central Japan and founded the Osaka Chamber of Commerce to promote this cause. And throughout the country literally thousands of middle-sized and small merchant houses and peasant families banded together into local "trust banks"—*shinyō kinko*—in order to fend for themselves and control their livelihood under conditions of extreme political and economic turmoil.

The list most assuredly can be expanded and, although the various items do not fall comfortably within a political narrative of events, they do not appear as merely sporadic and fortuitous occurrences. What conceptual resources were available to men of the *Ishin*, regardless of class location, and which ones did they draw from? From this perspective, it is far less important that the thought of a Nakai Chikuzan or a Yamagata Bantō, both men of the Kaitokudō, had direct consequences a generation or two later than it is to establish the structural basis of conceptualization from which fragmented bits were later reassembled into new analytical and critical perspectives. It is undeniable that the writings of Nakai and Yamagata were not isolated and unique events but were enmeshed in a broader intellectual engagement with issues of knowledge and polity. In this respect, their writings were also among the epistemological resources from which men later drew.

My readings of Tokugawa intellectual history, and recently that of the

Kaitokudō especially, suggest to me the greater utility of a less restrictive perspective than the narrow political one. There is the possibility of "alliances" across lines that stemmed from a complex set of conceptual events that I have provisionally called the "Tokugawa discourse on political economy." This study will elaborate on this discourse with regard to the formation of merchant thinking. The term "political economy" is a translation of the ideographic compound *keisei saimin,* which was often elided into *keizai. Keizai* came to mean "economics" in modern times. The conceptual and ethical foundations of "economics," in other words, are grounded in Tokugawa thinking on political economy or *keisei saimin.* This ideographic compound, it must be emphasized, meant more than economics in the specialized modern sense of the word and included within it broader spheres of political ethics, the art of administration, and epistemology. It connotes the acquisition of the proper knowledge needed to "control" external events both at the personal and public levels. The entire compound may thus be rendered more precisely as "ordering the social world"—*keisei*—and "saving the people"—*saimin.*

The main integrating idea in this cumbersome though often used maxim was this: How might governments and social institutions perform in ways that were ethical both in purpose and consequence, hence the importance of "saving the people" as the aim and consequence of the "means" of governance—"ordering the social world." As a dynamic intellectual concern that spanned the entire spectrum of the literate strata of society without regard to personal affiliation to school of thought, the discussion of political economy addressed problems of objectivity in evaluating institutions and the flow of historical events not only in domainal administration but in the workings of market, money, and trade. The result was a complex discursive interaction between a "political" view of economics and an "economic" view of politics in which merchants, far from being excluded, played a key role. Historians have not given adequate attention to this influence. As actors dominating the marketplace in cities and the finances of domains, merchants also developed an articulate grasp of how the nation ought to be administered, especially by locating economics as being central to the entire problem. We may see this broadly as the "bourgeois" input into the ideological dictum of "wealth and power" that undergirded Japan's first industrial revolution in the 1880s.

We have not on the whole been inclined to think of Tokugawa history in this manner. "Politics" and "economics" do not appear in monographic literature on late Tokugawa as dynamically interdependent elements within a coherent system of action but almost entirely in a superior-subordinate relationship. This despite our awareness that the late Tokugawa had generated two comprehensive and overlapping visions for national independence: political centralization and economic transformation through trade, both of which were steeped in the language and conceptualizations of Tokugawa political economism. Our view may in fact be obscured by the perception of classes as being authentic to the extent that they relate to each other in a conflictual manner, a legacy obviously drawn from interpretations of the French Revolution and the subsequent rise of industrial classes in Europe. A mechanical use of this formula, however, may be distortive in preindustrial contexts such as Tokugawa society in which class consciousness may be seen being shaped more properly out of "functional interdependencies."[7]

Although the superior-inferior relationship between samurai and merchant may never have been in doubt, the ideologies produced empowered certain kinds of perceptions and actions that allowed, over the long run, the inferior to assume dominance in certain ways, such as the management of industrial capitalism and the organization of regional and local investments. Far from being uninvolved in acts of ideological production, Tokugawa merchants offer historians impressive evidences of conceptualizations about political economy that carried important long-term consequences. We are aware that although merchants were viewed by the official class as being "inferior," they were nonetheless called upon by domainal lords and by the Bakufu to provide guidance in economic matters. Developing in the interstices of class interdependence, Tokugawa merchant ideology defined politics and economics as being entirely intertwined. If the aristocracy was to be responsible for bureaucratic administration, merchants came to see their rightful place in the political order as specialists in economic management. In other words, merchants developed an ideology that justified their acting economically in the public realm, thereby rendering their analysis and insights into the plight of the economy as being political ones. The intellectual history of the Kaitokudō clearly reveals this dynamic line of development.

Tokugawa history has not been narrated in terms of such conceptual interdependencies. The tendency has been instead to rely on conventional distinctions in dividing historical experiences: political and economic, samurai and merchant, high and low, urban and regional, mainstream and fringe, and so forth. While convenient, these divisions are also unstable and under close scrutiny do not hold up firmly as fixed boundaries. It would be wise to maintain a healthy skepticism about the adequacy of such distinctions in studying historical texts, for the utility of drawing from social, institutional, temporal and geographical markers in the enterprise of studying intellectual history is indeed dubious. Clusters and fragments of conceptual language tend to move about in a variety of reassembled forms, taking analytical directions unintended in their earlier incarnations. In other words, as conceptual fragments and formations "migrate," in the wording of J. G. A. Pocock, over geographical spaces and forward over time, they assume a life as epistemological instruments that often conceals their structural sources from immediate view.[8] Conceptual acts take on new meaning in an apparently unrelated context and arena. Peasants, we know, used the concepts of political economy to improve their lot. Due to the movement or "spillage" of ideas across social and geographical lines, overlapping conceptual spaces are shaped, suggesting the possibility of interdependencies and a much broader sense of social "participation" than might otherwise seem possible. Thus, whether located in a scholarly "treatise" or an "academy," the ideas found there must in the first instance be seen as "social," which is to say closely linked to a universe of language and moral and theoretical concepts.

The Kaitokudō, in this respect, may be framed together with segments of other classes, as with agronomists among the peasantry and political economists of the aristocracy. The education advanced at the Kaitokudō appears in a "graded" relationship with the ideas of these other social groupings and not as neatly enclosed and pertinent only to Osaka. Nor should it be concluded that the acceptance of widely available concepts at the Kaitokudō were simply attempts at emulating the aristocracy, for the reassembled ideas were put to creative use to confirm the work and moral worth of Osaka merchants and commoners more generally.

It is also a central contention of this book that the Kaitokudō is best situated in the continuous discourse on knowledge during the eighteenth century between those who claimed that "nature" was the ultimate source of knowledge and those who claimed "history" was the source. In addressing these two epistemological propositions, the Kaitokudō came to formulate a clear position for itself based on a theory of natural ontology. This informed the academy's intellectual history, especially in the latter half of the century. Although a good deal of Tokugawa thinking about political economy was identified with thinkers such as Ogyū Sorai (1666–1728) and Dazai Shundai (1680–1747) who analyzed problems of politics and trade with reference to a refined historical norm that was argued to be located in an ancient beginning, it was also the case that, among commoners especially, the more influential system of thought was grounded in a principle of nature as a fundamental premise to accurate knowledge. While nature could never be comprehended in its totality since nature was infinite and the human mind finite, it was reasoned that nature encompassed all visible and nonvisible phenomena and included, therefore, human beings and their internal virtue. This alternative epistemology based on nature played a central role in the evolution of merchant ideology at the Kaitokudō.

The development was not readily evident at the outset when the Kaitokudō was founded, and a number of moral concepts were presented to merchants, but it became increasingly important soon thereafter as the principle underlying the academy's curriculum and, in turn, as the basis upon which to critique the state of political economy. While obvious, the point should be emphasized that education at the Kaitokudō did not lead immediately to such criticism. Rather, as the title of this book suggests, it was to provide instruction based on concepts generally agreed to be of the highest scholarly standard that would confirm the "virtue" of merchants as members of the human community. How this subject of human "virtue" was worked out at the Kaitokudō, therefore, serves as the key subject in our analysis. It was over this very issue of "virtue" that scholars at the Kaitokudō turned against the thesis that "history" ought to be the sole source of moral norms, for this thesis was then formulated by Ogyū Sorai into saying that human virtue was not universal but highly particular to each individual. Political virtue, as well as the virtue of acquiring moral knowledge through scholarly inquiry, therefore, was said to be specific to a few individuals only and not intrinsic to the capabilities of all human beings. Scholars at the Kaitokudō, speaking for commoners in general, objected strenuously to this limited understanding of virtue and held consistently to a theory of virtue in which all human beings, regardless of class, possessed the capacity *to know*, albeit in relative degrees, the form and substance of external moral and political norms. It is this assertive claim to knowledge that shapes the critical thinking of merchants such as Kusama Naokata and Yamagata Bantō toward the end of the eighteenth century.

It should also be mentioned that the affirmation of virtue based on natural ontology is directly linked with the general eighteenth century Tokugawa problematic of engaging with Western science, and in turn, "technology." Again, the intent behind the reliance on this theory of nature was not, initially, to better understand Western science. The purpose as already mentioned, was to provide moral certitude among merchants—and to commoners more generally. The interest, we may say, was not in "applied" but in "moral" science. The theory of inexhaustible nature, however, lent itself to a certain tolerance toward those who experimented with nature. Since nature was absolute and universal, the human mind, it was argued, would constantly know more about it although al-

11

ways in an incomplete manner. Knowledge acquired in one era was thus seen as "relative" to that gained in the next, history providing not so much fixed norms as evidences of the continuing human effort to gain deeper insights into nature. On the one hand, therefore, the philosophical ideas of Chu Hsi, the main theoretician behind the system of thought known as Neo-Confucianism, were embraced as valid despite certain well-known limitations to his metaphysics. On the other hand, however, the scientific insights developed by Western scholars, and Dutch ones in particular, were similarly given due recognition as being "relative" but important and worthy of note and then, subsequently, as perhaps even being "superior" to that of scholars in Japan and continental Asia in the approach to scientific knowledge. It is certain, in any event, that in the late eighteenth century, such thinkers as Yamagata Bantō of the Kaitokudō had conceptualized their perceptions of money, market, and trade in terms of universal "mathematics" or "astronomy."

Equally worthy of note to further affirm the theoretical point made earlier, the concepts identified with natural ontology formed a tradition that embraced major figures of diverse social backgrounds. The pivotal philosopher in this tradition, Kaibara Ekken (1630–1714), and his colleague, Miyazaki Antei (1623–97), devoted their attention to the development of agronomy, the science of agriculture, and lived and taught among the peasantry. Nishikawa Joken (1648–1724) and Goi Ranju were of merchant background and involved themselves in the education of commoners. Goi in particular played a decisive role in the intellectual development of the Kaitokudō. Mentioned earlier, Miura Baien lived among the peasantry in Kyushu and sought from within that agrarian context new ways of thinking about the objective study of nature. Sugita Genpaku (1732–1817) and his colleagues in Dutch studies of diverse social origins revolutionized medical practices through their study of Western anatomical science. Ninomiya Sontoku (1787–1856) envisioned from within the peasantry the eradication of poverty in the nation through scientific farming and communal effort. Kaiho Seiryō abandoned his status in the aristocracy to live among merchants and peasant entrepreneurs to locate in their work the principle of "mathematics" and "calculation" that he believed foretold the future course of history. The Osaka financier, Yamagata Bantō, turned to astronomy and the heliocentric view of the universe to frame his view of received history. To round out this abbreviated list, Sakuma Shōzan (1811–64), while remaining firmly within the aristocracy, similarly identified a scientific principle, "mathematics," to argue the accessibility of universal knowledge regardless of the particular character of historical culture; science was not the privileged possession of certain nations—a view, as is well known, that had a far-reaching impact on Japan's emergence as a modern, industrial nation.

As these examples clearly suggest, the intellectual history of the Kaitokudō cannot be disengaged from a broader set of conceptual developments. Goi Ranju and Yamagata Bantō, noted above, were conspicuous figures at the Kaitokudō, and their ideas overlap unmistakably with those held by other thinkers occupying different spaces and social statuses. This phenomenon is in keeping with our view of Tokugawa thought as possessing a lively capacity for movement, adaptation, recombination, and transformation often concealed by formal status distinctions. The conceptual consciousness of thinkers in diverse classes reveals this pattern. From aristocrats to merchants to now nameless itinerant teachers in small country towns and villages armed with handbooks on agronomy and ethics, a dynamic articulation and dispersion of key epistemologies can be discerned. As participants in this broad intellectual history, the merchant scholars at the Kaitokudō provide us with a particularly clear set of texts that show the creative metamorphosis in the assembling of ideas for instructional use among commoners. By placing the conceptual events located at the Kaitokudō within a wider intellectual mapping, the academy sheds its often misrepresented position of being an institution serving the narrow needs of the "high commerical bourgeoisie" in their strivings to emulate the aristocracy.

The question still arises however, as to what might have triggered merchant leaders in Osaka to engage in scholarly and instructional activity. There is no simple response to this issue as it is open to interpretive disagreement. Although the subject will be dealt with later, suffice it to say here that the concerns that led to the creation of the Kaitokudō were intertwined with self-conscious reflections that took place in the aftermath of the commercial revolution of the late seventeenth century during the Genroku era (1688–1704). It hardly needs much emphasis to observe that merchants were thoroughly enmeshed in the turbulent events unleashed by that economic transformation. Questions arose as to the ethicality of economic passion and, more broadly, whether the course of history in the context of the new commerce might be properly grasped and brought under effective management.

From the early 1700s, and especially in the Kyōhō era (1716–36), strains generated by the uneasy structural relationship between agricultural production and commerce in the cities had rendered the celebration of "passion" and burlesquing of "virtue"—as in Ihara Saikaku's ribald novellas—to be somewhat inappropriate in light of the troubled conditions of the landscape. Spurred by poverty in the countryside, for example, peasants were known to spontaneously "pull out" of their villages to join religious pilgrimmages—called *nukemairi*—to revered national shrines located far away. Outwardly joyous, these pilgrimmages were rooted in famine and near-famine conditions that recurred in the country-side and reached disastrous proportions in west central Japan in the 1720s and early 1730s. At the most practical level, merchants in Osaka responded by establishing "relief food stations"—*sukuigoya*—to help combat famine. But at a deeper level, and especially in face of criticisms from indebted aristocrats that the cause of much of the misery was passion and greed, merchant leaders perceived that the problem at hand must also involve the establishing of moral and epistemological control of the un-steady present.

While available systems of thought did not offer simple solutions, they nonetheless provided merchants with the conceptual tools and the basic vocabulary about knowledge—often referred to comprehensively as "Tokugawa Confucianism"—that guided the search for intellectual order in the swiftly changing historical present. The question raised was how might the seemingly unpredictable and passionate fluctuations in the fortunes of men be brought into a moral perspective that would demonstrate knowledge to be accurate, truthful, and thus a reliable basis of action. The purpose here was to affirm that external evidences could be organized and controlled and to deny skeptical theories of knowledge that demeaned merchants or that claimed reality, as in Buddhist philosophy, was in a constant state of random flux and thus ultimately illusory and chaotic, something that men ought not rely on for order. Epistemologies that prescribed such a reliance were seen as merely the arbitrary handi-work of passionate and ambitious men; hence, such systems were consid-ered deceptive devices that caused suffering among human beings who wished for order when there was only ceaseless flux. To claim, as the early Tokugawa leaders and scholars did, that order was indeed possible, thus allowing for the prediction of peace well into the future did not, how-ever, overcome the actual evidences of disorder and unease generated by the commercial revolution. The general discourse on knowledge, within which the founding of the Kaitokudō should properly be situated, sought to extract from the intellectual universe concepts that affirmed "reason" and the logicality of external phenomena and events and denied the mere ephemerality of social existence. It was agreed all along the intel-lectual spectrum that human beings, regardless of particular cultural cir-cumstances, lived in a process of historical time (*toki*), a physical loca-tion that was a predetermined condition (*tokoro*), and a place or status within a general social order (*kurai*).

These "names," it was further argued, were not merely passionate contrivances aimed at fabricating order out of disorder but were "universal" to the human condition and were thus references to truthful realities that persisted despite the seasonal and life cycles that suggested constant change. The basic proposition that "names" could fix and order things into place, that "language" was not simply an artificial construct, clarified the project of controlling one's political and personal universes in ways that were predictable and thus ethical. The general consequence that ought to ensue from this epistemology was the alleviation of suffering among the people. The theory, however, was much more readily argued than realized in actuality. Poverty in the countryside, indebtedness among the aristocracy, and helter-skelter commerce in the cities all provided ready evidences of a severe discrepancy between ethical theory and historical actuality. Yet the crisis in knowledge that resulted was not over the question of whether "names" and actual "things" and "events" were, in theory, in accord with each other. The reasoned relationship here was not challenged. Rather, the issue centered on what should be the ultimate epistemological proposition upon which the meaning of "names" rested. Should it be anchored fundamentally in historical "text" or in natural "principle"? Over this alternative was then debated the meaning of human "virtue"—*toku*. Most crucial for merchants was the relationship between virtue and "righteousness"—*gi*—meaning "accuracy" and thus also "fairness"—*shin*—the entire ethical basis upon which a network of social and economic relationships might be articulated as ethically viable. As already noted, although the need to clarify that choice was not fully appreciated at the outset, the necessity to do so would become clear in the early decades of the Kaitokudō's existence.

In the chapters that follow, the conceptual metamorphosis at the Kaitokudō will be outlined beginning with a discussion of the epistemologies available to merchant scholars in the 1710s and 1720s. Although quite obviously many diverse intellectual fragments were melded into a whole, the emphasis will be placed on two authoritative claims to knowledge that served as the baseline to the Kaitokudō and much of eighteenth-century thinking. As already alluded to, one of these was the historicist claim formulated by Itō Jinsai (1627–1705) that contained extremely pertinent ideas for commoners; the other was the naturalism identified with Kaibara Ekken and Nishikawa Joken, which also was oriented in good measure to the moral concerns of the lower classes. The syncretic conjoining of these positions in the hands of the first professorial head, Miyake Sekian, and his colleague, Nakai Shūan, would come under severe attack from within the academy in the radical historicism of

15

the merchant scholar Tominaga Nakamoto. Using philological strategies, Tominaga denied the validity of *all* historical texts due to their competitive and passionate character whose historicity was no longer relevant to the present. Tominaga's expulsion from the academy would then be followed by polemical attacks on Ogyū Sorai's historicist theory of knowledge and virtue. The affirmation of natural ontology as the pedagogical principle of instruction at the academy was established by Goi Ranju in the mid-1730s through the 1750s.

The middle sections turn to the alternative visions that emerged from within that curriculum as embodied in the critical writings of brothers Nakai Chikuzan and Riken. Chikuzan shaped an expansive and radical vision of the academy within a reordered political system that would include universal education. Riken would see only continued historical decline, project the dissolution of the aristocracy, and seek refuge in an autonomous "kingdom of dreams" of his own making to pursue his scholarly curiosities in "science" and "texts."

The final portion of this book addresses the merchants' reintegration of the teachings at the academy into coherent ideological formulations in the late eighteenth and early nineteenth centuries. The key texts here are those of Kusama Naokata of Kōnoike on the "history of money"—*Sanka zu'i*—and Yamagata Bantō of Masuya on universal knowledge in his great opus, *In Place of Dreams—Yume no shiro*. In the latter in particular the theory of natural ontology that Goi taught can be seen as reintegrated into a worldview that includes the merchant critique of political economy.

It is of course hardly innovative to examine the lectures and treatises of critical and persuasive teachers in an academy in order to argue for the breadth of Tokugawa intellectual history. There is a great deal more to be done, needless to say, especially regarding the thinking about political economy among commoners in the lower strata of society. Yet, the case needs to be made that merchants developed a consciousness of politics and were not merely devotees of the new art forms, although they were indeed that; their engagement with Confucian epistemologies did not simply make them stodgy moralists, although they were mocked by critics such as the popular novelist Ueda Akinari. Obviously many diverse aesthetic and philosophical elements went into the making of what came to be called comprehensively as "The Way of the Merchants"—*Chōnin dō*. The task set here, however, is not to discuss this "way" in all of its cultural complexity but to isolate the ontological boundaries within which merchants thought about their place as marketmen in the political order of things and to discuss the conceptual strategies they employed within those boundaries to make their claim. It is this intellectual history that allowed merchants to absorb ethical and scientific ideas about political economy and to see critically beyond even that to distant lands and the universe of science. It was this history that generated the lively curiosity among merchants about natural history and world geography—about unusual fauna and animals found in Japan and elsewhere and the scientific instruments that Westerners employed to study the stars and the microscopic world of minute creatures. One can sense in all of this an intellectual history in which merchants acquired a conviction about the "virtue" of their work and their epistemological capacity to explore and control expanding spheres of knowledge.

T W O

THE PHILOSOPHICAL
ENVIRONMENT

THE CONVENTIONAL WISDOM AMONG HISTORIANS IS
THAT TOKUGAWA NEO-CONFUCIANISM, THE MORAL PHI-
LOSOPHY UPON WHICH THE RULING REGIME DEFINED THE STATUS STRUC-
ture, placed merchants at the bottom of the social order, below aristocrats, farmers, and craftsmen in descending order of importance, and
further likened that hierarchical sequence to natural reason itself. To that
wisdom is added the well-known fact that merchants did not revolt to
alter their formal status. But the conclusion usually drawn, that merchants simply abided by the ideological status quo, would seem to be unwarranted as it is doubtful to begin with that the self-conception of merchants ever accorded with the social order as defined for them from
above. The issue appears to be a good deal more complex than the usual
interpretive scheme would have it. Since merchants were not systematically discriminated against prior to the Tokugawa era—pre-1600—it is
probably closer to the truth of the matter to say that merchants in the
new status structure felt a pressing need to rearticulate the position they
occupied within that order. Out of the very Confucianism which defined
their lowly status, they sought a philosophy defining their own moral and
practical worth. Such an effort would aim to create a moral center for
merchants from which they could view themselves as not inferior in an
ultimate sense to the other functional classes. An examination of the philosophies being shaped toward the end of the seventeenth and on into
the eighteenth centuries clearly indicates such a development, as the discussion of Itō Jinsai and Nishikawa Joken will attempt to show. It is an
intellectual history, moreover, that began with the establishment of the
philosophical basis of "virtue" among commoners and carried with it in

the long run broad ideological implications in defining and giving purpose to merchant engagements in the historical process.

Tokugawa merchants did not create an intellectual history out of whole cloth with the establishment of the new Tokugawa order beginning in 1600. They inherited an ethical view of the social universe in which, according to the elegant analysis provided by Amino Yoshihiko, merchants saw themselves in ways other than being subservient.[1] Under conditions of generalized warfare among ambitious barons, merchants perceived themselves as being "disengaged" or "detached" from the world of military politics. The imagery decidedly suggests spacial distance rather than inferiority in a hierarchic sense. Market towns were thus called places of separation—*muenjo; engiri basho*—where entangling social and political relations had been "severed." The language is most certainly drawn from Buddhist thought in which detachment from society was taught to be a precondition for true religious experience. Merchants in this sense used religious concepts to define their secular spaces as "sanctuaries" that were detached from previous "ties"—*en*—and to which masterless warriors, poets, vagabonds, craftsmen, and itinerant priests could all comingle without interference from the outside. Furthermore, because these sanctuaries welcomed individuals of whatever social background to buy supplies, trade, create and sell wares, they also sometimes called their towns "public places"—*kugai*—a term suggesting at the same time as a homonym a place of shared "suffering." The hierarchical world of politics, the arena of personal loyalty and reward, by contrast, was deemed as being "private." Given the ironic twists imbued in these terms, it should not come as a surprise that these sanctuaries would also be called places of "rest" and "creation" which the word that was used (*raku*) implies, and as we see merchants in their more brilliant and elaborate metamorphosis in the "gay quarters" of Tokugawa cities. The concepts, then, of distance and separation, publicality and suffering, and rest—hence the terms "*Muen*," "*Kugai*," "*Raku*" that Amino has used to entitle his book—undergirded the intellectual life of merchant culture and were inherited during the early years of Tokugawa rule.

What is of special significance to our study is that this idea of detached market-town sanctuaries drastically lost significance with the construction of the Tokugawa political system in the first half of the seventeenth century.[2] The ebb and flow of "private" military fortunes lost its ephemerality and now assumed "public" form as a fixed legal entity. It is true that the presence of restless, rowdy, and masterless samurai served as reminders of the unpredictable conditions of the previous era. But with increasing forcefulness, it became an incontestable fact that the Tokugawa regime of "peace and tranquility under Heaven"—*Tenka taihei*—had come into place to stay and would not be easily dislodged in a generation or two or even for centuries, for that matter, by the personal, ambitious whim of regional barons. The ideology of "detachment" and "disengagement" made sense insofar as military politics remained in constant flux. Now that the bureaucratic system had been hammered into place as a public order, it steadily became less meaningful to retain an identity with the value of "detachment." Between 1600, when Tokugawa assumed power, and 1650, by which time the new order had come to be regularized, what had been "private" had been transformed into "public," and alternatively what merchants had called their "public" arena of "suffering" now had come to be redefined as "private." The population of that world was labeled "passionate," seeking only profit, and hence belonging, in the new ideological scheme of things, to the low end of the social totem pole.

The new hierarchic order as ordained by natural reason was also reinforced with concrete economic measures. Those confirmed in the new aristocracy would no longer be subjected to the iron law of uncertainty that reigned in the previous century but would be invested with guaranteed, hereditary stipends so as to assure stability from one generation to future ones in perpetuity. Such a luxury was not extended to merchants. Denied both stipend and agricultural land, the latter restricted to the peasantry, merchants now saw themselves occupying the world of "flux," a fact that gained psychological magnitude in proportion to the certitude gained by the public order. Once universal throughout society and confirmed in Buddhist thinking, the norm of uncertainty now seemed applicable primarily to merchants and more generally to city dwellers dealing in manufacture and trade. It was against this background of historical disjunction that early ideological efforts among merchants can be best appreciated. The key is the psychological sense of "disadvantage" that merchants faced in the new scheme of things, not the inherent "inferiority" that others believed characterized them.

A case in point certainly is the compilation of ethical injunctions by Mitsui Takafusa shortly after he assumed the third headship of the Mitsui House in 1716. Entitled a "record of things for merchants to consider"—*Chōnin kōken roku*[3]—it is actually the records of well-known merchant houses, some forty-six of them, bearing such names as Ishiko Jian, Hirano Yūken, Itoya Jūemon, Ryōgae Zenroku, etc., located mainly in the Kyotō area which without exception went bankrupt sometime between 1650 and the early 1700s. Despite initial successes, these houses were not able to maintain themselves as viable merchant enterprises beyond the second and third generations. Moreover, while in some instances the primary cause of failure was personal passion, indulging in excessive luxury and in song and games, by and large the main source of insolvency was the extension of badly conceived loans to the new regional barons, the daimyō, who needed funds to finance their luxurious needs in Edo. By relentlessly listing these negative evidences, the didactic point that merchant life is indeed precarious was driven home to those entrusted with the fortunes of Mitsui. Good, enterprising merchants had fallen by the wayside; carelessness and miscalculation had resulted in death to the house and all those relying on it for livelihood. On the other hand, even the most negligent and irresponsible of the daimyō would survive into the future because he and his retinue, by virtue of their birth, would continue to receive guaranteed incomes, like the "spring rains from Heaven." The indebted daimyō, however dishonorable, would survive; the good merchant whose loan was not honored by that daimyō would be destroyed. In short, earnings gained through trade were generically unlike the income of the aristocracy. Another theme, however, was also woven into the instruction. Through constant vigilance and wise management, merchants could assure their *social immortality* with dignity and without subordination to others.

As is readily evident, the *Chōnin kōken roku* was designed primarily to instruct leaders in the House of Mitsui on what to avoid. It is in this respect not unrelated to Ihara Saikaku's popular tract directed at a broader audience, the "Storehouse of Wealth"—*Nippon eitaigura*—which tried to explain what merchants needed to do to succeed.[4] The Mitsui account relies on negative evidences; Saikaku's relies on positive ones which show how wealth might be acquired. But underlying both is the recognition of the uncertainty and unpredictability that is a central fact in the life of merchants. Merchants must plan for the continuity of their houses. Nothing is inevitable. The language often relied on to describe merchant virtues such as "frugality," "calculation" or "intelligence," "diligence," "honesty," etc., were not simply moral platitudes or injunctions drawn from abstract principles but references to practical strategies by which merchants would struggle from one generation to the next and acquire a continuity directly paralleling what had been *guaranteed* to the aristocracy at birth.

The desire to maintain continuity over time gained in urgency as politics stabilized in the seventeenth century and as commerce expanded enormously as a result. The ideals of *detachment* and of *religious sanctuary* of the previous era were swiftly eroded in this historical reality. What had now come to assume heightened importance in the consciousness of merchants was their extreme disadvantage vis-à-vis the aristocracy, a reversal, in short, of how they had perceived their historical surroundings a generation or two earlier. The ideological project of merchants from the mid-seventeenth century onward had far less to do with the preservation or maintenance of their detached sanctuaries than with the search for ways to establish a more secure place in the new reality; in short, merchants tried to find bases of "attachment" and "engagement" despite the obvious drawbacks they faced and articulated accordingly a relationship of interdependencies upon which their work and contributions would not be denied.

The striving on the part of merchants to overcome the sense of disadvantage and the uncertainty they constantly faced involved other broader intellectual efforts besides practical prescriptions of the sort just alluded to in the case of Mitsui. These efforts often conceptualized the status of merchants in broad universalistic schemata based on philosophical principles that cut across hierarchic social placements. By holding firmly to these principles as ultimate propositions with which they could identify, merchants could speak of their human virtue and their capacity for moral action. These approaches often, although not always, bypassed the immediate world of power relationships to articulate those first principles with which merchants might reengage with the realities at hand and not deal with questions of superiority and inferiority and of high and low as fundamental concerns.

Some of the mediating concepts relied on especially in the mid-seventeenth century were drawn from Buddhism, although quite clearly it was not the ideas of detachment and disengagement that were emphasized. The Buddhist belief in the universal human capacity for compassion (*jihi*), for example, was used to counter the claim that merchants were somehow incapable of such action because of their work. Indeed, compassion was emphasized as essential to the life and work of merchants as with any other group of human beings. Ultimately, the reasoning went, all human beings inevitably encounter the truth of human existence, which is its ultimate "emptiness"—*ku*—the ontological principle that rendered all human beings "equal"—*byōdō*—a term which in modern Japanese means equality in the political sense and is Buddhist in origin and meaning. As used in the early shaping of merchant ideology, it meant the inescapable law that in some ultimate and absolute sense all sentient beings were equal before the unshakable law of change and hence death; social status, proximity to power, and possession of wealth have absolutely no bearing on this fact and render superficial human achievements in time as merely ephemeral. Phrases that said "in life and death all is equal" (*shisei wa kotogotoku byōdō nari*); or "there is only a single equality not two" (*ichi byōdō nishite ni nashi*), of which the writings of the time drew on frequently, were well known to merchants and were accessible throughout society. The emphasis given to these phrases varied from one Buddhist sect to another, some stressing the universality of Buddhahood in everyone, others the universality of "grace" extended to all by the merciful Amida, and still others the self-potential for transcendent enlightenment in the here and now. In the secular setting of daily merchant life, these all added up to a common meaning that stated the universal fate of all before the law of causation and change, the possibility of salvation or enlightenment for all regardless of social status, and hence the ultimately "horizontal" nature of human existence. Hierarchic structures erected in the new order could thus be "leveled" in this sense and kept at an arm's length. Far from simply conveying the pessimistic message which tolled the inevitability of death, these religious ideas stressed the absolute truth in the absence of ultimate distinction in the spiritual possession of human beings; and hence they also spoke to the potential of ordinary people to overcome the uncertainties imposed by the secular order by moral action and to thus continue from generation to generation.

These themes are readily evident in some representative works of the early didactic writings addressed to urban dwellers. Often cited is the "mirror" of teachings to bequeath to descendents, *Shison kagami* (1674), written by one Sango Masachika, an obscure former warrior of lowly status living as a merchant in the uncertain alleyways of the city.[5] The *Shison kagami* addresses the problem of "continuity" and asks what is there of "worth" to bequeath to the future for those who are not members of the aristocracy with guaranteed stipends? It is neither wealth nor status that is important, the *Shison* repeatedly asserts. It is a sense of absolute moral dignity that ought to be transmitted. This, rather than the lowliness of social status, is the idea that descendants into the distant future must be made to believe, thus joining present and future generations. Through aphorisms richly "punctuated"—*aru hito uta ni iwaku* etc.— with poetic references from Japanese literature, the theme is repeated that commoners ought to engage in moral action and do things out of their virtuous sense of fairness and compassion because they are morally "equal"—*byōdō*—with all other human beings regardless of differences in social status that the ephemeral world of practical necessity might impose. Such differences are finally inconsequential: "Heed instead that truly the way to Paradise is through work in daily life"—*Gokuraku wa tsutomete itaru michi to koso kike*; and again: "People all pretend to know

yet do not comprehend the basic teaching that all must inevitably die"—
Mina hito no shirigao ni shite shiranu kana, kanarazu shisuru narai ari to wa.[6]

The *Shison* does not waver in presenting the ontological perspective of
spiritual equality among human beings. Differences among human beings
are ultimately meaningless, moral values are applicable to all and not the
prerogatives of those with secular privilege. There is no such thing as a
hierarchy of virtues coincidental with social status. Moreover, one could
reach this egalitarian point of view from any one of the three major religions familiar to most Japanese: Confucianism teaches the universality of
Heaven's Way—*Tendō*—in which the potential for moral action is granted
without favor; Buddhism believes in spiritual salvation for all human beings; and Shinto nourishes the view that a divine spirit or *kokoro* joins all
beings and things without differentiation. Each of these religious ideas
lead to the common conclusion that in some absolute spiritual sense human distinctions as to status, power, and wealth lose their significance.
From this ultimate proposition merchants ought to begin to "order" their
lives though they are threatened by discontinuity. As a mediating conception, therefore, the idea of spiritual equality allowed merchants to distance themselves from the new hierarchic order, seeing themselves as
"classless" to begin with, and then, in turn, to perceive in the particular
function of their class a universal moral centricity that ought to survive
from one generation into the next. In this use of universalistic religious
ideas to provide a sense of moral order to a presumably hierarchically disadvantaged class, we see the shaping of an ideology pertinent to a merchant class that had experienced the commercial revolution of the late
seventeenth century and the rise and fall of the fortunes of merchant
houses of the sort documented by Mitsui.

The idea of "equality" as seen in the *Shison* was persuasive especially as
it was based on the ontological absolute of "death." It was, at the same
time, still linked with the concept of "disengagement" which was essential for universal salvation. The concepts of equality and salvation, in
other words, were closely intertwined and did not provide a consistent
philosophical affirmation of "life" as "virtue" that would allow the "re-
engagement" in a social reality no longer deemed to be merely ephemeral
but predictable into the future as an ordered whole. What needed to be
argued was that life as virtue was capable of "goodness" and of knowing
what was objectively "truthful." In the hurly-burly reality of the rise and
fall in the fortunes of merchant houses and as merchants came increasingly under criticism as never before for the ills of famine and indebtedness afflicting the land, the formulation of a life-confirming theory of virtue emerged as the central philosophical problem. As the robust and

ebullient Genroku era turned into the troubled Kyōhō in the early eighteenth century, the sobering realization of historical change steadily
spread among merchant leaders. By this period, a return to the previous
ethic of "detachment" and "disengagement" was widely viewed as point-
less. New moral propositions were required to incorporate merchants into
the existing order—moral propositions that would clarify the integral relationship between universal moral value and merchant commoners engaged in the seemingly passionate act of buying and selling.

Two philosophical orientations were especially crucial in serving as resources. They would remain central to the instruction at the Kaitokudō,
and they deserve special attention here. One of these was the historicist
theory of Itō Jinsai. A Kyōtō scholar of merchant origin, Itō commands a
distinctive place in Tokugawa intellectual history and has remained a
much revered thinker in modern times. Rejecting the metaphysics of
Neo-Confucianism, Itō turned to historical texts in ancient China, and
to *The Book of Mencius* in particular, to reintroduce into his Tokugawa
present a universal value for commoners. The other key philosophical
position is identified with Kaibara Ekken and, more pertinent to merchants, Nishikawa Joken, the merchant astronomer of Nagasaki who was
one of the most widely read and published popular writers on morals
among merchants in the Tokugawa era. These latter two men drew from
Neo-Confucianism the idea of an absolute, universal reason in nature—
Tenri. They understood it to mean the universal identity of all human
beings within the category of "humankind" and rejected the hierarchical
emphasis given to it by most scholars. By identifying with the universal
norm of natural reason, human beings could calculate action in ways that
were not arbitrary. Kaibara addressed this theory to shape an agronomical
science pertinent to peasants; Nishikawa addressed himself to merchants
as well as to peasants.

Both of these schemes of thought, it should be emphasized, are evidential in orientation rather than introspective and idealistic. In each an
ultimate proposition of knowledge is located outside of the immediate social and psychological context and then reintroduced into that same
present as empowering values for human action in ordinary life situations. The norms in each are universalistic.

While both epistemologies were empirical, the basic object of study,
however, was sharply contrastive as one isolated "historical text" as the
ultimate location of universal value while the other focused on abiding
"nature." Itō, moreover, relied on history rather than transcendent and
timeless moral norms in order to clarify the internal human potential for
moral action in all social and historical contexts. His evidentialism was

aimed at articulating a moral philosophy pinned to the positive idea of constant "life," not of passive quietude and religious meditation. Through this historicist procedure the "natural" active propensity in life is affirmed as integral to moral action and not as distortive manifestations of passion. Nishikawa relied less on written "text" and emphasized the absolute and infinite norm of nature that, by definition, transcended conventional "language." Yet, through this procedure based on natural ontology both men validated the human effort to use "language" to gain deeper insights into nature and thus also the relevance of previous philosophical and literary works.

Of these two alternatives, it was the naturalist views of Nishikawa that underscored more forcefully the judgmental capacity of the human mind to perceive and order objective things, stressing therefore the "accuracy" of that observation as being critical to moral action. For this and other reasons that will become apparent, men at the Kaitokudō would evolve a pedagogical position much closer to natural ontology than to historicism, although, in certain basic ways, Itō's understanding of "virtue" as the universal human capacity toward goodness would remain integrated as a value within the academy's curriculum.

·　　　·　　　·

No thinker in Tokugawa intellectual history is more pivotal than Itō Jinsai in articulating a broad historicist philosophy that endorsed "active life"—*sei-sei*—over the certitude of "death"—*shi*. This historicist philosophy allowed commoners to conceptualize new relational "engagements" in the fixed social order.[7] Due to his eminence as a scholar of ancient texts, however, Itō is invariably situated in relation to the other two great scholars of ancient historical studies—*kogaku*—Yamaga Sokō (1622–85) and Ogyū Sorai, rather than primarily as a philosopher for Tokugawa commoners and especially those that had come to occupy the new commercial spaces in the cities. While clearly sharing related conceptual approaches to knowledge with Yamaga and Ogyū, Itō at the same time retained a philosophical intent that diverged from them in certain crucial ways. The fact that Ogyū Sorai singled Itō out as an object of polemical attack throughout his systematic treatises no doubt added to the misconception regarding Itō's philosophical "place."

From Ogyū's point of view, Itō, while applying a historicist and philological methodology, had not reached similar conclusions to his own. For example, Itō's idea of potential goodness drawn from Mencius diverged from Ogyū's own focus on political creation in a much more ancient context, preceding even the articulations of Confucius. Because Ogyū situ-

26

ated Itō in this polemical relationship with himself, many subsequent commentaries tended to see these two scholars in potential debate with each other. This image was drawn largely from Ogyū's displeasure with Itō for not having responded to his queries to him. In a much repeated story reported by himself, Ogyū had written to Itō praising him for having developed a superb philological methodology that cut through the vagaries of Neo-Confucian cosmology and which accorded closely with his own thinking about how historical studies, as a mode of thought superior to metaphysics, ought to be carried out. Not knowing that Itō, already in the latter part of his career, had not responded to him for reasons of poor health, Ogyū took this as an arrogant personal affront and proceeded to attack Itō throughout a good many of his writings. Perhaps more than any one single factor, it was this polemical denigration by Ogyū that tended to place Itō, misleadingly, in a somewhat lesser light within the "genealogy" of ancient studies, a matter that was viewed with considerable displeasure by scholars at the Kaitokudō.

Well over a thousand scholars and aspiring scholars from various social backgrounds and regional origins are known to have studied at Itō's "hall to study ancient truthfulness"—the *Kogidō*—located in the Horikawa district of Kyōto. Scholars well known at the Kaitokudō such as Goi Jiken (1641–1721), Ranju's father; Keichū (1640–1701), the Buddhist philologist noted for his pioneering work in national literary studies; Kada-no-Azumamaro (1668–1736), also a key figure in the national studies movement; and Miyake Sekian, himself one of the founders of the academy, studied at the Kogidō. Indeed virtually every thinker in Japan came under the influence of Itō, and although most would not subscribe fully to his historicist propositions, many would retain his central moral purpose of shaping a philosophy inclusive of commoners. In particular, his appreciation of Mencius as the first articulator of a universalistic human value would remain a central theme in commoner ideology as at the Kaitokudō.

Thus the casting of Itō in terms of the ideas of Ogyū Sorai and his school of followers, while valid for comparing historicist approaches to knowledge, can also distract the historian from Itō's main achievement. He formulated what might best be described as an "empowering" philosophy for merchants and other commoners to make ideological claims about the virtue of their lives and daily work. While such an interpretive view hardly explains the totality of Itō's scholarly enterprise, it helps to clarify the social purpose underlying his existentialist view of moral action.

It is this often overlooked dimension that gives Itō's thinking a close relationship with the social world around him and relieves his scholarship of merely being an exercise in demonstrating a particular historicist methodology. Itō reminds us here of Quentin Skinner's warning that historians often tend to misunderstand texts by interjecting interpretive perspectives inappropriate to the "historicity" and thus of the "intentionality."[8] While it is true that uncovering such an intentionality is always treacherous business, it is suggestive in our approach to Itō. The criticism, begun by Ogyū and echoed by later scholars, that Itō was unconcerned with politics and especially with how the existing Tokugawa regime governed does not appear as the pertinent perspective of his thinking.

Although a fuller comparison between Itō and Yamaga and Ogyū cannot be pursued here, suffice it to say that unlike the other two, Itō emphasized the "horizontality" of universal human value rather than the conventional distinctions between "high" and "low," between those who governed and those who were governed. By seeking a value outside of metaphysics and beyond the hierarchical present, Itō sought to formulate a philosophical basis upon which human beings in general and commoners especially could claim a universal moral equivalence in terms of a shared potential. Relying on a language that affirmed "life" rather than "emptiness" and the inevitability of "death," he also shaped a broad philosophy that encompassed the human "passions" within a realm of goodness as praxis. For Itō, the potential of acting out goodness thus replaced the necessity of change as the ontological basis for articulating human "equality." It empowered "engagement" with, rather than "separation" from, social reality. Society itself was to be accepted as it is, as moral space, rather than the source of endless pain, suffering, and change.

Several premises for "engagement" with the existing social world stand out in Itō's overall structure of thought.[9] One cannot properly engage with that order simply by "observing" it. A stable reference point outside the present, established with a consistent method, is essential for observation to be meaningful. For Itō this meant uncovering a refined, unambiguous, text in a genetic moment in history when a universal human value was first articulated and readdressing that value as a relevant universal with which to engage in the present. Through this procedure, the world of daily life and work would be redefined as *the* field of moral potential and action. Itō's historicism does not point to antiquarianism but to active interaction in each particular, existential, historical reality, however humble in outward appearance, as the continuing universal moral present. History, in short, is transformed into an ongoing human field of moral potential.

Itō's identification of "history," documental human experience, as the source of moral knowledge, was posed as a polemic against the definition of human moral capacity in terms of abstract metaphysics. The idea of "timeless," "trans-historical" absolutes anchored to an ultimate moral principle as articulated in Neo-Confucian metaphysics, resulted, in Itō's view, in the authoritative confirmation of the "righteousness" (or "reason") of particular things as they were arranged in the objective present, confirming, in short, superior over inferior in both political and moral senses. Without directly objecting to the necessity of having a hierarchy to administer the country, Itō denied the moral implications that were infused into functional arrangements. Abstract moral norms were being used to confirm the status order as an extension of those norms, determining the moral significance of "engagement" in history as also being relative to the virtue that accompanied hierarchical distinctions. Itō found logical fault in the view that moral virtue coincided with social hierarchy as fixed by cosmology. The idea that the distribution of virtue coincided with the natural and social status was based, in the final analysis, on a speculative leap into metaphysics—*keijijō*—that posited the resolution of all differences in an ultimate universal of universals— *taikyoku*. By arguing in this speculative manner that each particular thing despite its differences with other things shared in an ultimate moral universal, that very abstract and timeless universal had in fact been utilized to confirm levels of moral differences and hence inequalities among human beings.

To avoid such a reckless metaphysical leap, Itō reasoned that knowledge about human virtue ought to be sought only where it could be evidentially persuasive, which was to say in human time, in history itself and not outside of it in a timeless absolute. Itō further theorized that evidence could be extracted from the historical universe of language and text to show the original point in an ancient past when the ideal of universal moral potential, or virtue, among all human beings was first unambiguously and purposefully enunciated. It was to that dramatic moment that scholars should fix their critical attention in order to make the meaning of universal value as moral potential clear for all subsequent human history, including, most crucially for Itō, the Tokugawa present.

Totally disregarding the narrative strategy in reconstructing the past, Itō defined history as a field of moral epistemology and not as the story of the rise and fall of political regimes. All historical epochs, in this view of the past, could not be viewed as being equally important. That genetic moment when universal value was first expressed must take precedence over all of the other eras. Itō's scholarly agenda, therefore, called for the isolation of that pristine moment and the analysis of it with a consistent philological method with which he could defend his particular reading of the past against others holding alternative views. This polemical stance, moreover, involved a prior "leap" out of his own present as an objective field into the world of the ancients. He thus severed intellectual ties with the received past as a structured present inclusive of Neo-Confucian philosophy. More expansively, he also disengaged himself conceptually from Japanese historical time and most of Chinese history as well, since much of this history had relied on deceptive metaphysics to organize knowledge. Itō thus bypassed not only indigenous history but most of Chinese history to focus his scholarly attention on the era prior to 221 B.C., prior to the construction of centralized, imperial dynasties, to locate in that ancient universe the genetic articulation of universal human moral potential.[10]

The radical pattern found in Itō is comparable to the Tokugawa historicist scholars Yamaga Sokō and Ogyū Sorai.[11] There is a common denial of the "observation" of things as an adequate approach to firm knowledge, because the observing mind is subjective and not conducive to deducing predictable conclusions. A reference point outside of the present and in a specific historical experience is seen as essential to gauge a given historical present in an orderly and controlled manner. And to specify this reference point in a distant past, a clearly defined philological "method" is also held to be necessary. While sharing these epistemological presuppositions with Yamaga and Ogyū, as a brief comparison with these thinkers suggests, Itō took his thinking in a distinctive direction, a fact that underscores the phenomenon of related thought structures being put to distinguishable social uses.

In Yamaga Sokō's case the separation from his own time led him back to a reconciliation with indigenous history, the rise of the Japanese aristocracy of the sword as creating value equivalences with that identified with the ancient sages.[12] Like Itō, Yamaga had a deep distrust of metaphysics and cosmology as a basis for morality and political ideology. A firm epistemological norm, or "measuring stick," as for cutting paper he would say, was needed to establish reliable ethical and political guidance. Convinced that such a norm could not be established by looking directly at his own immediate past, which indeed quickly strikes the eye as a history of indiscriminant warfare, Yamaga, too, leaves his own context for the ancient world, stressing the importance of maintaining a consistent method of textual analysis. Yamaga emphasized that the normative foundation of all ethical thought was to be found in Confucius's *Analects*. The interpretive mediation of Mencius is rejected. In particular Yamaga underscored the importance of certain ideals such as loyalty, filiality, trustworthiness, and so forth, first enunciated in the *Analects*. These moral norms, Yamaga reasoned, were created in historical time, not outside of it, and are nourished likewise by human beings in human time. By arguing in this manner that ethical ideals are products of human history and documenting this fact in ancient texts, Yamaga could then return to uncover those ethical values in his own historical past, as in the ideals found in the *Analects*: loyalty, filiality, honesty, trust, etc. He finds, moreover, that they were nourished over time by the samurai class, and hence, he proceeded to call the values of this class in their totality as the way of the samurai—or *bushidō*. These values are grounded in the social history of the Japanese past and are not anchored to a metaphysical absolute or, for that matter, to natural law. Rather, they are locked in the evolution of a class, and it is the responsibility of that class to nourish these ideals and use them as norms by which to govern society.

Yamaga's intellectual strategy of leaving one's immediate past and returning to it from a particular interpretive stance allows him to reconstruct a new evolutionary scheme of his own history in terms of the rise of the ruling aristocracy of the sword. Some 600 years of history can now be retold in terms of the creation of value by the samurai. The Japanese past can now be glorified in moral terms and not explained in terms of treachery among ambitious warrior chiefs, thus also raising that history to a par with Chinese history itself and indeed making it even superior to that vast section of centralized bureaucratic rule in China.

In the hands of Yamaga, ancient studies were forged into class ideology which while obviously supportive of the rise of the aristocracy was also critical of the epistemological foundation of the regime of "peace and tranquility" that relied on timeless metaphysical norm to mark a "break" between its rule and the immediate past of the "country at war." The use of cosmology to demarcate such a chronology, Yamaga warned, was a fabrication. Society and its functional parts and the values therein are the products of history and custom, being neither extensions of an abstract absolute nor of nature. The experience of the country at war, out of which the current regime emerged, cannot be disembodied from the rest of history and must be seen in its totality as the painful struggle to create and solidify ethical virtue. The ruling class must therefore identify and nourish those historical values that endow them with the only legitimacy they have. To fail to do so in favor of metaphysics is to invite the decline and fall of governance itself. That these pronouncements did not endear him to the Tokugawa rulers and led to Yamaga's expulsion from Edo to distant Hiroshima is easy enough to understand. Although his reasoning was conservative if idealistic, it was also a critical force against the prevailing thinking about the ethics of governing the country in peace.

Yamaga's manipulation of history is also readily evident in the thinking of Ogyū Sorai, although in interesting ways Ogyū occupies an intermediate position between Yamaga and Itō.[13] While he shares a similar thought structure with Itō, Ogyū's orientation to a political criticism of the present overlaps more extensively with Yamaga. As with the other two thinkers, Ogyū leaves his historical present and immediate past, enters into Chinese historical time, rejects most of that history for its reliance on obtuse philosophical reasoning, and settles on the ancients to find among their archaic textual remnants a generic explanation as to why society, and hence history, was created to begin with. He too proceeded from a deep skepticism regarding the use of abstract moral principle to define order in human society. And he, more than the other two, was explicit in his view that empirical observation could not show society to be an extension of nature. Only societies possess histories, and it is to that source, not to nature, that scholars must turn to understand the norms upon which society and politics rest.

Ogyū did not believe society and nature were dialectically related to each other, although this claim is sometimes made by historians. Nature for him was timeless, having neither beginning nor end, while history was timeful, having an actual beginning. If scholars could uncover the intention behind that genesis, however, human history, like nature, could also continue indefinitely into the future. "The Way of the Sages," he wrote in the Bendō, "is intertwined with Nature, actively developing both human and natural things, continuously and endlessly into the vast and infinite future."[14] Here we sense Ogyū's vision in which human history, while having an explicit beginning, could gain a stature equal to nature's and secure immortality through the Way of the Sages. The monumental problem that remained, of course, was to show through philological strategies what the original intent behind the creation of history was. While admitting the fact that a good deal of the texts no longer existed and that every available fragment would have to be examined for possible clues, including the songs of commoners, Ogyū nonetheless proceeded optimistically to formulate a bold theory of what he believed to be unshakably true.

Based on his textual readings, he theorized that the underlying intent of the ancient kings in creating society was to establish peace and well-being among humankind, separating social from natural existence and hence history from nature. Whereas in nature the strong overcame the weak and strife and struggle were intrinsic to the very order of things, in society under the kings all would be protected and nourished so that each human being could realize to his fullest the "little virtue"—*shōtoku*—that heaven had endowed him with at birth. This ethical purpose to nourish all is what the sages called Benevolence, which was the Great Virtue possessed by the creative ancient kings alone and not by human beings in history, princes and otherwise. What survived as a moral imperative in historical time was the original ethical intent of benevolence that later scholars and kings identified with and sought to actualize in an ongoing reality.

The similarity of Ogyū's structure of thought with that of Itō, more so than that of Yamaga, is clearly evident. Unlike Yamaga, Ogyū is not concerned with locating in his own Japanese past a "functional equivalent" to the creative ethic of benevolence and remained unwavering in his identification with the creativity of the ancient kings of China. And, having isolated the normative purpose of that ethic as "peace and well-being" in society, he then transferred it directly to his own present in the manner of Itō. He applied that norm, however, to questions of administrative policy: how ought the principle of peace be actualized in the immediate world of political economy, which, in his eyes, had deteriorated to a sad state of affairs. If the larger structures to nourish the people were in order, he would say repeatedly, then all the little items could be left alone to move freely to and fro and eventually to find their own places on their own accord. The key issue was "how" to operate such a set of structures so that this kingly vision could be realized.

Such reasoning led Ogyū inevitably to the matter of political prescription, to analyzing what was wrong with the workings of the system, why the view that "virtue" was a monopoly of the aristocracy as a birthright was intellectually untenable, and why it was, in the long run, completely injurious to benevolent rule. He prescribed that the aristocracy be returned to the soil, reduced to the level of commoners, and that talent be selected on a more objective basis. His thinking in this regard reveals a sharper critique on existing politics than Yamaga, who sought to redefine the aristocracy in terms of historical virtue. In Ogyū's thinking there is no attempt to embellish the rise of the aristocracy by resorting to national historicism, as this would have blunted his critical aim of injecting the norm of creative social genesis into the political present. Ogyū also attempted incorporating all of society, including commoners, within his theoretical framework, and in this respect, too, his thinking was closer to Itō than Yamaga. According to Ogyū's thinking, the ancient kings respected all human talent without exception and envisaged nourishing every variety of human virtue, as the following lines from section 7 of the *Bendō* indicate:

> Confucius' saying 'conform to your own personal virtue and rely on Benevolence' is an instructive one. What he meant was that no individual would lose his own special virtue if he conformed to his true nature. He meant too that while human nature may be infinite in variety, no human virtue can be harmful to Benevolence. It is only when human virtues cannot be nourished and consumated that there is deviation from the Way. . . . All human beings possess a virtue that is distinctive to themselves. By relying on the Way of Peace and Wellbeing of the Ancient Kings, everyone can realize fully their own personal virtues. This was the teaching of Confucius and his disciples. [15]

This theme that each human virtue was distinct to each individual is central to Ogyū's overall thought structure and the major point of difference with Itō's. Human beings, he repeatedly argued, ought not be coerced into being something they were not. In accordance with an abstract and unchanging norm of goodness taught in Neo-Confucianism, a view that again resonates with Itō's thinking, such coercion would be corrosive to the human personality. In the final analysis, a person's distinctive virtue cannot be transformed: ". . . while gypsum is fired, its essential character of producing coldness is not lost; and although aconite is buried in hot ashes, its inherent capacity to generate heat is not lessened. . . . What we learn is that the idea that human beings can change their essential specific character is quite erroneous. Indeed, one's fundamental nature is endowed to him by the grace of Heaven. However desirous, human effort cannot oppose and overcome the will of Heaven." [16]

Although Ogyū shared much with Itō intellectually, he was critical of him and praised him only grudgingly. "In recent years," Ogyū observed, "the eminent scholar Itō Jinsai presented some ideas that were close indeed to the central meaning of the Way. However, he examined the *Analects* through Mencius and interpreted ancient texts with the sight of modern language, so that, in the end, his position remained similar to that of the Sung period." And again in commenting on the coerciveness of the idea of human beings transforming themselves into sages, Ogyū wrote: "In recent years Itō Jinsai demonstrated his awareness of these erroneous ideas." [17] Ogyū, thus, recognized in Itō a philosophic brilliance that he found wanting in most other contemporary scholars, whom he treated with contempt. Ogyū believed, however, that Itō had erred in limiting the textual basis of his "ancient studies" primarily to *Mencius*, thereby failing to take into account those texts, notably the Six Classics, preceding Mencius and Confucius, relating to the creation of history and the formulation of the kingly ethic of benevolence. By restricting his view of the ancient world, Itō extracted the idea of human goodness found in *Mencius*, determined this perspective to be the correct insight into Confucius, and then articulated that ideal for the present; but he failed to grasp the most substantial legacy of the ancients—the idea that the purpose of history is social well-being. Had Itō broadened his scholarly vision, Ogyū argued, he might have noticed that Mencius was a narrow-minded polemicist and that Confucius was primarily an editor of received wisdom handed down from the epoch of the ancient kings and not the creator of fundamental ethical ideals. That Confucius deserved to be admired Ogyū would not deny, but this was because of his greatness as a teacher and his recognition of qualitative differences in the virtue possessed by each of his students, not because of his philosophical creativity. Ogyū concluded, therefore, that Itō had failed as a scholar, and his research into the ancient meaning of the *Analects* had not uncovered the true meaning of things in ancient times.

Despite the homology in their conceptual apparatuses, then, the agenda for Itō and Ogyū were different. Many years later in the 1890s, when Japan was in the midst of its industrial revolution, Nakae Chōmin (1847–1901), the theorist for modern participatory politics, would turn back to Ogyū and see his idea of general utility as somewhat analogous to Jeremy Bentham's thinking.[18] No doubt Nakae thought of Ogyū's enlightened despot as nourishing the little virtues of all and thus promoting the happiness of the social whole. Nakae makes no mention of Itō, although he too spoke of virtue being a possession of everyone regardless of status. But it would have been inappropriate to see Itō in the same light, for unlike Ogyū and Bentham, Itō's conceptual strategy was oriented toward circumventing the authoritative presence of immediate hierarchic politics and toward seeking an alternative, horizontal, moral premise on which to base a definition of human society.

Obviously Itō did not dispute the idea that governments ought to be benevolent and nourish society. But this did not, finally, satisfy what seems to have been the most pressing philosophical issue before him. Could all human beings be thought of as being morally equal in some ultimate sense without having to resort to definitions of power or to the Buddhist theology of the inevitability of change and death? While Ogyū theorized that all societies must have come into existence with a common ethical aim to establish peace and order, thus rendering politics inevitable to all social existence, Itō pointed his conceptual sights to show that social existence must, in the end, rest on the idea of the active moral worth of each of the several parts. Without such a moral foundation, the goals of benevolent government or social peace, however desirable, could not be attained.

Ogyū had a great deal of difficulty accepting this view, as reflected in his rhetorical questioning, directed at Itō, throughout the *Bendō* as to whether human beings in fact could determine internally the meaning of norms such as filiality. Since human virtue is variable, theoretically infinite, Ogyū believed it was logically unfounded to say that human virtue could generate ethical norms that were universally true. Norms were fashioned—created—by kings and sages for social ends. They were external, easily understood and hence accepted by all as a substitute for living in a state of nature.

Ogyū's confusion over Itō's reasoning is understandable; but it was not entirely warranted as Itō's position was somewhat more complex than Ogyū gave it credit for. In formulating a philosophy of social "engagement" that was divorced from both cosmological and theological reasoning, Itō sought to clarify the moral potentiality of the individual and did not commit the fallacy of claiming that each individual could generate "norm" from the interior, as Ogyū had unfairly accused him. The subjective human, Itō stressed, possessed the capacity to act in ways that have been called "good" since time immemorial. It was this existential moral potential rather than the self as source of norm that Itō believed to be fundamental to all fields of human endeavor, including politics. This moral potential encompassed all actual situations in society broadly conceived and every historical present regardless of context. Seen in this light, it made perfectly good sense that Itō would be drawn to *Mencius* as the ancient textual resource from which he could extract a moral philosophy that was relevant to his Tokugawa present.

Itō was attracted to *Mencius* because it articulated the idea of goodness as a universal human potential rather than as a static absolute according to which social arrangements could be fixed.[19] It was a concept Itō could apply to relativize existing normative hierarchies and place the burden of moral consciousness and action on each individual member of society. He proposed this potential to be the lowest common moral denominator in all human beings. Human beings, in short, were not to be seen as belonging to groups extending from the absolutely perfect to the least perfect at the lower levels of society, for example among merchants, as formulated out of Neo-Confucian thought. Neo-Confucian cosmology had imposed an unreasonable burden among commoners. On this score Itō was in agreement with Ogyū; but while Ogyū searched ancient texts for the ethical purpose behind the original creation of social constructions, Itō had searched instead for a different kind of "genesis" in which the first unequivocal statement could be found as to the universality of human goodness as an action potential, the ideal that, regardless of social origin, all human beings possessed a moral capacity inferior to no one else's.

Itō was convinced that this Mencian insight was the true meaning of Confucius's teachings rather than the hierarchic formations of later imperial bureaucracies and bureaucratic scholarship and became less concerned with why social rules were originally fashioned. He used that insight to endorse the reality of commoners acting in ways that were compassionate. All moral scholars, Itō concluded, ought to commence with a close reading of Mencius's work as the norm—*jun*—with which to understand Confucius, especially since all subsequent metaphysical glosses, he argued in polemical terms, had obscured that Mencian perception. The gravest error above all was to see in Mencius the idea that human beings were born with a pure and innate goodness that was identifiable with a timeless and absolute goodness, a goodness that was corrupted by social passions and which required the individual to then "recover" the original moral essence through meditative introspection or scholarly asceticism. Itō believed that the *Doctrine of the Mean—Chūyō—*and the *Great Learning—Daigaku*—two of the Four Classics along with *Mencius* and the *Analects*, were misinterpreted by Neo-Confucian scholars.[20] The *Great Learning* Itō found to be of spurious authorship and decidedly outside the Confucian intellectual tradition. The idea that through "observation" the ultimate essence of the self and universe could be grasped and the idea that "righteousness" could mean gaining advantage were in Itō's eyes contrary to the teachings of Confucius. As for the *Doctrine of the Mean*, Itō believed later scholars had tampered with it so that the internal discussion and chapters lacked coherency.

Here again, the idea that the "mean" was a "still" and "spiritual" locus was repugnant to Itō. By prizing these classics, however, the prime position of Mencius and his affirmation of active "life" in a moral field was distorted and rearticulated in terms of the metaphysical search for spiritual stillness. Indeed, Mencius was valuable not because he taught that the "mean" was a point of perfect quietude but because he argued precisely against quietism in favor of an activism in which all human beings participated in accordance with their potential of doing good in many different ways, beginning with the most elemental of all of these—being compassionate toward others in concrete and objective situations.

To Itō, then, all individuals had the immediate capacity, virtually intuitively it might be said, to grasp the authenticity of another life, such as when that other is in intense suffering or imminent danger. For Itō, this active compassion had nothing to do with later metaphysical interventions about the static and timeless goodness which human beings manifested in controlled and orderly ways. On the contrary, goodness was an active potential being lived in a continuing social history. In all times and places and regardless of political or social contexts, myriads of nameless human beings always continued to act in small and unspectacular ways that were in the relative judgment of things "good." In this everyday activity of being or doing good, the metaphysics of ultimate resolution or total reidentification with abstract and timeless essence is without human significance. To Itō, therefore, the *way* was better writ small as "pathways" that human beings in all walks of life traversed in the ordinary course of life. The Great Way or Tao, he went on, may be thought to exist apart from and prior to human experience—resembling here Ogyū's *Heaven*—and thus its transcendent meaning would be beyond human determination. "It is an issue best for men to set aside," as he put it, "for it cannot be argued over with words." It was indeed the very speculation on the meaning of the ultimate Way that had led to reckless conclusions about how some knew more about the Ultimate than others, that, in turn, justified moral hierarchy among human beings. Unlike the ultimate Way which is infinite, it was in the nature of the human mind to be limited, so that even the wisest of sages after much study could grasp virtue only in a relative way, never in an absolute identification of personal essence and the transcendent absolute.[21]

Itō's skepticism, based on the limited human capacity to ever know the meaning of the absolute, led him to reject all speculative claims as to the essential moral meaning of the absolute. It undergirded his own affirmation of the "byways" that the humble and unpretentious treaded on in daily life as the arena of human truthfulness and hence "goodness." At the same time this very skepticism also raised broader epistemological questions as to how the human mind might know and verify things close at hand in those "byways" to be truthful or good. This problem of empirical cognition and its relation to moral value was, of course, central to merchant intellectual history and it is crucial to Itō's thinking.

At a mechanical level, Itō resolved the issue by simply claiming that what could be known could be gotten through textual analysis, by penetrating language in terms of original meanings rather than through the interpretations of subsequent generations. Ancient insights into morality could thus be reconstructed and tested against action in the present. Through philology, distances in time and differences in language could be transcended, the gap between the ancient and the present bridged thereby allowing a perception of the present in terms of universal moral potential and seeing the individual and the collective society as a resource for moral action. The difficulty in Itō's reasoning is plainly evident. The connection between the exigesis of ancient texts and the affirmation of individuals as moral resources is uncertain and, thus, is initially persuasive more on emotive rather than logical grounds. Itō did not formally tie these two themes together, and they remained loosely present in his writings as continuous themes—a reading of Mencius on the one hand and a theory of active human personality on the other. A closer consideration, however, suggests a coherent relationship that is not readily apparent.

The key, as already emphasized, is indeed Itō's understanding of Mencius, although here again the presentation does not greet the reader's eye as a formal argument but as several outstanding concepts. One of these concerned the philological understanding of the term "elemental" or tan as in the four basic traits of human goodness, namely compassion, righteousness, humility, and wisdom. Itō contended that the metaphysicians of Sung Neo-Confucianism and Chu Hsi, especially, had misinterpreted the meaning of tan. These philosophers had rendered tan to mean "extension" or "manifestation," a visible and objective extremity of a fundamental and pure "internal essence" or sei, which was further characterized as innate goodness, stillness, imperturbable and consistent with a timeless and transcendent "reason." In disputing this philosophical construction, Itō identified the source of the difficulty to be in the misreading of Mencius's use of tan. Itō did not find Mencius speaking of tan as an extension or verifiable manifestation of a deeper innateness, but rather of it as referring to the "source," "beginning," or "root" of goodness itself. In conventional use, unfortunately, the term could be used in either way. Yet in philosophical terms, what seemed like needless hairsplitting carried with it, in fact, enormous significance regarding the interpretation of moral action. By focusing on tan as the crux of Mencius's thinking, Itō could then apply it to reject the metaphysical claims that the self and the ultimate absolute were essentially undifferentiated, with the various human virtues articulated simply as "extensions" of that unity. Such a speculative idea, Itō repeated, was not to be found in the writings of either Mencius or Confucius.[22]

Although his critics, such as Ogyū Sorai, maintained that the idea of "source" in Mencius was perilously close to that of "innate" goodness, Itō consistently denied this on the ground that the language in Mencius spoke of goodness as a human propensity or potentiality toward acting in concrete ways that were good. Nowhere, according to Itō, does Mencius speak of the "human" source as identifiable with an absolute and timeless moral essence. From Itō's point of view, then, "goodness" was "action" as an expression of a vital potentiality; it did not signify the manifestation of an unchanging inner pureness. The polemical implications of Itō's thinking were clear. Basing his claim that the human inner "source" was simply constant and irresistible activity on Mencius's thought, Itō then went on to argue this to be a possession of all human beings as a condition of their very being. Referring to this possession of "constant life activity"—*sei-sei*—as inevitable to every human actuality, Itō then denied the ultimate relevance of conventional distinctions that were made between the wise and the foolish, the powerful and the weak, the wealthy and the poor, aristocracy and commoners. The claim that some human beings were superior to others in moral terms and, in particular, the characterization of the uneducated and humble as being passionate in relation to the "still" and unchanging universal was prejudicial and based entirely on speculative reasoning. The "way," Itō repeatedly emphasized, is always "on the ground that men walk on"—*hito no fumu shochi*—and "close at hand and easy to grasp"—*mina sono chikōshite yasuki o iu.* In short, Itō insisted that whatever moral potential human beings possessed had nothing at all to do with superior knowledge or training in metaphysics and, by extension, with the distribution of power and status in society.[23]

Itō's reading of *Mencius* points to an existentialist position regarding human morality. The potential of all human beings to act in "goodness" was disengaged conceptually from an authoritative cosmological absolute with which human beings ought to identify their pure essences. Moral action should always remain relative and incomplete and thus continuous over time and never a salvational "moment" of total enlightenment. In Itō's scheme of thought, then, the human personality is placed within the broad natural propensity of all beings and things to be continuously active, filled with energetic movement—*ki* or *genki.* Everyday social existence, therefore, must allow for the "passion"—*jō*—that is endemic to that universe of constant activity. The passions of emotional likes and dislikes, fear, sadness, joy, and anger should not be shunned as distortions of universal moral truths but as inseparable from the world of human activity within which goodness is realized. As passion is endemic to human movement and also coincidental with the active "source," it is through human engagement with the energetic field of social interaction that is close at hand that compassion for others becomes a moral actuality. Passion and compassion, in short, are thoroughly intertwined in Itō's moral philosophy. To deny this fusion in terms of metaphysical absolutes would be to deny "life" and, in turn, the possibility of moral existence itself. To Itō, passion was inevitable but not inherently wicked.[24]

To underscore his argument that human nature was active rather than still and meditative, Itō referred to the often cited example from *Mencius* in which a person spontaneously saves a child about to fall in the well. Such an act, Itō emphasized, was not an extension of innate goodness or universal reason, but human compassion itself. Without concern as to reward or punishment, or social advancement, or quality of the audience, the act is carried out. Vis-à-vis the imminent death of the child, all distinctions between high and low, rich and poor, powerful and weak, disappear and human beings are reduced to their common source, which is a propensity to act with compassion. The conjoining of that propensity with action is goodness that is a continuous feature of ordinary life situations, the commonplace world of daily clutter and activity.[25]

On occasion Itō described the content of "goodness" in terms of the general virtues of compassion, righteousness, humility, and intellection—*jin-gi-rei-chi*. His preference, however, was decidedly in favor of benevolence—*jin*—above all of the others. Benevolence, moreover, he rendered as simply empathic "love"—*ai nomi*—as action. As he put it: "The central content of benevolence is love—*ai*—so that there is no greater virtue than loving others." and again: "If there is no love there is no virtue to be seen." Itō lamented, however, that in Neo-Confucianism, benevolence was misunderstood to mean one's spiritually pure self—*sei*—and, in turn, spoke of "love" merely as "passion"—*ai o jō to nasu.*[26]

The idea of benevolence, it will be recalled, was a pivotal idea in Ogyū Sorai as well, except that to Ogyū it captured the "intent" of the ancient kings to create society in order to nourish humankind and hence it was a Great Virtue unique to those kings. Itō's understanding of benevolence was a good deal closer to the Buddhist concept of compassion—*jihi*—although it was disengaged from the ontology of ultimate "emptiness." It meant spontaneously grasping the spiritual agony of a moment while simultaneously feeling deep empathy and acting to alleviate the suffering of another person, as just alluded to in the case of the child about to fall in the well. It meant, broadly speaking, possessing the capacity to understand the authenticity of an emotive truth in a situation, person, or thing and to act empathetically without regard to personal advancement. Although central to Confucius's teachings, the virtue of compassion was universal to all social contexts and hence totally pertinent as a source of moral action in the commercial surroundings of Kyoto and Osaka. It was not a possession of the "ancients" alone, but of all humankind that followed in every ongoing historical actuality. As there is no timeless norm that could show what compassion was as a perfect absolute, it must always be acted out in small and relative ways in the present so that goodness was as revelant to the present as it was for Mencius in ancient times.

A major difficulty remained in Itō's structure of thought, and this involved relating individual moral propensity to the social collectivity. Implicit in Ogyū's criticism of Itō is the question, what assurances are there that men will tend to act in ways that are common and hence predictable? For if individuals do not have innate norms, and if these are not transcendent and timeless, from whence do common moral norms emanate? Ogyū circumvented the problem by imputing infinite variety to human virtues and theorizing that the way of the ancient kings would nourish all virtues over historical time. Itō did not attribute such a grand capability to political benevolence. For Itō, princes, like commoners, must understand goodness and benevolence before they could carry out their duties properly. This view could easily be reinforced by Mencius's theory of regicide, that a king who is not benevolent is not a king. Presumably, however, if there is no outside norm to define the human personality in a moralistic manner, as both Ogyū and Itō agreed, then the possibility of variability must be taken into account. Ogyū's view that variety did not matter as long as there was benevolence could not serve as a solution for Itō.

While positing that each individual was endowed with a particular active "source," suggesting that action would also be varied and relative, Itō nonetheless argued that human beings exhibited a comparable propensity toward uniformity and similarity in acting out goodness. Individualized sources and the moral character of the whole, therefore, stood in some kind of coherent relationship in Itō's mind as he reasoned through the use of analogy. Just as different kinds of fruits (or minerals) exhibit different traits, they still share certain key features. Similarly human beings while different in many personal qualities also share a common propensity toward goodness. Since the Way is acted out by all in small paths in daily life, those acts that are close to the individual and are termed "trustworthy," "filial," and "compassionate," add up to moral coherence in society. Such a moral order could not be achieved through political direction from above, although without it effective governance would not be possible. Itō clearly argued the priority of morality over politics.

Despite the conceptual difficulty contained in his thinking in terms of social formation, Itō's overall importance in shaping a moral philosophy for commoners is indisputable. By focusing on history as a field of verifiable knowledge and applying the philological method of textual criticism—*kobunjigaku*—Itō had managed to extricate Mencius's philosophy from the metaphysical structure imposed on it by Neo-Confucianism. Neo-Confucianism in turn buttressed the hierarchical distribution of power and status as graded levels of moral worth with the moral worth of commoners being interpreted as an egregious deviation from refined and idealized norms. Having removed Mencius from this system of thought, Itō rendered Mencius's thought in ways entirely appropriate to commoners in their everyday lives. Indeed, the Mencian idea of the internal moral capacity of all human beings to act in ways that were compassionate without regard to their formal status would evolve into one of the central concepts informing the moral consciousness of merchants throughout the rest of the Tokugawa era.

Itō clearly appears as the key mediating thinker in shaping Mencian thought into an empowering philosophy of "engagement" for the merchant class. In his hands, "ancient studies" constituted a conscious strategy with which to articulate an essential meaning embedded in "text" and to render it in language pertinent to Tokugawa society. Through the ancient text of *Mencius*, Itō authenticated the present as ongoing moral space. Moreover, in relating "ancient" and "modern" in this manner, Itō infused into his philosophy a humanistic "compassion" for the inevitable "passion" that informs the daily lives of human beings, as in the activities of the new commerce so readily evident in the world in which he taught. It was no doubt this humanistic dimension that explains why Itō himself has persisted as a "text" into modern times.

.   .   .

There can be little doubt that Itō's claims for an active interiority tending toward goodness contained provocative instructional significance for merchant commoners. The problem of acquiring objective knowledge in the present, however, remained unresolved in Itō. Most would have agreed with him that ancient texts could be examined objectively, without arbitrary and subjective interpretation, and the moral meaning embedded in those texts appropriated through instruction. Could the same be said, however, of the marketplace? Could this too be dealt with objectively and be devoid of arbitrary and passionate expectations? Could the interior propensity toward goodness be acted out by marketmen deeply engaged in the act of buying and selling goods? Itō's philosophy would certainly allow this. "Benevolence," in words he drew from Mencius, "is the heart of the human being; righteousness—gi—is the outward way of men." Itō invariably contrasted inner benevolence with the external and objective paths that men took in the objective field of action. Through this scheme, he spoke of "love" and of "action" as being in accord, which allowed within his philosophy a theory of objectivity. Action, he insisted must be "accurate," "reliable," "measured," and "ordered"—*yakushin, ken, kei* etc.—rather than speculative and abstract; the acquisition of knowledge—*gaku*—must similarly have as its purpose, effectivity—*kō*.[27]

In the final analysis, however, "righteousness" to Itō was an externalized way and "supportive" of the primary concept—*daiichi ji*—of benevolence as an internal resource. In this respect, external action, while placed in a field of "passion" could not be directly related to the merchant calculation of fair "advantage," as measurable action must always be assessed in terms of "empathy" rather than "profit." The problem of "righteousness" clearly loomed large in the thinking of merchants and may be taken as the "code" term signifying the accurate assessment of external objects and events—*monogoto*—including the marketplace.[28]

How, in short, might one *know* with certitude that a particular act was fair and just. More than compassion and empathy were required to place the epistemology of effective calculation that Itō chose not to emphasize into an appropriate philosophical framework. Here, some of the insights that evolved out of Neo-Confucian philosophy, in what might be termed a metamorphosis from cosmology into moral science, proved to play a decisive role. In this "scientific" rather than "cosmological" dimension of that philosophy, the concept that general truths could be formulated through the careful observation of things took on a special significance in providing another ontological basis for "engagement" by commoners.

It will be recalled that Itō proceeded from the skeptical assumption that metaphysical absolutes could not be known by the limited human mind, so the "observation" of nature should not be thought of as a reliable epistemology that would lead the human mind to such grandiose discoveries. The very prescription of "observation," Itō argued, was a flagrant misreading by Neo-Confucian metaphysicians such as Chu Hsi of a passage from *The Great Learning*—*Daigaku*—which Itō labeled as a spurious and unreliable text of dubious authorship. All that "observation" can yield is the recognition that the natural and social world is always in a state of dynamic motion. And because this active natural order is infinite, it ought to be revered. But beyond that, "observation" cannot serve as an approach to reach conclusions as to transcendent and timeless norms of goodness that Neo-Confucian cosmologists have claimed. Nature from Itō's perspective was primarily a "given" condition rather than an object of precise study.

Despite this historicist critique of cosmology that Itō shared with Yamaga Sokō and Ogyū Sorai, the problem of "nature" as the primary field of knowledge to be "observed" remained tenaciously present in the intellectual world of the eighteenth century. The argument was advanced that while history was obviously important as an evidential base of knowledge, especially in demonstrating how great sages in the past thought about universal human problems, all human texts must, at the same time, be viewed as relative, if indeed the human mind is said to be limited. However valuable, history in this respect cannot serve as an ultimate or ontological basis for moral knowledge, and nature, while ultimately not knowable in a complete manner, could serve as such a basis because it was universal and infinite. That a good deal of cosmological speculation in Neo-Confucianism was unreliable was acknowledged. But that all human norms must finally be anchored in universal nature was retained as valid and superior to other approaches to knowledge.

The pivotal figure in this conceptual metamorphosis within Neo-Confucianism toward a moral science was Kaibara Ekken (1630–1714).[29] A country philosopher living in the domain of Kuroda in Kyushu, Kaibara dedicated his life to the refinement of agronomical studies and the ethics related to this science. His writings, which were read extensively during the Tokugawa era in the countryside as well as in all of the city academies, contain the epistemological point of view just alluded to. To him, history was valuable because it showed how particular societies developed social ethics and customs over time, demonstrating that all societies must shape an ethical system of some kind to survive in an orderly manner. It was an affirmation of history as functional and practical and not as fundamental knowledge. Similarly, he endorsed the importance of Mencius and, not unlike Itō, saw in him a down-to-earth philosophy about the universality of human action tendencies toward goodness. There were no claims, however, as to the superiority of ancient philology and textual exegesis compared with other approaches to moral knowledge. The issue for Kaibara, rather, was that if morality is universal and applicable to all human beings regardless of social status, as Mencius had said and to which he personally subscribed, what then might be the ontological warrant for making such a moral claim? The direct and intuitive perception of human action implied by Mencius did not resolve this issue; Itō, as noted earlier, did not address the issue squarely but resorted to a general theory of pervasive energy and movement to argue his case of "potentiality."

As a student of nature, Kaibara also accepted, without reservation, the idea of an energetic universe of ceaseless motion. He went beyond this point, however, to shape an alternative epistemology. Deeply concerned about the relationship between firm knowledge and the alleviation of the sufferings of the peasantry, Kaibara rested his philosophy on the ground that all knowledge, practical and moral, must ultimately derive from universal nature. As is well known, Kaibara immersed himself in the systematic and encyclopedic ordering of Japan's natural history—his collection of fauna and minerals known as *Yamato honzō* (ca. 1709)—to enhance his thinking on the science of agriculture. A small but influential group of like-minded colleagues gravitated toward him to promote the vital project of agronomy. The most famous of these was Miyazaki Antei whose compendium on agricultural knowledge—*Nōgyō zenshō* (ca. 1697)—served as the most widely used reference work in the proliferation of agronomical ideas throughout village Japan. While deeply involved with this work of "ordering and saving the people," Kaibara arrived at certain crucial philosophical conclusions that would serve as the key premises for moral science throughout the rest of the Tokugawa era. He set these forth in a number of treatises that culminated in a work completed late in his life, around 1713, which summed up his ideas and was entitled "a record of grave doubts"—*Taigi roku.*[30]

In this essay, Kaibara accepted the basic postulate in Neo-Confucianism that the ultimate source of human norms ought to be "principle" or "reason" in nature—*shizen no ri.* He departed drastically from that philosophy, however, by stating his "doubts" as to whether natural reason could be thought of as being intrinsically moral in the conventional sense that human beings understood it. From this skepticism, Kaibara developed the provocative idea that moral consciousness among human beings is not intrinsic to nature as part of its universal reason, but rather that it stemmed from humans' intellectual *awareness* of the natural life within themselves that they share with all other creatures and the ten thousand things in nature. Accepting this gift of life to be enjoyed as a Great Blessing—*Tai-On*—humans then expressed this in terms of a feeling of reverence and humility to nature as an all-encompassing universal. It was this reverence to nature for the gift of *life* that made humans compassionate and empathetic to all other forms of life without regard for conceptions of superiority and inferiority. The empathetic awareness of a shared "life-principle"—*seiri*—moreover, compelled men to relate to each other and to do things in ways that were not capricious, whimsical, and arbitrary, and thus to set forth clearly the rules by which such goals might be realized. All of the virtues that human society prizes, such as benevolence, righteousness, humaneness and trust, are not of nature but the result of reverential self-reflections about the vastness and universality of nature to which the human mind must always remain humble. Moral society, therefore, cannot be distinguished from nature as a mere fabrication as Ogyū had contended but must remain epistemologically related in a close and reverential manner to it. This was a relationship that every human being could engage in actively and was not a prerogative of those with privileged status; this resembles Itō's claim of moral potential for all regardless of class.

Of particular importance to our analysis, however, is Kaibara's empiricism regarding external things which Itō had not emphasized. While denying the dualism in Neo-Confucian philosophy of matter and spirit, phenomena and numina, physical and metaphysical and insisting that a unified and monistic natural principle must serve as the basis of knowledge whereby nature was reduced in this process to the world of matter, phenomena, and the physical; Kaibara nonetheless affirmed the epistemology of systematic *observation* as the basic approach to knowledge. Through the intellectual prepossession that says that spirit is *of* things and principle is *of* matter in a unified nature, the human mind informed with reverence could gain deeper insights into the workings of the "life principle." While it would be impossible for the human mind to know totally through observation the meaning of that principle, a great deal of knowledge could be acquired and incorporated into strategies for peasants in the countryside to alleviate their misery. Kaibara's monism thus presents the world of material reality as the only object of study as it is one with a unified and monistic universe of matter. Principle or reason similarly is of that immediate world of things and not a distant and removed universal abstraction. The most fundamental kind of knowledge, in turn, is made to be accessible to any discerning mind in any historical present. Kaibara's moral science taught that all human beings, including the peasantry, most assuredly possessed the reverential capacity to know objective things, order them in a principled manner, and to improve the lot of lives around them. Simply put, the message to the peasantry was to not wait for benevolent assistance by domainal administrators from above but to seize the knowledge before them to nourish nature's gift of life.

To Kaibara, then, every human mind could make intellectual judgments on objective things, provided these were based on the universal principle of nature. Through these judgments that lead humans to better understand the workings of nature, they also gain a clearer sense of their own moral character, in particular the values of reverence, humility, and benevolence. Unlike the historicist Ogyū Sorai, who denied the usefulness of speculating about morality in terms of nature as the human mind could not fathom its inner workings, Kaibara argued that reverence for nature was a universal human capacity and constituted the ultimate basis for self-reflection regarding the moral character of human beings. Moreover, he connected this idea of reverence with the equally universal human potential to observe nature and make accurate calculations of that objective world. As the workings of this natural order were principled and not arbitrary, it also followed that the human evaluation of them must likewise be principled and systematic. It was an epistemology utterly pertinent to peasants engaged in scientific farming and to merchants engaged in the workings of the marketplace.

The use of natural ontology such as expressed by Kaibara found its way to townsmen and commoners through the mediation of popular writers, the most effective and best known of these being Nishikawa Joken. A merchant astronomer from Nagasaki, Nishikawa compiled many of the naturalist perspectives in didactic treatises, or "bagfuls," of useful knowledge, for townsmen and farmers—*Chōnin bukuro* (1719) and *Hyakushō bukuro* (1721).[31] As miscellanies of ethical ideas, they were widely circulated and read; the one for townsmen, in particular, was reprinted at least eight times during the hundred years after its initial publication. As the title suggests, all sorts of useful ideas and perspectives are tossed into the "bag" so that it is devoid of any kind of apparent internal order. The topics commented on range over morality, nature, politics, society, history, language and custom, and such specifics as the evil of infanticide, and even the negative effects of consuming meat and wine, as witnessed in the short life span of Westerners. The entries are designed to serve as practical references for everyday use, and the language is easily accessible to commoners. The style is not convoluted, and the use of Chinese ideographs is kept at a minimum. There is, moreover, certainly far less grand conceptual design and elaborate philosophical speculation in Nishikawa than in Kaibara's recounting of his "grave doubts" about Neo-Confucian moral philosophy. While Kaibara's treatise is a reflective piece on the steady evolution of skepticism over his entire career; Nishikawa's is self-consciously didactic and aimed at persuading ordinary readers.

Yet, the themes that present themselves through repetition in the various entries add up to a readily discernible and provocative affirmation of moral equality among all human beings in terms of natural ontology and the capacity of townsmen and other commoners to acquire, evaluate, and make discriminations about knowledge of external things. In these ways, Nishikawa's miscellany outlines a relationship between epistemological control of objective reality in everyday life and moral purpose. If it may be said that Itō's function was to bring Mencian principles into the everyday life of commoners in eighteenth-century Japan, a companion observation might be made of Nishikawa. His function was to strip objective things of their mystery and to render them as falling within the range of the minds of commoners to know and to control these things in ways that were at once accurate and moral.

Although Nishikawa's miscellany directed at townsmen included merchants and craftsmen, in fact many of his comments are addressed primarily to merchants. Not surprisingly, Nishikawa is concerned with how wealth is to be understood. Although he does not provide a clearly formulated definition, his comments suggest a view of wealth that may be summarized as follows: wealth is the totality of goods produced, primarily agricultural, and the available metallic cash that is used to establish an exchange value for those goods in order to distribute them throughout society. Both goods and cash are seen as "social" items, that is, for the use and benefit of all. Money, as he explicitly noted, is not a private possession but a social one: "The money available in society belongs to everyone in the whole kingdom."[32]

Money then is "public," like other categories such as class stratification or law. "The ideograph for public is to be read in Japanese as ōyake," he writes, "and it means the natural principle—Tenri—which is devoid of the private."[33] Social stratification is inevitable in the public realm and is endemic to nations everywhere in the world. The same is true of laws. They regulate and order the public realm without concern as to private gain. The king—in Tokugawa Japan, either emperor or shogun—must govern out of a reverence for this natural principle of publicality and preserve the whole against treason. Whether the country is Japan, China, India, Holland, or whatever, no public order encourages its own destruction from within but seeks through law to maintain the peace for the good of all—the multitude or banmin. Similarly, wealth falls within this natural principle of publicality. It too ought to be viewed as social rather than private and, above all, natural, rendering in effect the actions of marketmen public, essential to social well-being, and anchored to natural principle.

More concretely, Nishikawa identified the dynamic process of the economy with the state of constant movement or momentum in nature—shizen no ikioi. Since wealth, as with nature, is in constant motion it cannot be in fact a stable "private" possession. There is no absolute position or locus to national wealth. It continuously moves from one place in society to another and is therefore relative and cannot be locked into "house" or "class" or "court" as some misguidedly seek to achieve by hoarding precious metals. Through exchange and transaction, or simply, trade, wealth is spread diffusely throughout the land: "Wealth does not remain stationary in a single place for any length of time. As soon as it stops it already has reversed itself and begun to scatter about. This is in accordance with natural principle."[34] In one of the more colorful images he sprinkled liberally throughout the miscellany for merchants, Nishikawa likened the distribution of wealth to cherry blossoms blown away by nature's wind onto what had been a barren yard next door. At any given point in time, wealth is always limited rather than unlimited. The spread of wealth in one sector of society means simultaneously the relative decline of it in another part. Similarly, therefore, poverty is relative and not permanent. The rise and fall in the fortunes of merchant houses of the sort described in the *Kōken roku* of Mitsui is a reflection of this turn and flow of wealth. For Nishikawa, his general theory also explained the overall shift in wealth from the aristocracy to the merchants.

What then might be the actual public function of merchants or *akibito*? Their work, he explains, is to exchange goods for money and thus facilitate public order by transferring goods abundant in one area to another area that needs them and vice-versa. More specifically, merchants make concrete calculations—*shōryō; keiryō*—to gauge the supply, the volume of goods at hand, and to judge the quality—*yoshiashi*—of those goods. Unlike in ancient times when exchanges were carried out with one type of good for another, the transaction is done entirely with money as the medium representing the value of any exchange. Without the objective mediation of merchants calculating supply and value, however, the flow of wealth could be seen entirely as the manifestation of arbitrary and passionate greed—*taiyoku*. The objective mediation of merchants proceeds on the presupposition that wealth is public and that publicality is based on natural principle—the idea that nature is devoid of selfish intent just as it shows no favor in running its seasonal course. Seen in this light, it is entirely reasonable for merchants to exact a just "profit" for their services, for through them the available wealth of the land is circulated throughout society, thus enhancing the nation's well-being—*kokka no yō o tassuru*. For merchants to exhibit "courage"—*buyū*—therefore, they ought not emulate the samurai and conceal their actual physical frailty, appearing only outwardly strong like them, and should possess instead the presence of mind to be objective and accurate and not take an iota more as profit than was fair. Integrity for merchants rests on economic intelligence, not on skill in the martial arts.[35]

Nishikawa drew on other themes to reinforce his claim for the public character of wealth and hence of the work of marketmen. Like Kaibara, Nishikawa was adamant in his endorsement of the basic proposition that all human beings possess a common moral potential. Indeed, merchants can act in ethical ways precisely because their moral character is no different from that of any other group of human beings: "When all is said and done, there is no ultimate principle that establishes superior and inferior among human beings. These distinctions result from upbringing. . . . How can distinctions be made as to high and low in terms of the fundamental essence of human beings." Nature does not establish these distinctions, as it treats all evenly without selfish intent. Nature does not determine that a child of illiterate commoners must remain so. A person born in China may be raised to become a Japanese, just as one of lowly birth could be raised to become a samurai. Like the digger wasp—*jigabachi*—that seeks to transform itself into something else, so too "the child of a wicked person will not grow up to become treasonous if raised by a good man." No human being is inherently inferior as all human beings possess a common moral potential endowed to them by nature. Nishikawa celebrated the natural human spirit with the following poetic line: "Plant and you will not find a meadow where flowers will not bloom"—*uete miyo hana no sodatanu sato mo nashi.*[36]

All existing social differences among human beings, then, must be understood in light of that prior principle of nature and viewed as resulting from historical custom and as not being intrinsic to the natural order. Each country develops along distinctive cultural lines that, over time, shape the personality of individuals. Thus the historical customs of China, Japan, and Holland for that matter, all develop different patterns. For example, China, from its inception, based its culture on "written language"—*moji*—while in Japan language was said to be a legacy of divine instruction so that its written component, the syllabary, is merely phonetic markings—*shirushi*. In Holland there are only twenty-four letters and words are formed by combining two letters together. Furthermore, Nishikawa notes, it is a custom in China for children of commoners to study and seek bureaucratic positions even as high as that of minister to the throne, but such a tradition is not to be found in Japan, although scholars in Japan have been abundant, and its custom does not preclude commoners from studying, acquiring wisdom, and demonstrating this in their received line of occupation—*shōbai*. Indeed, among Confucius's students, too, there were merchants and peasants and nowhere does he advise them to change their line of work to become "scholars." Still the cultural pattern determining the utility of scholarship in China and Japan are contrastive and rooted in the indigenous histories of each. But of fundamental importance is the point that while societies develop in different ways, they all proceed from an initial reliance on nature and the baseline proposition therein that distinctions do not exist as to high and low among natural things. Since nature always precedes society, the measurement of societies in terms of "superiority" and "inferiority" based, for example, on how "ancient" one is in comparison to another is a trivial point of view.[37]

However, while societies are different as to how they organize themselves and do things, there is also something that is analogous to all of them. They all begin with a relationship with nature, and out of this relationship all individuals come to act in ways that are deemed to be "ethical" in accordance with what each contributes to the well-being of the whole. How this is done in an organized manner is not determined by nature, so that the system of one country is dissimilar to that of another. Although Nishikawa offers no real explanation as to why this should be so, he is explicit in his view that within these different systems individuals act in ways that are ethical; and ethicality invariably involves the enhancement of social well-being inclusive of all commoners. The Dutch too, he observed, are loyal and filial as evidenced by the fact that they keep pictures of their mothers close at hand and also practice monogamy which is praiseworthy. Indeed, human societies may be likened to ant colonies. The ancients ascribed ideographs to ants to read "righteous insect" because ants, like human beings, are all involved in myriad different ways to sustain the entire community. This commitment to social well-being in the human world is termed wisdom, honesty, trustworthiness, frugality, and the like. They all point to the ethic of intelligent human involvement in the nourishment of society. In this respect, no single act or function that contributes to this end should be seen as fundamentally different from another. In short, there is no absolute hierarchical value of one kind of work compared with another. Just as flowers grow in fields everywhere, peasants are capable of doing the work of samurai if properly educated to do so and, similarly, the samurai of peasants.

The same held true for merchants as well. The issue for Nishikawa, however, was not so much whether merchants possessed the intellectual potential to perform as samurai, but rather if the actual work that they did produced beneficial social consequences. Could profit gained through competition and the passionate engagement in the exchange of goods be ethical with regard to the social good—*tenka no tame?* On what basis might the claim be made that the judgments of merchants are accurate and thus potentially *fair?* Was their epistemology of calculation sound? Or were they merely evidence of passionate greed as was often said?

As already emphasized, Nishikawa defined his epistemology in terms of a broad ontological principle of nature that encompassed all natural and social phenomena. The ancient sages expressed this unity well in epithets such as the following: "To deceive another person is to betray nature itself"; or, "Since Heaven is the parent of the ten thousand things, the spirit of human beings is one with all of those things."[38] Echoing the thesis advanced by Kaibara, Nishikawa declared the dualism in Neo-Confucian thought that separated "principle" and "matter" to be misleading and held instead to a monistic theory of nature in which all phenomena were integral parts of a unified material order. This order, moreover, was powered by a material energy—*ichi genki*—that manifested itself in the everyday world as constant life activity—*sei-sei*. The ancients called this natural energy the Great Virtue of Nature—*Tenchi no Tai Toku*, or the "divine spirit"—*kami*—of human beings. Far from being mystical religious ideas, these can be ascertained objectively through the systematic study of the movement of heavenly bodies in astronomy—*tenmon gaku*—and through the examination of the natural conditions of the earth itself or "geography"—*chirigaku*. These approaches to knowledge demonstrate conclusively that the ceaseless movement in the universe is not a religious or moral spirit but a principle of universal reason whose regularity could be recognized by the human mind. The most elemental aspect of this reason is what everyone calls Heaven's Time—*Ten no Toki*. All human beings order themselves with reference to that norm of time; their grasp of this is documented in the calendars—*reki*—that societies use. Politics is ordered according to this calculation of time. Time, however, is not a privileged possession of the powerful few; it belongs to the entire populace—*tami no toki*.[39]

In saying that the knowledge of time required to govern is identical with that used by commoners to order their lives, Nishikawa was not proposing that commoners should also govern the nation. While theoretically plausible, such a theory would have placed him totally outside his own historical context. His thinking nonetheless contained provocative and far-reaching significance. Knowledge of time, far from being an aristocratic privilege, was immediately accessible to the most humble of commoners. And as the ancient sages first constructed calendars, commoners like Nishikawa in the present could study astronomy and revise the calendar according to more precise knowledge. That Nishikawa would attract much attention for his work and even be invited by Bakufu officials to examine their calendar is less important than his main theoretical point that political regularity is actually based on natural time and natural time belongs to everyone. He taught merchants and peasants to have this perspective in seeking objective knowledge of nature. Without regard to their lowly status, commoners ought to see time as belonging to them; by applying that knowledge to rid the mind of superstition and divine expectations, they would be better able to work toward reasoned production and profit. Alluding to this view as one already outlined with great clarity by Miyazaki Antei in his compendium on agronomy, Nishikawa reiterated the conviction of all natural ontologists that the ceaseless activity of nature was not accidental flux as taught in Buddhism but a field of knowledge that human minds must engage in to contribute to the social good. "The reliance on time to enhance the productive advantages of land," he thus observed, "is especially important in the agricultural work of farmers. And merchants and craftsmen too should proceed with that same approach in mind."[40]

For merchants, this prescription meant calculating the precise moment of intervention in the flow of goods and cash and to determine from this timing where the proper point of "restraint" might be. Here it is quite plain that "restraint" does not mean the internalized exercise of "frugality" but the objective analysis and judgment made on a precise point of what is just and what is excessive in the calculation of profit. Nishikawa carefully pointed his conception of natural time away from a theory of profit maximization and toward the ethicality of reasoned profit taken as accurate, dispassionate, and "fair" by the most basic of natural norms. Just profit, within Nishikawa's framework, was simply the concrete and measured consequence of a controlled epistemological procedure—no different in its basic approach whether it was applied by a benevolent ruler, a calendar maker, or a farmer. The measurement of "volume" and the assessment of "quality" in which merchants engaged in the exchange of goods need not be arbitrary and passionate just as, in contrast, men who possess the status and power to govern need not necessarily be principled and just.

As suggested previously, Nishikawa used the theory of natural ontology in several related ways. Being universal and devoid of selfish and arbitrary intent, nature served as an ultimate norm for the principle of public justice. At the individual level, reverence for universal nature informed the moral values of compassion, honesty, trustworthiness, loyalty, and so forth. It endowed all human beings with a life spirit—honshin—that was universally shared without reference to actualities of status and power. While some human beings may be more or less talented than others, no individual could be denied his essential life spirit. That life spirit, moreover, contained within it an active potential to observe and order external things, to grasp patterns within a constantly moving natural field. The human mind could observe patterned regularity and formulate stable ethical concepts and rules of governance. It could also observe the stars and the movements in the heavens. It could make judgments as to when and what to plant in various geographical areas. And finally it could calculate significant points in the exchange of goods. In Nishikawa's thinking, all of these were fundamentally alike in their epistemological grounding. They all shared a common conception of knowledge oriented toward nature. To Nishikawa, rulers must identify with the selfless principle of publicality; peasants must harvest on time; merchants must calculate precise interest. In whichever way natural principle is used, one procedure should not be considered inherently superior to another. A samurai might succeed or fail at a particular endeavor just as a merchant might: the former, not knowing how to deal with the marketplace, might blemish the name of his lord; the latter, by seeking to advance himself into the aristocracy, might fail to acquire the more pertinent skills of economic calculation. One form of failure, however, is no worse than the other. Since nature's "blessing" of life is universal, how that gift is used in the human condition ought not be arranged in terms of a simple hierarchy; this view was quite explicitly intended to encourage his audience of commoners to engage dynamically in the world they had received.[41]

The ideological theme in Nishikawa's "miscellany" is unambiguous and provocative. While status hierarchies as they exist in the immediate world of class and authority may be useful for maintaining order, this should not be construed to reflect ultimate propositions about knowledge and life. The epistemological grasp of natural principle at whatever "level" was of vastly greater significance for acting systematically in ways that were hence potentially "moral" and not inferior to any other form of action. It was within this mode of thought that Nishikawa argued the ethicality of the creation of wealth through trade when it was grounded on sound objective judgments. According to his thinking, when merchants carefully gauged their work as traders in terms of the natural principle of measurement, the results were not arbitrary. Being determined by fair principles, the fruits of trade must also enhance the public good.

Convinced, then, that marketmen were fundamentally as ethical as anyone else, Nishikawa called on them to find joy in their world of work. Disregard illusions about salvation and reincarnation into another better social status, he told them. Why, as he noted in his summation, should anyone work to be reborn into another class, such as the samurai aristocracy. Life in that class is replete with unpleasant duties, such as serving a single lord to constantly embellish his prestigious name. And it is, after all, true that even the mighty fall in disgrace. Like the stork, therefore, better to live a thousand years—*tsuru ni umarete sennen*—than to possess a kingdom for three days—the reference here being to Akechi Mitsuhide (1528–82), the ambitious assassin of Oda Nobunaga (1534–82). Indeed, as for himself there is a life to enjoy merely as an ordinary merchant: *Tada kono chōnin koso tanoshikere.*[42]

.   .   .

Nishikawa's celebration of merchants relates to the thinking of his contemporary, Dazai Shundai, who was mentioned in the prologue. Being a member of the aristocracy, Dazai did not speak of the "virtue" of merchants so much as the political uses of their method of trade. And being a student of Ogyū Sorai, he identified history as being the primary anchor to knowledge rather than nature. But Dazai was familiar with the critical changes that had taken place within Neo-Confucian thought in the hands of Kaibara Ekken, a fact clearly borne out by the words of praise he had for Kaibara's treatise on "doubts." Dazai expressed astonishment in finding in Kaibara conclusions about the unreliability of Neo-Confucian metaphysics, in particular the dualism between matter and principle that was used to speculate about the "moral" content of principle as against physical things. Indeed, Dazai wondered why the widely respected Kaibara should be called a "Neo-Confucian" scholar at all. In a similar manner, Dazai himself, while maintaining his "historicist" frame of analysis regarding the normative intent behind the initial creation of history, arrived at a conclusion comparable to what Nishikawa Joken had concluded as a "Neo-Confucian" scholar of "nature." Nishikawa, in the manner of Kaibara, had posited that human intelligence possessed the capability of perceiving a nonarbitrary principle in nature from which external events, including economic exchanges, might be accurately calculated. At issue here for Nishikawa was the epistemological relationship between the human mind and nature in the present, not a normative warrant located in the texts of the ancient kings. Kaibara's dedication to agronomical studies and Nishikawa's to astronomy were both tied to that basic epistemology. Through this approach, they were convinced the livelihood of commoners could be improved, thus realizing from "below" the goals of political economism, namely "ordering and saving the people."

Dazai, on the other hand, was concerned with the political question of saving the people as part of kingly action. Yet, like Nishikawa, he too identified trade as a systematic art and saw it as the potential cure for the existing order. If domainal lords would but acquire the principle used by merchants to create wealth through trade, Dazai believed the Baku-han system would stand a chance of surviving into the future. "Like merchants," Dazai wrote, "stipended retainers and daimyō all satisfy their needs with money and they must therefore devise ways to acquire it. This may indeed be the most urgent task of our day, for there is, in fact, no better way to create wealth than through trade."[43] We sense that, for Dazai, trade is no longer errant "passion" but a controlled and disciplined activity capable of sustaining politics. Domains should export goods that are plentiful and exchange them for scarce items. Cash should mediate the transactions. If this entire process were executed with care, domains could create wealth and stem the tide of political decline which he saw everywhere around him. In a comment for which he came to be well known, Dazai warned that if such drastic measures were not taken, the sage had no alternative but to retreat into "nature" and simply watch the political system waver and fall. This, he concluded was the true political message of Taoism.

Although Nishikawa was not concerned with how political leaders utilized the principle of trade, he was aware that commoners must help themselves and not expect benevolent assistance from above. Commoners must do what is best for their well-being in terms of the knowledge they are capable of controlling. It was within this frame of reference that Nishikawa confirmed trade as a virtuous activity anchored to natural principle. Having placed the knowledge of commoners in this universalistic scheme, Nishikawa then went on to propose that the general activity of trade on a national level was crucial to the well-being of the nation and that, therefore, the principled world of merchants was not only moral but part of the "public" good. In this manner, Nishikawa articulates a "political" meaning to merchant trade activity that dovetails with Dazai, even though the specific social "actors" remain distinct. In the final analysis, however, Nishikawa's real didactic point to merchants was that their capacity to be objective and calculate precise "limits" to profit taking was a moral act inferior to no other; they ought not feel humiliated before the frequently made accusations of their rampant "greed," and they should engage in their work with the knowledge of it being within the public realm.

Another related interpretive point is worthy of emphasis here. It is pertinent to note that just as alternative epistemological positions, such as those of Nishikawa and Dazai, could converge in terms of the public meaning of trade, so too related epistemologies could be put to contrastive social goals. Itō Jinsai and Ogyū Sorai shared a common historicist structure of thought with each rejecting the cosmological moral philosophy of Neo-Confucianism and displacing it with ancient historical "text." But far from reaching similar conclusions as to the meaning of this epistemology, they diverged rather sharply. To Ogyū, how men ought to rule in the present was clarified in terms of the normative intent of historical genesis. For Itō, ancient text was utilized to affirm the universal moral potential in human beings, which thus empowered new moral spaces for commoners in the present. It is here in the distinguishable "intentionality" of common methodology that we see Itō as actually being closer in spirit and moral purpose to natural ontologists such as Kaibara and Nishikawa whose epistemology differed basically from his. Dissimilar conceptual premises nonetheless reveal related moral purposes which attempt to establish a firm philosophical basis for commoners "engaging" within an ordered political reality. Whether the reference is to ancient history, as in Itō's case, or nature, as in Kaibara and Nishikawa, the egalitarian basis of moral potential is emphasized so that commoners might grapple in a dynamic way with agricultural production and the new commerce without apology. Each philosophical position rejects the anachronism of "detachment" and "disengagement" as the ethical basis of defining living and working spaces and does so with clear epistemological reasoning.

Likewise, the ancient ideas of Mencius now become available to the daily intellectual lives of commoners through the scholarly mediation of Itō. Ancient text and the present universe of existential "action" are integrated. And similarly the ideas of moral science also gain a coherent place in the ethical and work consciousness of commoners. Kaibara promoted this through his study of agronomy and his encyclopedic documentation of natural history; Nishikawa turned his interest in astronomy into didactic writings persuading merchants and peasants of their natural capacity to control objective knowledge.

While Itō on the one hand and Kaibara and Nishikawa on the other shared a comparable social focus, their differing approaches to defining "action" are worthy of note. Seeking the broadest possible warrant for goodness as a possibility in the present, Itō did not concern himself with the specifics of what action should be like. All of the myriad acts that go into the constitution of everyday life must be viewed as being potentially good or contributing to goodness. One set of acts could not be prejudged as superior to others. Itō, therefore, emphasized the internal propensity within human beings to act empathetically toward their fellow men and toward creatures and things. The importance of empathetic relationships thus remained paramount to Itō.

In Kaibara and Nishikawa, action is defined in much more specific terms and keyed to objective physical knowledge that the human mind is capable of ordering and controlling as calculated rather than empathetic acts. Itō's philosophy is open-ended and avoids such specifics as how merchants or farmers should or should not act, even though his ideas quite clearly are aimed at affirming the expanding moral spaces that commoners controlled while Kaibara addressed himself specifically to the peasantry and Nishikawa to merchants as well as peasants to persuade them of their capacity to grasp natural principles through *observation* and thus make specific and nonarbitrary judgments on external things and events. While all phenomena in nature are in a state of dynamic movement, Kaibara and Nishikawa emphasized, this movement could be calculated in relatively accurate ways and ought not be seen as merely "flux" and "ephemera" from which the human mind should seek spiritual distance.

Both philosophical perspectives converged and metamorphosed merchant thinking regarding the moral place of merchant philosophy in society and its understanding of the workings of political economy. It is also evident, moreover, that Itō's ideas on empathy would be incorporated by merchant intellectuals *within* the evidential epistemology that affirmed the possibility of precise calculation, as our following chapters on the Osaka merchant academy, the Kaitokudō, will bear out. In combination, these two philosophical orientations can hardly be called subversive or accused of having shaped an iconoclastic theory of action from "below." Rather, they provided key philosophical references in the shaping of a merchant ideology that endorsed active engagement in trade as essential to the public order. It was out of this endorsement that a critical perspective of political economy would be shaped from the standpoint of merchant leadership.

THREE

⬜ IN SEARCH OF VIRTUE: ⬜
⬜ FOUNDING THE KAITOKUDŌ ⬜

THE VIEW, ADVANCED BY THE DISTINGUISHED HISTO-
RIAN TSUDA SŌKICHI (1873–1961), THAT TOKUGAWA CON-
FUCIANISM HAD LITTLE BEARING ON THE CULTURE OF THE GENERAL POPU-
lace, though convincing, is also misleading.[1] Slanted to minimize the
importance of Chinese cultural "influences" on Japanese civilization,
Tsuda's perspective tends to confine Confucianism within the boundaries
of the ruling aristocratic elite, so that his scattered comments admitting
the importance of China to Japanese history tend to be stylized and un-
convincing. Tsuda's view is valid insofar as commoners, as he demonstrates with vivid evidences drawn from popular literature, did not perceive of themselves as being anything other than Japanese. However
accurate this view, it can hardly be denied at the same time that thinking
in the countryside on agronomy and astronomy and on commerce and
education in the cities drew extensively from Confucian epistemology, as
is evident in the ideas developed by Itō Jinsai, Nishikawa Joken, Ishida
Baigan, and the scholars at the Kaitokudō. The often overlooked history
of commoners as they involved themselves in this critical activity of
teaching, learning, and shaping certain kinds of visions from this interaction is, indeed, a dynamic theme in the development of Tokugawa
thought—a theme worthy of analysis outside the framework used by
Tsuda and his contemporaries. The importance of Confucianism as a
source from which key mediating concepts were drawn to grapple with
specific moral issues confronting Tokugawa commoners is easily confirmed by the available literature of that period. In the case of merchants,
Confucianism offered a language with which to conceptualize their intellectual worth in terms of universalistic definitions of "virtue." Thus,
while Confucianism undeniably remained the preferred philosophy of the

60

aristocracy, to view it as being enclosed within the boundaries of that class would be to deny that system of thought its adaptive and expansive capabilities.[2]

Indeed, the stratum in Tokugawa society that specialized in the study of Confucianism—men known as *jusha*—was not part of the aristocracy at all and emerged out of the interstices of the various classes. Unlike the four legal classes of samurai, peasants, craftsmen, and merchants, the jusha did not have formal recognition as a status group, and entrance into that class was loose and informal, unregulated by such mechanisms as examinations and the possession of degrees as was the case in Imperial China. Coming from diverse and often lowly social origins, the bottom rungs of the aristocracy, and from commoner classes, jusha also referred to themselves as "physicians." A term indicative of a relatively impoverished scholar, "physicians" prescribed medicinal herbs from the front entrance of their homes and taught Confucian moral ideas in their back rooms. Because of their mixed and undistinguished social backgrounds, jusha were not uniformly held in high esteem by members of the aristocracy, and they were also often demeaned by writers of popular satires as impractical and pretentious men. These caricatures notwithstanding, the jusha flourished as a multiclass status group all through the eighteenth century and contributed mightily to the Tokugawa discourse on knowledge. They came to possess an intellectual "history" of their own that is documented by detailed biographical dictionaries and well-known critical historical summaries such as Hirose Tansō's *Jurin hyō* of 1836.[3]

Lacking formal status, the jusha, for the most part, pursued scholarly careers detached from the administrative apparatuses of Edo and domainal rule. The majority did not receive stipends—which explains the large number of "physicians" among them. Some, of course, did gain access into political chambers as advisors of Bakufu ministers, as in the cases of Ogyū Sorai and Arai Hakuseki (1657–1725). Others found employment in domainal schools and, in the example of Satō Issai, the directorship in the early 1800s of the Bakufu College—*Shōheikō*—itself. By and large, however, the jusha were men without firm guarantees as to livelihood and without clear links to the centers of authority, even though the ideas they studied were closely linked to the problems of ordering and governing. They carved out a living by establishing "private schools"—*shijuku*—in the urban centers such as Edo, Osaka, Kyoto, and the numerous domainal castle towns. It would not be farfetched to say that because the pursuit of knowledge in these schools (ranging from those with national reputations to the vast majority without such standing) was not specifically linked to "power," the intellectual evolution among the jusha was relatively open and unconstrained. The engagement with Dutch studies and, in turn, Western science and social science from within this stratum provides dramatic testimony of this tendency.

Jusha found Osaka a congenial city to teach and study in. It was not the Kyoto of courtly elegance nor, more importantly, was it dominated by the samurai aristocracy of the domainal castle towns and Edo. Over ninety percent of its population consisted of craftsmen and merchants. Well-known exiles from the aristocracy such as Asada Goryū, Hirose Kyokusō, and Kaiho Seiryō sought refuge there. Commoners who preferred not to seek employment in domainal schools staked their academic fortunes as teachers in Osaka. Scholars associated with the Kaitokudō in the early years were of such background as indeed were the two principal founders of the academy. Nakai Shūan came from a family of lowly "physicians" once under domainal employment, and Miyake Sekian, the head lecturer, refused numerous invitations from domainal schools and maintained a pharmacy while tending to his duties as a teacher.

In the early 1700s the poetry and reading groups, benkyōkai, that jusha had organized among their colleagues began to take on institutional form as "private schools" and "academies" reflecting, as mentioned earlier, the growing sense of crisis in the aftermath of Genroku. A number of such academies known generally as "regional academies"—gōgaku—and bearing such names as Gansuidō, Rinkakudō, and Kanzanrō were established at this time in the Osaka area. While the records of most of these regional academies are no longer available, the records of the Gansuidō shed light on the character of these schools on the outskirts of Osaka relative to the Kaitokudō which was situated in the center of the city. Founded in the country town of Hirano, which was located on the southern perimeter of Osaka with a population of 10,000, the Gansuidō was established around 1706 as a "study group" or "communal readership"—kōsha—for like-minded commoners, including well-to-do farmers and merchants, seeking to familiarize themselves with the secular philosophy of humanitarian action as taught in leading urban academies like Itō's Kogidō in Kyoto. With the financial support of "seven notable houses"—hichi myōka—the communal readership transformed itself in 1717 into an academy, the Gansuidō, which then remained active until 1870.[4]

Several suggestive themes are worth emphasizing here for purposes of comparison with the Kaitokudō. It seems quite apparent that the transformation of the Gansuidō from a readership into an academy was a self-conscious response to the crisis in the countryside at that time. More specifically, the men of the Gansuidō sought to establish their academy as a center of learning and practical philanthropy that would serve as a persuasive alternative to the Buddhist temple in the area—Faith Buddhism in this instance. In place of Buddhist charitable works based on the teachings of an otherworldly faith, the Gansuidō sought a secular ethic of *engagement* with that world before them as intellectually real and governable. Compassion and the alleviation of suffering among the people, in other words, would be undertaken in terms of the world of action that farmers and merchants in Hirano were engaged in, in particular the manufacturing of cotton textiles for which that area was known. In the affirmation of engagement with history, the denial of the Buddhist theory of the universe, and the search for ethics that would confirm commerce, the Gansuidō shared a common experience with the Kaitokudō, although as will be discussed later, the Kaitokudō concerned itself less with local charity than with addressing the general needs of the wider "public" order.

To realize the general aims of the Gansuidō, moreover, local leaders agreed to appoint a head teacher and several instructional assistants. Like the Kaitokudō, the academy would not be a "personal school" identified with an individual scholar and his descendants. It would instead be identified specifically with the local intellectual community. In short, the instructors would be interviewed and "hired" by a governing council of local leaders. This council, moreover, would schedule visiting lectures and make all major decisions regarding the expenditure of funds. This desire to maintain the definition of the Gansuidō as an academy founded by, and oriented to and for the local area, is clearly reflected in the council's choice of its first head instructor, one Tsuchihashi Tomonao (1685–1730).

A Confucian scholar of merchant upbringng in the Hirano area who was adopted into the prominent house by which he came to be known, Tsuchihashi studied under Itō Jinsai and with Miwa Shissai as a colleague in Kyoto. Drawing on the former for the universalistic theory of human virtue and the latter for philosophical idealism and Japanese poetics, Tsuchihashi brought to the Gansuidō a broad intellectual understanding of the relationship between secular moral philosophy and concrete action that contributed to "goodness." Under Tsuchihashi, the Gansuidō would gain justifiable fame for its charitable contributions to local commoners, especially in times of famine. Moreover, it is readily apparent from the "Outline of Schools in Japan"—*Honchō gakkō ki* (1721)—that he had a clear perception as to the "place" of the Gansuidō as an academy dedicated to doing good works among commoners. Although presented as a straightforward "outline," the *Honchō* states Tsuchihashi's claim for the Gansuidō as a school autonomous from the management of the domainal lord of the area. He began with a reference to the Bakufu's College in Edo and continued to describe other existing academies in the following manner:

> The Shizutani academy in Bizen was build on a grand scale; and in the castletown proper, another school was added. Even commoners were admitted to these schools so that the meaning of the Way was spread to all. In the domain of Aizu in Mutsu, two schools were also built and the ideas of the sages were taught. . . . Elsewhere, in Washū the Ekishūkan was built; in Jōshū the Kōkodō; in Ogo, the Kyūshidō; similarly in Sendai sagely halls were opened . . . and in Kii the Higakusha propagated the teachings. All of these schools were built by domainal lords.[5]

Unlike these schools that were founded by an authority from above, the Gansuidō was to establish its place as a private academy with the support of scholars such as Miwa Shissai, friends in Osaka, and notable commoners of Hirano. Tsuchihashi, therefore, took special pains to speak for the moral character and integrity of local leaders: "They were men of high morals who wanted to aid the people suffering from hunger. They became models of the entire nearby area."[6] Tsuchihashi went on to present his view. For very specific historical reasons, Japanese society had imposed a sharp division between the aristocracy and commoners, with the presumption that went along with this demarcation that moral knowledge was primarily to reside with the aristocracy because of its practical concerns for governing the rest of society. While conceding that moral knowledge should be central to governance, Tsuchihashi, however, denied the validity of the argument that such knowledge ought not be spread among the populace at large. Governance, he went on to assert, depended ultimately on the capacity of commoners to acquire moral knowledge and act in accordance with their virtue. And to realize this aim among commoners, schools such as the Gansuidō are crucial. The aristocracy that governs land, he noted, were concerned with broad questions of order and upholding regulations and not with the education of commoners, which Tsuchihashi believed to be quite appropriate. The entire line of argument behind his defense of heading a school among commoners led to the conclusion that commoners ought to educate themselves in order to be self-sufficient in moral and practical ways, especially in times of extreme crisis, as under conditions of famine. Above all, commoners ought not passively wait to be saved through political benevolence from above—on sukui—and, in fact, should take their destiny into their own hands. While commoners need not concern themselves with governing the nation as the aristocracy should, they could nonetheless acquire knowledge and control the immediate world around them in ways that, as Itō Jinsai would have it, tended always toward the realization of goodness in small, yet human, ways.

The importance here of Itō's moral thinking is beyond doubt. In Itō, the locus of "action" was always in the world of ordinary existence, the immediate field of empathetic interrelationships, and not philosophically related to bureaucratic and social hierarchy, or to the individualistic realization of sagehood. Itō's separation of moral action in the context of community from political action in the public realm is retained in Tsuchihashi's argument for education among commoners. The universal inclination of all human beings to act in ways that tend to be "good" is reaffirmed as the basis of commoners "controlling" their lives under uncertain conditions. Itō's philosophy is rearticulated here in terms of a practical theory of action more so than as a conceptual statement of the priority of "history" over "metaphysics" within a consistent theory of knowledge, even though Tsuchihashi often referred to himself as one who revered the ancients—*Kōkodō*. Yet this reverence, which Itō closely identified with ancient "text" and the philological "method" of unlocking those texts, is in Tsuchihashi an articulation of the principle that universal moral potential precedes politics and that commoners ought to stand on this philosophical basis, not to become scholars, but to actively "govern" their own history.

It appears quite certain that Tsuchihashi reinforced Itō's historicism with an idealistic theory of action, which he drew mainly from Miwa Shissai. A philosopher of considerable renown, Miwa rejected the Neo-Confucian moral philosophy that articulated hierarchy as a manifestation of observable "reason" and embraced, instead, a monistic idealism identified with the Ōyōmei (Wang Yang-ming, 1472–1528) intellectual tradition. External constructs and procedures were, from Miwa's point of view, necessary but not fundamental and certainly not manifestations of universal categories of truth. Avoiding thus the formalistic representation of nature and society, Miwa emphasized the universalistic value of moral truthfulness that resided in all individuals regardless of status. Moral purpose supplanted questions of administrative efficiency. Education among commoners was more important than the maintenance of a hierarchy of virtues. Miwa was personally involved in directly encouraging the establishment of the Gansuidō as well as the Kaitokudō and is said to have contributed funds to the founding of the Gansuidō.

Miwa reinforced Itō's universalistic theory of human "empathy" and "love" among human beings with a theory of idealistic commitment from within to a singularity of purpose—*sei-i seishin*. While Itō's conception of goodness as an action tendency left the definition of specific action open-ended and plural, there is in Tsuchihashi, through the mediation of Miwa's idealism, a sharper and more coherent focus on the meaning of goodness. It is specifically to alleviate the suffering of commoners in concrete and charitable ways. While the "way" to Itō was many different "pathways" that individuals traversed in the course of their lives, to Tsuchihashi, the "way," while not the grand *Way* that sages had philosophized about, was nonetheless "single" and not manifold. Tsuchihashi expressed this ideal of the unity or oneness of moral purpose in poetic language. The human spirit of autonomy—*shindoku*—he wrote, may be likened to the encountering of a solitary log that serves as a bridge over a ravine and which must be crossed as in making one's way through life: *Shindoku no kokoro o yomeru; Tanikawa ni kakeshi maruki no ichi hashi; Wataru kokoro ni yo o mo wataran.*[7] The image of unwavering, idealistic commitment embedded in these words points to a philosophy of action that is clear in its moral purpose. It is the concrete and objective world of human suffering pulled by the treacherous flow of reality that must be encountered and dealt with unflinchingly and directly. Empathy, in short, is fundamentally one path. And he referred to this path of practical moral action as his own inner truthfulness—*Tomonao no makoto.*[8]

Despite his idealism, which differed from Itō's affirmation of "passion" as inevitable to the human world of action, Tsuchihashi retained, as basic to his educational project, the proposition advanced by Itō that acting in ways that were good and seeking the "way" was not the exclusive privilege of the aristocracy or scholarly sages, but essential to all human beings and therefore to commoners in the world as they received it. And since commoners possessed moral knowledge like anyone else, they could also realize goodness through action in their own community without the intervention of politics. By this insistence on moral knowledge as being prior to political constructions and as being of greater significance than power and the authority to collect taxes, Tsuchihashi placed the responsibility of human nourishment squarely on the shoulders of the local community. The immediate local community, in short, becomes the arena within which goodness is to be realized; the Gansuidō would anchor that commitment as a center of learning and of practical resources.

Tsuchihashi's idea of "truthfulness," while located in the autonomous individual, becomes also the basis of faith and trust—*chūshin*—among members of a community. Emphasized in the instruction at the Gansuidō, therefore, was not the Neo-Confucian ideal of the individual transforming himself into a "sage" through meditation and diligent study, but rather the "horizontal" value of truthfulness that would serve as a universalistic norm—*kiku junjō*—to join together "the aged, weak, males and females, high and low, the wise and the foolish."[9] It was within this frame of reference that Tsuchihashi, as noted earlier, stressed the fact that the Gansuidō was not founded by the domainal lord but by a group of moral local leaders and that the academy was not "his" personal school, but belonged to the local community, the local fraternity of faithfuls known as the *kō*. The idea of a readership as a fraternity of faithfuls was retained fully as an ethical underpinning of the Gansuidō and projected its practical work for the local needy.

In the final analysis, then, the intellectual fusion of idealistic Confucianism and concrete empathetic action at the Gansuidō was determined by the practical consideration of maintaining the moral cohesion of the local community. This purpose took priority over all other considerations including, for example, the necessity to endorse all of the teachings of Itō Jinsai in their textual detail. Indeed, Tsuchihashi accepted all of the universal virtues of compassion, righteousness, propriety, and wisdom found in the great classics and did not feel it of great moment to discredit one text as against another as Itō had done, for example, in his rejection of *The Great Learning* on the basis of his philological method. Of greater importance to the men at the Gansuidō was the actual nourishment of "faith" and "trust" within community life and not the authenticity of textual resource. While Tsuchihashi made this difference between himself and Itō plain, his intellectual indebtedness to the latter as the philosopher who empowered commoners to build a moral world with things close at hand was also unmistakable.[10]

Within these intellectual contours, the Gansuidō shaped its mission to educate the local populace and to aid the hungry and poor. Outstanding scholars such as Itō Tōgai, Miwa Shissai, and Miyake Sekian visited the Gansuidō as guest lecturers, but scholarly achievement was secondary to the actual fact of doing good works. Unlike the scholars at the Kaitokudō, the teachers at the Gansuidō were not known for their academic treatises; nor did they train scholars of high repute. Focusing on conditions caused by uneven agricultural production and the demands of commerce, the Gansuidō established, shortly after Tsuchihashi assumed the directorship, as a practical and moral means to address this, an emergency "charitable fund." The aim of the fund was expressed as follows:

> This charitable fund is established because our society is in a state
> of extreme distress. Many are hungry and lack shelter and cannot be

saved by the action of a single individual. It is out of recognition of the conditions of famine and cold prevailing in the land that this fund was created. Contributions for relief will continue to be sought as such conditions persist.[11]

As the language here clearly suggests, relief of the suffering among commoners cannot be realized through the efforts of a "single individual," meaning the domainal lord, and must accordingly be sought in the communal resources available locally. The initial amount in the fund is said to have been the modest sum of about 775 *monme* to which contributions were made mainly by some eleven local notables as well as a few from merchant and academic "colleagues" from the Kaitokudō in Osaka proper. Yet, the modest beginning is also said to have contributed mightily during the devastating Kyōhō famines of 1732–33. The fund's entire savings of some six *kan* 310 *monme* were expended over a six-month period to provide famine relief to some 3,000 individuals in the local area. Unlike other nearby areas, not a single death due to starvation was reported in Hirano. Relief work among commoners remained central to the work of the Gansuidō, during the famines of Tenmei in the 1780s, of Tenpō in the 1830s, and of the last years of the Bakufu in the 1850s. The earnings that accrued from the charitable fund were also used to care for abandoned children and to assist in providing care for aged people who had no children.[12]

These activities "to save the people" gained the Gansuidō an enormous reputation as a center of knowledge and good works. And recognition also came from none other than the local domainal lord of Hirano himself, one Honda Tadayoshi, in the form of a letter of commendation and gratitude in 1738. Referring to the large number of deaths due to famine over the past years, he went on to say that "in your region not a single death has been reported due to lack of food."[13] Through this commendation, moreover, the lord extended a formal legitimacy to the Gansuidō and also allowed his retinue to study there. Despite this recognition "from above" by a "single individual," there was no recognition of this new status in the rules governing the school. No mention is made of special privileges accorded to samurai attending the Gansuidō. General rules governing teacher-student relations were left as they were, calling basically for respect between them as between parents and children, or among students as colleagues, and for proper regard for the decor and cleanliness of the school itself. Indeed, rather than special treatment to samurai who might attend the school, mention instead was made of the special importance of the children of the major contributors and "trustees" of the Gansuidō. The wealthy stratum on the local scene obviously counted more heavily than a distant aristocracy that would or would not utilize the academy on a regular basis.[14]

The Gansuidō serves as a valuable comparative reference in our discussion of the Kaitokudō as these two academies maintained an intimate relationship with each other. It is said that the name Gansuidō itself, meaning 'luxurious with greenness,' was selected by Miyake Sekian, the first head teacher of the Kaitokudō. Indeed, Miyake lectured at the Gansuidō often, especially on Mencius, and when his own private school, the Tashōdō was destroyed by fire in 1724, he was given a temporary home at the Gansuidō. Moreover, teachers at the Gansuidō had studied at the Kaitokudō, such as Hayano Yoshizō (1777–1831), Taki Chūshō (1777–1835) and Sawada Genryū (dates not known). And just as the Gansuidō contributed a sum of money at the founding of the Kaitokudō, colleagues at the latter reciprocated by giving to the Gansuidō's famine relief fund. Finally, many of the teachers of both academies were buried at the same temple grounds—the Shinkōji. They both also shared common intellectual ground. Neither would be a school identified with a particular individual but with a broad social educational cause. The importance of "like-minded" local leaders was emphasized. Above all, "virtue" was taught to be universal among human beings, and this was manifested in the acquisition of knowledge among commoners to "control" their world in moral and predictable ways. The acquisition of knowledge, moreover, would not be realized through the study of Buddhism nor would instruction be received from above.[15]

Despite the cordial relationship between both academies in personal and intellectual terms, certain distinctions clearly set the Kaitokudō apart from its counterpart in the country. Located in the center of Osaka, the Kaitokudō had larger ambitions. Its mission to impart moral knowledge to the local merchant community was accompanied by a dedication to establish itself as a major center of scholarly learning and training. Indeed, this mission may be seen as superseding charity work among lowly and suffering commoners in importance. "Saving the people" at the Kaitokudō was expressed primarily in terms of a scholarly and analytical venture dealing with the polity as a whole and not as alleviating suffering in the direct and immediate sense. In other words, as a "country academy" the Gansuidō turned its academic enterprise inward to doing good works for the local community. On the other hand, the Kaitokudō, besides educating local merchants, also sought to become part of a wider network of intellectual communication. This distinction emerges clearly in the manner in which they related to the public order.

The Gansuidō was given "public" recognition after it had demonstrated its utility during the famines of the early 1730s. The Kaitokudō, while established from "below," also set out to gain a formal legal charter for itself as a "public academy" in order to carry out its scholarly mission. In this regard, the Kaitokudō was charged with ideological potential from the beginning in a way that the Gansuidō was not, and the institutional and intellectual visions that would be generated from within the walls of the Kaitokudō would carry a distinctively critical and expansive flavor. Miwa Shissai would lament in 1733 the passing away of both Tsuchihashi of the Gansuidō and Miyake of the Kaitokudō as colleagues involved in a common cause. By then this was true only to a certain extent, for, institutionally, their academies had evolved in sympathetic yet distinct directions, with the greater expressive power embedded in the Kaitokudō, a merchant academy that insisted on its legal place within the public order.[16]

*　　　*　　　*

The beginnings of the Kaitokudō are traceable to a communal readership among a handful of merchants that had gathered around Miyake Sekian in the early 1710s to discuss classical Confucian texts. A student of Neo-Confucianism under Asami Keisai (1652–1711) and the idealistic tradition within that philosophy, Miyake studied in Kyoto in the heyday of Itō Jinsai's rise to scholarly prominence. There, he had also befriended Miwa Shissai. Unlike the latter who went on to Edo to establish himself as a prominent teacher at his Meirindō, Miyake sought a less conspicuous life in Osaka as a jusha teaching Confucian thought to merchants and running an herbal pharmacy, which he retained even after assuming the directorship of the Kaitokudō. It was due to his commercial success in this venture that his critics would later say that he was a scholar in name only and, in the shadows in fact, a merchant. He seems, however, to have been primarily a dedicated teacher who, due to this reputation, inherited the students of Goi Jiken, another prominent scholar of similar background who in his seventies, it is said, had retired from teaching to the game of go. It seems unlikely that Miyake's readership—known as the Tashōdō, which was quite unexceptional relative to any number of similar groups that had sprung up at this same time—would have transformed itself into a major academy under his leadership alone.[17]

The Tashōdō, as an educational project, shifted in emphasis and meaning in the early 1720s when a group of merchant leaders under the leadership of Nakai Shūan began to explore ways to establish the "readership" as a permanent and legal educational institution. In particular, the plan was shaped to gain a charter from the Bakufu itself to sanction the work of educating merchant commoners in Osaka. It has been suggested that this group sought legal certitude with the hope of receiving guaranteed public funds to support the academy. Yet this seems to be unlikely as a comprehensive explanation since the Kaitokudō survived for 150 years mainly through the financial contributions of the Osaka merchant houses, the counterpart to the family of "notables" that sustained the Gansuidō. The original aim, moreover, does not seem to have been to establish a legal beachhead in order to criticize the public order. No counterstructural thinking was involved, as the purpose was much more modest in scope—a case of merchants seeking to establish protective academic walls within which to teach young members about human virtue and thereby have them gain moral conviction in their work as marketmen. The fire that destroyed the Tashōdō in 1724 seems to have spurred the merchants on to find a permanent solution to the legitimacy of an academy among merchants that would surmount the realistic evidences that urban fires provided about the ephemeral nature of human existence.

Whatever the motivation, the confirmation of the Kaitokudō in 1726 as a public academy among Osaka merchants may be seen, in retrospect, as being an ideological act regardless of the original intent of the merchants. Within the walls that provided legal protection from outside interference, merchants could draw on universalistic ideas stripped of practical considerations as to existing political and social hierarchies and address the moral claims that merchants wished to make. The Kaitokudō, in this respect, served as a protected moral center, a visible construction within which the outside world's view of them had no significance whatever to the merchants. And in a reverse process, merchants could claim that the knowledge they had acquired at a "public" academy was not the special prerogative of the aristocracy. This is the kernel of thought that would evolve into the view that moral knowledge is necessary for proper governance and that merchants were fully capable of not only acquiring such knowledge but also of objectively knowing when that relationship was in a state of critical dissonance. The initial quest to certify "order" in the world around them rather than "flux" carried critical implications regarding the moral order of politics. It was through this education that Kaitokudō merchants, in turn, realized the significance of their work as marketmen and financiers as it related to the overall art of governance. The life of the Kaitokudō involves this complex intellectual history, and it seems clear that its capacity to "house" such a history is due in large measure to the initial act of gaining permanence as a "public" academy. Commoners could seek moral knowledge at an institution that was not inferior to any other place of learning in the country.

The key individuals engaged in the redefinition of the Kaitokudō from a private to a public academy were Nakai Shūan and a group of five merchant leaders. Known as the "five colleagues"—*godōshi*—this group included: Mitsuboshiya Buemon (1673–1732, also known as Nakamura Ryōsai); Dōmyōjiya Kichizaemon (1684–1739, Tominaga Hōshun); Bizenya Kichibei (1693–1768, Yoshida Kakyū); Funabashiya Shiroemon (dates not certain, Nakashima Kakyū); and Kōnoike Matashirō (1692–1755, Yamanaka Sōko). These were successful merchants, especially as financiers, who were also deeply immersed in developing educational activities in Osaka. They had studied with Goi Jiken and Miyake Sekian, identified with Itō Jinsai's lectures (the *Dōjimon* being one of their favorite texts), and had contributed to the Gansuidō and would bear the brunt of the financial burden at the Kaitokudō in the crucial early years.[18]

Nakai and these merchant intellectuals shared a complex sense of being disadvantaged relative to the stipended warrior class and of deserving a "permanent" legal place within which to seek moral knowledge that had been accorded to the aristocracy as a matter of privilege. Nakai drew on the support of these men to further the cause of the academy because, as his son Chikuzan would comment in his accounting of the founding of the academy, Nakai was a son of a household of "physicians" and had always lived among merchants. Compelled by destitute circumstances, the Nakai family had left the nearby domain of Tatsuno, half of the family seeking a livelihood with the father in Hiroshima, the other half, including Shūan, with the mother in Osaka, where sometime around 1713 he joined Miyake's readership. Located thus in the "interstices" of the Tokugawa status structure, Nakai was not only comfortable among merchants but could also take an aggressive role in advancing the claims of commoners vis-à-vis Bakufu authorities.

The actual details of the negotiations conducted by Nakai with Bakufu officials are not fully available. The general outline, however, was related by Chikuzan in his history of the academy.[19] What emerges from his son's account is a picture of Nakai Shūan as a consummate administrative politician who gained what he set out to achieve, at times despite reservations by Miyake Sekian himself. Some details are worth recounting if only to underscore the general point that the founding of the Kaitokudō as a public academy was a political act.

The desirability of a public academy for commoners in the Osaka area was a subject discussed between Nakai and his friend Miwa Shissai, probably during one of the latter's visits to Osaka and the Gansuidō early in the 1720s. Sometime late in 1724, Miwa wrote to Nakai indicating the appropriateness of presenting the case to the Bakufu for an academy under Miyake, since his contacts within the Bakufu had confirmed the receptiveness of the shōgun, Yoshimune, to such a venture. He noted that Yoshimune had indeed encouraged the scholar Shibano Ritsuzan (1680–1743) to open such a school for commoners in Edo. Between the time of that letter and the early months of 1726 when the formal approval was granted by the Bakufu, Nakai journeyed to Edo three times, once with Dōmyōjiya and Bizenya in 1725 when most of the details were worked out, but he also stayed alone in Edo for five months to develop support for the Kaitokudō cause.

Although there is no way of knowing what exactly transpired in the interventions of Miwa and others, there is no doubt as to the specific goals that Nakai pressed the Bakufu for on behalf of the Kaitokudō. Among these, he made certain that formal, written approval would be given, through the local Bakufu magistrate, so that the land upon which the academy stood would be declared autonomous and unencumbered of fiscal and other obligations—*gomen jochi;* that the present owners would be given alternative compensatory property of equal value; and further, that since the existing land was inadequate for the spatial needs of the academy, that additional space be assigned to it. The political implication of receiving such a prerogative was to declare the academy the equivalent of a chartered domain—*hairyōchi*—without a hereditary "lord" or a stipended retinue, but which nonetheless would enjoy the legal prerogatives of being a public space that could not be violated or subject to intervention as long as the academy respected the laws of the order. Although Nakai held firm to the above political course, the Bakufu showed some resistance to declaring the Kaitokudō a legally "autonomous" space. In one of Miwa's communications to Nakai he notes the great difficulty involved in achieving that goal—*jochi no gi naka naka nasugataki koto.* Miwa nonetheless commended Nakai for standing his ground in order to realize a truly unprecedented achievement—*mizou no ongoto.*[20]

Having gained this "domainal" status of legally unencumbered space, it should be pointed out that Nakai and his colleagues determined that some of the land assigned to the academy—in the Dotombori area—was undesirable for the needs of the academy. They promptly sold it for a profit and used the proceeds to create a fund to be invested among the leading merchant houses with the interest applied in perpetuity for the maintenance of the academy. The quest for "permanency," in short, was at once a "legal" matter as well as a "financial" one.[21]

A second issue that Nakai insisted on was that representatives of the academy be awarded the privilege of wearing two swords when calling on the magistry. That this may be taken as evidence of Nakai's desire to emulate the aristocracy goes without much saying. More fundamental was that he, as the administrative leader of the Kaitokudō, be received by the public magistry as one of relatively equal status appropriate to the legal stature of the academy. It was, in this respect, an aggressive request on the part of the leadership of the Kaitokudō that teachers of commoners nonetheless be treated as "peers" and not as "inferiors." Nakai, it should be noted, wore swords only while making presentations to the magistry on behalf of the academy and did not claim to have acquired the status of a samurai. The "external" image of the academy as a public place of learning for commoners was quite obviously at issue. Nakai consistently emphasized the "external" dimension of how the academy was dealt with by the legal magistrative authority and virtually dedicated himself to overseeing that sphere. In time, the magistry accepted Nakai into its inner halls and treated him and, through him, the academy with respect. The magistry engaged him and other teachers in intimate discussions—go kon'i—on scholarly matters.[22]

Nakai carefully guarded the special diplomatic role he had assigned to himself. In reviewing the events of the founding of the academy, he would specifically explain that he had been formally selected by the merchant sponsors—sewanin—to be the principal representative before the local magistry or "public authority" and, in turn, would report directly to the merchant leaders of Osaka's township councils. "After discussing the matter among colleagues at the academy," he noted, "it was decided that I would be the representative to be selected. We then discussed in detail before the town elders as to whether we should continue [as a governing committee] into the future. Joining me were the five: Mitsuboshiya Buemon, Dōmyōjiya Kichizaemon, Funabashiya Shiroemon, Bizenya Kichibei, and Kōnoike Matashirō."[23] These lines show Nakai establishing himself as the sole representative of the academy before the magistry in order to clearly distinguish between "externally" derived legitimation and "internally" managed, self-regulated space.

It was hardly accidental that his son Chikuzan's "history" of the academy is divided explicitly in terms of "external" and "internal" affairs—gaijiki and naijiki—for it effectively reflects the political reality present at the founding of the Kaitokudō. The division of labor between "administration" and "instruction," between external and internal affairs, contained an important principle. It allowed Nakai to specialize in one area and Miyake to devote himself entirely to caring for the instructional and intellectual life of the academy without having to endure the tedium of engaging with the public world. At the level of protocol, the head instructor of the Kaitokudō would therefore not be placed in an awkward situation of inferiority vis-à-vis an outside authority. At the personal level, this arrangement protected Miyake who was known to be an eccentric without much interest in political matters, which explains his inclusion in the Tokugawa biographical dictionary of eccentrics—*Kinsei kijinden* (1788). To Miyake the pursuit of scholarly knowledge was an entirely personal affair—*gakusha jiko bunjo*—which was not to be compromised with bureaucratic considerations. Indeed, Miyake seems to have harbored misgivings about acquiring a formal charter for the Kaitokudō in light of the complex political maneuverings involved. In a letter to Nakai, probably late in the spring of 1725 during Nakai's lengthy stay in Edo, Miyake conveyed the following warning: "To appeal [to authority] on behalf of scholarship," he advised, "may contrary to expectation have a baneful effect on scholarship itself . . . [*kaette gaku no tame ni gai arubeku koto nite sōrō*] . . ." While not opposed to the promotion of knowledge based on "public spirit" and contributing to the "public way," Miyake went on to indicate his reservations as to whether political intent and studying moral philosophy could be made to be consistent.[24]

Subsequent events provide irrefutable testimony that Nakai was not deterred from his immediate goal by Miyake's words. On the other hand, the clear delineation Nakai made between his administrative responsibility and Miyake's instructional one suggests a sensitivity to the latter's ethical stance. When Nakai called on the local magistrate in 1726 to receive the Bakufu's charter as the sole "representative" of the Kaitokudō, the magistrate expressed surprise and asked why he, Nakai, and not the head professor, Miyake Sekian, had appeared before him. Nakai later recalled: "I replied that Sekian was deeply involved in his studies and that it would be extremely difficult indeed for him to involve himself in affairs of this nature."[25]

It should be emphasized that Nakai Shūan described the previous events in a letter to the governing council shortly before his death in 1758. His purpose in doing so was to clarify the division of responsibilities between himself and Miyake. Perhaps equally important was the affirmation of the crucial role that the "five colleagues" had played in the establishment of the academy and why, as his days reached their end, Nakai felt obliged to remind the new generation of the five merchant leaders in order that their memory be preserved. He thus lamented that the "five" were all dead or retired, although a new group, fortunately, had emerged to continue to manage the academy's finances. He seemed especially pleased that Kōnoike's son had retained an active role in this respect: "While not actively involved in academic work personally," he wrote, "the current Matashirō [Kōnoike] oversees the finances of the academy."[26]

Despite the emotive spirit underlying Nakai's letter, it provides testimony as to how the Kaitokudō defined itself in terms of "inner" and "outer" spaces. The outside belonged to the political world of "verticality" that confirmed the Kaitokudō as an academic "domain" through the charter. A public trust had been granted to the academy as an act of princely grace—kun'on—from above. Yet this public act conferred protection to all who studied within the walls of the academy. Once within the academy, the spatial meaning lost all significance in relation to external statuses and hierarchies. The maintenance of this status, moreover, would be assured through skillful diplomacy by Nakai Shūan as the administrative "representative" assigned to this responsibility. The space "within" the academic walls, in short, belonged to the merchants—it was "theirs" and could not be tampered with or controlled from the outside. Insofar as it appeared unlikely that the Bakufu would either self-destruct or arbitrarily revoke the charter and confess error, Nakai and his "colleagues" could claim to have created a legally defined space within which commoners in Osaka could immerse themselves in moral and practical education as part of the public order.

No longer a private school identified with a particular scholarly personage, the Kaitokudō could project itself into the future as a permanent chartered entity that Osaka merchants could look upon as a center of institutional certitude akin to the domains of regional barons. It was "fixed" and its purpose was "moral" in the best sense of the term as it was understood at that time. Above all, legitimation acquired through vertical, political channels now could sanction the maintenance of the "inner" life of the academy as a horizontal and communal effort. Thus while the Kaitokudō had been transformed from an informal "readership" into a "public academy," law would serve to reinforce the communitarian ideal of the "readership" so that all within the legally fixed walls could seek knowledge at whatever level as "colleagues of like mind and purpose"—dōshi no hai.[27]

As with the Gansuidō, the idea of a community of faith and trust was vital to the underlying agreement at the Kaitokudō. This agreement, moreover, was expressed with a term widely used in Tokugawa society: kōsha and hence kōsha Kaitokudō, meaning a place to gather for intimate discussions. A brief elaboration of the ideograph will help clarify the meaning of "inner" space.

The compound kōsha refers to a community with a shared spiritual purpose—kō—gathering at a prescribed place—sha.[28] It was perhaps the single most important organizational concept among commoners in eighteenth-century Japan and found expression in a variety of unrelated ways, including educational activities. The underlying ethical principle of the kō is "trust" regulated by customary beliefs rather than formal law. Being customary, the idea of the kō was understood widely in Japanese society and could be easily grasped without detailed elaboration. The beginnings of this tradition can be traced as far back as the seventh and eighth centuries when Buddhist holy men gathered in small groups to study scriptures and hold prayer meetings. In time, however, the kō came also to be used as a proselytizing vehicle rather than as a meeting of ordained theologians that permitted ordinary individuals to summon other faithfuls to gather in a communal setting to recite, for example, holy words from a sacred text—nenbutsu kō. It was this tendency toward the popularization of communal religious practices that led to the expanded application of the kō as an organizing principle, informed always by the basic ethic of communal faith and trust, but applicable in a wide variety of ways and for multiple purposes, as in the organization of peasant rebellions, the establishment of mutual assistance cooperatives in villages, and the formation of investment confraternities of "unlimited trust" and mutual "reliance"—mujinkō and tanomoshi kō—that proliferated in the eighteenth century.

In the development of Tokugawa education, the kō functioned in two distinct ways: as an organizing concept for a stable and fixed space such as the Kaitokudō and the Gansuidō and as the migratory and expansive communal "cells" best exemplified in the educational movement founded by Ishida Baigan (1685–1744). Known as "the study of the human spirit" or Shingaku, this latter movement began with Ishida's opening lectures in Kyoto in 1729, some three years after the founding of the Kaitokudō, and spread among commoners of lower strata in Kyoto, Osaka, and other cities in the country. The movement expanded through the proliferation of kō or kōsha, as in the "seven kōsha of Osaka," each headed by a faithful disciple of Ishida dedicated to the proliferation of Ishida's moral concepts. To attract disciples to the kōsha, moreover, practical instruction in reading, writing, and the abacus was included so that these moral readerships served an important function as "elementary" schools in the spreading of literacy. The main points to be emphasized here are that the Shingaku kō expanded through moral confraternities of like-minded faithfuls that were duplicated into an ever broadening network and that, in this process, the moral principle of trust was anchored by an identification with the personal spirit of the founding "saint"—to Ishida's charisma.[29]

At the Kaitokudō, the kō was located within permanent and immobile space—the dō—and that space did not take its *raison d'etre* from a funding charismatic saint. At the Kaitokudō, the legal space superseded Miyake Sekian the scholar in importance and, indeed, gave his presence its meaning. In Shingaku, Ishida Baigan remained the informing spirit defining communal space. Since the Kaitokudō was not defined according to personal charisma but public law, all who attended that academy could relate to each other as "colleagues" in the pursuit of knowledge without expressing personal devotion to Miyake as the head teacher. Consistent with the foregoing, the idea of creating satellite academies in an expansive network was absent in the original founding vision. The same may also be said of the Gansuidō, where the aim of serving the educational and welfare needs of the local community remained central. All available surplus resources would be concentrated in that stable "center" rather than dissipated in the establishment of a network of related schools.

More specifically, the idea of the kō or kōsha served the Kaitokudō as a vital concept in the reception of broad ideological and hierarchical schemes of thought and provided it with a communitarian or "horizontal" bedding familiar to merchant commoners. Hierarchic ideas of Neo-Confucianism, blessed by the formal laws of the Bakufu itself, would be introduced into the academy in which the membership would be joined laterally by a common spirit of trust. This spirit did not come from a fomal dictate but was an essential part of the cultural understanding of merchants. Law is drawn upon through hierarchy to protect horizontality within the academy as a sanctuary of learning. In a society that ordered itself in terms of status differences and hierarchy, all reinforced by formal sumptuary codes, the idea of community and colleagueship found in the kō was essential to the maintenance of esprit de corps at the Kaitokudō. Formal status differences would be deemphasized or dropped completely within the academy. All involved in the common effort of moral education, at whatever level of advanced learning, would be considered "colleagues" having equal access to the academic space—*dōmon*. The sharing of educational purpose within a predictable space would form the basis of faith and trust.

Within legally sanctioned walls, then, commoner colleagues in search of moral knowledge could regulate their internal affairs without interference from the outside world.[30] The integrity of the project depended on certain key factors, beginning, especially, with the maintenance of as secure a financial base as possible. Merchant colleagues were expected to make an initial contribution of ten *monme* apiece that would be invested as an interest-bearing fund at the house of Kōnoike. The income would be applied in particular to cover the regular or daily administrative expenses of the academy. Meanwhile, income from lecture fees would be used primarily as salaries for the instructors—one or two *monme* to be paid regularly at the beginning of the first, third, fifth, and seventh months. Most important of all, the leaders at the Kaitokudō sought to stabilize the internal affairs of the academy by drafting a set of rules— literally an "agreement," *gojōhō*—that was posted in the main lecture hall. The overall importance of the academy as a place for commoners to seek knowledge was confirmed in these rules. All were welcomed to the academy to study Confucian ethics of loyalty, trust, and filial piety in order to carry out their occupation in life—*shokugyō*—consistent with these norms. No individual would be discriminated against in gaining admission to the lectures that presented these general and universal ideas. The rules also make it perfectly clear, however, that the academy would hold as closely as possible to the principle that public education was not free and that everyone capable of paying the agreed upon fee was expected to do so. Indeed, individuals incapable of paying in cash were encouraged to contribute a writing brush, paper, inkstone or the like that might prove useful to the academy. Those without personal possession of texts or writing equipment were welcomed to use these resources available at the academy for home use and to borrow them without charge or penalty for damages that might be incurred. But the basic *modus operandi* remained that education involved an "exchange" of fees for knowledge.

It is consistent with this that the rules would clearly acknowledge unexpected interruptions from the daily exigencies of the marketplace. Should an "unavoidable emergency" arise, it was thus stated, any individual could simply excuse himself from the hall and leave without permission during a lecture—*Tadashi kanawazu yōji dekisōrawaba, kōshaku naka ni mo taishutsu korearubeku sōrō.* This and another rider that once the lectures were underway free seating would be operative without discrimination as to status—*sono sabetsu kore arumajiku sōrō*—was clearly in the interests of merchants in the audience. Prior to the commencement of the lectures, the language read, members of the aristocracy in attendance would be given deferential treatment and allowed to sit at the front of the hall. Once the lectures had begun, however, that privilege would be denied them and they must sit alongside merchants. These merchants, on the other hand, were extended the privilege of leaving the lecture after it had begun without permisson. The weight of the "trade-off" is clearly advantageous to merchants. Indeed, in 1758, under Nakai Chikuzan and Goi Ranju, all seatings before and after the commencement of the lectures were declared, in the rules, to be on a first come basis. And the emphasis would be placed unequivocally on the egalitarian dimension of study which the founders had idealized: "Interchange among students will take place without regard to high or low status and entirely as colleagues of like mind"—*Shosei no majiwari wa kisen hinpu o ronzezu, dōhai to nasubeku koto.* At this time too the stipulation that guests attending lectures would require a formal permission either by Nakai Shūan or by a merchant official—Dōmyōjiya Kichizaemon—was also struck, allowing open entry to, and exit from, the lectures.

All the above were reinforced with a stern warning to students that the seriousness of the academy should be honored at all times. During lectures, as well as in seminars, frivolity would not be tolerated. Emotional austerity and earnestness would accompany the communality of intellectual purpose. The Kaitokudō would not deteriorate into a social club—*enkai.* Parties and drinking sessions—of which some of the scholars such as Goi and Nakai Chikuzan were fond—were to be kept entirely to a "private" indulgence and not be allowed to interfere with the formal life of the academy. The language of the posting speaks for itself:

> . . . not only will there be no dancing or singing in the halls, there will be no mischievous playing whatsoever. All colleagues of the academy must uphold this rule. There may be some exceptions to this as when the first annual lecture is held or at new year celebrations or at weddings. But it is to be understood that there will be no prolonged drinking that might lead to disrespectful behavior.[31]

Favored with a public charter, the Kaitokudō would maintain an atmosphere of moral austerity consistent with that status. Instructors and their aides would see themselves as "officials" and the head professor would be treated as a "national master"—*kokushi* and *kokurō.* Students, in turn, would study to enhance the well-being of the polity.

Enrollment figures have not survived, although a general idea of the student population can be gotten from the following. In 1790, five rooms were set aside to house between twenty and thirty boarders. Commuters from nearby are estimated conservatively to have been twice as many as boarders, so that at any given time, between sixty and ninety students were engaged in study at the academy. For youngsters, classes began at eight in the morning and continued until seven in the evening. Besides standard instruction in moral ideas, much emphasis was given to developing skills in reading, writing, and abacus calculation. Those designated

Curriculum of Kaitokudō*·

	Hōreki.8 (1758) Miyake Shunro, Director				Tenmei:2 (1782) Nakai Chikuzan, Director		
Time Date	Morning	Afternoon	Night	Time Date	Morning	Afternoon	Night
1	Rest day			1	(Tutorials)		
2	Lectures on *The Book of Changes* and *Record of Things Close at Hand*			2	Lectures on the *Book of History* and *Record of Things Close at Hand*		
3	(Tutorials)			3	Reading class on *Records of the Early Han*		
4	Lectures on *The Great Learning* and *Mencius*			4	Lecture on *The Great Learning*		
5	Rest day			5	Rest day		
6	(Tutorials)			6	Reading class on the *Tradition of Tso*		
7	Lectures on *The Book of Changes* and *Record of Things Close at Hand*			7	Lecture on the *Book of History* and *Record of Things Close at Hand*		
8	(Tutorials)			8	(Tutorials)		
9	Lectures on *The Great Learning* and *Mencius*			9	Lecture on *The Great Learning*		
10	(Tutorials)			10	Rest day		
	Other activities Informal seminars among "colleagues" on the 13th day				Other activities Poetry reading; informal seminars among colleagues on the 13th day		

*Based on Kobori Kazumasa, Yamanaka Hiroyuki et al , *Nihon no shisōka 24 Nakai Chikuzan—Nakai Riken* (Tokyo Meitoku shuppan sha, 1980), p. 155

as "advanced" students studied mainly in small seminars and tutorials along with boarders, such as the dozen or so students that Miura Baien sent to the Kaitokudō in the 1770s. The instructional schedule, moreover, suggests a fairly carefully thought-out plan oriented to small group learning. The month was divided into three ten-day cycles: of these, four full days and two mornings were blocked off for readings in texts and specialized tutorials; one day in each month was set aside for informal seminars among "colleagues" that were arranged according to student interest and which might include sessions in the reading and writing of poetry; all were expected to attend six formal lectures during the month, four of which were scheduled in the evenings to accommodate the local clientele; and finally, the fifth and tenth day of every ten-day cycle were declared days of rest.[32]

It appears that the formal lectures, although of considerable importance in the early years, declined into stylized presentations of well-known moral precepts and served as confirmatory rather than exploratory statements. The intellectual life of the academy was located mainly in the specialized seminars and tutorials rather than at these lectures. Thus, while elementary skills in reading and writing were taught to youngsters, this was primarily a "service" provided to merchant families living nearby in response to their "practical" concerns regarding the virtue of education. Instructors were carefully advised in the internal house rules not to turn away local youngsters seeking basic literacy so as to maintain cordial ties with local merchant families and not have them come to "dislike scholarship." The concern here reflects the demands from within the merchant community for practical elementary education for their children rather than specialized scholarly pursuits, which seemed to them to consume an inordinate amount of time, especially the philological examination of Chinese texts.[33]

While the Kaitokudō thus provided elementary education for local families, its preferred educational mission was training scholars and encouraging the discussion of moral philosophy at the most sophisticated level possible. It was believed that this high-level moral instruction would best serve merchants in their world of practical work. In this sense, the teachers of the Kaitokudō did not see themselves as trainers of scholars or jusha. On the other hand, they clearly left such a possibility open for students of outstanding ability who possessed the drive and inclination to pursue a scholarly career. Such a vision can be seen in the language of the house rules: "Should there by chance be a child excellent in character and rich in talent, and who potentially might become a teacher of others after he has completed his formal studies, then, with due consideration of the views of his parents, such a student may be encouraged to fulfill his academic virtue."[34]

When this ambitious language is placed in contrast with that admonishing instructors not to turn away youngsters seeking practical elementary skills lest the "public" come to "dislike" scholarship as being impractical, one can sense the tension that must have existed from the very outset of the academy's life. Merchants seeking practical knowledge and enmeshed in the daily uncertainties of the marketplace were expected to fund a "public" academy where much of the instruction would be "advanced" and "impractical." The fact that samurai would be expected to sit with merchants as "colleagues" or that merchants could leave the lecture hall as their practical work dictated did not mask the reality of practical need and scholarly vision, a tension that would remain as a dynamic presence throughout the eighteenth century. Not to be denied, however, was the emphasis on advanced training that established the reputation of the Kaitokudō. Seeking already literate students rather than individuals from the "poor" or from the "aristocracy," the Kaitokudō formed a number of informal and special seminars dealing with classical texts. It was in these seminars that subjects other than moral instruction were introduced, notably Japanese literature.

To pursue this educational vision, the academy dedicated itself to retaining the services of the best instructors possible, which by all accounts the early instructors were. Besides Miyake, Goi Ranju, Namikawa Kansen, and Inoue Sekisui served as instructors in the early years, with Inoue, a student of Itō Jinsai, assuming the role of chief assistant. Perhaps the most important regulation governing instructors was that they were strictly forbidden from running the academy as a personal possession of theirs or from promoting a school of thought they might favor. As with the Gansuidō, the head teacher and his assistants were hired by the academy's governing council and to reaffirm this principle the head teacher was explicitly disallowed from naming his own son to succeed him. As a public academy funded by merchants, the Kaitokudō envisioned the selection of instructors based on the principle of talent and not on hereditary succession such as utilized by the aristocracy. Even if a particular son happened to be extremely able, the rules of 1726 read he must first be sent away from the academy to do scholarly work elsewhere before being considered for the position of head of the academy. Hereditary succession, the wording went on, can only lead to the dissipation of intellectual vigor, as amply demonstrated in the rapid decline of Buddhist and Shinto sects shortly after the demise of the founding father.[35]

A later amendment to the previous rule suggests, however, considerable difficulty in upholding the original ideal. The language here would seem to indicate that it was not an easy matter to attract the very best scholars to head the Kaitokudō on a permanent basis. As instructors, these men could augment their salaries with fees from special tutorials in calligraphy, deciphering texts, and the like. It is doubtful, however, that the positions were lucrative enough to attract scholars with national reputations established elsewhere. For jusha such as Miyake and Goi, teaching at the Kaitokudō offered a basis of security and relative intellectual freedom that surpassed being a "physician" out of dire necessity or teaching at a domainal school or in an informal readership. Their dedication to the academy can be appreciated within this context. Yet, the fact remained that finding a head teacher of appropriate stature was clearly a difficult task indeed. Thus the rule of succession was amended to read that should an exhaustive search fail to result in the appointment of a professorial head of the highest order, a son may be allowed to serve in such an emergency. However, all administrative matters such as dealing with the academy's finances and the general overseeing of the academy would remain in the hands of an "advisory committee." In an extreme contingency, then, genealogical succession would be allowed, although total authority would again be denied the new head teacher. The principle that a successor should first and foremost be sought from outside the academy was reaffirmed as any head teacher who sought the headship for his descendents would be violating the basic spirit of the Kaitokudō. Ideal and reality converge in an ambiguous manner as the following summary suggests:

> The individual who becomes the academic head of this academy must have the deep respect of all the colleagues here. They must be able to entrust all matters to him. He in turn must feel as though he is one of them. . . . Now when that academic head passes away some feel that the successor should be his direct descendent. Basically, however, those who promote descendents in this way act inappropriately for this academy. A desirable head teacher is one who will discard everything else to study and teach the Way, although it may well be that the more desirable the person in this regard the less likely it may be for him to seek this place.[36]

Even with the ammendation just noted, the prerogatives of the "colleagues" of the academy whose interests Nakai purported to represent were recognized in the rules governing the duties of the professorial head. Since the protective blessings of public law—*kō on*—encompass all teachers and students within the academy, everyone shared a responsibility in maintaining the highest levels of education and training possible. The head teacher was not solely responsible for this. At the same time, however, the head teacher must clearly carry out the duties of a teacher or be held accountable to the other colleagues in the academy. Thus, should the teacher be ineffectual in executing his duties, his colleagues were expected to discuss the matter among themselves and, without fear of punishment, demand his resignation. Should a time come when the Kaitokudō as a community could no longer assure the intellectual respectability of the academy, due to poor instruction, or for that matter inadequate funding and the lack of an appropriate student population, then the academy ought to close its doors rather than abuse the public trust extended to it.[17]

Here again, the ideal and the actuality meshed in an ambiguous manner. Behind the principled assertions that the academy not be identified with a particular personality or school of thought since a public academy ought to transcend such personal considerations and the insistence that "colleagues" should serve as a corrective to poor instruction, there appears, albeit vaguely, a contentious reality. The inability to attract a scholar of national stature and the concession that a son might be named in such an emergency referred to a view among certain merchants that the Kaitokudō ought to be more firmly identified with Miyake Seikian as the "master" teacher, and hence the appropriateness of having his son Shunrō (1712–82) named his successor. Moved by a deep reverence for Miyake Sekian, these merchants no doubt believed such an identification would link the academy more closely to the Osaka merchant community. Not anywhere near the stature of his father as a scholar, Shunrō, it is said, preferred the life of a pharmaceutical merchant. Nakai's "revision" of the rules suggests a compromise with that merchant pressure in the event of an "emergency" while insisting on the primacy of the principle of talent and the avoidance of hereditary succession. Confronted with this obviously sensitive issue, Nakai sought to protect the public character of the academy while also retaining the allegiance of merchant supporters. From the early days of the academy, moreover, he nourished this position of his by concentrating on providing administrative leadership and entrusting the instructional end of things entirely to men of special talent such as Miyake Sekian and, later, Goi Ranju.[18]

It was within this protective framework designed by Nakai and his "five merchant colleagues" that Miyake addressed himself to his instructional audience. Distanced from outside authority as well as from his specific "place" within the merchant community and with the realization that the academy was not his personal school or that of his descendents, Miyake outlined a set of commonsensical, philosophical propositions containing universalistic values that transcended the realities of the world outside the academy. Specifically, Miyake reformulated the moral philosophy utilized by the Bakufu to confirm political and status differentiations. He turned it into a theory of universal human virtue that denied the ultimate relevance of those distinctions and thus rendered it as being entirely appropriate to a merchant audience ranked at the low end of the status structure. The ideas converged with those articulated by Itō Jinsai and other commoner philosophers such as his counterparts at the

Gansuidō. Like them, Miyake highlighted the dimension of the Confucian tradition that emphasized compassionate and trustworthy work by ordinary men without regard to status or station in life.

.   .   .

Miyake set forth the basic philosophy of the academy in his opening lecture on 5 October 1726 before an audience of some seventy-eight merchant leaders. Interestingly, the lecture carried two titles. A political heading read, "Lecture at the officially approved academy, the Kaitokudō"—*Kankyō gakumonjo Kaitokudō kōgi;* another stated the intellectual content, "Lecture on the leading concepts in the *Analects* and *Mencius*"—*Ron-Mō shushō kōgi.*[39] To be sure, the actual content of the lecture had nothing to do with government or politics as the merchants attending clearly had not come to pay homage to the Bakufu but to launch the Kaitokudō as a place of learning where merchants could study and discuss ideas about human virtue.

While Miyake's opening lecture can hardly be called dazzling, it was obviously put together with painstaking care, as evidenced by the unadorned and straightforward exposition of moral precepts. It was crafted so that there could be no misunderstanding as to where the Kaitokudō stood in terms of basic moral theory. The message that Miyake had to convey was well known to the audience. Hardly anything in it was new or innovative. But it was now being presented to them with official approval so that the very context invariably had the effect of clothing the message being conveyed with ideological dress. Articulated to local merchants rather than to public officials, Miyake underscored, in no uncertain terms, the universality of moral norms and their accessibility to all human beings without regard to class. Along the way, and in a manner that would not appear as a blatant apologia, he also related his discussion of morality with passion and profit, issues no doubt uppermost in the minds of the audience. The discussion is carefully modulated in understated terms. There is no vulgar plea for profit as being just. There could also be no denying that he had confirmed, in his lecture, the work of marketmen as moral within the universal framework of goodness and justice.

It is said in the *Analects*, Miyake started out, that the purpose of studying moral knowledge is to comprehend the way of being human—*hito no michi.* This means being able to grasp the basic ways in which men interact with each other, as between ruler and subject, parent and child, husband and wife, siblings, and friends. But these formal manifestations were not of primary importance; it was the universality of the moral in-

tent underlying them all. They are manifestations of an intrinsic goodness innate to all human beings everywhere regardless of time or place or
circumstances as to status. That intrinsic moral character is with everyone at birth, so that all human beings are *sages* to begin with: *umare no
mama naru ga seija nari*. In the proposition that at birth every human
being is equal and blessed with sagely virtue, Miyake found in the *Analects* a moral proposition crucial to merchants. Born as sages like anyone
else in all classes, merchants possessed in themselves a virtue endowed by
Heaven: *Ten yori umitsuke tamau mono*. Moral knowledge, the so-called
"teachings" of the great sages, are not intellectual contrivances to maintain order—*waza to tate oshie tamau koto ni arazu*—but are attempts at
clarifying the original meaning of human virtue. Together these teachings are called the Way, or the way of being human. As all human beings
are sages, the so-called "sages" are also human, "and we too," referring
here obviously to the audience, "are also human"—*seijin mo hito, kono hō
mo hito*. There is a polemical ring in Miyake's presentation. In carefully
selected language, he had separated the *Analects* from the problem of hierarchy and governance in the political scene and brought it down to the
level of moral philosophy for commoners, akin to the way Itō had also
done. The "Way" is to be found among human beings in mundane walks
of life. Moral knowledge is made up of articulate attempts, such as by
Confucius, to clarify its meaning. But Confucius is no more "human"
than any other human being, certainly not any more than "we" are. In
Miyake's understanding of "sage" as being "human" and in referring to the
audience as being "human," he had presented an interpretation of the
Analects that was utterly pertinent to his merchant constituency.[40]

Miyake elaborated on the universality of the way of being human in
another metaphoric line drawn from the *Analects*. "How deeply satisfying
it is," the aphoristic line reads, "when friends call on us from afar." The
meaning of this phrase, Miyake outlined in his interpretation, was that
being human was universal. Whether human beings visited from close by
or from distant places, they are all of the same order of things—*dōrui*—
hence should be treated as friends even though they may be strangers in
fact—*hito to tomo ni suru nari*. The imagery here is geographical and spatial. But it could easily be understood in terms of social distance, of hierarchic distinctions that separate human beings from one another, and in
this sense, the term "from afar"—*enpō*—might just as easily have been
read "from on high." Whether one is born low or high, powerful or not,
sage or commoner, all human beings ought to relate to each other in
terms of their common moral essence—*honshin*. Here again a moral concept of humanity is used in a particular way to intersect the hierarchical

uses of Confucianism and to reduce its ultimate meaning to a ground-level moral meaning that minimizes existing social and political differences. The intended audience impact is obvious. Great distances in "space" and "hierarchy" do not undermine in any way the moral conviction of "we" being human and moral like everyone else, thus to have this confirmed by friends visiting from "afar" is "deeply satisfying."[41]

The emphasis that Miyake gave to the *Analects* was based very much on the insights provided it by Mencius, and resembled Itō Jinsai's interpretation in his regard. It is true that the idea of common moral essence in human beings played a much more important part in Miyake than it did for Itō, for whom moral potential took precedence over innate sageliness. However, in using the *Analects* to underscore an ultimate moral proposition for all human beings, there was an overlapping of thinking. As with Itō, Miyake placed a great deal of importance on the text of *Mencius* as providing the key perspective into the *Analects*, especially into the argument that human morality was intuitive and spontaneous and thus prior to social experience. Moreover, *The Book of Mencius* provided him with a related yet somewhat different set of propositions regarding action.

In *The Book of Mencius*, Miyake found a theory of action based on the concept of justice, especially as it related to human passion, or *rishin*, the passion for profit, and because this text was juxtaposed to this key philosophical issue, it may be seen as the crucial text in Miyake's opening lecture to his merchant audience. During Mencius's day, Miyake explained passion for aggrandizement had become rampant, and rulers and their advisers barely seeing "beyond their noses" pursued shortsighted goals of gaining wealth and military strength—*fukoku kyōhei*. Deeply disturbed by this prevailing reality, Mencius formulated his moral philosophy in which justice must always be made to supersede goals of immediate advantage and profit. However powerful they may seem, kings too must abide by that norm or be destroyed in the end by the very passion for aggrandizement with which they ruled. In extreme cases, the result is regicide.[42]

In outlining these well-known ideas of Mencius, Miyake painstakingly elaborated his understanding of what Mencius meant by justice. The ideographic compound for justice, he explained, is *Jin-Gi*. The first of these ideographs, *Jin*, he read in Japanese ethical language as *megumi* and defined it to mean human compassion, the innate moral capacity in human beings to directly perceive things not in terms of their external shapes but their internal emotive, idealistic, and humanistic truth. What human beings see objectively and evaluate, in other words, are not merely objects, cut and dried things that might be manipulated according to the needs of power, conquest, and wealth. To believe this is to become a king who treats his human subjects as objects without feeling.

It is important to note that Miyake also referred to *Jin* with another Japanese phrase that he used for metaphoric effect, namely to know *mono no aware*, an expression deeply grounded in indigenous aesthetic vocabulary and meaning the innate and emotive authenticity in things that the human mind grasps and knows without formal, scholarly preparation. It · is an idealistic philosophy, often associated with Heian literature such as *The Tale of Genji*, in which human beings see in other beings, and things, or in an emotional landscape, a spiritual quality that informs their actions in an external setting. It is the basis of human generosity, compassion, and mercy. Here, the idea of *mono no aware*, which might be understood as a quiet and passive "appreciation" of fleeting emotive beauty outside the self, is interpreted via Mencius to mean the emotive force of compassion that ought to enlighten all human actions as they might effect things outside the self. Without this idealistic component, Miyake insisted, action could easily turn into a simply manipulative imposition of passionate ambition. Hence: "Knowing *mono no aware* is Compassion"—*Mono no aware o shiru ga Jin nari.* One can see from this idealistic stance of his why Miyake would be attracted to the philosophical idealism of Ōyōmei and that general tradition in Confucianism that he obviously traced to Mencius. One can also appreciate his careful choice of words and phrases—*megumi, mono no aware*—that were intimately rooted in the ethical and aesthetic language of his audience through which the ideas of Mencius could immediately be acclimated, without further mediation, in the world of everyday life.[43]

The second ideograph in the compound Gi—Justice or Righteousness—also carried a great deal of philosophical weight, as its importance to merchants was readily evident. It balances the idealistic proposition of the first half with a cognitive principle of reasoned assessment. It refers to the mental capacity to be accurate and hence fair, principled, and thus nonarbitrary, knowing exactly where the markers should be and to calculate accordingly with precision: hence, *kotowari; wakachi o shiru*, etc. In a few terse lines, Miyake confirmed the universal human capacity to evaluate external evidences, to avoid erratic mistakes, and to reach just and fair conclusions. The ideal of justice without this epistemological dimension meant little, if one could deal with objective things only with skepticism and uncertainty. Indeed, one of the key intellectual themes in the Kaitokudō was this confirmation that the human mind could know objective things and deal with them without being arbitrary. Thus, in contrast for example to Ogyū Sorai who insisted that natural objects could not be known as their ultimate secrets were infinite, the tendency at the Kaitokudō was to see external nature as less mystical, to consider it as provisionally knowable, and to calculate in ways that were within reason. Nature, in other words, was not simply an emotive external object but a measurable set of things.

This view, of course, had everything to do with the mentality of marketmen having to calculate the forces of nature on the production of rice and hence of its price. But the philosophical implications went deeper and, in turn, would feed the curiosities of students concerned with nature as phenomena. The assertive epistemological position in comparison with Ogyū's skepticism coincides exactly with that of Nishikawa Joken's principled naturalism that he presented in his popular treatise widely read among merchants. Even as it related to textual matters, the Kaitokudō took the position that external markers could be ascertained and, hence, what was accurate, known.

This stance differed with Ogyū Sorai's criticism of the *Doctrine of the Mean* which he said, in the opening section of his *Bendō*, was a polemical defense of Confucius written by Tzu Ssu, a disciple of Confucius, against Lao-tzu the naturalist. In advancing the view that the idea of the "mean" was not simply a fabrication but based on the ideal of human "truthfulness," Tzu Ssu confused matters by identifying it with the Way, whereas in fact the "mean" was but one polemical "position" that one "chooses" to identify with. In other words, in the world of argumentation, there is no such thing as a permanent "center" and to identify an unchanging moral value with it is an intellectual error.

The position developed gradually at the Kaitokudō was that, on the contrary, the "mean" could be ascertained and that the doctrinal enunciation of that principle by Tzu Ssu was valid. The issue here was not simply a matter of correctness in textual and philological exegisis. Involved was the epistemological position of merchants that they could recognize the "mean" or the "center" in any exchange without being arbitrary or unjust. From this point of view the ancient classic was more than of symbolic value. It contained practical meaning in the Tokugawa present. Miyake's opening lecture, while not dealing with the treatise on the "mean," affirmed through a discussion of objective "righteousness"—*gi*—the human capacity to know external things, evaluate them, and make intellectual judgments as to what was, or was not, just.

The dualistic components of *jin-gi* the ideal and rational, intuitive and judgmental, empathetic and sensible, combined to make up Miyake's conception of "virtue." Each was necessary to the other in obvious ways, for emotive idealism without reason could lead to prejudicial and pas-

sionate action; and reason without empathy could similarly result in manipulative and coercive behavior. While Miyake avoided the political
theme in Mencius's philosophy that had been directed against corrupt
ministers and ambitious kings who had surrendered the "substance" of
their "names" and hence their legitimacy, he extracted the universalistic
implications of that philosophy. Substance superseded "name" in importance. Thus, although often accused of lacking compassion and of being
arbitrary in the determination of profit, thereby causing chaos throughout
the country, "merchants" need not passively accept that understanding of
their "name." Indeed, as affirmed in the *Analects*, human beings, without
exception, are originally "sages" and sages are "human," merchants are
first and foremost human and sagely, and this comprehension of humanistic substance ought to inform the essence of their being, whatever the
"name" outside authority imparted to them as a collectivity. The name
"merchant" ought in no way preclude one from acting in accordance with
the universalistic idea of "justice" that Mencius idealized in terms of compassion and reason.

The specific problem of marketmen seeking profit, however, required
special attention. If this be passion, then how was it to be regulated by
compassion and reason? Miyake addressed this issue, with no doubt of its
crucial importance to the audience, in understated and judicious choice
of language, without, however, obfuscating his main intent. Miyake explained "passion" to be determined externally through sensation and thus
as being akin to "habit"—*kuse*—and not intrinsic to the original self.
Miyake denied, however, that merchants who dealt with the seeking of
material advantage in the "external" world were necessarily doomed to a
fate of immoral passion that Mencius had assigned to wicked ministers
seeking wealth through the illegitimate use of power. The widely held
view that seeking profit—*ri*—was in and of itself the result of passion,
and hence morally inferior, was erroneous because it was not related to
the principle of justice that was central to all of Mencius's thinking. Profit
sought in accordance with that norm ought to be judged as moral action
so that the accusation leveled against merchants that their acquisition of
profit violated human standards of goodness was entirely misplaced.
Profit was nothing other than an extension of human reason, of the epistemology of "righteousness"—*gi*. Indeed, merchants should not even
think of their occupation as being profit seeking but as the ethical acting
out of the moral principle of "righteousness." When righteousness is
acted out in the objective world, Miyake went on, "profit" emerges
effortlessly and "of its own accord" without passionate disturbances: *Ri
wa senedomo mizukara ri ga tsuite mawaru nari*. If profit be righteous—*ri*

wa gi nari—then, indeed, "profit" ought not be affixed as a "name" on that mercantile activity of buying and selling. The livelihood gained through the marketplace was no different, therefore, from the efforts of men in other occupational groups in society, be they samurai, peasants, or moral philosophers. The actions of merchants, like those of other members of society, must be judged in terms of their "righteousness" and not in accordance with prejudices identified with names.[44]

The didactic message in Miyake's initial lecture that profit need not be mere passion but a moral extension of righteousness would become one of the key ideological convictions at the Kaitokudō. It was a conviction, moreover, premised on the epistemological proposition that the human mind, regardless of social status, could calculate objective things in ways that were precise and true, as in determining the "mean." Reinforced by the "sacred" texts of the *Analects* and *The Book of Mencius*, this epistemology that was taught within public academic space encouraged marketmen to see themselves and their work as being virtuous, compassionate, and fair, and as possessing, therefore, a moral center in their community equal to that of any other class. Through repetition over time, this moral affirmation would acquire enormous significance for the academy's ideology. Often, the statement would be made in assertive and polemical language that went beyond Miyake's lecture, as in the case of Nakai Shūan.

That merchants take profit to maintain their livelihood there can be no denying, Nakai would say in his frank "unsolicited viewpoints" of 1728.[45] But if this be wretched, then more wretched still are the samurai who squeeze "stipends" from poverty stricken peasants: "Indeed should this not also be taken as being truly despicable—*kore o mo hata iyashi to sen'ya.* Classes of human beings, Nakai went on, are different from one another only in terms of their special occupational "skill"—*waza.* The exercise of each skill brings a "profit," a measurable amount of material reward by which human beings survive in society. When this is done with righteousness, that profit emerges naturally and in and of itself—*onozukara no ri*—echoing here the language of Miyake. The actual skill of merchants is in the exchange of goods—*akibito no kaegoto*—for which a just profit is exacted. Within the exercise of this skill, some are more effective than others qualitatively, some are more exact and fair, some are lazy and abuse the skill. But regardless of the particular skill in any of the classes, the same ethical truth remains constant, "the diligent flourish, the ineffectual languish"—*tsutomureba shōji, okotareba kiyu.* This is a matter of knowledge and ethical self-control and not of the intrinsic moral superiority in the substance of one skill as against another. Nothing in the classical canons says that being an aristocratic administrator is morally superior to being a merchant, and this is because no human being is intrinsically morally superior to another. Whether a skill is executed in excessive ways is a matter to be judged by the objective and universal norm of "righteousness" and of "compassion." The actions of the samurai, in this framework, may be excessive and immoral, just as that of a passionate merchant might be. The judgmental norm, however, is identical for both, the skill of one not being inferior or superior to the other, and the moral worth of each being equal. The fact that men of commerce specialize on the objective calculation of market forces does not, in any way, mean that compared with men of other classes, they are heartless and devoid of compassion. "It is said," Nakai concluded, "that since merchants practice the skill of acquiring profit . . . that they are incapable of true inner feelings. This is a despicable view"—*asamashiki ron nari.*[46]

To take this theme one step further, Nakai Shūan's son, Chikuzan, who would emerge as the dominant figure at the Kaitokudō in the latter half of the eighteenth century, would incorporate the views of his mentors into the elementary instructional handbook he compiled on how to "nourish one's house"—the *Kayō hen.*[47] In this key textbook of moral instruction written in elementary language, Chikuzan reiterated the basic ethics of profit taking by merchants. "Like the stipend of the samurai and the produce of farmers, the profit of merchants," Chikuzan wrote, "is to be seen as a virtue"—*toku nari.* Indeed, as all of these forms of income were morally "righteous," profit ought not be singled out as being inferior, so that the term "profit" itself should not be used in the conventional derogatory sense. Profit in this latter sense, Chikuzan went on to note, is "avarice"—*riyoku*—and indicates excessive and inappropriate profiteering, not guided by the principle of "righteousness." Although Chikuzan does not elaborate further on this theme and states it in a brief and terse statement, the message was crystal clear. Exacting a righteous profit was a virtue, inferior to no other means of nourishing life. Profit may be motivated by greed, but this need not be so if marketmen retained an identification with the moral norm of accurate calculation or "righteousness." The fact that these lines appear in Chikuzan's textbook for youngsters, makes it clear that the early articulation of Miyake on this subject and as reiterated by Nakai Shūan was also worked into the introductory primer of the academy itself.[48]

The openness with which Nakai Shūan and Chikuzan confirmed the work of merchants suggests once again the importance of Miyake's maiden lecture in which he outlined the philosophical basis for this. Using con-

cepts readily understood by his audience and avoiding an egregiously polemical stance appropriate to a "public" academy, he endorsed the virtue
of merchants and their capacity for righteous action. Unlike Itō, who did
not take his philosophy to such a pointed confirmation of particular action, Miyake also avoided a discussion of the scholastic procedures espoused by Itō. Itō, it will be recalled, concentrated a good deal of his
intellectual energy on clarifying the epistemological procedure—the systematic explication of ancient texts—by which firm knowledge was to be
attained. Lacking such a clear procedure, he had reasoned, metaphysical
speculation would replace the articulation embedded in the classics. To
preserve an authentic epistemology, Itō did not address his philosophy to
clarify "action" as it pertained to a particular class, or to a restricted audience of merchants such as Miyake attempted to do.

On closer observation, therefore, Miyake's lecture can be seen as a series of assertions rather than well-founded philosophical propositions. It
was this didactic aim rather than academic rigor that made Miyake effective as a teacher. But it also left him vulnerable to critics skeptical of the
worthiness of teaching Confucian moral thought to merchants. Miyake's
critics would say that although his formal training was Neo-Confucian,
he was also ambiguously attracted to Ōyōmei idealism and drew on language reminiscent of Itō Jinsai. While this criticism pointed obviously to
the eclectic and inconsistent philosophical basis of Miyake's pedagogy,
behind this seemingly valid criticism lurked the barbed implication that
such a discrepancy in intellectual orientations stemmed from his being a
Confucian in the light of day and a merchant in the shadows, in short, of
not being truthfully dedicated to moral scholarship. This was a view,
moreover, that would come to be voiced among teachers within the academy itself, such as Goi Ranju, who were sensitive to the pointed criticism
of scholars skeptical of the Kaitokudō's mission.[49]

Yet it is clear that Miyake's eclecticism was inherent in the very strategy he had taken in his first and decisive lecture. Leaving unsaid the specific scholarly methods to be utilized in the search for moral knowledge,
Miyake turned his lecture, endorsed by a public charter, into a didactic
statement—kyōkun. Telling the audience that they, as merchants, possessed the virtue to control the public academy as their "communal"
space where, as "colleagues," they could seek the knowledge taught by
the ancient sages, Miyake, through this approach, transformed the moral
philosophy of Neo-Confucianism that the Bakufu utilized to confirm hierarchy and social distinctions as extensions of natural reason (and which
Itō had found conceptually flawed). In Miyake's formulation it was now
a theory of moral equality of high and low that also legitimated the work

of merchant commoners. Since sagely virtue was basic to all human beings, all could acquire knowledge and act in accordance with the norm of righteous reason. By affirming the epistemological capacity of commoners, Miyake had "selected"—*setchū*—a dimension of Tokugawa Neo-Confucian philosophy that was quite at odds with the conventional political use of it as affirmation of formal hierarchy. It was this self-conscious selection from within Neo-Confucian thought that made it also consistent for Miyake, despite the views of his critics, to see worthy elements in a variety of intellectual positions, as in the idealism of Miwa Shissai, the universalism of Itō Jinsai, the spiritualistic Confucianism of Yamazaki Ansai (1618–82), (even though Miyake had serious reservations about his excessive tendencies), and finally, the philologism of Ogyū Sorai, minus Sorai's exclusive adulation of the ancient kings. Having chosen one key aspect in Neo-Confucianism, even while stating his allegiance to the whole, Miyake could not deny the virtues of other points of view, although on a selected and limited basis.

Miyake's eclectic tendency was important. Beyond the commitment to compassion and righteousness and a formal identification with Neo-Confucianism, a good deal of intellectual exploration could be allowed within it. The approach to knowledge was not molded in terms of a consistent procedure—such as Itō's textualism—and a variety of methods could be tried out. This eclectic flexibility, however, created potential as well as real intellectual difficulties. While the inquisitive search for knowledge was to be encouraged, were should limits be placed? Eclecticism from the point of view of Miyake and his colleagues should not be tantamount to intellectual license. Here, the epistemology of "righteousness" played a key role in serving as a pedagogical guideline. Knowledge must be selected from those ideas that affirm the human capacity to grasp this norm, which thus precluded the use of religions such as Buddhism and Shintoism that were determined to be destructive to the goal of realizing objective righteousness. Knowledge at the Kaitokudō must be what men know to be verifiable and accurate, not ultimately how one believed in spiritual mystery.

The eclecticism of Miyake was thus to be sharply distinguished from that of Ishida Baigan's Shingaku, who was mentioned earlier. While sharing broad concerns with Itō, Miyake, and other commoner philosophers, Ishida formulated a moral philosophy that drew from Buddhism, Shintoism, as well as Neo-Confucian idealistic thought. As he would repeat in his "Questions and Answers about Town and Country"—*Tohi mondō*—(1739) and "On Nurturing the House"—*Saika ron*—(1744), possessing faith, whether in Buddha's Law to attain salvation, or in the virtues of the

Sun Goddess Amaterasu, or in the universal spiritual essence in Neo-Confucian thought, is a manifestation of the Way of Heaven—*Tendō*—and thus ought not be differentiated with doctrinal sophistry. Relying on this religious syncretism, Ishida affirmed some of the same ideas taught at the Kaitokudō: All individuals regardless of status are endowed with a universal essence that is sagely and that goodness is to be acted out in the everyday world of work. In their work, moreover, merchants contributed through trade to the well-being of the whole. The ethics of trade are accuracy and thus the affirmation of human trust. The labor of commoners, in short, was not morally inferior to that of the aristocracy, and the "profit" of merchants was no different from the "stipend" of samurai as both are forms of "gifts" from Heaven—*Tenka no onyurushi no roku nari.*[50]

Despite certain similarities between Miyake and Ishida, especially regarding the virtue of marketmen, crucial differences also stand out. While in Shingaku economic action is viewed as a means through which to transform the spiritual self toward "goodness"—*zen ni kasuru*—by defining itself as a religious and introspective movement, the idea of spiritual self transformation was not a central concern at the Kaitokudō. Goodness, it is true, is a sagely possession at birth. But it is to be expressed in ways that are objective and fair and that can be calculated in accordance with the norm of righteousness. The emphasis at the Kaitokudō, therefore, fell on the problem of acquiring knowledge outside of the virtuous self in ways that were not arbitrary thus to place the virtue of "fairness" in an objective social setting. Claims to intuitive self awareness as taught in Shingaku were viewed with deep skepticism, since "righteousness" depended on what men "knew" and not how they "believed." Syncretism that included religious ideas drawn from Buddhism came under especially harsh treatment at the Kaitokudō, beginning with Miyake and continuing throughout the eighteenth century in the thinking of Goi Ranju and Yamagata Bantō.

It was entirely consistent with the foregoing that the Kaitokudō would place a special weight on objective scholarship—reading, commenting, writing, and so on—which contrasted with Shingaku, where scholarship was downplayed. Students were not to meditate on their inner goodness but to confirm it through the actual engagement with difficult texts. Thus, while scholars at the Kaitokudō did not espouse philological theory as absolutely essential in the manner of Itō or Ogyū, much of the academic training did in fact focus on reading classical texts, including ancient ones. Unlike Shingaku, which held that spiritual self-awareness was transcendent of the world of form and change and resembled the Zen conception of enlightenment (thus it could be taught to commoners without concern as to their literacy), the Kaitokudō set its goals on scholarly excellence and proceeded to collect a library to support such a vision.

Thus, while the Kaitokudō as a public academy was limited by its "territorial" warranty and could not duplicate itself physically in the manner that the Shingaku could as a spiritual movement, it stood quite importantly for another kind of principle. Stable and predictable academic space would promote the study of moral philosophy in an "eclectic" manner that, at the same time, would not "retreat" to meditation and spiritualism. Individuals from all classes were welcomed to study there within this limit, as many from within Osaka and the regions in fact did. The institutional self-perception, based on a theory of righteous knowledge, moreover, stirred scholars within the academy to see the "objective" problems beyond the enclosed sanctuary in more abstractly conceived terms, including problems of political economy and educational structures. In time, a conception of the Kaitokudō's "place" within a broadly conceived educational order would be shaped. It is quite plain that the emergence of such an institutional projection rested firmly on the prior awareness of the need to manage the academy in an orderly and self-reliant manner that accorded with the epistemological commitment to "righteousness."

The systematic avoidance of haphazardness in the instructional program and the insistence on regularity as a matter of maintaining the public trust were clearly related to the "limit" drawn against spiritualistic eclecticism. Within the boundaries drawn to exclude that religious view, a wide variety of concepts could be discussed and critiqued in formal and informal seminars. Even here, however, crucial problems remained. While ideas such as those identified with Shingaku could be kept at arms length outside the walls of the academy, other equally "threatening" concepts could not be excluded quite as neatly. In particular, there was the matter of how much tolerance the Kaitokudō should allow in the "objective" reading and interpreting of "texts." Should the academy tolerate eccentric historical interpretations that through "righteous" reading of texts directly questioned the central philosophical propositions of Miyake's teachings? The ideological character of the academy emerges with stark clarity over this issue much more so than it did by defining the boundaries against religious movements such as the Shingaku. The test to this question would arise quite unexpectedly soon after the instructors had regularized the curriculum, and since the issue involved in this instance was not introspection and meditation but the objective reading of texts and the ethical meaning of this exercise, it carries special significance for the subsequent intellectual life of the Kaitokudō.

The case involved the brilliant young scholar Tominaga Nakamoto. The son of Tominaga Hōshun of Dōmyōjiya, one of the "five colleagues" that had funded the academy to begin with, Nakamoto, in a precocious outburst, utilized the knowledge he had acquired at the academy to challenge the textual resources upon which basic moral claims were being made by leading scholars of the day, including his mentor Miyake Sekian. A clear and decisive line would be drawn against Tominaga Nakamoto. Yet in doing so, the Kaitokudō would also move toward elaborating how limits were to be determined in the pursuit of knowledge; how, in short, intellectual permissiveness might be regulated in terms of a rational epistemology. This development owed much to the instructional presence of Goi Ranju. Indeed, it was out of the decisive impact of his teaching that the scholarly life of the academy would undergo redefinition and serve as the basis for the reflective visions that would be shaped by the brothers Nakai Chikuzan and Riken.

FOUR

BETWEEN ECCENTRICITY AND ORDER: HISTORY OR NATURE AS FIRST PRINCIPLE

IN RETROSPECT, THE CONSTRUCTION OF A LEGALLY STABLE ACADEMY PROVED TO BE FAR LESS CONTROVERSIAL THAN THE MAINTENANCE OF CLEAR INTELLECTUAL LIMITS WITHIN THAT space. Practicing his syncretist approach to Neo-Confucianism, Miyake Sekian continued to lecture formally on Mencius and Confucius while conducting specialized seminars on the idealistic writings of Ōyōmei (Wang Yang-ming) that he preferred. Among the guest lecturers, moreover, Itō Tōgai presented his father's extremist position on ancient studies while Miwa Shissai addressed himself to the contrastive theme of the introspective Confucian idealism of the more recent past. Among the assistant instructors, Inoue and Namikawa were protégés of Itō Jinsai's historicism while Goi Ranju was skeptical of that approach and preferred to base his thinking on universal "principle" in nature. To the extent that there was agreement on "compassion" and "righteousness," with the epistemological emphasis on the latter, a clear boundary could be set between the academy and Buddhism with its teachings on meditation, faith, and salvation. This was a line, as we shall see, that would be reconfirmed consistently.

Of more pressing importance was the development of controversial and "irregular" conceptual tendencies shaped within the framework of permissive syncretic "righteousness" and which required critical reflection and ideological monitoring. While Buddhism could be kept at arms length as being "external" to the Kaitokudō, "heterodox" ideas developed within the academy could not be ordered philosophically within Miyake's syncretism. That there should be confusion among onlookers as to the real banner under which the academy sailed can be thus readily appreciated. Looked at favorably, it meant the intellectual life at the academy was tolerant and permissive, allowing for exploration into a variety of intellectual areas, as indeed was the case to a significant degree. Viewed unfavorably, the academy seemed to lack coherence and, hence, intellectual integrity. The question was sure to be raised as to where the limits of "tolerance" were; whether the "walls" of the academy stood as conceptual markers or merely as protective barriers; and whether these walls were indicators of what would be disallowed without standing as obstacles to the pursuit of appropriate scholarly study. At issue, of course, was the intellectual identity of the Kaitokudō. If extreme intellectual irregularity was not to be allowed despite the spirit of tolerance, then would this require a conceptual clarification of the interior itself?

Beginning in the 1730s, and especially in the two decades after that, a sturdy tradition, which the academy would come to be identified with, took shape. External boundaries would indeed be set; certain kinds of conceptual propositions would be judged inappropriate; and within those guideposts, a wide variety of intellectual pursuits would nonetheless be encouraged. The outer limits would be drawn with the expulsion of the merchant student Tominaga Nakamoto from the academy as *persona non grata* in 1730 for proposing a theory of history believed to be intolerable to the scholarly life of the academy. The critical work of defining the internal intellectual space would fall on the instructional shoulders of Goi Ranju. The academy would have to make a stand between eccentric irregularity and intellectual order. Tominaga and Goi, each in his own way, however, were "eccentric" and articulated polemical positions that would both come to be identified over the long run as parts of a related history of the Kaitokudō. Excluded from the academy, Tominaga would leave behind an intellectual legacy and would be remembered and admired, especially in modern times, as the *enfant terrible* of the Kaitokudō. Goi who shaped the intellectual destiny of the academy would live on especially through the thinking of his students Nakai Chikuzan and Riken.

The tense demarcation that we see being drawn between Tominaga and Goi should not be viewed in terms of a personal dispute. Although Tominaga studied at the Kaitokudō when Goi was an assistant instructor, no mention is made by one of the other. There is no record of a face-to-face debate. At issue here, from the point of view of the intellectual history of the Kaitokudō, is the conceptual choice offered by two contrasting approaches to knowledge best articulated by Tominaga on the one hand and Goi on the other. Each tries to answer the question of what, in the final analysis, should constitute the ultimate field of human knowledge and hence of moral reference. Tominaga oriented his thinking with scrupulous consistency toward "history" and language texts while Goi, with equal coherence, devoted his mind to universal "nature."

Due to his historicist preference, Tominaga's ideas clearly overlapped with the theoretical views advanced by Itō Jinsai and Ogyū Sorai; yet his thinking contained a radical eccentricity unique to himself. Had he remained at the Kaitokudō, he probably would have steered the intellectual life there in an iconoclastic direction. The history of the Kaitokudō would in all likelihood have been a stormy one indeed. Goi possessed a rigorously logical position as well, but his ideas were less reductive and extreme, exposing an open-ended view of knowledge from which new visions might be shaped. His juxtapositioning of the limited mind and the vast universality of nature produced a variant of rational evidentialism, akin to that of Kaibara Ekken, that would come to permeate the Kaitokudō and be realized as a full statement in the grand synthesis provided by Yamagata Bantō at the end of the century. Yet, in this conceptual interfacing of reductive philologism and open-ended rationalism, we see the creation of a merchant intellectual history that would go far beyond the ideas outlined by Miyake in his opening lecture. In this respect, Tominaga's position, being shaped just beyond the shadows of the academy, and Goi's position within its gates, deserve our attention one next to the other.

.   .   .

TOMINAGA NAKAMOTO
(1715–46)

Although only the bare outlines of Tominaga Nakamoto's brief and meteoric life are known to us, the ideas he recorded in his writings testify to a precocious brilliance which has assured him a firm place in Japanese intellectual history. He was the son of Tominaga Hōshun, known also as Dōmyōjiya Kichizaemon, one of the five merchant colleagues directly responsible for the establishment of the Kaitokudō and its earlier incarnation at the Tashōdō. His father's financial contributions to the Kaitokudō were vital to the academy's survival, and both Miyake and Nakai Shūan trusted Tominaga Hōshun as a close confidant. Nakai even took him to Edo to assist him in the negotiations to gain the official charter for the Kaitokudō. Through his father, Tominaga Nakamoto's education at the Kaitokudō began at an early age, and it was no doubt expected of him to further strengthen the intimate ties with the academy that his father had established. He studied under Miyake from about 1725 until his expulsion from the academy in 1730. His fall from favor was severe and final, as evidenced even by the conspicuous absence of his grave in the family burial ground.[1]

During his studies at the Kaitokudō, Tominaga Nakamoto quite obviously read deeply into the historicist writings of Itō Jinsai and Ogyū Sorai and was greatly influenced by their approach to scholarship. The key to moral knowledge, these thinkers had said, was to be found in human experience as recorded in historical texts; the method of analysis was to be philological, the precise and critical scrutinization of language. The conclusion Tominaga drew from this general approach, however, would hardly have pleased either Itō or Ogyū, as he came to reject the idea that ethical norms were embedded in ancient sagely articulations for scholars to uncover. In his first essay, completed at about the age of fifteen, a work called *Setsuhei,* meaning roughly "a critical discrimination of doctrines," he challenged the integrity of the classical texts upon which the entire Confucian moral tradition rested. The empirical scrutiny of ancient texts did not justify the conclusion accepted by most scholars that moral norms could be found in ancient texts. On the contrary, these texts, without exception and hence including those held to be sacred at the Kaitokudō, the *Analects* and *The Book of Mencius,* were all polemical, passionate, and unreliable as sources of norms for later history.

Ancient virtues, Miyake Sekian had said, echoing a position held by Itō Jinsai as well, could be identified in certain classical texts and these could serve as moral norms for commoners to identify with in the contemporary world in order to guide their actions. It was this basic proposition that Tominaga found uncritical and deceptive. His readings into ancient texts indicated to him that such a transference of value from the past to the present was to use fabricated ideas as though they were normative in an abstract moral sense when, in fact, what is truly normative in ancient texts cannot be determined since ideas undergo constant distortion over time. For this appallingly disrespectful theory, Tominaga was forced to leave the Kaitokudō. The strange disappearance of his *Setsuhei* at this time points to the likelihood of it being destroyed, although he incorporated the thesis of that essay into his two main subsequent works, the *Shutsujō gogo*—"Interpretations Subsequent to Origination"—and *Okina no fumi*—"Jottings of an Old Man." Worthy of note is the fact that Tominaga then enrolled in a nearby school under one Tanaka Tōkō (1667–1742), a disciple of Ogyū Sorai, where he pursued his philological studies for several additional years before taking on employment at about the age of nineteen at the Zen temple in Kyoto, Manpukuji, to assist in the preparation of a new edition of the Tripitaka. Most of the materials on Buddhist history that he used in the *Shutsujō gogo* were drawn from his work on that editorial project. Both the *Shutsujō* and the *Okina* were published in 1745, a year before his death at the age of thirty-one. In his last few years, he is said to have turned to writing a history of Japan, which, had his health not failed him, would certainly have resulted in a most interesting work given his clearly defined theoretical orientation toward historical knowledge.[2]

Shutsujō gogo and *Okina no fumi* are provocative treatises. In a style that manifests a fresh sense of intellectual discovery, Tominaga proposes that historical texts invariably embody a silent polemical intentionality that cannot be readily detected on the surfaces of the pages and which reveal upon closer examination an ambitious contestation on the part of the author vis-à-vis another point of view against which that author wishes to gain intellectual advantage and supremacy. The sages of the past, he argued, did not compose their so-called classics divorced from some sort of doctrinal contest, and this invariably involved rival claims as to the exact meaning of the original principle or vow and thus as to what constituted the true tradition that ought to prevail in the present. To achieve persuasive advantage, the sages, without admitting to doing so, embellished received ideas with interpretive excesses and extraneous glosses, thus distorting the very tradition they claimed to be true. Sectarian and factional lines were then formed around the various contending claims. Their varying views were then "anthologized" and imputed to contain authoritative moral truths. Each successive era repeated this polemical distortion of received ideas and anthologized positions as being the authoritative interpretation of true tradition, further distorting moral precepts in the process. "It is invariably the case," Tominaga observed in *Okina*, "that one who expounds on an ancient philosophy always founds his own school of philosophy . . . and seeks to improve on the positions of his predecessors. His own view in turn becomes part of tradition, and later generations follow this derivative philosophy without knowing its origin."[3] The history of moral ideas, in other words, is not at all the unfolding of insights into what is true, but ambitious struggles over orthodoxy that produce falsifications and that render them utterly unreliable as a stable source of ethical authority for the present. To teach these ideas as though they were unshakable certainties is to deceive well meaning and unsuspecting human beings in the everyday world.

In Tominaga's view, all of the major religions were vulnerable to the same set of charges. The entire history of Buddhism (the central subject of his *Shutsujō*) is one of polemical contention based on mystical distortions and ungrounded speculations, all of which began over a struggle as to whose position was heterodox—*gedō*—literally, "outside of the way." After the historical Buddha had formulated his religious ideas, he is said to have conveyed their basic meaning to his disciples shortly before his death. Nothing but disagreement ensued as to what exactly had been said. Some say he made a "vow" that all would be saved; others said he conveyed all he had to say without words. After centuries of inconclusive debates, sectarian lines hardened into what is sometimes called the "greater" and "lesser" wheel, or Mahayana and Hinayana, within which the disputes were carried on. Even within a major contending tradition, sectarian lines developed—Ritsu, Tendai, Shingon, Shin, Zen, etc.— with each sect striving to outdo rivals as the recipient of true history and relying on devious intellectual methods to deceive the ordinary people.[4]

Confucianism too, while not given to the mystical and superstitious excesses of Buddhism, reveals a similar history of ambitious sectarian debate. Here again the contention down through the centuries has revolved around what is true history which is based on what exactly the sages might have said and over which scholars argued and formed sectarian lines to establish the supremacy of their views over those of others. Confucianism thus reveals a history of deception through dogmatic overemphasis, convenient deletions, and excessive generalization. The tradition, Tominaga observed, has reached the Tokugawa intellectual world itself, as witnessed in the polemical writings of Itō Jinsai and Ogyū Sorai.

Referring to Ogyū's critique of the *Analects*, the *Rongo chō*, as entirely a "subjective" interpretation and no different in its polemical distortions than those whom he attacked, Tominaga accused Ogyū of presenting ideas that looked attractive but in fact were not the views of the ancients as he claimed them to be—*koi ni arazaru nari.* In particular, Ogyū had committed the fallacy of reducing all of the key concepts into creations of the ancient kings—*sen'ō no gi*—thus offering "laughable" arguments such as the absence of a stable thesis in the *Analects* and excessively distorting the views of other scholars. From Tominaga's viewpoint, Ogyū, to defend his absurd thesis, was compelled to argue that "righteousness" and "principle" and "accurate center"—*gi, ri, chū*—were not relevant to the ancient classics that the Sung scholars such as Chu Hsi (1130–1200) had relied on. Yet anyone reading those texts, Tominaga argued, could readily detect these concepts in them, as in the *Book of Songs, Analects,* and the *Doctrine of the Mean.* By accusing Ogyū of being mistaken in not accepting the "center" of a fact as being "principled" and claiming this to be a nonargument—*ri arazaru nishite nanzo*—we detect Tominaga defending the Kaitokudō epistemology of objectivity and of "righteousness" possessing a calculable and "principled" center. It was this defense of the ethic of "righteousness," or "truthfulness" as his preferred term would put it, however, that was the premise of Tominaga's theoretical position that no historical text or scholarly interpretation of it were reliable sources of stable knowledge for men to resort to in grasping the meaning of action in the present.[5]

He summarized his overall view of Confucianism in the following manner:

> Kao Tzu said 'human nature is neither good nor evil' to improve on Shih Tzu's theory that 'human nature is partly good and bad.' Mencius' view of innate human goodness is a betterment of Kao Tzu's view of human beings as being neither good nor evil. Hsun Tzu, meanwhile theorized on the innate evil character of men to outdo Mencius. Yueh Cheng Tzu singled out the idea of filial piety, based on the dialogues of Tseng Tzu, to write a canon on the subject, and thereby abandon a wide range of previous doctrines. Unaware of the details of this history, the Sung philosophers took all of these various doctrines as parts of a single orthodoxy. More recently, Itō Jinsai observed that only Mencius had a true insight into Confucius and that the views of the others were all heterodox. And Ogyū Sorai argued that the ideas of Confucius were actually part of the Way of the Ancient Kings and that Tzu Ssu, Mencius and others taught things that were adverse to that Way. So many of these views are mistaken as they fail to see the real truth.[6]

With relentless consistency, Tominaga leveled his defiant attack against Shintoism. He refused to romanticize it as later scholars of national studies would. Nothing in its history moved Tominaga to modify his critical evaluation of religious history. The same kinds of distortions spawned by competitive polemics are to be found in the religious history of his own land as in Buddhism and Confucianism. It too unveils a history of deception. His language from *Okina*, voiced through the "old man," leaves little doubt as to his harshly negative opinion of Shintoism as a history of polemical distortions.

> As for Shinto, people several hundred years ago called it the ancient way of Japan, and superior to Confucianism and Buddhism. . . . Clearly both [Confucianism and Buddhism] were formulated by later thinkers for their own particular age. Now Shinto too did not have its genesis in divine antiquity. It was first taught as Dual Shinto, combining elements from Confucianism and Buddhism in ways that were convenient and suitable for the time. Then came Honjaku Engi Shinto, which reflected the attitude of Buddhists who envied the growing popularity of Shinto and outwardly taught Shinto while ac-

tually reducing it to the stature accorded to Buddhism. There followed Yūi Shinto, which separated itself from Confucianism and Buddhism and claimed to be the pure Shinto. These three forms of Shinto all flourished several hundred years ago. Recently a new type of Shinto called the Imperial Way has gained prominence. Except to say the Imperial Way is Shinto, it lacks specific doctrines. There is also a teaching which claims to be Shinto, but is essentially the same as Confucianism. None of these types of Shinto is derived from divine antiquity. As just outlined, they competed for superiority under the pretense of teaching the people. Unaware of this fact, the foolish in the world believed them to be true, practiced their erroneous teachings, and invariably quarreled among themselves. The old man thought this to be pathetic and laughable.[7]

The main thrust of Tominaga's iconoclastic and critical ideas about history are easy enough to discern as the previous passages cited from his writings clearly reveal. His thinking, however, takes on added complexity in the simultaneous introduction of concepts about language and culture. Tominaga was squarely within the broad framework of eighteenth-century historicism in exhibiting these interests. The supposition that firm knowledge is to be located in history, which Tominaga shared with his predecessors Itō Jinsai and Ogyū Sorai, led scholars of the historicist persuasion to an intense interest in language itself as an objective datum and, in turn, to the related matter of distinguishable uses of language in different cultures. Tominaga, as already emphasized, had oriented himself toward the historicist position which argued that the proper object of knowledge is history. He deduced from this approach the lesson that fixed moral norms could not be located there. Assertions to the contrary were irresponsible, and to make such claims such as Itō and Ogyū had done, therefore, was to simply repeat the ambitious polemics of their predecessors. The problem remained, however, that the language that human beings used was inherited from the past, and if language is manipulable according to emotive human intent, how is the ethical person in the present to avoid the excesses to which received language has been subjected? In other words, if moral language is encased in sectarian exaggeration, how does one then disengage himself from that reality?

Tominaga does not provide us with a clearly defined solution to this knotty problem embedded in critical historicism. In pursuing his study of "one-upmanship" in religious history, however, he had begun to address the possibility that language revealed regularly repeated patterns of use through which emotive purposes were articulated and which could be objectively identified. The idea being suggested here was not that the study of "language" could show "norm" but that it could clarify how distortions took place. Sectarian contention, in short, does not occur haphazardly but within identifiable contexts and also with a reliance on rhetorical strategies that were repeated in the various historical eras. Although Tominaga did not formulate a comprehensive theory of language, his historicist reasoning went beyond the debunking of religions to an analysis of patterns in the use of language, a discussion that situates him in the wider eighteenth-century intellectual concern with this problem.

Tominaga outlined his conception of language in his *Shutsujō gogo*. Language consisted of three distinguishable elements—*gen ni sanbutsu ari*. He called the first of these the "human" dimension, by which he meant the subjective, individualized, and hence relative perspective found in the use of language. Language always expresses a discrete point of view, and in its polemical form this is a sectarian view. Language, in this sense, is never neutral and therefore varies in rhetorical content depending on the context and thus must not be thought of as being the bearer of fixed truths. Applying this thesis to show the revision of Buddhist concepts over the centuries, Tominaga concluded with a few terse lines: "These are all sectarian words [*kagon*]. The variety of views we see expressed illustrates the observation that a human viewpoint is embedded in the language"—*iwayuru gen ni hito aru nari.*[8]

A related dimension is "historical time." While the subjective element refers to the individualized use of language representing different viewpoints in a certain situation, the dimension of historical time points to language change in a broad and comprehensive sense. Thus, while language ostensibly remains similar in external form, as Japanese remaining Japanese over time, it nonetheless does not remain static and in fact undergoes substantial alteration in both sound and meaning from one epoch to the next. Again, while this idea reinforces the point that moral concepts do not remain unchanged over time, the emphasis here is not on sectarian differences but on the inexorable change in language as history passes comprehensively from one era to another. Despite certain obvious continuities, for example, the language of ancient Japan, Heian, and Tokugawa is quite distinctive to each respective period. Evidences from the history of Buddhism demonstrate, Tominaga observed, that Sanskrit terms from the immediate post-Han period (ca. fourth century A.D.) are quite different from those of the early Sui three centuries later, and these are not merely cases of differing dialects but of actual language change. "These differences," he observes, "are often referred to as one of dialect. But language in fact differs with each age, so that pitch and voice undergo change as language changes with time. The so-called dialect is not at all a true dialect and should be seen as embodying the history of an era"—*gen ni yo aru nari.*[9] Thus, differences *within* an age as manifested in doctrinal contests and similarly *between* disparate time periods, as evidenced in the dynamic change of language, combine to relativize moral assertions made in the past. All human beings, even the greatest of sages, must rely on the language of their day, not that of another era in the past. Each historical present, in short, must deal with the contentions of the time and the language available to it. However, quite aside from the specifics of any given historical context, certain functional, rhetorical patterns are observable, Tominaga noted, that make it possible for scholars to see language in terms of these regularly repeated patterns and thereby enhance one's critical understanding of how language is used in any given historical situation, including the present.

In this third and most intriguing of Tominaga's ideas, he referred abstractly to language as containing "patterns"—*gen ni rui aru nari*—that clarify how concepts are presented. Tominaga's discussion unfolds rather casually, as if this theory of language came to mind somewhere midstream in his composition of *Shutsujō*. Moreover, while he spoke of "five patterns," he discussed only four in one place and belatedly introduced the fifth in the very last section of the treatise, practically as an afterthought. The evidences are also cryptic and presented as though they should be obvious to the reader, which hardly seems to have been the case then, and obviously less so for the modern historian. Yet, a provocative intellectual drive at work is discernible in this discussion that goes considerably beyond the previous two elements in theoretical curiosity. We see an attempt being made by Tominaga to abstract from his use of the philological method a broadly applicable set of rhetorical categories that transcend the constraints of polemics and historical change. We see a theoretically bold turn of mind displayed as he groped for ways to deal with language as an objective problem of knowledge.

Tominaga's basic thesis may be summarized as follows: If distortion is endemic to the history of moral ideas, certain basic rhetorical patterns that are related but distinguishable in function should be discernible. Following this line of inquiry, he then proceeded to identify "five" such patterns, all of which add up to impressive evidence that he had taken his historicist reasoning quite far indeed into the area of language study.

In the first of these patterns, Tominaga perceived "expansive"—*chō, haru*—use of language. The meanings of terms are stretched far beyond the limits of their original identification with a specific, physical object. Metaphoric references are used to facilitate this "stretching" process. In Buddhism, for example, a term that literally means "physical arena"—*dōjō*—is used metaphorically to depict a spiritual or religious state, so that a term used conventionally to describe a concrete empirical object is distorted through this rhetorical mode of "expansion" into an abstract religious concept denoting a spiritual world of saints and bodhisattvas. Similarly in Shinto, the physical reference to the "high plains"—*Takama no hara*—is extended to mean the heavenly realm of the gods and, in turn, as the source of spirituality in all things. Regardless of the philosophical content or the historical context, religions exhibit this rhetorical pattern of exaggerating the concrete or the actual—*jitsu*—into an abstract concept without verifiable empirical reference, and thus, he concluded, "Examples of this kind all belong to the pattern of expansiveness"—*kaku no gotoku no rui wa mina chōsetsu nari.*[10]

Precision is sacrificed in the next pattern as well, although the nuance here is somewhat different. While in the previous pattern concrete terms were extended in meaning, in this second variant abstract and all-inclusive terms—hence, *han*—are used from the outset to define the particular. Discrete physical references are not used metaphorically to make abstract claims. Through the argumentation from the general, all particularities are invested with spiritual meaning. Thus in Buddhism, the universal absolute is authoritatively presented without the mediation of empirical references and is claimed to have a cosmic reality prior to experience and to the emergence of differences in the universe. It is said to precede even moral distinctions of good and evil. As the absolute pervades the universe, it is said also to reside as an essential spirit in each particular individual as his "buddha-hood" or "buddha-nature." Here, neither the authoritative premise nor the particular embodiment is verifiable in terms of empirical references. However, by arguing that the spiritual essence of the particular is identical with the universal, by underlining spiritual similitude over particular physical differences, the idea can then be advanced that all human beings were endowed with a spirit of goodness or a buddha-nature that could transcend the physical and attain salvation. All of the particulars are thus made to seem to be "afloat"—*ukabu*, an alternative reading of *han*—on a common spiritual sea, eradicating in the particular the blemishes of age, poverty, lowliness of status, and so forth and thus dignifying all in terms of the assertion of universal spirit. It is an argument that is captured best, in Tominaga's view, in the phrase, "The entirety of humankind each and all is blessed with a buddha-nature"—*Issai shujō wa mina nyoraizō.*[11]

The third pattern is a direct extension of the previous one and is distinguishable from it in intensity and hence in quality. The pattern may be thought of as being a form of logical reductionism, or taking an authoritative premise to its logical limit—hence, *ki* or *uchitsukeru.* Whereas the former pattern is somewhat static in its description of the spiritual commonality of all beings, in this particular pattern a dynamic dimension is made to intervene in the form of concrete human action. Similitude is replaced by differentiation through this. The idea of universal Buddhahood is now expressed in terms of the individual realization of moral virtue in concrete ways as in acts of compassion and mercy, or simply "good works." Ultimate spiritual essence comes to be expressed in terms of concrete virtues. The individual is no longer only blessed with buddhanature, he is now also a "scholar" or a "saint." As the universal is taken to its logical limits in the form of concrete human action, distinctions emerge between the wise and the ordinary, the imperturbable and the passionate, the saint and the vulgar, the high and the lowly. Thus, while all particulars may be said to be afloat on a vast infinite sea, some are claimed to be enlightened, others ignorant. The rhetorical function of language used in this manner to show qualitative differences is to elevate those who understand true tradition from the heretical and unenlightened, from those who grasp the way and those who remain outside it.

Yet another rhetorical strategy, the use of ironic opposites—or *han*—is used to distort language. As in the previous case, the universal is reduced to the level of the particular. Here, however, language is twisted so that conventional terms are made to mean something other than usually expected. The device is used when concrete acts presumed to be good become habitual and customary and lose their ethical significance. Conventional language no longer suffices to convey what is good. The device of twisting and reversing the meaning of terms is thus relied on as argumentative strategy. "The term *jishi*," Tominaga writes, citing from Buddhism, "originally meant something evil as in passionate self-indulgence. But this was used instead to mean goodness. Among the patterns in language, this is called the use of opposites."[12] Tominaga might well have drawn additional examples from Zen Buddhism in which opposites are juxtaposed to transform meanings, in asymmetry being symmetry, the bent straight, the aged beauty, the rustic pure, the blind having true sight, and so forth. In all of these, what is true in the conventional and empirical world of meaning is transformed through the device of ironic reversal—or perversion if one is reconstructing the history of polemical contestation and intellectual distortion. In other words, one of the key patterns by which language and moral ideas undergo change is through the conscious twisting of conventional meanings for, at first, purely rhetorical effect but which, in its perverted form, comes to be conventionalized.

At the end of his treatise, Tominaga introduced a fifth pattern he referred to as "transformation" or "change"—*ten*—which is linked directly to his discussion of ironic opposites. While in the previous pattern the passionate is said to be good, the angular straight, the blind sightful, in the fifth pattern or "transformation" evil is said to *become* good. The emphasis here is on *process* rather than ironic effect. Language is thus employed to convey change from one state into another that is totally different: a hopeless and totally passionate person transforms himself into his opposite being; from absence of spirit, one is delivered into total spirituality. "Is it not said," Tominaga thus writes, "that a thoroughly evil person devoid of buddha-nature nonetheless transforms himself? And this is said to be realized on one's self-strength and not on the aid of others. Indeed, is it not here that the source of buddha-nature is said to be found even though such a buddha-nature is said not to have been there? The use of language in this manner is transformation." [13]

Drawn from Zen Buddhism, Tominaga's example points to the argument that rejects the idea of a universal spiritual essence as an authoritative given and places the generating source of religious deliverance in the concrete individual, thus transforming the individual from one totally devoid of buddha-spirit to a saintly bodhisattva. Tominaga's main point, however, was that in this rhetorical strategy language was used to focus on the process of change from one state to another, and this pattern was thus distinguishable from the other ones and should be included as one of the ways in which religious ideas were shaped into polemical form historically.

These examples provide suggestive evidence as to the analytical orientation of Tominaga's thinking. Disputes over moral ideas may be endemic to all histories, but they occur for different individualized purposes in different times and through distinguishable patterns. Rhetorical patterns in particular may be utilized in distinct religious histories, as in Buddhism and Shintoism, and as they are regularly repeated in different times and places may in this sense be said to be "universal." To be sure, the net effect is always the same: ordinary human beings are deceived into believing religious and moral assertions that have no grounding in existential human reality.

In contrast to rhetorical patterns that may be universal, Tominaga also advanced the theory that language systems contained within themselves certain characteristics that were culturally specific and not universal. Thus while arguments of "expansion," "universal authority," "logical differentiation," "ironic opposites," and "change" may be utilized in a number of different contexts, certain basic cultural characteristics that are historically particular cannot be transferred and grafted into other contexts through rhetorical devices. In short, Tominaga superimposed yet another dimension to his understanding of language, that of *cultural* distinctiveness. While this view was consistent with his overall historicist mode of reasoning, he used it to argue that change and distortion over time took place in historical time sequences that were parallel and distinct and not interactive. Attempts at grafting religious systems across these distinct lines were thus totally artificial and arbitrary and a major source of distortion. Tominaga found it ludicrous, for example, that the Ōbaku Zen sect at Manpukuji, where he had been employed as an editor, was a thoroughly sinicized form of Buddhism in which the monks in Japan continued to wear Chinese-style mandarin dress while living within a Japanese language and cultural context. He took to task his fellow countrymen who deluded themselves into believing that foreign customs could be duplicated in Japan. "Buddhists in Japan," he observed, ". . . are intent on emulating the customs of India. Indulging in practices that are inappropriate to this country, they fail to understand the meaning of the true way. The old man detested this and ridiculed it." Similarly, he went on, "Confucianists in Japan . . . are unquestioning in their emulation of Chinese manners and customs. To imitate Chinese customs that are foreign to this country is to misunderstand the essence of Confucianism." [14]

Each historical sequence, Tominaga reasoned, contained within itself a comprehensive quality informing the process of change, creation, and distortion. Buddhism was produced within a dynamic cultural context specific to India and similarly Confucianism to China and Shintoism to Japan. Except through drastic distortion, Buddhism could not be transplanted into China, nor Confucianism into Japan. And since each sequence changes in terms of a momentum specific to it, religious forms of the past are no longer relevant to the respective present, certainly not to his Japan. Tominaga set forth his thoughts by arguing that Buddhism is the way of India; Confucianism is the way of China; and as one country differs from the other, so the teachings of these countries are not the way of Japan. Similarly, Shinto is the way of Japan, but time changes and Shinto is no longer the way of the present. What we perceive here is the use of disparate historical development to further reinforce the argument that history is relative. Exogenous history is unrelated to Japan; ancient Japan is irrelevant to the present. Tominaga's purpose in making history relative in order to affirm the judgmental capacity of ordinary individuals in the social world of the present is clear enough. The idea of cultural distinctiveness, however, was a potent concept that was subject to appropriation by later thinkers to reaffirm the uniqueness of Japanese culture and language, even though it does not appear to have been Tominaga's main aim to privilege Japanese history.

The ambiguity can be traced to Tominaga's discussion of cultural types in the *Shutsujō gogo*. He discussed this problem in terms that were not entirely negative, suggesting for example that the use of language to persuade the people had to be in accord with the cultural preferences of the populace at large and that each society possessed a "preference"—*sono minshin no konomu tokoro*—that was distinctive to itself. "The custom of India is an extreme attraction to mysticism," Tominaga thus wrote, "and it is analogous to the fondness for scholarly studies in China. In general those who prepared the teachings and explained the way invariably proceeded with these [customs] in mind. Were it not so, the people would not have believed in them." In discussing Japan, he presented what he saw as the people's cultural preference in a positive light.

In contrast to the mysticism and scholasticism of India and China respectively, the Japanese prize "direct, unadorned, honest language"—*seikai shitchoku no go o konomu*. As already alluded to, however, Tominaga lodged this cultural preference in the general populace as a customary value belonging to the people and thus set it apart from the formal religion or the elitist schools of scholarship. The idea is tantalizingly presented here that popular preferences are not simply flawed "habits" continued over time but also the source of cultural virtue. Although irrelevant to other societies, India's mysticism is essential to India. The same may be said of scholasticism for China. And so too the Japanese attraction to the straightforward spirit—*naoki no kokoro; makoto no kokoro*, etc.—and to the down-to-earth ethic of precision—*kō, shimeru*. These may be taken to represent, in Tominaga's eyes, the cultural resources for Japan's own "virtue." Tominaga seems, therefore, to have erected a dichotomy between formal or doctrinal religions, which although intertwined with distinctive cultures were nonetheless fabricated over time, and popular cultural orientations or preferences, which were not in and of themselves flawed and which constituted the basis of divergent cultural virtues.[15]

His general thinking on this interpretive twist deserves recounting, especially his scathing denunciation of organized or "fabricated" religions, as this then sets the stage for the presentation of his view of "virtue" as being the way of "truthfulness"—or, in short, the Japanese cultural preference for "straightforwardness" and "precision." He began in his *Okina* with this irreverent attack on Indian Buddhism:

The flaw of Buddhism is its reliance on magic. By this is meant the use of chicanery to create illusions. India is a country that finds fascination with sorcery, even as a means with which to explain the Way. When magic is not woven into religion, the people will not be responsive to it. Because he knew this, Buddha taught himself the techniques of sorcery, engaging in six years of ascetic exercises in the mountains to learn the art of creating illusions. The miracles and supernatural events that are described in the various sutras are all magical illusions. . . . All sorcery. To add still another point, Buddhists believe in the transmigration of the soul and invent stories about the previous lives of the Buddha's disciples and of Buddha himself, and then they explain the truth of these stories with various supernatural means. While these were all devices to convert the Indians to Buddhism, surely they are unnecessary to the Japanese.[16]

Predictably, the denunciation of Chinese Confucianism is equally vehement:

Confucianism is excessively scholastic. Our society thinks it is eloquence. The Chinese adore it. Even in explaining an idea to the people, if the language is not proper, the audience will not be responsive to it. Take for example the explanations of the meaning of rites. Originally the term for rites meant those ceremonies performed at puberty, marriage, mourning, and at festivals. Today it is used to mean the duties of a son to his father and of a retainer to his lord. It is tied to the moral character of human nature, as it is to sight, sound, speech, and action. As you are well aware, it is even said to transcend heaven and earth and to embrace all things. . . . All of these examples show how in Confucianism commonsensical things are explained with rhetorical excess and verbosity so as to attract a popular following. Like Indian sorcery, Chinese verbosity is unnecessary.[17]

Tominaga then plunges his sword with unflinching consistency into the religion of his own land:

The blemish of Shinto is obscurantism, the reliance on mystical formulae and injunctions that conceal reality. It is the source of deception and thievery. In the least, sorcery and rhetoricalness may be worth either seeing or listening to and hence may be tolerable. But obscurantism has no such redeeming features. Since people in ancient days were simpleminded, obscurantism may have been useful for purposes of instruction. When corruption, lying, and stealing are as rampant as they are today, the teachings of Shinto priests reinforce these tendencies. . . . Even teachers of the lowly No drama or the tea ceremony are influenced by them. They sell certificates for profit.

114

> How wretched they are. . . . Any doctrine . . . that is obscure, de-
> mands a price, and is mystical, cannot be thought to be the way of
> truthfulness.[18]

Having totally rejected historical religions, foreign and domestic, as irrelevant to Japan in the present, Tominaga then proceeded to "the way of truthfulness" which he prescribed as the only realistic alternative available to his society as it was deeply enmeshed in the commonsense mentality of the people. The "way" is not to be identified with moral absolutes and philosophical truths but closely to the individual self in everyday life, a view that closely reflects Itō Jinsai's philosophy. "The way of truthfulness," he thus comments, began as practice. "A way that cannot be acted out is not the way of truthfulness . . ." Tominaga then goes on to elaborate what he means:

> The answer is simply doing what is reasonable, making daily work
> in the present to be of highest importance, and being correct in
> thought, careful in speech, discreet in conduct, filial to parents. With
> diligence one should serve masters, educate one's children, guide
> those below, respect older brothers, be kind to younger relatives,
> care for the aged, be warm to children, remember ancestors, pro-
> mote harmony in the home. One should be honest among men and
> avoid debauchery, respect superiors, and be compassionate to the
> foolish. Most of all, we should not do to others what we should not
> want done to ourselves. . . . Do not steal even a grain of sand. Give
> when you must without the fate of the kingdom in mind. . . . Do
> not immerse yourself in wanton pleasure and drink. Do not kill a
> living thing that is not harmful to human life. Nourish your own
> individual self. . . .[19]

Underlying this brisk endorsement of conventional ethics as taught at the Kaitokudō and understood by the world around him is Tominaga's central existential thesis. One ought to do these things not because it is sanctioned by tradition to do so, or because a wise sage prescribed them, or that a classical text explains their meaning, but simply because they are essential to human life in the present, making human interaction regular and orderly rather than violently chaotic which is intolerable. Moreover, if one were ethical in these practical and commonsensical ways without indulging in time-consuming debates as to their ultimate underpinning in the cosmos or in historical texts, then one could, in fact, devote himself to an intellectual or aesthetic pursuit of his own interest. "When one has time to spare," he notes, "he should study a special art and thereby seek to realize excellence. . . . Commenting on this view, the old man observed that the *Analects* advises one to do what should be done and then apply himself to an art."[20] Even in the Buddhist tradition, Tominaga politely observed, monks were encouraged to study literature and mathematics: "These too are insights into the way of truthfulness."

By disengaging the self from all of the "useless" things of the past and not making of ethics any more than what they were, that is, practical guidelines for human existence, the individual could then realize his own particular talent or what Ogyū Sorai had called the distinctive "little virtue" that each individual was blessed with at birth and which should be developed to its fullest expressive potential. Believing that the essential purpose of kingly benevolence was to allow human beings to do this, Ogyū also had written toward the end of *Bendō* in language that clearly resonated with Tominaga's. In the "way of human nourishment"—Ogyū reasoned, one relies on "benevolence" and gains mastery of an art. As Confucius taught, all human beings possessed a virtue that was distinctive to themselves so that by relying on the way of peace and benevolence of the ancient kings, everyone could realize fully their personal virtues." It is this idea of immersing oneself in the "enjoyment" of and "devotion" to a special art—*gei ni asobu*—that is woven into Tominaga's ostensibly commonsensical idea of "truthfulness." In Tominaga's eyes, a mathematician and a student of literature were worthy of respect, but not a scholarly monk, for while the latter claimed to teach about grand, ultimate truths, the former were devoted to their personal "virtue" writ small.

Tominaga's idea of "goodness" would also be writ small in the manner of Itō Jinsai. Being good is doing the obvious—*sono atarimae*—in the actual world of daily work and play, being compassionate to others and supportive of one's self. It means doing good "in countless little ways"—*moro moro no yoki o okonau*—and from doing these things goodness is generated—*okonawaruru yori idetaru.* Truthfulness, then, as it is articulated as part of the world of commoners in daily life, resembles closely the ethics of Itō. Although Itō relied on Mencius as a source of norm and Tominaga did not, both men nonetheless immersed themselves in textual analysis to emphasize the ethical potential of commoners in the present. To both of them, goodness is not a distant absolute but a way of life that is close at hand in the narrow byways of the immediate world. Goodness and truthfulness are thus generated from below by commoners who possess the capacity to know and to judge and not imposed from above as a fixed absolute. Ethical potential, in this important respect, belongs to everyone, not to sages or men with high status, and it is rooted in the cultural preference of the Japanese people as a whole for honesty, precision, straight-forwardness—in sum, "the way of truthfulness," *makoto no michi.*[21]

The convergence of Tominaga's ideas with those of Itō and Ogyū is grounded in a skepticism toward the use of cosmology to anchor moral absolutes. It is a skepticism that led them intellectually to history, or concrete human experience, as the primary field of knowledge for scholars and to rely on philology and textual criticism as their method. From their reading of history, they formulated ethical perspectives into the present. In the case of Itō and Ogyū, the intellectual procedure of leaving indigenous history and returning to it after identifying with a normative basis in an alternative tradition is of vital significance, as evidenced by the crucial role that "Mencius" and the "ancient kings" play in their respective systems of thought. They shared a tendency to seek out a universalistic norm by which to explain history and ethical action in the present, seeing all histories, in this regard, as being comparable at some deep moral level, thus justifying the transference to Japan of norms drawn from an unrelated historical past.

As already emphasized, Tominaga strenuously denied that such transference was valid. Changes within a single sequence were too extensive and the cultural difference between parallel cultures too deep. In the final analysis, Tominaga did not believe in the comparability of historical experiences and denied the utility of introducing refined norms uncovered in ancient texts into the present. Itō and Ogyū had erred in trying to do that and thus revealed themselves to be in that unfortunate historical stream of polemical scholarship. These critical reservations notwithstanding, Tominaga most certainly shared a related epistemology and methodology with Itō and Ogyū. Like them he exhibits a logical inclination to take a particular philological method and hold firmly to a clear set of conclusions rather than to indulge in eclecticism. In these various respects, Tominaga was not a unique and isolated figure, detached from the historicist discourse on knowledge that captured the attention of the scholarly world in the early eighteenth century. However eccentric and nonconformist he may have seemed to colleagues at the Kaitokudō, beginning with Miyake and subsequent historians, he shared a broad common ground with Itō, Ogyū, and their historicist schools of thought.[22]

It is not mere coincidence, therefore, that his thinking should parallel that of his contemporary Dazai Shundai, Ogyū's leading student of political economy.[23] Both share a decided impatience with historical texts as sources of truth. Although Dazai retained Ogyū's idea of kingly benevolence, he, like Tominaga, tended to use historicist reasoning to deemphasize the authority of the past and to comprehend the present in terms of current realities. There is a coherent relationship in their thinking that situates them within a common frame of reference, even though the emphasis of Dazai was on assessing the state of the economy while Tominaga was concerned primarily with ethics for commoners, especially those in the commercial world of Osaka where he lived.

Equally intriguing, although here again hardly accidental, is the admiring evaluation of Tominaga's ideas by leaders of the National Studies Movement—*Kokugaku*—notably Motoori Norinaga (1730–1801) and Hirata Atsutane (1776–1843). These thinkers also sought to bring to present reality what they believed to be its true meaning without the mediations of foreign religions, language, and aesthetics. Tominaga's idea of cultural distinctiveness and the nontransferability of values across parallel historical lines certainly found a sympathetic response from advocates of national cultural uniqueness. The fact that Tominaga did not spare Shinto from his caustic comments went unnoticed while his attack on Buddhism in *Shutsujō gogo* offered the leaders of national studies a scholarly critique that reinforced their dislike of that religion as being foreign and intrusive to indigenous culture. Motoori certainly was deeply impressed by the *Shutsujō* and recorded his evaluation of it in his intellectual autobiography *Tamakatsuma* (1799):

> In nearby Osaka there lived a person by the name of Tominaga Nakamoto. During the Enkyō years [mid 1740s] he published a work called *Shutsujō gogo* in which he discussed the way of Buddhism. Drawing on a wide variety of canonical texts from that tradition, he presented detailed documentation many of which are wonderful to read. It seems to begin with that this person [Tominaga] felt it fruitful to study Confucianism as well, so that his Chinese-style prose is also quite polished. Though himself not a Buddhist priest, his extraordinarily lucid insights into Buddhist texts reveal a depth of knowledge that is not to be found in the various sects. How truly impressive his method is.[24]

Brushing aside the attempts of Buddhist scholars to refute Tominaga (such as Musō Bunyū in *Hi Shutsujō gogo*, 1759) as "frankly speaking, useless"—*muge ni iu kai naki mono nari*—Motoori concluded that, try as these critics might, they would not be able to undo or contain the importance of Tominaga's scholarship, which is the literal meaning of these words—*Kono 'Shutsujō' oba, eshimo yaburaji to koso oboyure.*[25]

Motoori's elegant words of praise could not escape the attention of his protégé Hirata Atsutane. "Our teacher," Hirata wrote, "read this book, and in his collection of scattered essays, *Tamakatsuma,* praised it over and over again"—*kaesu gaesu homeokaretaru de gozaru.* Hirata then began a search for the *Shutsujō* in Osaka and Edo bookstores and, after initial difficulties, ended up with more copies than he needed and went to construct from it his own denunciation of Buddhism, which he called *Shutsujō shōgo* (1817). The title itself is obviously drawn directly from Tominaga's work, save for the insertion of the term "words of laughter"—*shōgo*—for ironic spice. Hirata, in any event, left no doubt in the introduction to his own work as to his indebtedness to Tominaga:

> How marvelous it is that there should be written during the reign periods of Kanpō and Enkyō for which the Emperors of Sakuramachi are known, a fine scholarly thesis by a merchant scholar, one Tominaga Kichiemon of Naniwa in the region of Settsu. At first he studied with the widely known Miyake Mannen [Sekian] a great Confucian scholar of the time, and discovered in the course of his learning the great harm brought upon our country by Chinese scholarship. He wrote this in a book now lost entitled *Setsuhei,* which he showed to Miyake only to incur the latter's wrath as he, Miyake, was a Confucian scholar. His relationship with Miyake ended thus, Tominaga proceeded to read Buddhist canons and turned the extraordinary talent he possessed to study all the various texts. With reference not only to Buddhist scholars in China and Japan but India itself . . . he presented an insight that had not been expressed or thought of before him. He said that every single one of the Buddhist scriptures did not contain the true view of the Lord Buddha and that they were all falsifications of later ages. Thus even the title of his book is called *Shutsujō gogo,* meaning to make verbal pronouncements long after having departed from the original law. Tominaga refers to himself in the introduction of the edition published in the first year of Enkyō as having attained the advanced age of thirty, so that it would seem likely that he had not yet approached being forty . . . .[26]

Although Hirata found Tominaga brilliant just as Motoori had, he also felt that most scholars would find the *Shutsujō* too difficult to read and doubly so for ordinary readers. Its relative lack of readership, he thought, was due to a high level of complexity, which he believed should be corrected by adding phonetic Japanese comments—*kana no chū*—so that it would receive the popularity it deserved. It should be noted that due to his desire to simplify the *Shutsujō* for a popular readership, Hirata tended to underestimate the accessibility of the work for scholars. While it is unlikely to be counted among the most widely read works of the Tokugawa period, it was still republished a dozen times following its first appearance in 1745.[27] Of greater importance is the fact that, intricate as it may have been, the *Shutsujō* presented little difficulty to Motoori and Hirata who proceeded to appropriate Tominaga's work for their mission in national studies, in Hirata's case, emphasizing his agreement with Tominaga that Buddhism was a hindrance—*samatage*—to Japanese culture.

Despite this important appropriation of his ideas, it is best not to connect Tominaga with the National Studies Movement. His unflattering comments on Shinto, as noted earlier, were passed over without comment by Motoori and Hirata. The theoretical drive in Tominaga's thinking was to disengage the present from all religious systems including ancient Shinto, which was a point of view decidedly at odds with national studies. In the final analysis, it would seem to be far more appropriate to place Tominaga near the Kaitokudō and its intellectual environs. The unexplained disappearance of his essay, *Setsuhei*, is evidence that he represented an eccentric and iconoclastic historicist dimension that the academy, despite its eclecticism, would not formally acknowledge. It was a well-known fact, however, that Tominaga had incorporated the main ideas of that maiden work in his subsequent writings, the *Shutsujō* and *Okina*, both of which were included in the academy's library.

In point of fact, despite his iconoclastic use of historical texts, Tominaga's ethics were not by any means totally unrelated to the views discussed at the academy, namely that the mind of ordinary commoners in the present could organize the external world and "know" what was accurate and valid and thus make judgments on what might be fair, just, and "truthful." This proposition that endorsed the epistemological potential of commoners was central to the ethic of the Osaka commercial bourgeoisie and had found expression in Miyake Sekian's concept of "righteousness." Tominaga called this human capacity to know "the way of truthfulness." These concepts are closer to each other than they are sometimes thought to be, although Miyake, reacting to Tominaga's iconoclastic procedure, could not appreciate that possibility. Thus while Tominaga's interpretation of history was not likely to be discussed openly within the academy, the awareness of his works persisted, and it is thus best that he be situated in the course of Tokugawa intellectual history as being just beyond the walls of the academy where his scholarly life was placed. The line drawn against him (and the historicist mode of reasoning more generally) would be scrupulously maintained, but it placed him in a curiously vital relationship with the history of the school.

Maintaining that demarcation and defining the nature of intellectual order within the Kaitokudō would be taken up by the scholar-teacher Goi

Ranju whose task it was to keep the academy's scholarly life consistent with the public trust it had received. A highly complex and individualistic intellectual, Goi would exercise decisive influence in establishing the theoretical basis for the line drawn against iconoclastic historicism.

GOI RANJU
(1697–1762)

In the view of the journalist-historian Nishimura Tenshū, who wrote in the early twentieth century what is still the most elegant historical account of the Kaitokudō, it was Goi Ranju, more than any other scholar, who gave decisive intellectual direction to the academy (following a period of uncertain leadership through the better part of the 1730s) and thereby established its prestige as a place of learning. Among Tokugawa scholars too, Goi was acknowledged as having been a much more influential intellectual presence at the academy than the earlier founders, Miyake Sekian and Nakai Shūan. The third son of Goi Jiken, a scholar of commoner background of considerable reputation in Osaka, Goi Ranju was an assistant instructor to Miyake Sekian in the early years of the Kaitokudō even before it had gained official status. Partly out of a sense of uncertainty with Miyake's approach to scholarship, Goi took leave of the academy in 1727 to further his studies in Edo. Following this he served sporadically for periods amounting to two years as an instructor in the domain of Tsugaru in northern Japan. It has been said that this was a most trying experience since the young lord entrusted to him for instruction was poorly motivated in matters of learning. He returned to Osaka in the late 1730s (the exact time is not known) and rejoined the Kaitokudō with an invitation from Nakai Shūan who was concerned about the lack of intellectual purpose at the academy. As Nishimura records it, Goi returned and corrected that situation before his death in 1762.[28]

Little more that is factually reliable is known of Goi's life. Although he emphasized the importance of maintaining one's house from one generation to the next in his personal teachings, he himself, for reasons that are not clear, did not do that. His only offspring, a daughter (Setsu), was born out of wedlock. He was, however, deeply affectionate toward her throughout his life; he educated her personally, and the last poetic lines he wrote at his death bed were of her sad and tender presence. Frankly critical of the self-denying views of Buddhism, Goi apparently enjoyed life with a certain philosophical exuberance, though he felt that the clever writings of the "floating world" such as those of Saikaku were "useless." One gets a sense from scattered bits and pieces of information that Goi was an intense and outspoken scholar, unafraid to voice his views and given to impatience in matters relating to ritual and formal protocol. Something of this is hinted at in Nakai Shūan's letter, mentioned earlier, of instructions written shortly before his death in 1758.[29] Addressed to the advisory council of the academy headed by Goi, Nakai wrote that he would very much have wanted Goi to assume the sole leadership of the Kaitokudō—*hitori Goi . . . gokurō ohikiuke kudasaretaku.* He refrained from asking him to do so, however, because of Goi's age— "being not that far apart from mine," Nakai observed—and because of the great deal of energy required to maintain the academy's diplomatic relations with the public world. It was here, responding to the views of some of the merchant leaders, that Nakai proposed the name of Miyake's son, Shunrō, who was not expected to distinguish himself either in academic or administrative matters. Yet Nakai's carefully chosen language conveys the impression that, in his view, Goi probably would not have been the right person even if he had been younger.

His forte was not in matters of protocol but in teaching, in which he was acknowledged by all at the Kaitokudō as a brilliant master. It was a well-known fact that Nakai had by then turned over the scholarly side of the academy entirely to Goi and that he had also entrusted the education of his sons Chikuzan and Riken to him. Goi, on his part, seemed perfectly amenable to the role assigned to him and distanced himself from the external affairs of the Kaitokudō. During his lengthy tenure as head teacher, he came to identify himself closely with the academy, making his home there and not teaching privately elsewhere to acquire personal wealth. Born into a family of poor scholars, Goi dedicated all of his energy to daily instruction at the Kaitokudō for which he received housing and a moderate stipend; true to the family legacy of some three generations, he also died in poverty.

Thus, although Goi remains one of the less remembered figures in Tokugawa intellectual history (his works still remain largely unpublished in modern form), his impact on the Kaitokudō during his instructorship was deep and lasting. First and foremost, he steered the academy from an easygoing eclecticism toward a consistent philosophical basis and, in doing so, provided the academy with a sense of intellectual enclosure, of controlled academic space, within which scholarly instruction might take place. Goi was especially sensitive to the opinion commonly circulated in the scholarly world that the Kaitokudō was an academy for merchants and hence somehow inferior and biased in its outlook and, further, that the school lacked real intellectual substance. Goi strongly believed the earlier eclecticism should be altered. He was not against making choices and hence in this sense may be said to have been eclectic himself, but he insisted that the conceptual basis of choice must be made explicit. His displeasure with uncritical eclecticism can be seen in his reference to the academy's image in the scholarly world:

> It is said that Miyake does not have a consistent scholarly point of view, as he is engaged in selling medicine and enjoys talking about the art of healing. To most observers he sounds like a mysterious night bird. His head is Neo-Confucian; the backside resembles Riku Shō Zan; the arms and legs are like Ōyōmei; and his language reminds one of a physician.[10]

This rather unkind commentary was circulated in the scholarly world and recorded in a number of places, the language being altered sometimes to say that Miyake sounded like Itō Jinsai, as noted earlier, rather than a "physician" as in the passage just quoted. But whatever the variation, the main point was the same. Scholars had a difficult time identifying Miyake's intellectual stance, and this no doubt hurt the image of the Kaitokudō. Somewhat impatient with this evaluation, Goi perceived a clear need to cultivate a stable intellectual identity by clarifying the boundaries within which knowledge would be pursued since, in his view, the mission of teaching commoners did not justify inconsistent eclecticism.

Goi therefore tended to reverse the permissive strategy implicit in Miyake's syncretism to underscore the weaknesses of the various schools of thought rather than their strengths as Miyake tended to. He accused Ōyōmei idealism of denying the commonsense world of natural things so that it differed little in the end from a religion such as Buddhism. Yamazaki Ansai's brand of Neo-Confucianism he found to be too dogmatic and intellectually inflexible, thus fostering intolerance. Itō Jinsai was taken to task for neglecting the idea of action in a public context and unwittingly encouraging opportunism since goodness could refer equally to virtually any kind of action. His sharpest barbs were reserved, as will be elaborated on shortly, for Ogyū Sorai and through him to radical historcist thinkers that would include Tominaga. By referring to the various schools in terms of their limitations, Goi could then emphasize his own intellectual position and, in turn, that of the academy as well.[31]

As is readily evident from extensive lectures and commentaries compiled in his *Meiwa,* meaning roughly "casual observations over tea," Goi based his philosophical position on the Neo-Confucianism of Chu Hsi—*Shushi no gaku.*[32] Although he does not develop his philosophy in a sustained and systematic manner in *Meiwa,* which was a collection of Goi's views conveyed to students on any number of subjects ranging from nature, religion, language, custom, superstition, and the like, resembling in this regard Nishikawa's "bagful" of knowledge, a remarkably clear and coherent epistemology emerges from his teachings. His approach to the Neo-Confucian system of thought was entirely rationalistic and, like Kaibara and Nishikawa, devoid of the cosmologism and moral metaphysics for which it had been known and often criticized for by Tokugawa thinkers. The introspective idea of identifying the spiritual self with an abstract absolute he similarly kept at a distance, underlining instead the epistemology of "observation" as the first pinciple in the acquisition of knowledge. Regardless how limited human intelligence was, men must proceed from the elemental proposition that the universe was not organized in a random way and things did not move about in a state of meaningless flux. While the details as to the shape of things may differ slightly depending on the locale, the general theory that things must ultimately cohere in terms of categories possessing internally consistent and hence defining principles must be held to be valid. Human beings, therefore, ought to be able to relate abstractly to all human beings because of this generic and categorical identity. Ethics, dealing with others in ways that are not arbitrary and prejudicial, stem from this basic conception of observation of the commonality in things. His position is stated in unmistakably clear language as in the following:

> If an ant is indeed an ant, its life principle cannot be any different from ants [in general]. The same is true of human beings. Their life principle cannot be said to be different because they live in different countries. The Tang people [Chinese] refer to foreign groups other than us [sic] as barbarians differing little from the birds and beasts. They fail to understand the Way of Nature, and thus also the life principle common to all human beings. The sages were not like that. It was after all Confucius who once said he would like to live among the nine barbarian tribes.[33]

Not only sages but every individual, regardless of status, belonged first and foremost to that category of humankind. All human beings, moreover, possessed the inherent intellectual capacity to observe and to know basic truths. In affirming the empirical potential of the human mind, Goi reinforced the idea of "righteousness" as taught by Miyake. Goi's empiricism, however, was grounded less in sacred text than in the ultimate proposition of the universality of nature, and in this respect, he was intellectually much more closely linked to thinkers such as Kaibara Ekken and Nishikawa Joken discussed in the previous chapter. Goi was not an agronomist or an astronomer as these latter two figures were. His mission was the moral education of commoners. Like these men, however, he pegged human reason to universal nature as an ontological first principle. Unlike Buddhist theologians and historicists such as Ogyū Sorai who said that the human mind could not possibly comprehend the workings of nature and that it ought not be looked upon as a normative principle, Goi, along with Kaibara and Nishikawa and others of this naturalistic persuasion, claimed that as human beings gained knowledge of nature in ways that were ever expanding yet always incomplete, they reaffirmed over time their grasp of the regularity and nonarbitrary manner in which natural events unfolded. Thus they also renewed their sense of reverence for other beings and things in the natural order as a whole. Nature, therefore, must precede all other forms of knowledge as an ontological reference, as Goi reveals in this passage that very closely resembles the language employed by Kaibara Ekken:

> The great virtue of nature is life itself. In some indefinable way the principle of continuous life pervades the universe. As life goes on, there is death. Death may also be said to be part of that process of ongoing life. . . . Without the natural order that we see before our very eyes, there would be no humankind, no historical events, no rules of nature, neither men nor laws can be seen apart from it. Thus when we speak of the Way of Nature as being outside of us, we should also see it as being within us as well. It is the discussion of this subject that we call the Way of the Sages.[34]

Goi's natural ontology informed all aspects of his thinking, and it remained a fundamental premise he held to and from which he would not waver. From it, for example, he encouraged a certain and unashamed engagement in the physical aspects of human existence. Human beings shared with other things in nature the same instinctive drives such as to reproduce and survive. Although he certainly did not endorse the reckless pursuit of pleasure to satisfy human passion, he nonetheless denied that human life was a matter of spirit alone. It is natural that human beings should interact to sustain life, and this should not be interpreted merely as the manifestation of human passion. He writes for example in the following vein:

> As I see it, the endlessness of that great energy [onki] is truly the universal grace of Nature itself. Thus . . . should people in society not reproduce beyond one or two children, saying this is adequate, should those children pass away, that house will come to an end. If things continue in this fashion human life will steadily decline, and the principle of active life will disappear, and in the end only the birds and beasts will remain. Distinctions between the wise and the

125

foolish, the poor and well-to-do will likewise be done away with. What is proper and improper human interaction will meet the same fate. Yet it is only when there is interaction between male and female is life reproduced, and this indeed is the principle of continuous life—*sei-sei no ri.*[35]

Morality, in other words, does not arise out of the avoidance of the physical nature of humans but in recognizing its place within a natural universal whole. While rules may regulate human appetites for functional reasons, they cannot eradicate them, and it is thus the "human way" to abide by this general principle of life—*kono kotowari ni shitagau o hito no michi to su.* To deny the physical self its natural passion, as in Buddhism, was to sever the individual from the real world of sensation, which is unnatural and fundamentally impossible. Even the great poet Saigyō (1118–90), Goi observed, could not achieve this religious goal of physical detachment and admitted it. Thus, Goi went on, as Saigyō gazed at the wintry storm from his religious sanctuary he could not help but feel the biting cold which then moved him to compose a poem about that feeling—*yuki no furu hi wa samuku koso are.* Laudable as it may have been that Saigyō, for whatever tragic reason, should have detached himself from the world of human passion, Goi found that abdication of life to be unacceptable and ironically toasted the renowned saint with *sake* that he personally enjoyed without apology: "With admiration for Saigyō's honesty, I raise to him a cup of warm *sake.*"[36]

The problem of good and evil in human beings was conceptualized similarly within the previous philosophical frame of reference. As with all natural things, human beings possessed a living "essence," but this was not inherently evil. It was nothing more than a natural life principle— *hito no sei wa tada sei nari.* Human societies, however, assign "names" to certain kinds of action which are said to be good or not good, so that what human beings ordinarily speak of as "evil" may be best thought of as being part of human custom rather than a universal absolute anchored in natural human personality. Thus, for example, when human beings are attacked by tigers or stung by mosquitoes, unfavorable terms are used even though it is their natural virtue to do so while similar kinds of acts by human beings on fish and fowl are described in different and favorable terms. A general theory of wickedness is therefore theoretically weak, being too human-centered and restricted, and lacks the overall perspective of universal nature. Evil is nothing other than a *social* definition of what is believed to be the "excessive" pursuit of human wants. The sages, therefore, formulated rules to define where those limits might be placed in order to foster the well-being of society. Rules are functional. They set limits. They are not to be confused with "goodness" in the universal sense of that term.[37]

Again, Goi takes his stance from the premise of nature. Like evil, goodness must be seen first, not from a human-centered point of view but in terms of nature. "Being incapable of taking a view from universal nature," Goi wrote of the advocates of human evil, "they were also unable to grasp the general theory of goodness." Goodness pervades the natural order as the nonarbitrary principle governing the life process of all things. Beyond specific social rules, human goodness is rooted in the human recognition of the place of human life in the broader scheme of nature. Goodness as manifested in social rules must always embody the purpose of nourishing the "life essence" of humankind. It was the purpose of the sages to teach men to treasure human "life" as the "seed"—*tane*—of goodness and it is central to Mencius's theory of human personality as being basically good.[38]

It is important to note that the endorsement of Mencius is made in the context of a critical rejection of Hsun Tzu's theory of knowledge and human personality. Arguing that men were basically passionate and wicked, Hsun Tzu had said that what is referred to as "goodness" was actually a human "fabrication"—*itsuwari*—in which human beings acted in accordance with the formal teachings of the sages. Goi did not deny that the sages formulated ethical rules or that human societies were better off for having these guidelines to conform to. He rejected the idea, however, that ordinary human beings did not possess the intelligence to know that the norms they relied on were of sagely formulation. By endowing the sages with an exclusive genius, Goi claimed, Hsun Tzu had reduced ordinary human beings to a state of ignorance and failed to understand Mencius's theory that human beings did possess the capacity to know goodness even without the formal instruction of the sages and acted out this goodness intuitively, as witnessed when the individual saves a child spontaneously without reference to established "norms." But Goi's point in siding with Mencius, and hence also with Miyake, was not so much to say that all human beings were inherently good, in the sense of having fixed moral principles, but that they possessed the mental capacity to know and hence also to internalize knowledge—*mizukara no mi ni oshie o ukuru zensei.* Referring to this intellectual capacity as "something precious"—*tōtoki mono*—in all human beings high and low alike, Goi stressed that, indeed, without it the moral norms of the sages would not be recognized and appreciated and would mean very little. Moral potential in human beings, then, resides in their intellectual capacity to know things beyond the immediate physical interests of the self to broader issues of society and beyond that to nature. That capacity was not a sagely property but a human one; a concept vital obviously to the Kaitokudō's project of scholarly education among merchant commoners.[39]

It was in this broad epistemological frame of reference that Goi endorsed the general position of Mencius against that of Hsun Tzu over the basic nature of human personality. While the endorsement of Mencius makes it evident that Goi remained within the received moral framework of the Kaitokudō, clearly he had also shifted the philosophical foundation for it. Nature is the decisive mediating construct for Goi in a way that it was not for Miyake. To Goi, goodness is not simply penetrating such classical texts as the *Analects* and *The Book of Mencius* and uncovering in them a timeless moral principle that might be acclimated to the present. These classics are obviously valuable because they provide insights about human "life" and its "continuity" in social form within the broader natural order. But it is this latter that is absolute; the former, the writings of the sages, is relative and limited despite the creative intelligence manifested in them for which they deserve deep reverence and scholarly concentration. The view, however, that moral norms are embodied in perfect form in the classics required modification in Goi's view because nature as a universal reality could not be totally known by the human mind which is always limited.

However, it would be fallacious to assume that because men cannot know all there is to know about nature that some phenomena transcend reason, as in afterlife or immortality and an assortment of other myths and superstitions. It would be equally erroneous to conclude from the fact of limited human intelligence, as Hsun Tzu tended to, that men have no choice but to rely on what the ancient sages said and be good thereby. More appropriate Goi felt was the view that since the human mind, including those of the sages, is always limited, men in every historical present must strive to constantly seek to understand more of what there is to know in the universe, recognizing all along that the limited mind can never fully fathom its workings. Goi cites, by way of example, the phenomenon of thunder. "We do not know what this is," he writes, "because our intelligence has not yet reached the level to understand it"—*kore o shiranu wa waga chi no imada itaranu yue nari.* He went on to comment that after much observation and study, men would someday be able to explain thunder as a phenomenon of nature. It is most surely the case that the ancient sages did not understand it and indeed were not knowledgeable about many other things as well—*seijin to iedomo shirazaru tokoro ari.* Had they known what thunder was, they would have explained it. Sages of more recent times did not do much better: "Even Chu Hsi did not possess the intelligence to understand it, and thus harbored superstitious views." The human mind, however, has already gone beyond the ancient and more recent sages in certain areas of knowledge and will no doubt continue to do so as it explores new areas of a limitless natural universe.[40]

Goi's expansive view of knowledge based on nature as the first principle, and the human mind as being always limited and relative to it, undergirded his discontent with scholars who sought refined moral truths in classical texts, a viewpoint already mentioned in his critique of Hsun Tzu. One of the clear boundaries that Goi drew from his philosophical stance, therefore, was vis-à-vis the historicist school and that of Ogyū Sorai in particular. Consistent with this position, he did not question the demarcation that had been established between the Kaitokudō and Tominaga Nakamoto, who had received methodological inspiration from Ogyū. When Goi returned to Osaka, Tominaga had already left the Kaitokudō. Tominaga was frail and died young, while Goi continued beyond the former's death for another seventeen years as a teacher. Given these sets of facts, it is unlikely that there were close personal interactions between them, although in retrospect this is not as important as the conceptual tension arising from their divergent epistemological propositions and which, as previously noted, remained part of the intellectual history of the academy.

The significant areas of overlap between Goi and Tominaga should of course be underlined. Both were deeply distrustful of Neo-Confucian cosmology as intellectually unreliable; Buddhism and other religions dealing with afterlife and mysterious spirits were discounted as totally irrational; the purely subjective and idealistic philosophy of the Ōyōmei school that Miyake tended to favor was also kept at arms length as unpredictable and unsound as a theory of action; but, most importantly, and on the positive side, they affirmed the evidentialist position regarding knowledge that the human mind possessed the capacity to judge external things and to reach reasoned conclusion that were, if not perfect, nonetheless fair and truthful. In other words, they believed that the mind observes, organizes, and makes judgments and that this was the bedrock of scholarship. Tominaga would not have found Hsun Tzu's philosophy any more acceptable than Goi did, for it denied analytical human intelligence to commoners. Both men in this respect were grounded in the intellectual environment that had produced the Kaitokudō in the first place. But the conceptual division between them was very deep indeed, separating the "inner" from the "outer" as far as the Kaitokudō was concerned, and Goi made certain that that line was maintained. The heart of the matter was their disagreement as to what ultimately constituted the proper object of knowledge to be cognized, ordered, and evaluated.

Although not opposed to the study of history by any means, Goi, like Kaibara, understood the *ultimate* object of human knowledge as being "nature," as already emphasized. Historical texts must always be seen in relation to that vast backdrop and hence as *fragments* of human insights into it and through that of the human self or "human nature." All of the major texts down through the ages that shed light on this problem were valid objects of study, not because they contained fixed norms, but because they informed the ongoing effort in the present to gain new human understandings of nature, which is vastly more universal than man. The idea set forth by Ogyū and others that moral norm could be located in a single set of texts in an ancient epoch was to Goi a reckless and irresponsible claim, an argument he dealt with at some length in a piece he wrote against Ogyū Sorai.

Although this polemic against Ogyū Sorai, *Hi-Butsu hen* ("Butsu" being a pen name by which Ogyū was known), was edited by Nakai Chikuzan and Riken and first published in 1766,[41] it had been written a good deal earlier, probably sometime in the late 1730s, and had already been read in manuscript form in the various academic circles, especially in Edo and Osaka. From the perspective of this study, this work is of considerable significance as a defense of the basic precepts subscribed to at the Kaitokudō. More than the scholastic question of whose readings of the texts were philologically more accurate, this critique by Goi is what concerns us here. A set of persistent arguments can be detected that provide a structure to his criticism of Ogyū. Much of Ogyū's scholarship, Goi reasoned, was inspired by an antipathy to Itō Jinsai to whom Ogyū in fact owed a great deal intellectually. Driven by this passionate aim to surpass Itō by denigrating him, Ogyū had proposed a theory of Confucianism that was argued to absurdity. If accepted, this theory would cause extensive damage, Goi believed, to Confucian moral philosophy.

Goi began by observing that Ogyū had rejected Itō's claim that the basic perspective into the Confucian morality should be through Mencius to Confucius's *Analects*. Quite aside from denying the stability of Mencius as a guideline, claiming it to be subjective and thus unreliable, Ogyū went on to question the normative importance of the *Analects* itself as the text of ultimate importance as Itō had claimed it to be. And with unshakable dogmatism, at least in Goi's eyes, Ogyū went on to locate the source of all Confucian norms in the great ancient kings who had first created society. Thus benevolence itself was no longer the "principle of human empathy" but the great virtue of the ancient kings and, as Goi quoted from Ogyū, "Righteousness is the Righteousness of the Ancient Kings. Reverence is the Reverence of the Ancient Kings. Mercy is the Mercy of the Ancient Kings." Ogyū had removed all of these values from the human interior and with a single-minded consistency, had invested all virtues containing general human moral meaning into the kings. And, finally, his assertion that these virtues of the kings were all to be understood as being part of the way of governance made their importance ultimately political. The Way of the ancient kings was the Way to govern the people—*tami o yasunzuru*. The "base"—*hon*—of Confucian knowledge, therefore, was nothing other than the way to order the kingdom—*Tenka kokka o osameru no michi o iu*. It followed that "scholarship" must have as its sole purpose the examination of the textual basis when that original concept of the "way" was first formulated, as in the ancient classics of Songs, History, and Rites.[42]

Goi objected to Ogyū's entire structure of reasoning. By imputing all ethical norms beginning with "righteousness" into the ancient kings, Ogyū had committed a number of fallacies. All human beings, like physicians, in all times and places, use "norms," and this is not a matter that can be reduced to several texts identified with the ancient kings. To deny a normative content in Confucius's *Analects*, is therefore, highly prejudicial and idiosyncratic in the extreme. Secondly, Ogyū had forced a thesis that scholars like himself could penetrate the spirit of ancient language in its totality. Aside from specific errors that demonstrate that Ogyū himself was flawed in this effort, the fact was that the language of ancient China and that of Japan could not ever be in perfect accord—*gengo awazu*. The search for spiritual identicality through "language," therefore, was an extremely deceptive idea and ultimately irrational.

Indeed, Goi went on, there is an element of irrationality running all through Ogyū's historical theory. His "purpose" is to venerate the "spirit"—*kishin*—of the ancient kings by claiming a transnatural intelligence on their part to grasp the mandate of heaven at the beginning to bring peace among men. In this manner, Ogyū imputed into original structures created by the ancient kings a "Divine Gift"—*Tenpu*—an assertion that could not be documented and had to be accepted on faith because Ogyū had said so. This irrational dimension went even further. To Ogyū only few could know this historical truth, since it would be beyond the intellectual grasp of ordinary human beings—*bonjin*. For himself, however, Ogyū claimed the mental powers of a genius and likened himself to Confucius, as a "sage" born in the wrong age, after the created fact, and distanced from the actualities of doing creative political deeds.

When Ogyū spoke of Confucius understanding his "mandate" or "imperative"—*mei*—in his fifties to mean his realization that he would not be in a position to influence policy—*seisaku no nin ni ataru atawazu*—he, Ogyū, analogized this to be true of himself in his own age as well. The presumptiousness here, Goi reasoned, was consistent with the mystical adulation of the ancient kings who received the Divine Mandate which, in turn, only the most talented would comprehend.[43]

The ramifications of Ogyū's mystification of the ancients disturbed Goi. It fostered a radical elitism that Goi rejected. Heaven does not grant "imperatives" to "kings" alone, in his view, but to the "people" at large. To study, moreover, does not mean to examine a few of the most ancient texts in the original form. It must mean to grasp certain broad moral concepts and to embody them in "everyday life"—*nichiyō*. Ogyū's argument that only a few intelligent individuals—*kenjin*—in the "upper" levels of society—*chūjin ijō*—would be equipped to study the ancients had the net implication of separating the bulk of society from moral concepts and from the wider normative universe of "Heaven." By doing so, "inner" and "outer" spheres would inevitably be torn asunder. Yet if one saw the *Analects*, in fact, as not being about "politics" or the transmission of the ideas of the ancient kings but as containing a commonsense human morality stressing the coherency of inner thought and outward action, or "language-learning" and action that was "truthful and faithful"—*bungyō-chūshin*—then, indeed, the opposite conclusion must be drawn from that of Ogyū, namely that "inner" and "outer" are in accord—*mina kore gai nai o gassu*. To Goi, therefore, the value of "benevolence" was not located with the ancient kings, but in the "spirit of the people"—*jinshin*—and the theme of control through "righteousness" that Ogyū had rendered as the "way to govern the nation" Goi believed to be first and foremost in Confucian philosophy as "ordering the self"—*onore o osameru no michi*. Thus while to Ogyū, "political action" was entirely an externally determined way of kingly governance, to Goi, as for Chu Hsi, Ogyū's principal target, "politics" was at once "public" and also "private"—*kō, shi*. The first part of the ideographic compound for politics—*sei-ji*—Goi understood to mean the public act of governing the nation, while the other he took for ordering personal affairs. Both spheres ought to be evaluated in terms of a common moral framework and not politics as being totally external and divorced from the norms of private virtues. Goi stressed that political virtue must be in accord with human virtue and understood at the commonsense level of human existence.[44]

Goi believed the key source of Ogyū's errant theory was his misunderstanding of the meaning of the natural "principle." As he believed this to be ultimately unknowable, Ogyū had reasoned that the ancient kings had not relied on "principle" in creating society but had done so only on the basis of "things." But Ogyū had failed to grasp the simple truth that "principle," while invisible, abstract, universal, and ultimately unknowable in its totality, was still the "principle" that gave internal coherency to all "things." Things are not separate from "principle." Indeed the latter is the organizing "norm" in all things—*mono no soku.* In creating, the ancients could only have relied on "thing" and "norm" in it. By separating these, however, Ogyū invested "norm" into the genius mentality of the kings alone, thus removing infinite nature as a "text" for human understanding and also distancing the source of human norms from ordinary human beings throughout the rest of history. Yet, while human beings might not in general be likely to approach the intelligence possessed by the kings, the conclusion Ogyū drew that ordinary minds would not be able to grasp in some fundamental manner the meaning of universal values was a prejudicial and dogmatic fallacy of reasoning on his part.[45]

The "Way," Goi went on, was never intended by the ancient sages to mean something human beings could never achieve. Indeed, what Ogyū calls the "Way of Ancient Kings" ought more properly be termed, "The Way of Human Beings"—*hito no michi;* and "governance" in the specific sense of "fabrication"—*sakui*—that Ogyū also discusses should be seen within this broader "human" way. Within this human way, the sages taught that individuals could transform themselves through study and self-reflection—*kishitsu henka.* It was not so much that anyone could become a sage, as Ogyū distorts it, but that all human beings were able from within to act in ways that were good and truthful. Goi expressed only "dread" in Ogyū's lack of faith in the human self—*hito no onore o shinzezaru o osoru*—and commented ironically that rather than accept that pessimistic view he would prefer to gaze at the grasses and find joy—*kusa o mite yorokobu mono nari.*[46]

Equally as disturbing as Ogyū's distancing of moral norms from the general populace was his insistence that those norms, and hence their application in historical time, were distinct from nature. The ultimate source—*daigen*—of all human and social things, however, must be nature, and hence the "ways" men devise stem from that source and are not artificial as social history against the state of nature as Ogyū had conceived it. Without universal principle in the universe, the "way of the ancient sages" would not have come into existence. Similarly, there is no such thing as heaven that gave the original "mandate" to the kings as against "nature." Heaven and nature are one and the same thing. The "mysterious spirit" and the "divine way" of heaven—*kishin* and *shintō*—

are terms that refer to the invisible workings of the way of nature. By recognizing that the human interiority is also part of the natural principle in the universe, men are also inevitably empathetic to the life spirit in other things and beings. The ancient sages did not separate heaven from humans but referred to them as simultaneous and integral to a vast natural order—*Tenchi no dai; uchū no kō.*[47]

As is readily evident, Goi leveled his critique against Ogyū consistently from the viewpoint of a commoner scholar committed to the education of ordinary men. It is the assumption of Ogyū's school, Goi observed, to recognize only those who are superior, but "he seems unmindful that recognizing only wise men at the exclusion of others is to be ignorant of the meaning of wisdom itself"—*ken o shirazu.* Goi took strong exception to Ogyū's favoring of the talented few, namely, those "possessing virtue"—*yūtoku*—for these were invariably contrasted with commoners, ordinary men without moral and intellectual potential—*bonjin.* To Goi, all human beings were blessed with "virtue," and the accumulation of pedantic scholarly knowledge, such as amassed by Ogyū, did not guarantee virtuous action. And conversely, ordinary human beings without extensive scholarly knowledge could, indeed, act in ways that were compassionate and virtuous as Mencius had taught. Thus, while Ogyū rejected the idea of "striking" the "center" (*ataru*, to strike, written with the ideograph *chū*, center), as being uncontrollable with a constant norm or principle and therefore useless to human beings, Goi countered that in the commonsense world, human beings need not possess a philosophical grasp of "principle" to know that what they knew internally could be realized externally in an accurate manner. This indeed is central to the "way of humanity" which teaches human beings things that can be realized and which encompasses all, including kingship and the way of governance. Since the way of the sages is about "people" and not exclusively about "politics," it prizes each knowing human self. In the Way, reverence for heaven means also "reverence for the human self"—*keishin.* The values of "empathy and righteousness" are located prior to political mandate: "How is it possible to speak of human beings as human without [them]?"[48]

Although Ogyū had not subscribed to Hsun Tzu's theory of human wickedness, he had advanced the related view that ordinary human beings did not possess the individual intellectual capacity to comprehend complex moral norms such as "benevolence" and that these were in fact created by the ancient kings. Thus, "benevolence" was always "outside" of the individual, located in the articulations of the kings, and not a virtue that individuals possessed within themselves. In Ogyū's language, "To speak of managing the human spirit totally divorced from rites [external norms] is an arbitrary and subjective idea. The regulator and the regulated become identical. In short, one is expected to regulate his spirit with his own spirit, which simply reminds us of a madman trying to cure his own madness."[49] The provocative point in Ogyū's theorizing was that each person should concentrate on the self-realization of his own heaven-endowed "virtue," "talent," or "calling" and not be deluded into believing that he could identify his subjective essence with others or with nature, which he believed to be ultimately a coercive and "legalistic" idea that convinced individuals they could become something other than what they were.

Goi too affirmed the idea of individual virtue and talent, but he remained unmoved on the theoretical reasoning. Besides gaining an awareness of one's own particular talent, Goi insisted that all individuals could also "know" from within their natural selves what was externally "good" or, for that matter, what might be wrong as well. In his critique of Ogyū and Hsun Tzu, Goi would not surrender the idea that ordinary human beings possessed an independent capacity to organize knowledge and make judgments and that this was in the nature of being human in a universal and categorical sense. For Goi, the human capacity to know was more fundamental to any moral system than the assertion that the ancient kings were geniuses and created norms for all of subsequent history.

To Goi, then, Ogyū had erred in trying to show through his philological method that ancient texts were normative and that all subsequent texts from Mencius's time especially were polemical distortions. All of the Confucian texts from the ancients down through the Sung philosophers must be studied without prejudice, not in terms of one set of texts being superior, for this is to undermine the effort of the present in contrast to some mythic and creative origin. The usefulness of "philology" was not that it could make that origin factual, because it could not, but that it helped to clarify the long historical unfolding of the human intellectual effort to understand nature and of man's place within it. Scholarly efforts in the present must likewise be seen as a direct continuation of that long history. All too often, however, philology in the hands of students of ancient studies simply resulted in antiquarianism and the beautification of obscure language. Goi did not mask his disapproval of ancient studies and conveyed his feeling to his students in no uncertain terms:

> Of late, scholarship has come under the influence of ancient studies. Thus the four classics are not studied and even recent books with grammatical markings are not examined. . . . In the end, books that

in fact cannot be read and understood are talked about as though they made perfect sense. One can hardly feel sympathetic toward this. Those who join such scholarly groups do so simply to deceive the people around them.[50]

The last line above probably referred to scholars who made a fetish of studying archaic poetry. But it could easily include thinkers such as Tominaga as well. The latter had utilized Ogyū's idea of intellectual decline since the creative "origin" to argue that all historical texts were polemical fabrications and hence irrelevant to the present. Although, Ogyū had insisted that the proposition of the ancient kings that society was created for peace and well-being among humankind was valid for the present as a standard of judgment, Tominaga had said that that origin could no longer be empirically ascertained. While sharing with Tominaga the view that historical texts were relative and imperfect, Goi advanced a sharply divergent explanation for this phenomenon. Although unreliable as a source of absolute norms for the present, to Goi those historical texts were crucial resources for intelligent minds in the present to reach back in order to know more about the meaning of nature.

The dogmatic search for a clear and refined norm in Confucian texts was a misguided pursuit. While historical texts are in fact imperfect, they are not merely fabricated falsehoods and are indeed appropriate for study in the present, for no single text in the ancient past or in the distant future is ever likely to fully express the meaning of universal "principle." It is from this perspective, Goi insisted, that the philosopher of Neo-Confucianism, Chu Hsi, should be properly appreciated, for it was he who consistently called attention to the theory of a nonarbitrary principle in nature as being central to the quest for moral and practical knowledge. Thus while the historicists of ancient studies denounced Chu Hsi for his cosmologism, his basic contribution ought not be uncritically scuttled.

At the same time, however, Goi vehemently opposed the use of Chu Hsi's personal idealism as the premise upon which to "choose" historical texts, claiming instead the rational concept of "principle" to be the key reference. He resisted in particular the tendency among certain intellectual movements such as Ishida Baigan's Shingaku to utilize Chu Hsi's idealistic cosmologism which confirmed the internal "heart," the "little universe"—shō tenchi—as the premise from which to "select" whatever religious text that affirmed that link between cosmic goodness and the essential self. Ishida, it may be recalled, had encouraged the selection of key concepts from different religious systems precisely from that point of view. While basing his teachings primarily on the Neo-Confucian idea that emphasized the ultimate coherence between cosmic moral ideal and the spiritual self, Ishida also admitted a close affinity between this idea and, for example, Buddhism. "Having faith in Buddha's Law," Ishida thus commented, "is in order to gain spiritual enlightenment; and hence there can be no difference at all between spiritual attainment realized through Buddhism and the Way of Confucianism." The realization of enlightenment taught in Buddhism through introspective effort—*kufū*—"is very close and difficult to separate" from the moral essence—*ri*—in Confucianism—*chikōshite wakaregatashi.* Similarly, Ishida went on to note that his spiritualism was not any different from the ideals embedded in the Japanese imperial virtues of the "jewel, mirror, and sword." The Sun Goddess Amaterasu was thus said to be one with heaven itself, and while he did not approve of the popular beseeching for special favors from the gods, Ishida agreed that the "divine" spirit emphasized in Shinto was identical to his idealistic philosophy, not denying in this framework of teaching the idea of Japan being blessed by divine deities from the beginning of its history.[51]

Goi objected just as vehemently to this idealistic mode of thinking as he did to Ogyū's historicism. The ideal in Shingaku that the "little universe"—*shō tenchi*—could fully "know Heaven"—*Ten o shiru*—through diligent introspective meditation was unacceptable to Goi as a basis of intellectual syncretism. To Goi, "Heaven," being infinite, could never be fully "known." Texts were to be selected not to show the spiritual oneness of the self with a universal moral essence but to provide evidences of something of the human potential to acquire accurate knowledge in the present. Texts, in other words, verified the epistemology of controlled reason intertwined with empathy or compassion that had meaning in the specific and objective arena near at hand. The spirit of empathy was not to be confused with a knowable ultimate spiritual norm but invariably to be realized in concrete empathetic action, doing things in imperfect yet ethical ways in an objective field composed of the other beings and things. Action is always for others or in relation to others, not as "self-realization" of an inner ideal essence. Analysis always superseded intuitive introspection. Goi thus rejected mysticism of all kinds, including myths about divine origins of the Japanese nation as well as claims of enlightenment and salvation. Goi would not, therefore, select texts from Shintoism or Buddhism, the former because of its superstitions and the latter because of its skepticism regarding reason in nature.

At the same time, however, Goi was not adverse to selections from indigenous and religiously inspired "literary" and "poetic" texts because

some of these offered authentic aesthetic glimpses into something fundamental about nature. Goi's philosophy of knowledge thus carried decisive
significance for the curriculum at the Kaitokudō. It clarified the conceptual basis upon which choices would be made in fields of study and explained why all the great texts extending from Confucius and Mencius
down through Chu Hsi and the recent past would all be treated as serious
objects of study. As Goi refused to privilege one epoch over another in
the quest for universal knowledge, he drew a clear line of demarcation
for the Kaitokudō against historicist thinking of the sort that held most of
the past except the "ancient" (for Ogyū) or all of it (for Tominaga) as
useless to ongoing history. Within this broad definitional framework,
however, Goi proceeded to open the internal spaces of the academy to a
wide variety of academic pursuits that somehow added valid insights into
the universality of nature. Committed to an expansive view of knowledge in which ultimate truths about nature would never be fully known,
Goi created a pedagogical environment of intellectual breadth and tolerance. His approach is best captured in the addendum to the rules of the
academy drafted under his inspiration in 1758 that reads, in part, as
follows:

> Although the lectures will focus on the moral concepts of the four
> books and the five classics, to the exclusion of miscellaneous texts,
> special approval will be given to private seminars and reading groups
> being held on Chinese literary culture, medicine, and Japanese po-
> etry and literature. Even Sekian privately taught from medical and
> poetic texts. Of course, these latter should not be used as the basis of
> public [omote muki] lectures as previously stipulated in the rules of
> understanding.[52]

As the passage indicates, a clear distinction was made between formal
lectures given to maintain the academy's public status and personal seminars within the protected sanctuary.

Goi's domain as instructor was quite obviously in this latter sphere
where, without question, the interesting work went on, minus, of course,
the radical historicism of Tominaga and Ogyū and the idealistic syncretism of Ishida Baigan. Under Goi, for example, the study of Japanese
literature came to occupy an important place in the curriculum. Under
Goi's direction, classical works such as the Manyōshū, Tale of Ise, and The
Tale of Genji, were annotated for seminar use. Goi, moreover, drew extensively from the scholarship of the famous Buddhist scholar Keichū
(1640–1701). Keichū was especially important to Goi, and their intellectual relationship must have been a close one indeed as it was he, Goi,

who would pen the epithet engraved on Keichū's gravestone. A student of Itō Jinsai and the Kogidō, Keichū used the methodology of "ancient studies" to uncover the "original" poetic language, and hence the "spiritual" resource, of the great saint and founder of the Shingon sect, Kōbō Daishi (774–835). Keichū's deeply religious quest led him to locate the genesis of the Japanese poetic impulse in the first songs of the impetuous mythic god, Susano ō, who, while in exile in the harsh environs of Izumo, discovered in those utterances a sense of the sublime in himself.

Although unimpressed with the saintliness of Kōbō or the godliness of Susano ō, Goi, reminiscent of his celebration of Saigyo's human "passion" mentioned earlier, was nonetheless deeply inspired by Keichū's literary discoveries. Like Motoori Norinaga a generation later, Goi found in Keichū a perspective into literature that went beyond the religious quest of a scholar-monk. While this perspective opened a vista to the origins of Japanese poetics for Motoori, Goi gained aesthetic light on his rationalistic epistemology. Unreserved in his criticism of Buddhism and Shintoism, Goi praised Keichū's understanding of the "truthfulness" in ancient Japanese literature about an objective natural reality. Thus, while Keichū viewed the study of Japanese literature as a way to clarify the poetic impulses informing the religious aestheticism of Saint Kōbō, Goi saw them as textual evidences of how creative men in another era documented their sharp perceptions into one aspect or another of nature with aesthetic language. Goi did not challenge Keichū's religious quest but, from his own point of reference, indicated that ancient poetry offered evidences of ordinary men possessing the creative intelligence to penetrate nature and grasp a sense of its universality without having to refer to external historical norms as Ogyū, for example, would have insisted. Indeed, without the artificial mediations—*itsuwari*—of formal ethical rules, pedantic exegisis, sagely advice on propriety and the like, ancient poets had often stated pure human insights into nature, and in this sense, their meaning was utterly pertinent to the contemporary mind seeking ways to understanding the vastness of nature. "In looking over the *Manyōshū*," Goi observed admiringly, "it seems every aspect of nature is somehow touched on with elegant language. The same is true of the *Book of Songs*" [of ancient China]. Revealing a "historicist" point of view he did not allow in other subjects, Goi admitted that unlike the poetics of later times, the emotive quality and the original freshness of the ancients declined over the ages—*moto o ushinaeri*. The ancient poems seemed to be direct, authentic, and utterly honest. And in this respect, they were valid textual resources for human beings in the present to deepen their insights into nature. Rational observation did not preclude aesthetics for

Goi but indeed was confirmed by it. While thus teaching admiringly of the naturalistic aestheticism of ancient poetics, Goi strenuously resisted the tendency he detected in some to mystify ancient literature into a genetic world of the ancient kings or of the utopian origins of the Japanese people.[53]

While poetry had a firm place in Goi's rationalism, "dreams" did not. Here his instruction to youngsters at the Kaitokudō was clear. Poetry should be appreciated for reasons already noted. It should not be viewed with prejudice as mere romantic projection but as an articulation of a phenomenon conceived in language and thus ordered by rules. In an absurd yet conceptually related manner, "gambling" too is not *prima facie* "wicked." Like "poetry" one must know what the form of expression is. It is, of course, stupid for men to *choose* to gamble, but to say that gambling is unwise and that it therefore lacks operational "rules" would be "prejudicial." "Wicked" though it may seem, "gambling" does operate upon agreed rules and hence must not be seen as being totally arbitrary and outside the range of human reason. Now, it would be equally fallacious to say that because gambling is governed by rules that it is, therefore, "moral." The key here, Goi insisted, is that men must be wary of judging without knowledge and of reaching fallacious conclusions without valid information. Both are forms of prejudicial knowledge. "The virtue of study," in his words, "is that it teaches the avoidance of prejudice and slander." This was true whether the subject was "poetry" or "gambling."[54]

But with regard to the "dream" for which he could not discern internally consistent "rules," Goi drew the line. His message to students—to rather young ones it would seem judging from the language—was consistent with his general epistemology. Superstitious speculations have proliferated about "dreams," Goi's comments to students say, because men do not fully know what that "phenomenon" is about. From the ancients to *his* present, the situation had changed little in this regard. Yet, on this subject, one most likely pressed upon him by his students who wished to clarify the relationship between "reason" and "dream" even if they accepted "poetics," Goi held to a firm course. Poetry students should study for reasons already noted. Unregulated by norms of human consistency, dreams should be discarded with the beginning of each new day. As this theme of "dreams" was an important one at the Kaitokudō, virtually standing as a *code term* for "heart," "salvation," "enlightenment," and other more philosophical concepts, Goi's language to his students is worth recounting here:

> It is sometimes said that wisemen do not dream. This is not to be
> taken to mean that they actually do not have dreams but that to

them dreams are like memory. Even when an ordinary person spends the night wrestling about this and that and everything seems at times to be so troubling, the next morning things hardly seem to be so. . . . It is noted in an ancient book of terms that dreams defy explanation. While asleep, the human spirit sees only darkness, and thus the ancients assigned the ideograph for darkness to mean dreams. Because a wise man . . . possesses a clear mind, it is said he does not dream. In *Mencius* we thus read that the spirit of the morning should be celebrated for it dissolves the darkness of the night and ushers in the clear light of day. [55]

The celebration of dawn here is Goi's affirmation of reason. Dreams are to be relegated to the realm of darkness which men do not yet understand in a controlled manner. Without this admission of ignorance, Goi argued, dreams are all too readily dealt with in superstitious ways as being part of the "objective" order of things just as ghosts, devils, and goblins—*hito tengu*—are often said to be. While it is true that the human mind cannot ever totally fathom the workings of natural principle, it was erroneous to say, therefore, that all of the unknowns, including dreams and imaginary creatures, are also manifestations of that "principle," rendering them presumably "natural." Yet, even within the Confucian tradition, Goi lamented, such irrational leaps of logic could be ascertained. By using "principle" to encompass all of the mysteries in the universe, imagined fears also came to take on a false concreteness in the guise of goblins and bewitching foxes, the latter sometimes being reported to possess human beings, assume their shape, and occupy a mysterious sphere of their own from which they came and went to do mischief among men. These fallacies are all to be avoided, Goi taught, by first "setting aside what is not known as being just that, something that is not known"—*shiranu wa shiranu shite okubeshi*. But this admission of ignorance ought not lead to the conclusion that some things in the universe are outside the organizing principle of nature, which is consistent with the advice of the ancient sages. Indeed, everything must still be assumed to be within it—*Tenka ri gai no koto nashi*. In short, "dreams" ought not interfere with or lead the human mind away from the continuing effort to study "principle" in nature. [56]

Goi's theoretical position that human knowledge is always incomplete led him quite consistently to recognize that others might possess more knowledge about particular phenomena, much in the same manner that he claimed to know more about some things in nature than had the ancient sages. It was entirely consistent with this view that he would accept the possibility that the Dutch might possess superior approaches to the study of nature. Reflecting on reports that had begun to filter from Nagasaki into Osaka and especially to the Kaitokudō by traveling scholars, Goi offered the following comments. The general hypothesis of the Dutch that the "energy" that permeated the universe was ultimately traceble to the sun was probably correct. Similarly the dynamic principle that regulated the natural order was generated by that same source. More specifically he believed the Dutch had been able to formulate these general hypotheses because of superior empirical methods that had led them to penetrate their subject effectively. He wrote down his views in the following passage:

> Unless a fact has been ascertained by what we commonly call precise visual calculation [menokozanyō], and beyond that to gauge that fact with a fixed standard of measurement as through the use of optical devices [kenkibutsu], the Dutch do not offer statements about it, nor do they attempt to utilize it. They avoid making reverential comments about Heaven; Buddhism does not attract their sympathy; and they do not rely on superstitious beliefs. I have heard reports from one Watanabe Chōyō of Edo, who twice accompanied the Dutch from Nagasaki to Edo and back, about their scholarship and the substantial command of astronomy that they have.[57]

Goi reveals no prejudice or surprise at the fact that the Dutch were more knowledgeable about certain things than he and his fellow scholars were. He felt that the questions being posed by the Dutch still tended to be somewhat narrowly gauged. But there can be little doubt but that within his expansive conception of knowledge, Dutch science occupied a comfortable place as yet another example of the continuing human effort to know nature. Through Goi, the Kaitokudō thus established itself as a sympathetic touchstone, and sometimes sanctuary, for scholars engaged in the empirical study of nature from a rational "Confucian" point of reference yet closely intertwined with Dutch studies.

As alluded to in the opening prologue, some of the distinguished men who frequented the Kaitokudō were scholars of this scientific persuasion. These included Asada Goryū who taught near the academy and Miura Baien's students, including Waki Guzan and Hoashi Banri, all of whom were welcomed at the Kaitokudō during Goi's instructorship. This intellectual ambience allowed students to study with Goi (or later Nakai Chikuzan and Riken) and also with Asada Goryū without any sense of intellectual constraint. The study of "principle" through relative "texts" or through Dutch scientific instruments was conceptualized as reinforcing activities rather than bifurcated ones along "Eastern" and "Western" lines. The culmination of this tradition can be seen in Yamagata Bantō and his use of "astronomy" to organize his thinking, as we shall see in a later chapter. Goi's open-ended view of knowledge, therefore, is of decisive importance to Kaitokudō learning. It is at the same time true that Goi did not see himself as an "experimental" scientist but rather as a teacher within the epistemological universe of "moral science." Thus he did not attempt to alter the basic aims of the Kaitokudō from an academy dedicated to the study of "virtue" to one committed to Dutch science. There can be no denying, however, that while the Kaitokudō did not openly teach Dutch studies, its reputation, beginning with Goi, of being sympathetic to all systematic studies of nature, including those of the Dutch, was hardly a secret.

Goi remained true to his life-long mission of moral education, of teaching merchant commoners how to reason and act in the everyday world. His approach to nature was ontological in the moral rather than in the technological sense. It served the purpose of instructing commoners that they and not only sages or men with swords could observe, make decisions, and act in ways that were ethical by universal standards. His basis of instruction in this regard was clearly sympathetic with the instructional vision outlined by Miyake Sekian, notably that action based on reasoned judgment could be "righteous." Goi affirmed this view, saying that human beings were indeed capable of acting in ways that were at once "fair"—*chūsei*—and "effective"—*kōri*—as in striking a target on the mark. Goi, however, went beyond these early propositions in two interesting ways that added nuances not readily apparent before. They speak to issues of intellectual skepticism and informed and disciplined choice.

He warned first against making dogmatic claims of an act being "fair" or "effective." These terms should not be taken as normative but as relative to the knowledge that informs the act. Thus, Goi argued, rather than judging an act, it was of greater importance to examine the basis upon which that act was *chosen*, the various factors that might have been weighed, and how the consequences of the act might have been assessed. The quality of the deliberation upon which a choice is made, in short, outweighs the act itself. Goi brought to bear a simple example drawn from military history to illustrate his general point: A military envoy sent on a special mission by his commander is presented enroute with the possibility of choosing an alternative road that would reduce the distance of the journey by one-half; after deliberating on the situation at hand, although realizing the desirability of completing the mission in shorter time, the envoy chooses nonetheless to stay with the original course. The anecdote illustrates, Goi explained, that crucial choices must be based on firm knowledge. The envoy could not acquire reliable information regarding the actual conditions of the shorter route and thus, while tempted to take it, decided against doing so out of deliberate prudence. The risk in this case outweighed the ostensive advantage. His choice of action may thus be said to be fair and effective, since by shunning expediency he assured the execution of the mission entrusted to him.[58]

His second general argument about action is perhaps of greater importance than the commonsense prudence advised in the previous example. If reliable knowledge is available to choose an alternative course of action while already embarked on a mission, Goi went on to say, then obviously the individual envoy should opt to take it and depart from the safer preplanned route. The quality of the information is of course the key. The evaluation of this information and the decision to choose an alternative course, Goi emphasized, is entirely a matter of the independent "judgmental authority" of the individual enroute on the field. There are no "fixed rules"—gojōhō—that guide such actions and determine what is fair or effective. Decisiveness, in short, rests on independent judgment and initiative. It is especially intriguing that Goi used the political terminology of "power"—ken—to describe choice based on independent judgment. The ideograph for this term denotes a concept of action that says in an emergency of unexpected contingency, the leader or "prince" must reach deeply into his mind and choose to depart from conventional rules or the presumed course of action and arrive at an alternative solution. The wise prince, in other words, does not limit himself to the broad and safe highways but at certain moments takes decisive risks, departs from convention and custom, for which there are no preconceived rules to predict "effectiveness." The image Goi sketched here clearly was that of a political reformer.[59]

Goi himself did not draw explicit political conclusions from this theory of action, although the implications were clear and certainly determined a good deal of thinking about political economy by his students Nakai Chikuzan and Yamagata Bantō. Goi tended to state his concern about governance from the perspective of commoners possessing a naturally endowed capacity for reason rather than that of the reformer prince. Ordinary men, Goi had reasoned, echoing the ideas of Nishikawa Joken, could be fair and effective by adjusting their actions to natural time, as in knowing when to prepare, plant, and wait for the results. Goi went beyond Nishikawa, however, by arguing that since commoners possessed this capacity to know and to judge, they should also be allowed to carry out certain administrative functions that relied on that intelligence. Governments decline in effectiveness, Goi noted, to the extent that trust and understanding deteriorate, and this is usually evidenced by those "above" seeking to exact more taxes than they should and those "below" conspiring in turn to put forth as little as possible. Bureaucratic function-aries appointed to bridge this situation only aggravate matters as they uti-lize their role as mediators to personal advantage. These functionaries should be done away with and the responsibility of fiscal administration entrusted to the peasants themselves. "Peasant leaders," Goi com-mented, "should be selected at appropriate intervals and made to take on official functions. Even though they perform well, they should be re-placed once every three to five years. . . . Those above should concern themselves simply with regulating mischievous irregularities."[60] Having broached this intriguing and potentially radical idea, however, Goi did not develop it further. As we shall see, Nakai Chikuzan and Riken would indeed take this idea of reform from Goi and address themselves to the question of administrative initiatives that should be taken to improve conditions in society.

Since Goi's audience was primarily merchant commoners and not as-piring administrators, the subject of political reform remained a minor subject. The evidentialist theory of action he advanced, however, was certainly applicable to merchants in their engagements with the market-place. A merchant could easily place himself in the position of the mili-tary envoy in the example mentioned earlier and relate to the issues of knowledge and action, deliberateness and decisiveness. The emphasis Goi placed on the one hand on the importance of prudence, of avoiding reckless choices that might undermine a plan of action and on the other hand on the intellectual preparedness to make independent decisions based on one's "judgmental authority" were both entirely pertinent to the daily life of the Osaka financier. What is important in this regard is not that Goi instilled political thought into his curriculum for commoner education, but rather that he justified the decision making of merchants within a broad ethic of action in which knowledge must always precede choice and action to achieve ends that were "fair" and "effective."

．　　　．　　　．

The previous themes in Goi's teaching add up to an intellectually consis-tent position which, as presented regularly by him over nearly twenty-five years, would come to be identified with the Kaitokudō itself. Whether we examine Goi's naturalistic philosophy, his engagement with literature, his denunciation of religion and superstition, his open-mindedness to-ward Dutch studies and to empirical scholarship on nature in general, or his clarification of practical action, all are related themes within an integrated whole, and it was for this reason that Goi's presence at the Kaitokudō was of such importance. The assessment of the Kaitokudō as intellectually "eclectic" would persist, but the meaning of this would change from suggesting the incorporation by Miyake of bits and pieces from here and there to intellectual choices based on a coherent philosophical premise. The consistency with which Goi held to this position fully justifies the reputation he gained as an outstanding teacher and intellectual and which Nishimura Tenshū found to be impressive.

As we have emphasized in this chapter, however, the maintenance of such a consistent philosophical basis from which to choose meant also the exclusion of the historicist approach to knowledge that Tominaga Nakamoto had championed at first within the academy and then in the intellectual world just beyond it. Finding the historicist approach too reductive and restrictive because it applied the philological method to debunk huge segments of creative human history, Goi shaped a perspective that was expansive and pointed ultimately to gaining deeper understandings of nature. Tominaga, it will be recalled, used the philological method to show, unlike Itō Jinsai and Ogyū Sorai, that the lesson to be drawn from human history was that all of the texts available contained precious little of existential value in the present. While sharing his view that historical texts were relative and not absolutely normative, Goi cast this in terms of the limitation of the human mind vis-à-vis universal nature, so that historical texts, however imperfect, were useful for purposes of moral education in the present. Goi felt Chu Hsi's idea of "principle" underlying nature was especially crucial, and he accused the historicists, most pointedly Ogyū Sorai, for being reckless in bypassing that perception and proceeding (like a misguided envoy, as in the fable mentioned above) directly to a set of ancient texts to find a perfect "norm" for all subsequent history. Goi found especially annoying the view that norm created by ancient sages and kings could not be recreated in the present, thereby effectively denying commoners any kind of critical ethical independence. The only choice that commoners had was to rely on a norm that was outside of the ethical self, a "fabrication," as the philosopher Hsun Tzu had said in ancient times and which Ogyū Sorai had echoed in Goi's age. As an academy dedicated to the mission of teaching commoners regarding the meaning of "virtue," such a position was intellectually untenable. Goi, therefore, held forth with the concept that all human beings, high and low alike, possessed a universal capacity for reason and hence to order, organize, and to know and judge what was fair, accurate, true, and good. This epistemology, in retrospect, clearly occupied the ideological center of the commercial bourgeoisie that supported the academy. It would obviously have been untenable from the viewpoint of the Kaitokudō and its audience to simply cast the present adrift from the past as Tominaga would have done. To deny that a discussion of "virtue" in the present had nothing to do with what had been said on the subject in the past would have placed the actions of merchants without the historical moorings needed to justify those actions as virtuous. The exile of Tominaga, therefore, was complete and sealed with unforgiving silence. Goi never mentioned him by name; and as already noted Tominaga would not be buried in the family plot. He would be denied the chance of saying again within the academy that Confucianism (along with all other systems of moral thought) revealed a history of polemical contests over what was true tradition and thus it was intellectually unreliable.

The line that separated Goi and Tominaga, then, was substantial and transcended matters of personality differences. Indeed, their philosophical division tells us a great deal about the intellectual history of the academy, clarifying for us what the academy would not allow and therefore where the outer limits would be placed, as evidenced in the regularly repeated polemical stance against Ogyū Sorai's historicism. However, there can be little doubt that Goi and Tominaga were both products of a related universe. This is revealed in their displeasure with uncritical eclecticism; their identification with the empirical approach to knowledge; the rejection of superstition and ideas about salvation; and the common focus on the question of ethical action in the present. Tominaga's "truthfulness" and Goi's "fairness" and "effectiveness" suggest a resonance with each other as well as with Miyake's "righteousness." Yet, by having chosen divergent epistemological positions as to the ultimate underpinning of knowledge, it is in retrospect doubtful that they could have shared the same academic space for any length of time.

At stake was an ideological position within the academy that insisted on the moral and intellectual capacities of ordinary merchant commoners to know virtue as expressed in philosophical texts and thereby to articulate their actions as being ethical within broad and universalistic moral propositions, such as those formulated by Mencius on universal human goodness or Chu Hsi on natural principle. Without this affirmation that commoners possessed the potential to acquire general moral knowledge, the academy would have lost its *raison d'etre*. Goi understood this well and provided a stable philosophical position to sustain it. More meteoric and radical in his thinking, Tominaga tended to be less sensitive to that concern for moral ideology. Thus, while Tominaga would be forced to occupy a place just beyond the walls of the Kaitokudō, Goi de-

147

fined the conceptual uses of the spaces within those walls; and while Tominaga's ideas would make their way into the undercurrents of Tokugawa intellectual history, as through national studies and the concern for critical historical consciousness in the modern era, Goi through personal instruction created the basis from which intellectual visions would be generated from within the academy. His thinking would thus live on through his students, most remarkably Nakai Chikuzan and Riken.

FIVE

☐ VISIONS FROM THE ACADEMY ☐

CRIPPLED IN HIS OLD AGE WITH PARALYTIC ARTHRITIS, GOI RANJU WOULD BE REMEMBERED AT HIS LAST BY RESIDENTS NEAR THE KAITOKUDŌ FOR THE DEVOTION HE WOULD RECEIVE FROM the young Nakai brothers Chikuzan and Riken. Stories spread through Osaka about their exemplary behavior toward Goi. They were said to have taken him regularly to hotsprings for therapy and to have cared for his one daughter, Setsu, as their sister although she was born out of wedlock. Later they would formally adopt her to assure her a proper marriage; and in turn, her son—Nagashima Yoshiyasu—would study with them at the Kaitokudō and edit some of Goi's writings, in particular the *Meiwa* referred to in the previous chapter. For their reverence and esteem for Goi, who had devoted much energy to their education, the Nakai brothers received the respect of Osaka's merchant communities, and they were praised for the magnificent burial they gave Goi, an affair befitting the most eminent of scholars in all the land.[1]

Yet of the many good memories Osaka residents had of Chikuzan and Riken, the fondest was of them as youngsters, when they were still known as Zenta, child of "goodness," and Tokuji, child of "virtue," practicing their calligraphy playfully, one with a wooden ladle, the other with a broom, on the white, frost-covered ground near their academic home.[2] From their childhood it was believed they were destined to become great scholars who would raise the banner of the Kaitokudō for all to see. This they would do. Following Goi's death in 1762 and continuing for the better part of the next fifty years, the Kaitokudō would come to be known as the school of the Nakai brothers, and their reputation would dramatically overshadow Goi's, to whom they owed their intellectual upbringing. Their prestige was such that the great philosopher Miura Baien would not only send his students to them for special study, but would ask, although he had never met them personally, that one or the other write the epitaph for his gravestone.

Alike as they may have appeared to observers of the above winter scene, Chikuzan and Riken were quite dissimilar in temperament and style. Their differences would be clearly revealed in calligraphy and vision as mature scholars. Chikuzan's ideographs were firm, dark, and orderly— "geometric" one is tempted to say—while Riken's were thin and delicate—mysteriously "moist." Their personal lives reflected this difference in calligraphic preference. Chikuzan championed the institutional mission of the academy and devoted himself to the politics of expanding its voice beyond the immediate world of Osaka merchants to a wider scholarly and politically articulate audience, thus dramatically altering the previous emphasis enjoyed at the academy. Drawing on Goi's teachings and his father's administrative practices, Chikuzan oriented the ideas of the Kaitokudō toward the creation of a new vision for the academy with a vastly expanded role in a reordered national educational system. He thus projected the Kaitokudō into the broader polity, seeking a secure place for it as an institutional leader in the field of moral education for all classes.

Riken, in contrast, prized his independence and scholarly autonomy and chose to live the last forty years of his life away from the academy to pursue his studies in romantic and splendid isolation. He, too, drew on Goi's pool of ideas, but he turned it into an exhaustive reconsideration of the ancient classical sources and, on occasion, with Asada Goryū, toward scientific experiments. Rejecting institutional life within the public order, Riken fashioned what he would call his "kingdom of dreams" to study as he wished, freed from the constraints of administrative duties. Riken's calligraphic style, however, should not be interpreted to mean "weakness" or "frailness" in comparison with Chikuzan's. Chikuzan's strength of personality is easily understandable given his expansive vision for the Kaitokudō. But Riken was also strong-willed, passionate, and often temperamental. His avoidance of public visibility in favor of solitude was an intellectually self-conscious choice. He chose the "dimness" of seclusion out of a deep sense of discontent with the larger world around him and fashioned a little "kingdom" to maintain his fiercely independent commitment to "virtue."[3]

Quite interestingly, their different characters are also reflected in the names they took as scholars. While both are romantic and idealistic, they carry different meanings. Chikuzan literally means a "bamboo grove in the mountains," but the image is decidedly of balance and regularity as found in the structure of the bamboo stalk itself, and "mountain" does not refer to the wilds but the aesthetically landscaped hill in a garden that only symbolizes a craggy mountainside. Riken, which comes from the phrase *riken yūjin*, refers to a solitary spiritual recluse treading firmly, yet effortlessly, on the Way, unperturbed by superficial distractions. Their names were entirely in accord with the lives they led as scholars.[4]

It need only be said in passing that despite their differences, which came to be widely recognized in Osaka and elsewhere, they nonetheless remained deeply respectful and, finally, affectionate of each other. This in no small degree was due to their common devotion to their mentor Goi and the philosophy of knowledge they received from him. They remained true to Goi's identification with a moral philosophy for commoners. And within this, each in his own way went on to shape a vision that reflected an uneasy sense of general crisis and political decline.

.   .   .

NAKAI CHIKUZAN
(1730–1804)

When Nakai Shūan passed away in 1758, Chikuzan was already 29 and well versed in the administrative workings of the Kaitokudō. This can be surmised from his father's final letter of instructions to the chief council of the academy in which, as mentioned earlier, he refrained from naming Goi his successor and recommended Miyake Shunrō instead due to support for the latter among Osaka merchants—*sejō ni mōsu gotoku*.[5] The choice of Shunrō was a controversial one in that his scholarly presence at the Kaitokudō was at best tangential. His preference was to operate the pharmaceutical shop that he had inherited from his father, an activity which he seems to have been quite adept at, earning thus the high regard of merchants and the vaguely concealed contempt of Goi and Chikuzan. To Goi, the teacher of virtue to commoners ought to consider education his full-time occupation and not an activity that one engaged in as work on the side, an opinion he harbored against Shunrō's father Miyake Sekian as well. Regardless, there was little respect for Shunrō within the academy, particularly since Chikuzan was clearly superior in intellectual power although younger in age by some seventeen years. Besides handling the administration of the academy, Chikuzan also took the responsibilities of delivering most of the formal lectures after Goi's death in 1762. Shūan was clearly aware of his son's abilities. Thus he went on in his letter, in a subtle way, to create a firm place of leadership for Chikuzan. As one of the achievements of his administration, Nakai pointed to the establishment of a fund of twenty *kan* at the banking house of Kōnoike Matashirō (one of the original founders) to cover emergencies such as fire. The management of that fund, he suggested, should be handled by Chikuzan as he was already familiar with the details of the investment and the interest accruing from it over the years. Thus while Shunrō might be entrusted with "formal" activities, Chikuzan should be included in the managing council of the academy as its financial officer and thereby help to assure the immortality of the academy—*eitai sōzoku no yo.*[6]

A tension between the academy's role as a public institution as perceived by him and his son Chikuzan and the expectations of it as seen through the eyes of local merchant leaders can be detected from Shūan's letter. The division of labor between Miyake Shunrō's "formal" duties and Nakai Chikuzan's "financial" duties, or internal administration more generally, reflected this tension. A merchant himself, Shunrō had the support of local leaders. Chikuzan, while deeply respected as a "commoner," was known to have strong views about the Kaitokudō being more than a local school for merchants and a "public" one in the broad meeting of that term. Chikuzan's father had presented himself before the local magistrate as representing his merchant "colleagues" and not as an individual scholar, but Chikuzan wished to reduce the dependency on those "colleagues" somewhat in order to project the image of the academy as an independent public academy and, in turn, to offer its scholarship ultimately to the Bakufu itself. The merchant "colleagues," however, saw the academy as belonging to them and under their jurisdiction. Shūan's letter reflected the compromise settlement in which the "public" academy would still retain, through Miyake Shunrō, a close link with the local merchants who provided the financing. The discrepancy, however, could not be breached with ease and would resurface soon after Shūan's death.

One issue involved how best to use the living quarters that had been occupied by Goi. To Chikuzan that space belonged to the academy and should thus be applied to educational needs determined internally by the administrative head of the school. Chikuzan thus simply assigned it to scholarly guests or boarders as he saw fit. No doubt fully cognizant of their regular contributions to the academy, the local elders took exception to Chikuzan's use of discretionary authority and demanded that the space be "rented" to generate income. Chikuzan rejected this plan on the grounds that as a public academy the Kaitokudō was legally autonomous and not subject to the jurisdiction of the local town council—a status, as noted earlier, rendered as *jochi gomen,* which indeed the Bakufu had extended to the Kaitokudō at its inception. Insofar as the academy survived on local support, however, the town elders insisted that the academy should be responsive to the wishes of their council. To verify this relationship, Chikuzan was summoned to appear before them to affix the seal of the academy as a member of their council. Chikuzan declined the invitation, stating the academy was legally exempt from the jurisdiction of local authority. Despite a personal visit by a delegation from the council, Chikuzan held uncompromisingly to his position.[7]

Although a record of the exchanges do not exist, the disagreement was of such severity by all general accounts that personal ties between the chief elder (one Kawai Tachimaki) and Chikuzan were at one point entirely severed. Only with the personal mediation of Miyake Shunrō, it is said, was the relationship grudgingly reestablished. The elders held to the view that despite the Kaitokudō's public character there were certain local administrative issues from which the academy should not be exempted, the handling of abandoned babies being the case most often cited. In emergencies such as this, the town council was directed by law to assume responsibility and collectively find a proper solution. The academy could not be independent of local jurisdiction in issues of this kind. As fate would have it, a child was indeed abandoned before the front gate of the Kaitokudō in the spring of 1774. The council assumed an unresponsive posture to Chikuzan and the academy's specific predicament. The local magistrate, while entirely sympathetic to his overall argument, had no quick solutions to offer with regard to the particular case at hand. One thing led to another and, despite all that could have been done within the academy, the child died.[8]

This crisis prompted Chikuzan to seek adjudication from the local magistrate and resolve the jurisdiction issue once and for all. The Kaitokudō would indeed be reaffirmed as an *autonomous* public academy exempted from local administrative duties, and whatever obligations that might accrue to it of an emergency nature would be distributed evenly throughout all the town councils in Osaka. The net effect was to disengage the Kaitokudō from the authority of the immediate town council and its elders and to pluralize and broaden its relationship to councils on a city-wide basis. In order to retain its integrity as a public school for commoners, Chikuzan insisted the Kaitokudō must protect its autonomy and pursue its mission as a public academy. To reduce itself to being a local school would contradict the purpose for which the Kaitokudō had been founded, the clarification of which Chikuzan set forth with great care in his historical reconstruction of the establishment of the Kaitokudō— *Gakumonjo konryū ki*. And he reaffirmed this purpose in a pledge of his own in 1782 to local leaders entitled "memorandum of understanding among colleagues"—*Godōshichū sōdan gaku:* As the Kaitokudō is not a private school, it is not to be thought of as belonging to a single individual or family; being a public academy, the Kaitokudō is to be treated as being entrusted with legal autonomy from local authority, not unlike the domain granted by the Bakufu to daimyō even though the academy's space differed in not possessing agricultural land or a hereditary lord; the maintenance of that public trust was *sine qua non* for the life of the academy. Presented to his colleagues at the time he assumed the overall headship of the Kaitokudō, the memorandum may be seen as a declaration of Chikuzan's "victory" over the possessive claims of the local elders. It states his view that the Kaitokudō will enhance the cause of education for commoners not as a local school, but as a public academy oriented intellectually toward the country as a whole, thus gaining prestige and eminence that merchants and commoners in Osaka and elsewhere might feel justifiably proud.[9]

The previous discussion serves to highlight the pivotal role that Chikuzan came to assume in defining the institutional character of the Kaitokudō. Although Miyake Shunrō provided mediation with the local council as academic head and as a merchant leader, his stature within the academy was clearly a diminished one, while on the other hand, Chikuzan can be seen as the decisive figure in seeking to shape a new destiny for the academy. In his hands, the Kaitokudō would come to be known as a place for the serious pursuit of moral knowledge without the encumberances of local administrative duties. It nonetheless would hold firm to the pedagogical concept that as a public academy its gates would be open to commoners to study the meaning of "virtue" while being fully protected by law and who could then return to their world of practical work with moral dignity.

The rules, summarized below, that Chikuzan enforced give credence to this understanding he had of the Kaitokudō. All lectures would be open to the public and would not require a verbal or written introduction from an officer of the academy as had previously been the practice—thus also rendering irrelevant the administrative responsibility held by a leader of the merchant community to regulate attendance; knowledge would be sought by all as colleagues—*dōshi dōhai*—in a common quest and distinctions between classes would not be made; although deference is to be shown to the elderly or those of advanced scholarly achievement, seating privileges would not be determined by class; the aristocratic privilege of sitting in the front of the hall would be discontinued; in accordance with this spirit, all instructors would be selected according to talent and moral character and not social status; students without regard to social background should organize among themselves special seminars on a regular basis on such diverse subjects as Japanese literature and medicine that might not be dealt with in the formal lectures; and finally, again in keeping with the public trust, students were reminded sternly to avoid fighting, drinking, gambling, and horseplaying in general within the halls.[10]

Besides these general guidelines, Chikuzan made it unambiguously clear as to the moral principles upon which the academy rested. As summed in the following passage, his ideas echoed the basic propositions articulated by Miyake Sekian a generation before:

> Virtue is the basic nature of the human spirit. Human beings are endowed by heaven at birth with a virtuous essence, consisting of compassion, righteousness, propriety and wisdom. In the classic of the *Great Learning,* this is referred to as clear virtue; in the *Doctrine of the Mean* as heaven's imperative; in *Mencius* as inner goodness or basic spiritual essence. These all refer to the spiritual nature of the individual self. With the virtue of compassion, things are empathized with genuine feeling; with righteousness the validity of a fact is determined; with propriety there is deep reverence; with wisdom moral imperatives are seen clearly.[11]

This idea of virtue and the implications stemming from it, moreover, were rearticulated on elegantly crafted scrolls and hung strategically in various parts of the academy, making it impossible for students to avoid them.[12] The ideas embedded on these scrolls tells us a good deal about Chikuzan's pedagogical philosophy, or those ideals that he hoped to imbue in his students.

Students and visitors approaching the Kaitokudō were greeted by two scrolls mounted on either side of the entrance. Although simply homolistic when rendered in English as compared with the dramatic calligraphic form, they affirmed moral propositions basic to the academy: "Know your original goodness and doubt it not"; and "Grasp those norms that are true and waver not from them." Commenting on these lines, Chikuzan spoke of them as being synonymous with the name of the academy, "understanding virtue," as in *kaitoku.* The idea of original goodness—*koyū no zen*—and obvious norms—*tōzen no soku*—he noted were identical with universal "virtue" or *toku.* The active terms such as knowing, doubting, grasping, and the like he equated with the act of "understanding" virtue, as *kai* in Kaitokudō. These paired calligraphic lines at the entrance, then, stood as affirmations of the ideal of universal goodness and the equally universal capacity to know, for all to acquire knowledge, which together had served as the moral warrant for commoner education at the Kaitokudō from the beginning. Reminded thus of the inherent dignity of all human beings regardless of status, students encountered additional scrolls along the hallways. Another set of lines were hung on either side of what was called the "middle doorway" leading to a small inner garden and the central lecture hall.

Here firm ideographs established the relationship between acquisition of knowledge and self-control and governance: "Through exhaustive study, one regulates the self"; and the other read, "On the basis of firm knowledge, one governs others." The quest for knowledge is drawn away from self-centered enlightenment to broader concerns of governance, or to matters of political economy more generally—*hito o osamu*. While the language might be interpreted to mean simply the ordering of lives in a familial or commercial context, it is clear that Chikuzan was implying a broader concept. Thus he noted that in China, where the phrases were first created, the lines pointed to the possibility of rising up in society through study to contribute directly to the governance of society. Although such a pattern was precluded in Japan due to "national custom," Chikuzan made it clear that he would not abide by that "custom" and would state his views without hesitation as to how he believed the country should be governed. This was a responsibility of all who studied virtue. Indeed, the relationship between scholarship and governance, or knowledge and power, was boldly asserted again in still another pair of scrolls on the southern wall of the main lecture hall. "The art of governing," one line read, "rests on the human spirit"; and the other, "Language provides wings to the Way." Here, virtue, or the human spirit, is said to be the basis of governing—*keijutsu*—and through "language"—*bunshū*—meaning knowledge, virtue is made to soar and permeate the land. The primacy of knowledge and virtue as a precondition for governance is unmistakably articulated in these words.

And finally, on either side of the north windows of the main hall, the philosophy of intellectual courage and universal potential was enunciated: "To live in timidity and fear is like facing the dark abyss or stepping on thin ice"; and also a line that defies easy translation as it is not exactly symmetrical with the other, "The morning flower yields to the day not knowing of the bounteous fruits that will ripen at evening." Chikuzan admitted the awkwardness of the paired lines, but despite the lack of symmetry, he justified them in terms of the content that he personally valued. Every individual ought to live life with moral conviction and not with fears about nightmarish dreams and the unknown and the fragility of human existence. Thus one ought to seek knowledge and nourish one's virtue precisely because, as a youth, one cannot foretell what his potential might turn into. The optimism here is plain enough. Each individual regardless of status can undergo a transformation through study. Commoners are potential sages or critics of the polity. The fruits of moral knowledge cannot be enclosed with "customs" mechanically applied.

The reformist impulse that one detects in Chikuzan's open-ended vision of education was endemic to the academic project of the Kaitokudō. Commoners need not remain lowly. Unlike Ogyū Sorai who emphasized each individual virtue as particular and unrelated to society or politics, Chikuzan quite emphatically emphasized the opposite. Since human beings were endowed with the capacity to know, they could grasp general problems of social and political norm. The privilege should not be restricted to a few geniuses or extraordinary scholars. Scholarship, in short, was thought of as appropriate to all, not to the few whose "virtue" inclined them in that direction. "To be born a human being and not engage in scholarship," he thus observed, "will make it difficult to realize the way of being human. Scholarship, however, is not necessarily limited to reading books. Learning about all those things that men ought to do and to hold them within one's spiritual self is entirely within the realm of scholarship." While he further mused that the wisdom which men refer to to make judgments and distinctions as to moral issues have been compiled in "books," so that studying these works is sometimes called "true scholarship," Chikuzan believed that even those with little interest or time or aptitude in reading these books should engage in acquiring moral knowledge through elementary Japanese. To deny them access to knowledge would be to deny their humanity. Education, in short, is not for the elite, the geniuses and members of the aristocracy but for everyone.

Chikuzan thus remained true to the original mission of the Kaitokudō. Clearly the scrolls were not decorative embellishments but expressive of a philosophical baseline regarding human epistemology that was also entirely in agreement with the teachings of his predecessors and more pointedly of Goi Ranju. Indeed, Chikuzan's instructional orientation concerning a number of related themes reveals, without question, Goi's indelible imprint on him. Some of these are worth underscoring as they indicate the themes Chikuzan emphasized in his classes.

Echoing Goi, for example, Chikuzan spoke out impatiently against religious syncretism as employed by Shingaku. This is readily apparent in his response to a query from a student who asked why the selection from different religions might not be valid since the quest for universal knowledge would lead to a common end, as expressed in the ancient Japanese poem: "While at the base of the mountain the paths leading upward are many, is it not the same moon in the sky that all see in the end?"—

wakenoboru fumoto no michiwa ōkeredo onaji kumoi no tsuki o miru kana.[13]
To use this poem to say that all major religions and philosophies were
different paths leading to the same god, was to distort the meaning of the
line, Chikuzan replied. Just as there are many different kinds of mountains and the conditions in the sky are not the same at every peak, so too
the moon in the sky means something quite different in Confucianism as
against Buddhism—the clarity of "principle" in the former is hardly identical with the "ephemeralness" of life in the latter. While the poem
speaks to the "beauty" of the moon, it cannot be generalized thereby to
encompass philosophical perceptions.

Moreover, as with Goi, Chikuzan felt the confusing of Buddhist with
Confucian ideas was especially unfortunate. The concept of "enlightenment"—*satori*—was a case in point. Again it is in the form of a response
to a student's query that we learn of this. Asked to comment on the credibility of the Zen monk Hakuin's announcement of personal enlightenment following a retreat of several years deep in the mountains at the age
of seventeen or so, Chikuzan responded that any sudden realization
of a truth may be called "enlightenment." What is meant by this in
Buddhism, however, is again totally different from Confucianism. In
Buddhism, enlightenment, or *satori*, was the sudden awareness that the
universe is empty, the objective world is illusory, human actions tran-
sient; while in Confucianism it referred to gaining insight with universal principle, the reality of things, the predictive worth of moral action.
In the final analysis, Buddhism discards the self as a knowing agent and
Confucianism does not; the former seeks salvation only for the discrete
self *disengaged* from other human beings, while in the latter, the continuity of human life in social form, or as interrelationship between individuals, is crucial. "What a comfortless way of thinking," Chikuzan
comments of Buddhism to his questioner—*sate-sate fujiyū naru omoitsuki
nari.*[14]

Chikuzan reinforced his statements with a thoroughgoing rejection of
all superstitious ideas, again revealing his indebtedness to Goi. Scattered
in Chikuzan's writings is the affirmation that all phenomena visible and
invisible are within a comprehensive universal principle, and that ghosts
and goblins and cagey foxes and badgers were all figments of human
dreams and imagination and not grounded in reality. Students, however,
no doubt exhibited a lively fascination with happenings that somehow
went beyond the pale of conventional reason, a fascination that Hino
Tatsuo has discussed in his essays on the "unknown" in the imagination
of Edo society.[15] Foxes and badgers in particular fascinated the young stu-

dent as these were invested in popular folklore with the miraculous spirit of bringing either good fortune or evil misfortune. A question to Chikuzan was thus couched in the following language: ". . . having received instructions last year, my doubts as to the incredulous ideas of foxes and badgers possessing the spirit of men have been dispelled . . . On a related matter, though, what about their using human language on occasion or changing into human form?" Responding to the broad implications of the question, Chikuzan admitted that scholars were unable to explain many things and that if knowledge were to be construed from what they did not know, they would be compelled to admit ignorance and claim one explanation to be as good as another, superstition being equally true as other forms of firm knowledge. One ought not proceed from the assumption, however, that because men do not have perfect knowledge that ghosts are real. Chikuzan closed his response with the following affirmation of natural ontology as the basis of knowledge:

> One ought to discriminate and examine things carefully and penetrate to the heart of any matter by holding firm to the general rule that nothing in the universe exceeds the bounds of true principle. Is it logical to compare the often alleged phenomenon of foxes and badgers transforming themselves into human form with the caterpillar changing into a butterfly, a silkworm into a moth? These latter are part of the pattern by which opposite forces engage to further the life process by undergoing transformations . . . and are thus examples of true principle. As people often observe this process they do not think of them as mysterious. If foxes and badgers transform themselves into human form, would their offspring revert to being a fox or a badger . . . or would they be half human and half beast? Just as a moth or a butterfly cannot return to their previous form once they have evolved out of them, so too, all transformations of natural shape must follow their necessary course. Neither human nor strange beast can alter the principle that regulates that process. Foxes and badgers cannot do miraculous things outside of nature any more than any other life form can. Stories about such strange and unnatural happenings are fads circulated among the foolish, and if anyone claims to have seen such events, surely they must be ill in eye or spirit.[16]

In similar thoroughgoing manner, Chikuzan discussed "dreams," a subject that recurs in discussions within the Kaitokudō as we saw beginning with Goi. As in the case with superstition, the problem of dreams presented itself in the following related pattern: If the world of things could be observed, cognized, ordered, and determinations made about it as to what was fair, just, truthful and so forth, then how does one explain the dream that is *beyond* observation, is sometimes remembered, yet for which concrete evidences do not remain. Chikuzan dealt with this problem as he had the question of superstition, affirming to young students what might best be termed commonsense reasoning:

> There are no clear explanations among previous scholars as to dreams. The confusion brought about by the comment of Chuang Tzu that a sage does not dream has made it almost impossible to understand even the dreams of the Duke of Chou . . . To begin with, one must examine very closely the true nature of dreams. Generally, when the human body falls asleep, its spirit does so too. When the spirit awakens so does the body. On occasion, however, the body awakens while the spirit is still in sleep, and the person either sleep talks animatedly or gets up and thrashes about. Youngsters often do not remember anything at all about it the next day. We call this sleep-drunkenness in everyday language. At times the body is fast asleep but the spirit alone awakens. This is the dream. While one in this state goes forth to other places and back, or talks about all sorts of things, or converses with others, the body does not move at all. Only the spirit is awake and moves about. When one is fatigued and in deep sleep, one tends not to dream. Dreams often occur just before one is about to awaken.[17]

This commonsensical discussion of dreams, however, contained within it a didactic message based on an experiential view of knowledge. There were limits, Chikuzan argued, as to what one dreamt. And the limits were determined by daily life, that is, by what men did and hence "knew," not what they did not do and hence had no knowledge. In his words, "A farmer dreams about harvesting his crops; a merchant about his enterprise; a craftsman about his wares . . . A farmer does not dream about manufacturing wares, a craftsman or merchant about harvesting crops." Dreams, in short, are grounded in concrete human reality. A king does not dream about living in a village, nor a fisherman or lumberjack about life with horse-drawn carriages. And so the dreams of the sagely prince in the classics are made to make sense:

> Thus it is entirely appropriate for the Duke of Chou to dream about spreading the way of the sages to all in the kingdom for it was about this that he was so deeply concerned. In old age when such aims were no longer uppermost in his mind, the Duke no longer dreamed this. . . . Dreams are the shadow of one's spirit.[18]

Dreams, then, are not evil, or mysterious, or ominous signs, or predictive in significance; but they are connected to human reality, and hence limited by the experience of that reality. Chikuzan's analysis also confirms the authenticity of ambition as revealed in the Duke of Chou's dream. The Duke's dream is not a mere "dream" or total chimera as Chuang-tzu tried to make it out to be but grounded in a credible vision in which he had sought to provide moral order to a chaotic land.

While "rational," Chikuzan's analysis of dreams also reveals his identification with the reformist vision of the Duke. Chikuzan too was ambitious. He too sought to prescribe ways, which he would outline in his writings, to alter the course of history from its unsteady course to one that would bring justice and order to the populace. Chikuzan's conception of dreams, in short, was somewhat different from Goi's, whose classical reference was not the Duke of Chou but Mencius and the joy he expressed in encountering the light of day when reason could once again rule.

In all of these themes—the rejection of miracles, heaven and hell, magical foxes and badgers, the mystery of dreams, and finally, in the reliance on an ontological premise of reason encompassing the universe, Chikuzan held to a set of presuppositions that were very close indeed to the teachings of his mentor Goi. It was, however, in his extremely hostile view of the historicist ideas advanced by Ogyū Sorai that Chikuzan took Goi's rationalistic humanism to its most contentious and polemical limit. Goi's opposition to Ogyū was well known to Chikuzan through his essay against him, Hi-Butsu hen, which Chikuzan and his brother Riken had edited and to which Chikuzan added his own scathing summation of the Kaitokudō's antagonism in his Hi-Chō (1785).[19] The particular emotional vehemence with which Chikuzan couched his criticisms is worthy of some attention here since it speaks to a passionate defense of the Kaitokudō's ideal of the moral education of commoners.

Scattered throughout Chikuzan's writings is his impatience with Ogyū Sorai's restrictive view of human epistemological and moral capacity, which he believed ought to be refuted head-on. Thus, while he felt little sympathy for Yamazaki Ansai's school of Neo-Confucianism, particularly in its disdain for complex scholarship and its favoring of the repetition of carefully preselected sacred phrases, Chikuzan was far less disturbed by it than by Ogyū Sorai precisely because the latter had formulated a philosophy that contained demeaning implications for the bulk of society. Taking the proposition that the moral classics were entirely "language"—rikkei wa mina bun nari—a view that Chikuzan accepted as well, Ogyū pro-

ceeded to draw a set of conclusions that Chikuzan found totally repugnant: individuals were denied the internal potential to transform themselves, thus limiting them to their "little virtue," which may be taken to
mean a natural talent, and disengaging them intellectually from general
moral norms. Having separated internal knowledge and external norm,
Ogyū had further argued that human beings by and large were incapable
of comprehending the organizing principles of society and hence had
no alternative but to "rely" on them without seeking to identify with
them internally, a proposition that appeared to Chikuzan as an enormously problematical position that challenged the very foundation of the
Kaitokudō.[20]

Vital to Chikuzan's thinking was the idea that subjective and objective
spheres of knowledge be rendered consistent philosophically. The cognition of virtue ought not be exclusively internal as claimed by idealists,
nor totally external, the result of direct experience only. Since action
must be accountable in terms of certain identifiable norms, their exter-
nality cannot be denied: "Thus one should first gauge carefully the clear
rules of the *Great Learning* and then grasp the truthfulness of one's action."[21] Tominaga had said that such norms were unreliable; and Ogyū
said that ordinary human beings could not discriminate and "know"
them and that even if they did, most of the so-called norms were faulty.
Realizing this latter to be the case, Tominaga had emphasized direct experience as the only guide to truthfulness while Ogyū set out to find the
one unshakable norm in history that men in history might rely on—the
way, in his favorite phraseology, of the ancient kings. While Chikuzan,
like Goi, held to the need for textually grounded references to serve as
ethical guides, he also insisted in the general capability of the human self
to know which norms were valid and what their purposes were, in short,
acquiring knowledge to apply personally and as a basis to discriminate the
actions of others—the theme of "governance" mentioned earlier in connection with scrolls. Thus, while Ogyū believed such an approach to
scholarship was a wasted effort for most of society, Chikuzan adamantly
held to the view that all human beings innately possessed the capacity to
know the universal moral norms of compassion, fairness, truthfulness,
and the like. One's "imperative" in life, in his eyes, was not to be a "merchant" but an individual who knew "virtue." And precisely because Ogyū
Sorai denied the internal human capacity to know universal morals,
Chikuzan perceived him as a fraudulent thinker:

> Sorai simply discarded the ideas about the internal capabilities of
> human beings to judge truthfulness, honesty and rectitude and cal-
> lously talked about the economy. How can this be in keeping with

the teachings of the ancient kings? He simply asserted this view as the norm proposed by the ancient kings. One is reminded of a show-man who paints an eagle on the signboard when there is only a simple kite behind it to see. The audience cannot help but feel cheated by such a fraud.[22]

Moreover, Ogyū's denial of interior moral potential left him with only "rites and rules," entirely external norms that for Chikuzan were totally unacceptable. The following lines clearly indicate the displeasure he conveyed to his students:

> As for rites and rules we must think of them in the broadest sense of the basic principle pervading the universe and see them as essential to all things in life, from the insignificant individual spirit to the vast kingdom, from the weighty matters of ethics to household manners. These serve as standards of virtue . . . Sorai [however] detested discussions of the human spirit and universal principle. As his rites and rules were all about external activities, they end up only as jewel and fine fabric, as bells and drums, leaving for later generations nothing to identify with when those rites and rules no longer hold sway. All of this stems from his idle talk about rites and rules . . . being situated in the Western Chou the spirit of which he believed to be embedded in the language of the ancients of that time. He thus divested the individual self of any center. . . ."[23]

Left only with ancient rites and rules, empty historical artifacts—jewels and fabric, bells and drums—containing little of persuasive moral value, human beings in the present would be denied by Ogyū their most precious gift of all, to discriminate and understand "virtue" and render ancient norms relevant to the vastly different circumstances of the continuing present.

Believing then that Ogyū's historicism posed a major challenge to the Kaitokudō, Chikuzan launched a sweeping polemic, best outlined in his *Hi-Chō*, a critical review of Ogyū's commentary on the *Analects*, the *Rongo chō*, and rearticulated in other places as well. Of the several strategies Chikuzan employed, one was to repudiate Ogyū's claim to originality. Ogyū, Chikuzan claimed, owed all of his ideas to Itō Jinsai and to late Ming textual scholars. Conceptually and methodologically he did not go beyond Itō, for example, in the identification of history as the primary field of knowledge and the seeking of basic concepts in explicit texts through the philological method. However, while Itō had concluded in a humanistic manner with ideas drawn from Mencius, Ogyū had taken Itō's approach to extreme and unwarranted conclusions. This fallacious tendency toward extremism in argumentation, moreover, was based entirely on personal rather than logical grounding. As Ogyū himself admitted feeling "disdain" for Itō, the latter having died without acknowledging Ogyū's letter of high praise to him, Chikuzan pointed to this personal pique as underlying the unusual vehemence with which Ogyū had denounced Itō. Although Itō had then been in his eighties and Ogyū was in his forties and about to enter the prime of his scholarly career, Ogyū set out nonetheless to discredit Itō with arrogant and excessive statements, denouncing him for succumbing in the end to the idealistic view of human essence that made him little different from the Neo-Confucian moral philosophers he deigned to criticize. He also accused Itō of lacking courage, of being timid like the individual burned too often with hot food who then blows on a cold salad—*atsumono ni korite namasu o fuku mono to iubeshi.* Ogyū justified himself in making these assertions by claiming a special spiritual blessing or mission from heaven—*Ten no chōrei*—while in fact his basic method did not come from such a source at all but from a group of Ming scholars whose ideas he "stole"—*shoron o nusumi*—and dressed up to make them seem like his own.[24]

Thus reminiscent of Tominaga's interpretive theory of "one-upmanship" in which philosophers manipulated received ideas for purely selfish and ambitious reasons, Chikuzan accused Ogyū of using ideas from recent Ming history and from Itō himself to discredit the latter. In doing so, Ogyū had hoped to establish for himself the creative role of having rediscovered the ancient origins of true tradition after centuries upon centuries of intellectual decline—*masse matsugaku.* From the time of Tzu Ssu, the author of the *Doctrine of the Mean*, and *Mencius* on down through the Sung moral philosopher, Chu Hsi, and to Itō Jinsai, scholars had deviated from the original way. Ogyū foolishly believed he alone had stemmed that downward course of history. Yet, such a claim was deceptive in the extreme since Ogyū's perception of the ancients was not direct and unmediated as he announced, having drawn it entirely in fact from Ming scholars and Itō. Their scholarship, in turn, had emerged out of a history of scholarly and philosophical debate in which the thinking of Chu Hsi and others of the Sung era whom Ogyū found wanting was in fact pivotal.[25]

The deceptiveness of Ogyū's historicism, to continue Chikuzan's critique, can also be readily seen in his use of ancient texts. The classic Ogyū relied on most heavily was the Book of Rites—*Reigaku.* But this text according to Chikuzan was not "ancient" in the manner that the ancient kings presumably were, since it was actually a product of the Han Dynasty—postdating the *Doctrine of the Mean* and *The Book of Mencius.* Thus, ironically, these latter texts that the Neo-Confucian philosophers based their thinking on turns out in actuality to be more "ancient" than Ogyū's own source on "rites." Not only is his methodological perspective not grounded in ancient reality; his most important textual evidence is not entirely "ancient" either.[26]

Similarly as regards "language," Ogyū had theorized that ancient Chinese could be read directly and even be pronounced—*kaon chokudoku*—as originally done. Chikuzan joined Goi in accusing Ogyū of proposing an extreme "sinophilism." Refusing thus to recognize differences in time that could not be bridged, Ogyū even denigrated the use of diacritical markings—*kaeriten*—in reading ancient Chinese, an absurdly dogmatic point of view that no one in the current scholarly world agreed with or tried to live up to in fact. Even in China from the Ming era onward, Chikuzan observed, classical writings were punctuated to aid contemporary Chinese scholars in reading these texts; and, needless to say in Japan, even his followers Hattori Nankaku (1683–1759), Yamagata Shūan (1687–1752), Inoue Kinga (1732–84) and others all relied on diacritical aids to read Chinese prose. Ogyū's view of ancient language was totally idiosyncratic and informed by an irrational belief that through ancient words the contemporary mind could mesh with the spirituality of the ancients, a view that totally overlooked the fact that language was primarily functional and expressive of certain kinds of ideas but not "pure" and comprehensible without mediations. All important ideas in the Confucian tradition, Chikuzan thus concluded, could be read with diacritical aids and in fact be rewritten into Japanese and understood without prejudice—*Wago nite wa ashishi to iu koto mo arumaji.*[27]

Chikuzan pressed his attack from there, accusing Ogyū of intellectual reductionism, of oversimplifying complex problems in clear "black and white" terms. Thus, instead of disagreeing with the sages Tzu Ssu, Mencius, and Chu Hsi only on certain issues while seeing their virtues in others, "selecting what is worthy and discarding what is not, as is the responsibility of all who study texts," Ogyū denounced them totally. According to Chikuzan, Ogyū was driven by the dogmatic belief that he could uncover in ancient culture the single norm with which to explain the essence of all human history. He also believed this norm to constitute the central truth in Confucian scholarship from the outset—*Kōshi no gaku no dai ichigi to nasu.* Yet nothing in ancient language warranted such a monistic and reductive thesis. While concentrating on language as the primary object of study was a worthy position, the claim that such an approach could uncover the one norm for social existence was grossly deceptive. Having accused all the great sages from Mencius's time on for having distorted the true way of the ancient kings, therefore, Ogyū himself must stand accused similarly of having created an even greater distortion than any of his predecessors by coercing meaning into terms that even the ancients could hardly have recognized.[28]

The intellectual tendency toward extreme reductionism, in turn, appeared to Chikuzan to be deeply rooted in Ogyū's irrational temperament. Beyond his "illness" of striking at the individual scholar—*hito no onore o semuru no yamai*—was the profoundly irrational dimension in his aim to establish the historicity of divine transmission of heaven's mandate to the ancient kings, which finally can only be taken on faith and not on written evidence. The retracing of history backward to the point of absolute genesis had led Ogyū to the point when "language" and "text" did not exist and to speculate that, blessed with divine suprahuman intelligence—*jinshu setsu*—as this is called, the ancient kings comprehended the mandate from heaven to inaugurate history based on the norm of benevolence, that is, of providing peace and well-being to humankind. Due to this intense adulation of the ancient kings as virtual deities, Ogyū went on to construct the argument that the norm of benevolence created once at the beginning must therefore be "external" to human personality in social history and that later kings, sages, and scholars must study and identify with it and articulate it for the rest of society to "rely" on. While individuals might study that norm, or seek to make it operative as a governing principle in the present, they could not transform themselves and approximate the suprahuman greatness of the ancient kings. Despite the rational facade of Ogyū's philological method, Chikuzan found this resulting deification of the ancient kings to be implausible, irrational, and distortive mystification in the extreme.[29]

As confirmation of his argument, Chikuzan pointed to Ogyū's mysterious behavior shortly before his death. Ogyū was said to have proclaimed to the disciples at his bedside that when a great genius passed away, the transnatural forces of the universe would respond by filling the sky with scarlet tinted clouds. Anticipating his demise, he is said to have advised those near him to step outside to witness the changing color of the sky. Chikuzan worked this anecdote into his critique of Ogyū as evidence of his general insight into Ogyū as an irrational and ambitious pedant. While offering absolutely no sympathy for Sung Neo-Confucian scholars because of their "irrational" metaphysics, Ogyū in the end turns out to be, by Chikuzan's light, far worse as a ludicrously superstitious person believing that his mind was like that of the ancient kings and possessing a suprahuman dimension that could influence the cosmic spirit.

As reported from Edo to Chikuzan by his friend Rai Shunsui, the responses to his emotional critique of Ogyū were, by and large, unfavorable.[30] The reasons as Rai described them were complex and as follows: Chikuzan had raised issues that did not bear on Ogyū's accomplishments as a scholar of political economy; as to the strange utterances attributed to him at his deathbed, their authenticity was doubtful, and even if they were true they did not reflect on his historical theories; and finally, due to the severity of his denunciation, defenders of Ogyū had begun to say that the critic, Chikuzan, could not be an honorable prince of high stature. Chikuzan responded to this latter point in his rejoinder to Rai. Bristling with anger, he reaffirmed the dignity of his position as a scholar of commoner backgrond. The fact that he was not a "prince," he noted, was indeed true; but from his childhood, he had been taught by his father to avoid being a small and petty individual; and although living up to this teaching was not always easy, he, Chikuzan, had absolutely no desire to become a stipended domainal "prince." The barbed language was hurled at samurai aristocrats who lived on guaranteed income and, as men of leisure, dominated the scholarly ambience in Edo, and who also, for the most part, were hardly princely themselves.

Putting that matter aside, Chikuzan then went on to authenticate Ogyū's irrational behavior prior to his death. Although scholars in Edo may have suppressed the incident out of embarrassment, the fact is, he noted, that his disciples close to the event had talked about it openly. In particular Hattori Nankaku, Ogyū's leading student in matters of poetics, often described the incident, and this was attested to by Chikuzan's close friend, one Ayabe Isho, who had studied with Hattori. Ayabe, a scholar hailing from Bungo in Kyushu, often called at the Kaitokudō on his visits to and from Edo. His younger brother, Asada Goryū—a colleague of Miura Baien who left his domain to live near the Kaitokudō to carry out scientific studies—also confirmed the story in all of its details. Both of these men, Chikuzan made plain, were utterly reliable and had no ulterior motive to lie about it. To discount it as evidence of Ogyū's overall irrational adulation of himself and the ancient kings was to misunderstand the arrogant purpose underlying his historicism. He rounded out the response by brushing aside the accusation made of him that his use of the anecdote was irrelevant as it had nothing to do with Ogyū's political theories. Most of Ogyū's commentaries, Chikuzan pointed out, had little or nothing to do with political economy and were simply antiquarian polemics hurled against individual scholars whom he detested. All of the distortions and simplifications that Ogyū had indulged in, the trivilization of the human self as a knowing agent, the positing of absolute norm as being entirely external and based in "history," the imputation of divine qualities in the ancient kings, were all pointed out to confirm his own claim to being a genius who had uncovered the truth of historical origin, relegating everyone else to relying on that discovery of his. However severe his criticism might appear to his detractors, Chikuzan insisted that they were entirely appropriate to Ogyū's own extremist claims.[31]

Had Ogyū stated his reservations regarding Neo-Confucian metaphysics in the manner that Kaibara Ekken had in his "record of grave doubts"—*Taigiroku*—he, Chikuzan, would have chosen less vituperative language. The discovery of philosophical difficulties in Chu Hsi's cosmological reasoning, after all, was not new with Ogyū. From the philosophical stance of natural ontology, Kaibara had found excesses, as did Goi, in Chu Hsi's system of thought. Unlike the measured commentary of Kaibara, however, Ogyū had indulged in such reckless thinking as to deny creative scholarly insight into problems of human moral reason over vast epochs and saw only decline before his time. Confucius was thus said not to have been creative but a mere editor of received ideas; Mencius was made out to be an advocate of anarchy in his thesis on regicide; and Chu Hsi's profound insight into Mencius about the goodness of the human spirit was trivialized.[32]

It is clear from comments of this sort, that Chikuzan's emotional outburst against Ogyū was profoundly intertwined with a passionate defense of the philosophical position of the Kaitokudō. On other matters, Chikuzan could allow a hint of generosity, involving himself in poetry seminars with former students of Ogyū and admitting that Ogyū's ability to compose Chinese-style prose was of the highest order—*nan to ittemo Busshi dai ichi narubeshi*. No other scholar, including his best students such as Hattori, could begin to compare on this count—*haruka ni ochitari*.[33] But on the central philosophical concepts that were crucial to the Kaitokudō as an academy, Chikuzan was uncompromising: All human beings were born as sages with virtue; the ancient sages including the kings were human as were commoners in the everyday world; all human beings ancient and in the present possessed the capacity to know from within goodness as externally recorded in philosophical treatises; through study, human beings could transform themselves and produce "fruits" of unexpected quality; commoners such as merchants could thus acquire the moral knowledge and evaluate the secular world without sacrificing their own practical activities as marketmen.

The crucial moral link in all of these propositions was the insight that Chu Hsi had brought to *Mencius*, that all human beings possessed an inner human compassion or benevolence—*Mōshi no kokoro o motte kokoro to nasu*. While to Ogyū "benevolence" was a norm of kingly governance historically grounded and "external," to Chikuzan it was universally human, as it had been for Itō Jinsai. It was the ultimate philosophical warrant for the education of commoners. Without that fundamental per-spective, Chikuzan affirmed, "our Way is unclear"—*waga Michi fumei nari*.[34] Thus, while both Chikuzan and Ogyū spoke of "virtue" as "potential"— *toku wa toku nari*—they meant profoundly different things by it, to one it was the universal capacity to know goodness as righteousness and to the other it was a particular gift specific to the individual. Chikuzan's attack on Ogyū was at one and the same time a defense of the internal moral capacity of humankind as theorized first by Mencius and conceptualized philosophically by Chu Hsi in terms of natural "reason," the premise from which marketmen were taught at the Kaitokudō beginning with Miyake Sekian, that what they did functionally was not contradictory to their moral endowment to know goodness and righteousnes from within.

To Chikuzan, as it had been with Miyake Sekian, his father Shūan, and his mentor Goi, merchants and other commoners while retaining their particular occupational talents were also by their very humanity, men of virtue, capable of knowing and doing good and compassionate deeds as recorded in sagely books. The separation of individual "talent" and "benevolence" as philosophized by Ogyū cut diametrically against the grain of the academic walls. The moral justification of the academy as a public school for commoners would have been unquestionably dissi-pated. The practical implication was hardly trivial. While Ogyū as head of a private school could use his pedagogical philosophy to instruct only those students convinced of their heaven-endowed "virtue" to become scholars of ancient historical studies, Chikuzan was dedicated to instruct-ing all who, even if only briefly, would wish to study virtue in a serious academy protected by law without any reference as to their becoming a scholar as a heavenly "calling." Seen in this light, Chikuzan's contentious attack on Ogyū was inspired by more than a simple *ad hominem* purpose, although Rai Shunsui's report from Edo hinted at that, as it served to rearticulate in a formal and organized fashion the Kaitokudō's pedagogical philosphy and, hence, also its ideological foundation as a public academy for commoners.

As alluded to in this discussion, Chikuzan further found it extremely problematical that Ogyū would claim for his historicist theory a superior critical insight into present history. Chikuzan's conviction was posted with bold ideographs on scrolls on the academy's walls: Governance— *keijutsu*—at some basic level must be consistent with "virtue" as embod-ied in every individual, so that the study of virtue was inseparable from gaining insights into the field of regulating society. While he did not insist that his students engage in political criticism—examining "righteousness" in the polity around them—he most assuredly felt his philosophical orientation provided insights into the state of political economy with superior clarity to the historicist approach offered by Ogyū. Thus, although Goi, his mentor, had not pressed the matter of taking Kaitokudō epistemology into the problematical area of the polity, Chikuzan did so in good measure with Ogyū self-consciously in mind. Knowledge acquired at a public academy ought to be addressed in a substantial manner to the problems besetting the polity. It was incumbent on the Kaitokudō to fulfill this responsibility in a formally recognized manner, such as within a broader structure of general education. Chikuzan's polemic against Ogyū, in short, was deeply enmeshed with an expansive institutional vision that he had begun to shape. As a public academy oriented to educating commoners on the basis of the Mencian theory of human personality, the Kaitokudō would at the same time serve the cause of governing in accordance with "virtue." This ambitious vision which he had for the Kaitokudō was a deeply personal matter. Scholars of commoner background like himself ought to be formally recognizied for the knowledge they had to offer those who ruled. It was also interwoven into Chikuzan's profound sense of the general crisis pervading the polity that he believed must be rectified in accordance with effective knowledge.

·   ·   ·

As already mentioned in connection with the scrolls which graced the academic walls, Chikuzan taught the idea that "virtue" was the foundation of governance and that human beings in general possessed the capacity to know what virtue meant in terms of goodness, compassion, righteousness, propriety, and wisdom. The political identification with virtue preceded, in importance, governance by law. However well designed the laws might be, without virtue the people would not be governable. Unlike law, virtue is not an external "instrument" to use in order to rule; virtue exists prior to politics and law and must be relied on in order to rule—*Sei o nasu wa toku o motte su.*[35] Virtue resides in human beings and not in law, the latter's virtue being dependent on how wisely they are formulated and used. Governance must rest ultimately on the moral character of individuals and their ability to discriminate and choose to realize the purpose of government, which is the well-being of the people. And, more important than concrete law, the most important "method" of governance is the precise calculation of the state of the economy. A benevolent prince does not spend first and then seek the resources later at the expense of the people. He calculates to begin with what justly ac-

quired resources there are and then determines their use. Without this
"budgetary" principle of calculation, Chikuzan reasoned, government
will not exist for the people and will exploit them instead.

Chikuzan reaffirmed these ideas in the prescription he offered to one
Lord Imamura in 1794 on how he should govern his domain. The ethical
purpose of governance, he wrote, is to nourish the people as a whole. "It
is said in the Book of History," Chikuzan noted, "that the people are the
base of the nation. When the base is firm, the nation shall be at peace.
When national base is in turmoil, there is no reason to expect peace and
well-being in the land. Relief for the people (*banmin ando*) therefore must
be carried out at once. . . ."[36] Chikuzan's language is drawn directly from
the discourse on political economy, on how to order the polity and
save the people, which he saw as the *sine qua non* for peace in the kingdom. The issue, then, was not the social objective of policy, but how to
achieve it. Although Chikuzan's prescriptions to the lord are moderate,
they directly address the domain's capacity to plan and reform: all expenses must be reduced by one-third; expenses incurred to and from Edo
in the system of alternative attendance must be tightened; annual expenses must be adjusted to income as determined by natural conditions
that change from year to year; maintenance of the martial arts must be
more than matched by a reduction of the aristocracy's engaging in superficial displays of elegance; a sum should be set aside annually to repay
debts incurred of Osaka financial houses.

Stripped to its barest minimum this sums up Chikuzan's understanding
of the concept of "political economy"—*keisei saimin*. The implications of
his thinking, however, were quite extensive as he elaborated them in a
detailed treatise entitled *Sōbō kigen*,[37] a title that meant "frank words"—
kigen—on a wide variety of current issues. It was directed to the individual about to become the most powerful figure in the Bakufu at that
time as chief councillor, Matsudaira Sadanobu (1757–1829). In the early
summer of 1788, Matsudaira, enroute to Kyoto on an official visit, called
on Chikuzan in Osaka to hear his view about conditions in the country.
Chikuzan, fifty-nine by then, prepared his materials in great detail and
presented them in a lecture format to Matsudaira, only thirty-one at the
time, through an entire afternoon and on into the late evening. These
materials formed the basis of his *Sōbō kigen*, his most important and best-
known work on political economy. The *Sōbō* is in many respects a remarkable document as it sets forth far-reaching proposals for reform. It
also embodies Chikuzan's ambitious vision for his academy. Some of his
critics detected this and referred to the work as an "ambitious" tract typi-
cal of the "Osaka style" of furthering the cause of "merchants." But the

work gained the respect of the scholarly world and along with Dazai Shundai's *Keizai roku* and Ogyū Sorai's *Seidan* would indeed be one of the three most widely consulted works among political reformers and activists during the last fifty years of the Tokugawa era. The issues Chikuzan dealt with, as outlined below, clearly show why his work would achieve such a status.

The most important feature of the *Sōbō* is that it speaks directly to the problem of reform of the "national system"—*kokka seido*. Chikuzan makes it clear from the outset that while changes should be planned with great deliberation and executed over a reasonably long period of time, thus avoiding drastic and sudden measures for which the people are unprepared, broad reforms—*kaikaku*, *henkaku*—must be carried out nonetheless to prevent the country from continuing on its course of steady decline. Demanding immediate attention was the system known as *sankin kōtai* which required the domainal lords and their retinues to confirm their loyalty to the Bakufu by going to Edo periodically for extended stays. To begin with the system was objectionable on moral grounds, since leaving behind wives and children as hostages in Edo was inhuman and cruel. It was also indefensible on practical grounds. Should there be general internal disturbance, the system was unlikely to prevent regional rebellions. Moreover, it was unfair as it placed an unduly heavy burden on some domains, especially those in distant places, which resulted in crushing indebtedness. Chikuzan advised that the system be revamped so that lords in distant domains would journey to Edo only once in five years and those in domains closer to Edo would make the excursion every three or four years. The period of residence in Edo should not exceed three months.[38]

Reducing the burden of periodic attendance would have immediate and extensive ramifications. Since the political authority of the Bakufu was hardly a matter of dispute, and loyalty to it beyond doubt, the system should be altered according to a calculus other than the political one, namely the economic factor. To throw the entire economy into disarray was totally self-defeating as it eroded the nation's strength. Furthermore, since the need to service the large aristocratic population in Edo would decline proportionally, the demography of that city would be dramatically altered by the steady decline in its population, thus bringing welcome relief from the present congestion. Because the city had grown so enormously due to the system of periodic attendance, vagrants and unregistered laborers had increased accordingly. This created a demand for food and materials that the countryside could not provide and disrupted the economy as a result. By reducing the number of aristocrats in Edo at any given time, Chikuzan reasoned, the net effect would be a reduced demand for goods by that city, thus allowing a more balanced distribution of food throughout the regions and minimizing the dangers of periodic famines. Even in strategic terms, Chikuzan went on, a large concentration of people at the political center was unwise as it was an all too easy target in the event of unexpected invaders such as the "foreigners of the northeast"—meaning, of course, the Russians.

If carried out, the reform would obviously have a drastic effect on the financial houses of Osaka as domainal lords, relieved of much of the expenses of traveling to and from Edo, would rely less on the rice market and banking houses of Osaka. While damaging in this respect, the reform should be carried through with the provision that merchant houses be allowed to purchase the vacated mansions of the domainal lords in Edo and manage them as hotels, further reducing the financial and administrative burdens of the domainal lords and increasing the responsibilities of merchants in regulating the orderly flow of people to and from Edo. Similarly, all serviced facilities along the major roadways would be administered by merchants. The major beneficiaries of these reforms would be the peasantry, the bulk of the population, and the object of humane governance, for they would be relieved of crushing taxes and of having to produce rice and other goods merely to finance the extended journeys of the domainal lords and their retinues.

Chikuzan offered the following special plan.[39] Since the system of periodic attendance had produced a pattern of indebtedness stemming from excessive administrative and ritualistic activities (including the normal costs of travel) which led to punishing taxes, Chikuzan advised a systematic study to document the depth of this disruptive economic situation. Specifically, he would have precise data gathered on the extent of indebtedness by each domainal lord over the previous thirty years, documenting in exact detail the extent of loans taken out and the actual interest paid over these years. This data should then be used to establish new categories of domainal lords (not according to who were allies or enemies of the Tokugawa house when it came to power in 1600) based on the economic terms of indebtedness caused by the system of periodic attendance. A reduction of financial and administrative burdens should be made in accordance with these new economic categories. In return for this reduction, the domainal lord in question must agree formally to carry out a strict retrenchment policy within his home domain.

As implied by this last point, Chikuzan had advanced the provocative idea to Matsudaira that the Bakufu ought to provide centralized direction over the nation's economic life rather than simply serving as a larger version of competing domainal governments. It ought to guide its economic policy according to the principle of virtue, which is that no major policy should be adopted by the center that produced a negative effect on the populace at large—*shimo no gai arashimubekarazu.* It should therefore press forward without hesitation in reforming the anachronistic system of periodic attendance which is counterproductive to the people in virtually every respect.

Similarly, it should exercise firm and consistent management of the country's money. For example, copper should not be exported to Korea and China because it is less "precious" than gold and silver. On the contrary, it is valuable because it is socially functional in a more universal manner than these latter two metals. In this regard Chikuzan's view is similar to Miura Baien's who had argued in his treatise on the "origins of economic value"—*Kagen*—that the most valuable metal was "iron" since it was plentiful and socially the most useful, and therefore all commodities ought to be gauged in terms of this metal and not in relation to metals that were scarce and hence "valuable." Chikuzan was especially harsh on the Bakufu's manipulation of this concept of "scarcity" by debasing the content of money and generating distrust. When money is uneven in quality, he warned, poor money will remain in circulation and good money will be hoarded, resulting in more money being needed to buy the same amount of goods. Chikuzan's views would be presented in greater detail by one of the students of the Kaitokudō, the merchant scholar Kusama Naokata, as we will have occasion to see in the next chapter. Whether Chikuzan drew his ideas about money from Miura Baien or from Kusama is not certain. As used by Chikuzan in the *Sōbō,* they added up to a plea to the Bakufu that it serve as a central government to unify the content of money throughout the country. Only it should mint money, and its seal and year should be clearly affixed. Then he added, rather gratuitously, that since social utility should determine the minting of money all the major temple bells and statues of Buddha should be confiscated and melted down for use as cash.

The Bakufu should serve as a central government in other areas of the economy as well. The practice of monopolistic merchant guilds to fix prices should be forbidden. Similarly the cost of transporting goods from one region to another should be standardized and transit taxes between domains abolished. Furthermore, the Bakufu should sell bonds or certificates to merchant financiers to build granaries to stabilize the price of rice over the long run and to provide a more systematic way of distributing rice throughout the general populace during lean years. The Bakufu must be the sole authority, as these matters embrace the needs of the people as a whole and cannot be solved by a domainal lord acting alone or, for that matter, by merchants as a group.

But these prescriptions appear somewhat trivial and insignificant when compared with Chikuzan's recommendation to the Bakufu that it, as the central authority, take the initiative and abolish the most sacrosanct of institutions within the Tokugawa order, namely the granting of fixed stipends—*roku*—to members of the samurai aristocracy as a matter of hereditary right. It was this practice, he explained to Matsudaira, that had as much to do with the plight of the economy as any other single factor. Because income was fixed and guaranteed, samurai could and did use it as credit and borrowed off it well into the future. No amount of moral exhortation to this class to be "frugal" could stop this pattern—an argument that reflected Chikuzan's knowledge that merchants were frugal not because they were told to be moral, but because their income was not fixed. Hence they were compelled to save to assure continuity into the future. While each generation of merchants had to create its own "stipend," samurai, not faced with this fact of life, lived off their future and thus fueled the pattern of excessive demand and consumption that had placed an enormous strain on the economy. The remedy was quite simply to terminate stipends as a hereditary privilege and adjust them according to the nature of the duties and responsibilities of the individual involved. Although Chikuzan stopped short of advocating the abolition of the aristocracy, the practice of pegging stipends to merit and ability and not to hereditary privilege carried with it that iconoclastic consequence. For surely, as administrative responsibilities in Edo and on the journeys to and from that city declined, the number of jobless samurai without stipends would perforce increase. It was these unemployed samurai that Chikuzan viewed as a potential pool of talent for the new educational system he had in mind. They would become teachers like himself, working among commoners, taking moral knowledge and enlightenment to them, all in the cause of the well-being of the entire nation. His critique of the stipend system was closely interrelated with the future he had in mind for scholars of commoner background like himself and for the Kaitokudō as an educational center.

The perspective that Chikuzan brought to bear on reform was shaped by the deep frustration that "Confucian scholars"—*jusha*—especially commoners like himself felt during the eighteenth century because they belonged to a stratum without a clearly articulated place in the status structure.[40] They were not seen as members of the aristocracy, in the sense that a samurai could certainly be a Confucian scholar, but the latter need not be one of the former. The stratum came to include a complex mixture of diverse class elements. While it is fair to say that commoners such as Itō Jinsai, Miyake Sekian, and Goi Ranju interacted with the aristocracy and gained the respect of certain segments of it, it is also the case that they were often looked upon with contempt because they lacked high status and were often quite poor, as was Goi, and were compelled to make a living in ways other than in scholarly work. By comparison, as Chikuzan was well aware and often commented on, a "scholar" in China belonged to a status commanding respect throughout society and he was expected to engage in some kind of public service during his lifetime. Commoners like himself in Japan lived with the awareness of the improbability of his becoming a member of the official aristocracy. Some, such as Goi who had taught as a domainal teacher, preferred not to be part of that aristocracy, choosing instead the life of the independent scholar and teacher rather than serving a domainal lord. While Chikuzan agreed with this mission of teachers to immerse themselves in the study and teaching of "virtue," he also believed that the study of this subject carried with it a broad social purpose. "A Confucian scholar," he thus observed, "is not one who simply discusses books and writes poetry."[41] Chikuzan believed in a public purpose to being a "Confucian scholar," and he defined this before Matsudaira as educating the talented of the nation for the good of the polity.

In 1783, several years before his meeting with Matsudaira, Chikuzan outlined his thinking about schools in a preliminary way in a response to Lord Suge, a Kyoto courtier, who had queried about establishing a public school in Kyoto. Chikuzan began by noting that while Kyoto was just beginning to think about a school for its city, Osaka had created one fifty-seven years earlier:

> . . . based on the exalted thinking of the virtuous Shōgun who wished schools to be established in the Kyoto-Osaka areas, my now deceased father Chūzō submitted a request for a school in Osaka. Just as he requested, official permission was granted in Kyōhō 11 for the Kaitokudō to be built. Open to all the people including aristocrats and the most humble, and although occupying within the city a small area hardly amounting to anything, lectures have been given without interruption down to today with great care and diligence. With regard to this, it appears that no teacher in Kyoto responded as communication concerning it had not been reported. That both areas are not on a uniform basis as the Shōgun had wanted is to be lamented.[42]

As to the principles upon which the school should rest, Chikuzan resorted to the well-worn formula that all schools should include the cultural and military arts—*bunbu*. The main thrust of his thinking, however, was that this formula should not be applied mechanically to the Tokugawa present and that schools appropriate to current realities should be built. Thus, if the Bakufu established a school of the military arts in Edo, it would be entirely appropriate to have a parallel school in west-central Japan specializing in literary studies—*bungyō*—and contribute greatly to the governance of peace and tranquility in this manner.

> Presently, in the Kantō area to the east, the way of the military arts has been highly developed. Its glory now permeates the four seas as a rule of great peace. Thus in Kyoto there should be complete concentration on cultural studies, enhancing even more the flowering of the great peace.[43]

According to the way of the ancient sages, schools should be divided into six areas: rites, music, archery, administration, history, arithmetic. But since the military and administrative arts are cared for thoroughly in Edo, Kyoto should replace these areas with poetry—*shi*—and prose—*bun*. The result would be a school specializing in cultural studies with the martial and administrative subjects left entirely in the hands of the Bakufu college in Edo. Chikuzan proposed that the school bear the classical name of Kankōin, which suggests perceiving reality with jeweled clarity, and the main lecture hall the name of Meishindō, a place to clarify the good spirit of the people. He also recommended that carefully selected scrolls with parallel lines be strategically hung from the walls. But, squarely within his intellectual position, he went on to say, "Why indeed should the present necessarily adhere to ancient ways." He also urged the school to staff itself with men of ability without regard to class background and warned that it should avoid the excesses of Yamazaki Ansai and especially Ogyū Sorai.[44]

What is especially intriguing in this "personal view on schools" is Chikuzan's prescription that there be a clear division of instructional labor between Edo on the one hand and Kyoto-Osaka on the other. The implication quite clearly is that there should be a new integration of learning within a broadly conceived educational structure in which Edo would specialize in certain things and west-central Japan in others. These implications were expressed in greater detail in his presentation to Matsudaira.

As in his communiqué to Lord Suge, Chikuzan began his comments to Matsudaira on education in a forthright manner by reviewing the purpose and achievements of the Kaitokudō. It was, he observed with obvious pride, the first public academy to provide lectures for commoners. He quickly went on to observe, however, that academies such as the

Kaitokudō or the Bakufu's own college in Edo, the Shōheikō, were hardly adequate to meet the needs of the nation. The absence of an official school in Kyoto, for example, had diminished the luster of that great city—*hikari o ushinai.* A comprehensive national educational system seemed to be in order, he proposed, with three major centers located in Edo to the east and Kyoto and Osaka in the west and center, with numerous additional public schools on a lesser scale placed in smaller cities such as Nara, Sakai, Ōtsu, Ikeda, Nishinomiya, Hyōgo as well as in regional towns throughout the country. Private schools for children should all be given official status and renamed as secular "schools for reading and writing." In cities such as Osaka, these should be distributed evenly according to township units. In the countryside, every village should have schools to teach the young the basic skills of literacy. Under present conditions, Chikuzan observed, such a program of general education was not feasible given the size of the population and the limited educational facilities that existed. A new system should be devised which provided schools for youngsters of lower-school age, and these would be integrated with higher-level training. Upper-level study groups should number no more than 150 students, and the schools should be built with public funds on public lands. Finally, advanced-level academies at Edo, Kyoto, and Osaka would coordinate and administer the system from positions of academic authority directly under the aegis of the Bakufu.[45]

In justifying such an expanded role for his Kaitokudō, which caused his critics to label him as "ambitious," Chikuzan offered a line of reasoning that the education of commoners and the promotion of talent were morally sound and politically beneficial. General education for commoners, however, should not be done in a haphazard way as this would allow unqualified teachers, especially Buddhist priests in his view, to assume that responsibility. Indeed the very designation of many of the schools for youngsters as "temple schools"—*terakoya*—must be altered, as it was a misnomer to begin with. In the sixteenth century such a designation may have been appropriate, since Buddhist temples were the only place where such education was carried out, giving rise to the metaphor of a young student as a "temple child"—*terako*—but the realities were now vastly different and temples ought not be allowed a privileged place in the education of the young. Commoners should study "virtue" and acquire practical skills. Buddhism ought not be taught, as it encouraged "disengagement" from society and polity. A public school for commoners from its inception, the Kaitokudō was entirely suited to assume the overall administrative responsibility of general education of the populace. It was located in the "major city" of Osaka which was inhabited almost entirely by commoners—*heimin nomi ōki tokoro.* Thus, Chikuzan went on without disguising his own interest in the matter, "if this place that I uphold—*gu no mamoru tokoru*—were to be expanded only slightly," then the Kaitokudō could assume the educational role for commoners appropriate to it in west-central Japan that presumably the Bakufu's Shōheikō anchored for the aristocracy in Edo.[46]

The division of labor that Chikuzan had made between the study of military and administrative arts in Edo and cultural subjects in Kyoto is thus presented again but with a slightly different twist. The division is between Edo as the college for the aristocracy and Osaka the center of education for the commoner population in general. While remaining within the original purpose of the Kaitokudō to teach commoners within the protection of law, Chikuzan's proposal provided that aim with a much expanded pedagogical and structural significance. Although it is clear that his plan was inextricably woven into his personal ambition to assume, on behalf of the academy, a place of high authority within the public order, it is also undeniable that it contained a more general vision of systemic universal education for all commoners. Moreover, while it would be a "public" system under the authority of the Bakufu, it would not suffer from the substantial presence of the aristocracy, again making Osaka suitable in his eyes. The overall idea of a college in Osaka open to commoners and at the pinnacle of a vast educational system reaching down to the lower classes and determining the instructional content of the curriculum was a bold one indeed, as it would have elevated the Kaitokudō from an academy for merchants to a status of enormous authority in matters of national education.

Chikuzan rounded out his ideas on educational reform with specific recommendations. Consistent with his general philosophy, he insisted that teachers ought to be selected on the basis of talent and not class—*heimin nitemo mibun no sabetsu naku.* Buddhist priests with ability would be allowed to teach but must first go through a retraining program appropriate to the needs of the revised system. Unemployed samurai, no longer with guaranteed stipends, would especially be called on to serve as teachers. Their ties with domainal lords would be severed, and they would gain compensation according to their ability to teach at an appropriate level. Their formal status would be changed from "samurai" to "teacher." Using language thoroughly familiar to modern Japanese, Chikuzan recommended that teachers and scholars from commoner background be formally recognized by law with "certificates"—*menkyo*—designating them as "scholars of letters"—*hakushi bungaku no shoku*—who "profess"—*kyōju o suru*—on matters of virtue. They would be allowed, moreover, to post their certificates on the front door of their homes. As their status would not be hereditary, however, new talent would be continuously promoted from below to replace them and assume responsible duties in society.[47]

The overall boldness of Chikuzan's proposals reflects not only his ambitious vision but, at the same time, his sense of a general crisis encompassing the political order that called for far-reaching educational reforms. This need would be felt with increasing intensity in the fifty years or so after Chikuzan's death in 1804 and on through the Meiji Ishin of 1868 and the establishment thereafter of the national educational system of the modern era. Proposals similar to Chikuzan's for a unified educational system based on merit were made by a number of other individuals, such as by the political economist in Edo, Honda Toshiaki (1743–1820), who advocated the establishment of a central "great university" to train the nation's talent in the arts of modern technology, and by Shōji Noriyoshi (1793–1857), a Nagasaki merchant who wrote at length on the importance of universal education particularly for the lower classes. Among scholars who had come under the direct instructional influence of Chikuzan and maintained close ties with the Kaitokudō, two in particular, Waki Guzan and Hoashi Banri, both eminent intellectuals and teachers in their own right, wrote essays that bear the distinct markings of Chikuzan's thinking.

A scholar of peasant background, Waki was a student of Miura Baien in Kyushu and studied at the Kaitokudō in 1787 and again in 1796. After serving as a teacher in the domainal school of Kumamoto, he then opened a school of his own. In his "personal" view on schools—*Gakkō shisetsu*—Waki echoed Chikuzan's proposal for a unified educational system open to commoners through which talent would be promoted from below. The system would be double tiered, a comprehensive "lower" or "elementary" level—*shōgakkō*—and an "upper" stratum or "great school"—*daigakkō*—for advanced and special students, culminating at the top in special academies. It was Waki's student Hoashi Banri, however, who would take Chikuzan's ideas and develop them into a fuller statement. Like Waki, Hoashi was primarily a Confucian scholar interested in science and was similarly deeply indebted intellectually to Miura Baien the philosopher scientist and to the Nakai brothers at the Kaitokudō where he also studied. Hoashi established a school of his own, just as Waki had done, and taught, literally, hundreds of late Tokugawa students, including for example Fukuzawa Yukichi's father and brother. Hoashi's particular contribution to Chikuzan's ideas on education was the incorporation of the study of Western science within the "humanistic" curriculum of a university located in west-central Japan. The manner in which he reworked Chikuzan's thinking to add this dimension deserves brief attention.[48]

Following Chikuzan's model, Hoashi proposed two major academic centers for the nation, one in Edo and the other in west-central Japan embracing the Kyoto-Osaka area. The academy in Edo would specialize in the administrative and military arts—hence, *bugei daigaku*, as it would be responsible for servicing the needs of the Bakufu there. In west-central Japan, preferably in Kyoto for cultural reasons, the academy would concentrate on general "letters"—*bun*—and it would bear the name of college of humanistic arts—*gakugei daigaku*. Within this division introduced earlier by Chikuzan, Hoashi would broaden the range of the subject matter, going well beyond his predecessor in this regard. Rational Confucianism would remain central to the overall curriculum and serve as its ethical and epistemological baseline. All of the major texts, however, would be translated into current Japanese—*wagon*—and taught accordingly because the main purpose of education was to teach youngsters basic moral concepts. Instruction, nevertheless, ought to be introduced as early as possible rather than after the mastery of Chinese-style prose.

Unlike Chikuzan, Buddhism would be included in the curriculum, but Hoashi, revealing his bias here, recommended that it be taught in Chinese-style prose rather than in Japanese, rendering it far less accesible. As at the Kaitokudō, Japanese literature would be one of the major subjects of study. Unlike it, however, a special bureau of research—*tokushu kenkyūjo*—would be created to study Western science. A position of chief translator of Dutch science would be established to direct translation projects of works in astronomy, geography, medicine, and engineering. To Hoashi, the study of science involved the problem of epistemology—how to better grasp the ultimate meaning of natural law or principle and not that of technology, as in the study of making gunpowder and explosives for strategic purposes advocated by Honda Toshiaki. Despite this innovative incorporation of Western science into the formal curriculum, which reflects Hoashi's deep engagement in the study of Western physical science (as documented in his major opus, "the exhaustive investigation of things"—*Kyūri tsū*, 1837), it is beyond dispute that the basic concept for national education is derived from Chikuzan. The plan for general education among commoners, the reliance on small study groups organized on a communal ideal—colleagues in learning—*dōshi, dōhai, kōsha,* etc., the promotion of talent from below regardless of social background, and above all, the division of the educational structure between an administrative college in the east and one on cultural studies in the west, all point to a closely articulated relationship between Chikuzan and the younger Hoashi.[49]

Yet, when all is said and done, Chikuzan's vision was unlike Hoashi's. While Hoashi's agenda, if we may speak of it as such, was to create a formal space for the study of Western science in an educational system, Chikuzan's was decidedly a political agenda for establishing a constructive and "permanent" place within the broader legal system for his Kaitokudō. The restless sense in Chikuzan that the Kaitokudō, public school for commoners, was not being given the just recognition it deserved is given suggestive confirmation by his attempt at writing a laudatory history of the Tokugawa house and bearing his name as author and head of the Kaitokudō. The use of history to legitimate his educational enterprise and the vision he projected for it lends additional weight to the view that Chikuzan's proposed extensive educational reforms were based primarily on his political goal.

Chikuzan's history is essentially an apology of the Tokugawa house, a glowing account of its rise from among contending regional barons into the shogunal authority that graced the land with "peace and tranquility." It is of particular interest that he began to draft this history in the 1750s, while still in his mid-twenties and while Goi was still alive. He redrafted it at least five times before settling on the final version to submit to the Bakufu as *Isshi* in 1797. It is a history that sought to establish the very crucial ideological fact that Kaitokudō scholarship stood in a formal and sympathetic relationship to the Tokugawa house, the authorizing source of the academy's very existence, and was not related to an alternative history as the "history of Osaka" was identified with the ill-fated Toyotomi Hideyoshi and his descendents. Behind Chikuzan's historical narrative lies the fact of social memory in Osaka; the Hideyoshi bastion in Osaka was felled by the Tokugawas' chicanery, and the local population continued to retain a romantic adulation for the tragic hero, Hideyoshi, a baronial giant of peasant stock who came so very close to being the ultimate unifier of Japan. That alternative history had to be replaced with the history of the rise of the Tokugawa's because the Tokugawa history resulted in the ongoing present in which the Kaitokudō must be formally located. The *Isshi* disengages Chikuzan and the Kaitokudō from the history of the romantic and defeated to the source of formal law as it had come to be constituted in the Tokugawa Bakufu.

Scholars close to the Bakufu College responded with much enthusiasm. His colleagues there, Shibano Ritsuzan and Koga Seiri, and one of his former students, the famous Satō Issai, brought Chikuzan's work to the attention of the Shōgun himself, who, in turn, rewarded Chikuzan in

1799 with two elegant ceremonial outfits of the highest artistic quality bearing the Tokugawa insignia of the hollyhock. Such recognition of the Kaitokudō from the source of authority was, needless to say, unprecedented. That Chikuzan wanted more than ceremonial garb also goes without saying. He no doubt wanted a newly designated role for the Kaitokudō within a freshly conceived educational system, as he had proposed in his *Sōbō kigen*. Scholars somewhat distant from the Bakufu felt less kindly toward Chikuzan's use of history to "flatter" the Bakufu. Most painful, his brother Riken took strong exception to Chikuzan's history, seeing it as a ploy to gain bureaucratic advancement and as unvirtuous in the light of the moral premises of the academy. For a while all personal relations between them were rumored to have been ruptured over this issue.[50]

As Chikuzan's history was not ideologically innocent, Riken's disappointment can be readily understood. Yet it was also entirely consistent with the overall purpose Chikuzan had in mind, which can be seen in his dealings with the local town elders as well as in his prescriptive *Sōbō kigen*, to establish a clear and authoritative relationship between the source of legal power and the Kaitokudō as a "public" educational space unconstrained by Osaka's social geography. It was not enough by his lights that the Bakufu allowed commoners to study virtue; as a responsible legal authority, it must also be responsive to the measured voice of scholars who were commoners. The academy, in short, should be permitted to address itself to the problems of the polity writ large. This was, after all, the duty of scholars regardless of status and not that of the aristocracy alone. Such a claim for himself and the Kaitokudō, however, could remain legitimate only insofar as the academy remained strictly "public" and unequivocally identified with the "true" history behind the rise of the Tokugawa house. Viewed in this light, Chikuzan's ideological history was not simply a strategy for individual advancement. It was also a way to legitimize his plea on behalf of scholars of commoner background trained in public academies such as the Kaitokudō to gain equivalent stature with those in the aristocracy who by *birthright* were expected to advise lords as to how to govern the land. As noted earlier, he would have these scholars of commoner background awarded legal "diplomas" to formalize their scholarly achievement; he would redefine the Kaitokudō so that it would oversee general education among commoners as a whole. Thus, although hardly innocent, Chikuzan's history was intertwined with a broad and critical reformist vision that went beyond personal ambition in the narrow sense and should be seen as part of the same fabric as the more concretely prescriptive *Sōbō kigen*.

Having written the *Isshi*, it was entirely appropriate that the Bakufu would summon Chikuzan in 1796 to become the chief of the newly created bureau of historical studies. A more prestigious appointment for a scholar of commoner background is hardly conceivable. The same friends who had arranged for the reward of ceremonial clothing, Bitō Nishū and Koga Seiri, again were said to be his supporters for this post. It was also consistent and appropriate, however, that Chikuzan would decline the invitation by feigning poor health as his ambition had always been tied to the future of the Kaitokudō and to the education of commoners in general rather than to the acquisition of office for himself in the Edo Bakufu.[51]

*   *   *

When offered the post of chief historian in the Bakufu, Chikuzan had already acquired a firm reputation in scholarly circles through his *Sōbō kigen,* which had come to be widely regarded as a carefully reasoned, if provocative, treatise. He had also cultivated academic friendships along a broad front to enhance the visibility of the academy. Scholars whose names are now obscure called on Chikuzan from at least a dozen different domains, mainly from west and west-central Japan but including Mito from the east. As Nishimura Tenshū lists them,[52] we find a Taki Sōtei (dates not known) who would later teach at the Gansuidō; Iwamura Nanri (1784–1842) who would instruct at the domain of Marugame in Shikoku; and Maruyama Shōin, similarly a domainal teacher in Niimi. The example of Miura Baien and his students has already been noted several times. Waki Guzan studied with Chikuzan as did Hoashi Banri. Another dozen students can be identified as hailing from the domain of Tatsuno, where Chikuzan's father, Shūan, lived as a youngster. Studying under both Chikuzan and Riken, some of these men from Tatsuno would return to form what came to be known as the "reform faction" within that domain and would suffer defeat in a political struggle in which its leader, a close friend of Chikuzan, would be forced to commit suicide. We also know that the head of the Bakufu College in Edo, Satō Issai, studied under Chikuzan in 1792 at age 21. Although Satō leaned intellectually toward a much more idealistic position than Chikuzan favored, he revered Chikuzan as his esteemed teacher. Undoubtedly, however, his most important colleagues were Rai Shunsui, Bitō Nishū, and Koga Seiri, influential academics close to the seat of power in Edo and at the forefront of the scholarly world of the day. Rai, as mentioned before, was deeply concerned over Chikuzan's outburst against Ogyū Sorai; and Bitō and Koga had supported Chikuzan for a position within the Bakufu. These men had frequented Osaka from the early 1750s, invariably making extended visits to the Kaitokudō.

Through his scholarly writings, teaching, and cultivation of a wide circle of acquaintances, then, Chikuzan had indeed taken the Kaitokudō to a level of visibility and prestige that went well beyond the achievements of his predecessors. Chikuzan's pride over this is reflected in the enormous effort he expended in rebuilding the Kaitokudō following its devastation in the early summer fires of 1793. Ironically, although Chikuzan had struggled with the town elders to orient the Kaitokudō outward rather than to the limited local setting, in the end it would be these Osaka merchants that Chikuzan would turn to for the bulk of the funds to rebuild the academy. The Bakufu's response to Chikuzan's appeal for 1,400 *ryo* would not be generous, some three hundred only. The remaining rebuilding cost would be covered with local funding. For the better part of four years, Chikuzan devoted himself to this project, and the resulting structure, while adequate, would not be the authoritative university overseeing a vast education system that Chikuzan had envisaged all along. Still, there was much that Chikuzan could feel proud of. Since its beginnings as the Tashōdō in the early 1710s, the Kaitokudō had survived through the very lean years of the early 1890s. The academy had gained the respect of scholars throughout the country, and a steady flow of students and visitors from outside Osaka came specifically to Osaka's "public" school. Believing the rebuilt academy was assured continuity into the future as a public academy for commoners, Chikuzan went into retirement in 1799.

The problem of succession that had weighed heavily on Chikuzan's mind also appeared to have been settled. Chikuzan had been deeply concerned that, although the Kaitokudō had received appropriate recognition, the fact remained that scholars tended to come and go rather than remain in Osaka, and few expressed interest in staying on to become its academic head. Goi Ranju had stayed because his home was Osaka, he was poor, and he disliked serving in domainal schools. Outstanding scholars of Goi's stature, Chikuzan had come to conclude unhappily, would seek and find more lucrative employment elsewhere. In view of this general situation, Chikuzan settled on his son, Shōen, to succeed him when he retired. By all accounts a truly gifted young scholar, Shōen, however, was also frail. One of the three of Chikuzan's nine children to survive childhood, Shōen would pass away in 1804, a year before Chikuzan.

With Shōen's death, Chikuzan turned in his last testament to his brother Riken to assume the leadership of the Kaitokudō despite the fact that Riken had self-consciously kept his distance from the academy for many years. His final appeal reveals his respect for Riken despite his idiosyncratic intellectual style. In carefully chosen language that Chikuzan no doubt wrote with some uneasiness, he advised the managing council of the Kaitokudō that he wished the headship of the academy to go to Riken who should be persuaded to return to live within the school itself—*dōjin kono hō e hikiutsuri*. If Riken should not agree to such a move, he should still be made responsible for the regularly scheduled lectures, and students from the academy "should transport him to and from his home on a palanquin"—*kono hō tekago nite subeshi*. Then to Riken personally, he wrote the following lines:

> After I pass away, I should like you, my wise brother, to assume the duties of the headship. Although it will be burdensome due to your age, I hope you will accept this and return to live in the academy. You will have absolutely no formal responsibilities as far as dealing with the outside world is concerned. You may, in other words, continue to teach in exactly the same manner as you have been at your separate residence. There will be hardly any additional work of note at all.[53]

This plea to Riken, combined with a letter through the house of Kōnoike to the Osaka merchant community in general for continued support of the Kaitokudō after his departure, brought an end to forty-five years of Chikuzan's intellectual and administrative dominance of the Kaitokudō. His years marked, without any question, the most vigorous and expansive period in the history of the academy which would not again be duplicated in large measure due to the problem of succession. Very much present, although unstated in the above lines to Riken, is the premature death of his son Shōen. Had he lived, the letter to Riken would have been unnecessary; without him, he felt compelled to turn, not without a sense of desperation, to his brother, knowing all along that Riken had no ambition at all in this direction. Thus it was that he pleaded to Riken to return "home"; allowed him his idiosyncratic methods even so; but if he chose to live away, wished him to agree to deliver the regularly scheduled lectures. Despite their differences, Chikuzan admired and openly admitted Riken's superior scholarly ability.

NAKAI RIKEN
(1732–1817)

Chikuzan's respect for his brother's scholarship notwithstanding, Riken in fact was not suitable for the headship of the Kaitokudō. Already seventy-three at that time, he was only three years younger than Chikuzan and could not provide the detailed administrative attention that the academy needed. Moreover, he had for many years chosen an alternative personal style from that fostered at the Kaitokudō, as Chikuzan clearly acknowledged in his letter. It was not surprising, therefore, that Riken did not honor Chikuzan's plea that he take up residence again at the Kaitokudō. While aware of his brother's strong preference that he be physically present at the academy, Riken chose to continue to live away from it, wary perhaps of Chikuzan's assurance that not much administrative work would be involved for him. He did, however, agree to deliver the formal lectures at regularly scheduled times, although it is said that he left immediately after having fulfilled this duty. While Riken owed his intellectual and scholarly training to the Kaitokudō and to Goi in particular and retained a strong sense of loyalty to the academy and to his brother as well, he would not surrender the autonomy and solitude that he had come to cherish. Unlike Chikuzan, who had shaped his scholarly vision entirely in accordance with the fate of the Kaitokudō, Riken had severed himself from all concerns relating to academic administration. Indeed, it would be more accurate to say he had come to harbor a profound disinterest in bureaucratic formalities, which he often expressed in such frank and fearless ways that he came to be known as an eccentric. Rai Shunsui would say of him that he was "somewhat prickly"—*ya-ya henpeki naru mono*— and the historian Naitō Konan would describe him as brazenly "temperamental"—*kimagure*.[54]

Fiercely independent about his work as a scholar, Riken declined Matsudaira Sadanobu's invitation to consult with him during his visit to Osaka—Chikuzan, it will be recalled, turned the affair into his *Sōbō kigen*. As already noted, furthermore, Riken took strong exception to his brother's laudatory history of the Tokugawa house which he believed to be contrary to the purpose of scholarship. True to the image evoked by his name, Riken chose to tread on the Way in his own "effortless" manner with inner strength, evading the temptations of institutional life, and limiting his circle of scholarly acquaintances and students to a small group of individuals. He agreed to teach only those students who came to him with a strong and worthy scholarly project in mind. Still, all of the students and scholarly visitors at the Kaitokudō continued to view Riken as part of the Kaitokudō, so that although he lived "beyond the gates"— by choice and not out of expulsion as had been the case with Tominaga Nakamoto—everyone at the academy referred to him with esteem and affection as Riken Sensei or Yūjin Sensei.

The dramatic contrast between Riken and Chikuzan should not limit our view of them in a broader intellectual context. Chikuzan, as emphasized, relates to the entrepreneurial and bureaucratic field. And Riken, far from merely reacting to his brother's ambitions, interrelates with an alternative critical eccentricity that permeated a good deal of late eighteenth-century Tokugawa intellectual history. What we discover among the "eccentrics"—*kijin*—of this era is a deeply felt sense of crisis in the ongoing present and the need to somehow shape a basis of creative independence apart from it. In Riken's case, the break seems to have come around 1767 when he left the Kaitokudō to take on a teaching position for a year at a noble household in Kyoto, although it is entirely likely that the tendency in that direction was present in him well before that time. In any event, Riken did not return to the academy but rented a personal hideaway in the commercial center of Osaka. It is said that while in Kyoto he imbibed the loyalist thinking being discussed among court nobles under the influence of Takeuchi Shikibu (1712–67), a *cause célèbre* for his defense of "imperial justice" against Bakufu rule.

It is clear that Riken developed around then a profound pessimism about the existing order and, in particular, the unlikelihood of political "righteousness" or justice ever coming to pass among the people under the authoritative presence of the Bakufu. Like other eccentrics of his day, Riken came to conceptualize "justice" as a "dream." The dream to Riken, however, was not the unknown phenomenon that occurred at night discussed by Goi, or extensions of everyday experience as taught by Chikuzan. To Riken, the "dream" referred either to a fabricated space designed to protect one's intellectual autonomy or to an ideal that may someday be realized but that remained totally outside the realm of possibility in the present. Realizing this, Riken could not identify personally with the political world around him and, as might be said of a modern intellectual, felt alienated from it. He is thus reported to have said of himself shortly after his year in Kyoto: "Yūjin already knows that he does not belong to this age. So he will leave it and cease to be."[55]

It appears that Riken's decision not to return to the Kaitokudō was determined by the disturbing sense suggested in his language that injustices would persist and that the sage who knows this fact had no choice but, in the manner of Lao-tzu, "do nothing." The central political message of that Taoist philosopher can also be identified in Dazai Shundai's appraisal a generation earlier. The sage, Dazai had said, must disengage with things as they are. Yet, by disengaging that personal world from the public order, that personal sphere was now also abstract to Riken and, ironically, dreamlike. Enclosed in such a disengaged world, Riken hoped to create his own reality without compromise to the political order. In this regard, he was entirely in the company of some outstanding contemporaries such as Buson, enclosed in a little hut and writing abstract poems about the national landscape broadly conceived; Jakuchu, in the upstairs of a greenery store painting roosters with devilish eyes; Shiba Kōkan, declaring himself dead on a public poster and then leading a new life as a creative recluse; and Kaiho Seiryō, exiling himself from the aristocracy to seek "objectivity" in the world of "play"—*asobi*—among merchants in and around Osaka in order to see social reality as it actually was. The list can be easily expanded. Riken clearly belongs with these "risk-taking" eccentrics, for like them, he had lost faith in the present; in his case, more specifically, with expanding the role of the Kaitokudō within the public order, or engaging in writing ideological history, or sharing his ideas with a Matsudaira Sadanobu.[56]

It is also worth reemphasizing that Riken and other eccentrics held a deep fascination with Taoism that one does not find in Goi or Chikuzan. To Riken and others like him who were disenchanted with the course of history, Taoism served as a mediating philosophy of disengagement from that history which allowed one to gain a new basis of objectivity and see things in their true and unadorned light. As in the case of Kaiho Seiryō, who utilized Taoism to leave the artificial world of social "classes" to clarify the true underpinning of political economy, which he came to identify with the principle of mathematical calculation as exhibited in the marketplace, Riken too made self-conscious use of that philosophy in distancing himself from social artificialities in order to construct an autonomous space defined exclusively in terms of his own scholarly purpose and totally under his intellectual control, and hence also potentially the basis of an objectivity beyond outside influences. It is therefore intriguing yet perfectly understandable that Riken should call his autonomous space "the kingdom of dreams"—*kashokoku*—a utopian land where the legendary Yellow Emperor is said in Chinese folklore to have freely played and sought wondrous adventure. As the sagely scholar and teacher within that kingdom, Riken referred to himself as its "king"—*kashokoku ō*—autonomous and free to dream in his utopian land as he pleased and wander in adventurous pursuit of his scholarly mission. The physical structure of that utopian space, his "castle," also bore the reinforcing name drawn from Taoist imagery of "heavenly bliss"—*Tenraku*. The scholar in complete control of his "kingdom of dreams" lives in the supreme mental state of inner peace, freedom, and profound joy—a blissful state apart and transcendent of social artificialities. It comes as no surprise that he would list the romantic Taoist philosopher Chuang-tzu, along with Confucius and Mencius, as among the three greatest writers of all time. Unlike any other thinker, he observed, Chuang-tzu possessed the gift of writing at once about the vast and expansive and the minute and delicate, incorporating the infinite and the sentient minutiae. Riken thought of Chuang-tzu in this regard as completely original and never again to be surpassed.[57]

The themes to be detected in Riken, of separation, objectivity, and intellectual control, all encased in the romantic metaphor of the "dream" and of the distant utopian "kingdom," tend to reaffirm the interpretation that Riken's Taoism had little to do with an escape into or a return to "nature" as an alternative to social reality. His underlying concerns are rational epistemology, controlling knowledge, seeking an autonomy essential to objectivity, and investigating things in terms of their truthfulness. In Riken, therefore, we do not witness a flight into nature. Nature remained for him as it had been for Goi—an objective universal order to be examined for its underlying "principle." His "escape" was within the city itself as he fabricated within this environment his "natural" autonomy. It is said that the six or so different places that he located his "kingdom" in Osaka were all in noisy commercial sections. Stirred by a restless spirit, Riken also moved his utopian kingdom frequently to protect his anonymity. Rejecting the idea of establishing a "fixed" school, Riken, in the words of Nishimura Tenshū, floated from one place to another as though in a "dream."[58] Dreams and "utopian" yearnings, as Hino Tatsuo has written about,[59] were important themes in eighteenth-century Edo popular culture, symbolizing the unknown, the mysterious, and the inexplicable. We see this, for example, in Ueda Akinari's famous *Ugetsu Monogatari* (1776) or in Tsuruya Nanboku's *Yotsuya kaidan* (1825), the chilling popular tale of aristocratic decline, treachery, and ghostly vengeance. Though Riken did not appreciate Ueda's writings about dreams and mystery, he shared with him and other contemporaries the fascination with the "dream," as can be discerned in the idealization of his own dreams within his "utopian kingdom." Yet, as he was steeped intellectually in the rational epistemology taught by Goi, his conception of the "dream" was not a mediation with the "unknown" or the "mysterious," but a conscious fabrication to define an autonomous space in an abstract manner within which he might pursue scholarly knowledge in the light of day. In this regard, his understanding of the dream did not deviate from that espoused by Goi and Chikuzan in their attack on popular superstitions and religions. The utopian metaphors employed by Riken established for him enclosed boundaries within which to "play"—to freely "observe" and seek knowledge. It allowed him a space where, to refer again to his own language, he could "cease to be," terminating one kind of existence and immerseing himself totally in another, which, being detached from a reality that he no longer "belonged" to, must therefore be seen as a distant "dream."

In his hideaway "kingdom of dreams," Riken devoted himself for more than forty years to the scholarly task of "encountering the original classical resources"—hōgen—which he used to entitle a series of key textual studies such as the Analects (Rongo hōgen), Mencius (Mōshi hōgen), and the Doctrine of the Mean (Chūyō hōgen).[60] In "encountering" and "interpreting" these texts Riken compiled some one hundred volumes of dense commentaries in which he imprinted the name of his scholarly approach to textual studies, Suisaigaku, a phrase drawn from Mencius suggesting the slow yet inevitable flow of the river's current beginning from the tiny wellspring to the vast sea, or some ultimate and truthful destiny. True to that image of persuasive momentum, Riken deliberately and meticulously pursued his personal aim of engaging with the original sources. He made clear his dedication to penetrate the ancient texts, disregarding physical needs and the deepening of age, and maintaining an "even spirit"— heishin. He would avoid the excesses of Ogyū Sorai, the complacency of the Hayashi school, the reckless approach of Yamazaki Ansai and his followers, and in general, discard the prejudices of the past. By approaching the original textual sources directly, he hoped thereby to transcend personal polemics and reach empirically unshakable conclusions.

As the historian of Chinese thought Takeuchi Yoshio (1886–1966) notes, the list of conclusions Riken drew were long and rendered "without regret" that much of what had been said by previous scholars about the classics was erroneous and required rethinking.[61] The Book of Changes was basically unreliable, as it lacked internal consistency and sections attributed to Confucius' commentary were spurious; The Book of Songs that attributes to Confucius the reworking of ancient poems is a fabricated story as these so-called "reworked" pieces existed long before Confucius, and whatever he might have selected to anthologize was destroyed with the burning of the books around 200 B.C.; The Book of History was substantially inauthentic, made up of totally unreliable additions of later eras; The Book of Rites was badly fragmented and unreliable as historical evidence; The Spring and Autumn Annals was not the work of Confucius as claimed, and the language about exercising power in the "autumnal" season of an empire cannot be attributed to him.

Quite aside from the authenticity of these sweeping conclusions, the verification of which is not our task here, there was, more importantly, polemical intent in them despite Riken's claim to even-spiritedness. The aforementioned texts that Riken discredited were, with the Analects added, those that Ogyū Sorai had identified as the crucial "six classics" to uncovering "the way of the ancient kings." In declaring them to be unreliable, Riken focused, in the end, on only three classics as authentic original "sources" the scholar should encounter in order to extract the moral foundations of the Confucian tradition: the *Analects*, *The Book of Mencius*, and the *Doctrine of the Mean*—the latter two being labeled by Ogyū to be polemical exaggerations and inferior to the others. Set forth in terms of these broad features, it becomes apparent that Riken's objectivity was also informed by an agenda. By approaching the original textual resources directly, he hoped to clarify once and for all to his satisfaction what the classics had to say about those issues as regards nature, virtue, and righteousness that had been subjects of such intense debate all through the late seventeenth and eighteenth centuries—a debate in which the revisionist historicist interpretations of Ogyū Sorai and, to a lesser extent for Riken, Itō Jinsai had occupied especially prominent positions. Riken, in short, was not an antiquarian but profoundly engaged in the discourse of his generation regarding the human capacity to make moral judgments and to assess and give meaning to social and historical reality, that is, "to know," morally, the character of empirical events. This project involved a deep commitment on his part to meet the challenge presented by historicists such as Ogyū to all scholars of the eighteenth century in terms of his own textual analysis and thus to encounter their challenge on their own grounds. And as his studies deepened over the years, Riken steadily moved toward the view that the moral concept of "accuracy" or of the "center" to be found in the *Doctrine of the Mean* was fundamental to moral epistemology in the Confucian tradition and, as we have emphasized throughout, also crucial to the ideology of the Kaitokudō.

Certain themes that suggest the working out of a basic philosophical position grounded in the classical texts repeat themselves frequently in Riken's dense commentaries. The parts may be summarized with the following points and elaborated on in the pages that follow: (1) a frank and, at times, what must have been to him, disturbing admission that the moral philosophers of Neo-Confucianism, Chu Hsi in particular, had indeed overinterpreted the ancient texts; (2) this meant that some of the precepts enunciated by the founders of the Kaitokudō required reappraisal, perhaps even the interpretive glosses advanced by Miyake Sekian, although Riken diplomatically does not refer to him by name; (3) while thus pointing out the errors in Neo-Confucianism Riken nonetheless made a sharp and firm distinction between his knowledge of the classics and Ogyū's historicism, a position of his that he pinned in the final analysis to a perception of the moral concept of the "mean"; and

(4) in staking his philosophical banner along that boundary, Riken articulated a moral philosophy for commoners consistent with the teachings at the Kaitokudō as he had received them from Goi.

With striking frequency, Riken scattered throughout his textual commentaries the conclusion that the philosophical ideas, grounded on ancient sources, advanced by Neo-Confucian scholars from the Sung Dynasty on were, virtually, in their entirety erroneous and deceptive and hence untenable as social morality.[62] Riken entered terse lines that repeatedly insisted that the ancient texts reveal nothing about the following concepts central to Neo-Confucian thought: "principle in nature"—shizen no ri; "exhausting principle through disciplined observation"—ri o kiwameru; the "inevitability of universal natural principle"—ri no tōzen; and, personally "realizing universal principle"—shiri. All of these philosophical concepts were "entirely at odds"—mina somuku—with the textual sources and throughout other texts as well. While the Sung Dynasty philosophers erected a vast philosophical construct based on these excessive interpretations, the ancient texts, in fact, contain precious little that even suggests abstract universal theory that might embrace the cosmos. For example, the Analects, the ultimate source of the Confucian tradition, is basically down-to-earth human morality. Indeed, the beauty and virtue that make it the greatest single source for moral ideas is precisely that the Analects is addressed to humanity and to concrete human concerns. It is "timeless" for this reason and not because it provides insights into the "timelessness of the universe." In Riken's eyes, then, ancient Confucian thought addressed itself exclusively to humankind—moppara hito o iu nari—and later Sung moral philosophers erred egregiously in confusing these insights in terms of cosmology.[63]

Specifically, Riken identified one of their key misinterpretations as being the rendering of the ancient ideograph "thing"—mono—to mean "nature," when in fact in the ancient passages, "thing means fact and does not refer to the ten thousand things in nature"—Mono nao koto nari; banbutsu o sasu ni arazu. And "fact" in this textual context is nothing other than "things" that people do. The primary philosophical significance of the classics was the emphasis given to "acting from within"—mizukara nasu—and "doing something" outside the self—mono o nasu. Action required "internal" moral awareness or "knowledge"—chi—and the externalization of that moral knowledge must inevitably be compassionate—jin. His summation goes as follows:

> The term thing [mono] is used to distinguish the self [onore] with reference to other individuals. It does not refer to nature, or even to

facts in general [but to specific acts] . . . The virtue of the moral
essence of human beings is compassionate intelligence [jin-chi] . . .
and these refer to the fulfillment of virtue through the realization of
truthfulness in objective acts. Thus is it said that moral essence is
based on truthfulness, which joins external action and internal
knowledge [gai-nai au].[64]

While human action may be judged in terms of its truthfulness—*sei* or
makoto—nature cannot be judged according to that human norm. When
the ideographs for "The Way of Heaven and Earth"—*Tenchi no Michi*—
are used, the reference is indeed to the universal natural order. However,
in these passages, Riken went on to observe, the moral concept of "truthfulness" is not used—*mata makoto no ji nashi.* Being exhaustive and infinite—*kiwamari nashi*—nature was viewed with reverence by the ancients but not looked upon as a moral norm for human action.[65]

Finding the Neo-Confucian perspective in the ancient texts as regards
nature to be deeply flawed, Riken felt compelled to qualify some of the
sweeping assertions as to universal human goodness. What results is a
critical revision of a view regarding human nature that had been incorporated into the teachings of the Kaitokudō beginning with Miyake Sekian,
although it is important to observe that as Riken went through this exercise, he also retained certain essential points of that early instruction as
well. Miyake Sekian, it will be recalled, organized his opening lecture on
the *Analects* and *The Book of Mencius* to enunciate, within the Neo-
Confucian frame of reference, the philosophy of the natural and innate
goodness of human beings so that merchants identifying with this sagely
goodness could progress to become men of virtue. Relying on the opening
lines of the *Analects* on "studying and learning," Miyake had defined the
purpose of "study"—*manabu*—as being "to learn"—*narau*—about the
"human way"—*ningen no michi*—and gain deep satisfaction thereby. Although Riken did not address himself directly to Miyake, as his critique
was pointed toward the Neo-Confucian position, he did, in fact, depart
significantly from the founding teacher of the Kaitokudō.

Confucius's language on studying and learning being deeply joyous—
mata yorokobashikarazu ya—Riken tersely commented, says nothing about
human beings possessing innate goodness at birth to which one identifies
and then proceeds forward toward greater moral awareness. All it says is
that "to study" and "to learn" are distinguishable items in the sense that
the former speaks to the acquisition of knowledge possessed by others
from whom one might get direction—*shidō*—as in studying the moral
precepts of the sages. To study, in short, involves the examination of a
specific and definable object. In the case of the latter, "to learn," ac-

quired knowledge at whatever level of sophistication is translated in a direct and immediate way into action in a particular context. The real import of Confucius's language on studying and learning, therefore, had nothing to do with the universality of human goodness. It taught that some may study but never learn, insofar as learning involves acting out knowledge, and that, therefore, how "joyful" it was to be engaged, at times, in the act of learning. In this interpretation, "learning" is in time, in the continuing present, and does not involve exhaustive or lengthy scholarly meditative preparation. Riken detected in Confucius's language the possibility of studying a great deal and learning little and denied the accumulation of knowledge through "studies" as the source of joy but weighted his view on the egalitarian concept that however little one may in fact know, there was profound joy in realizing knowledge in one's actions. It was in bending Confucianism from elitist scholasticism to a philosophy of humankind that Riken's thinking retained sympathetic links with Miyake Sekian, for both in the end saw Confucius as the articulator of moral thought appropriate to all commoners. But in Riken, the proposition of universal goodness based on natural philosophy was deleted as being unwarranted in light of the language in the text itself.[66]

Riken's interpretation of another statement by Miyake reveals a similar discrepancy. In this line Confucius is recorded to have said that when friends call from afar, it is truly a source of great pleasure—*Tomo enpō yori kitaru araba. Mata tanoshikarazu ya.* Following Neo-Confucian glosses, Miyake had interpreted that line to mean as human beings were universally alike in their fundamental essence, human beings close by and afar being of the same "category"—*dōrui*—of things, it was deeply satisfying when one could relate to strangers visiting from afar as "friends" in terms of their common virtue. To realize that a stranger is a friend thus confirms the basic principle of the universality of human existence.

Riken disregarded that interpretation, offering instead an alternative view that reflected his own eccentric perspective into his surroundings. What Confucius meant by that line, Riken offered, was that friends who called from afar usually had a *purpose* for doing so and thus were a source of much stimulation and pleasure. By comparison, those living nearby could not provide intellectual satisfaction as they were moved by the habits and conventions of routine requirements. The image of a friend calling from afar was used to characterize that point. "It should be known," Riken thus noted, "that people close by have nothing provocative to say." Familiarity, in short produces routinized relationships and the intellectual edge in conversations disappears, whereas a visitor uses his time differently, engaging in discussion and debate before having to depart. Thus the "pleasure." Riken offered another possible interpretation: in his old age Confucius who was known to have called his students "friends"—*tomo*—lamented the fact that as these friends passed away they could no longer return to visit him; thus when a "friend" did manage after long years to call he was moved to remarking how deeply pleased he was with the reunion. And thus, Riken noted, Confucius said the following in a related passage: "When friends pass away and no longer visit, I say treasure them within yourself"—*Hōyū shishite kisuru tokoro nakereba. Iwaku ware ni oite hin seyo.*[67] Regardless, neither interpretation resembles the use Miyake made of it referring to human beings near and far belonging to a universal category defined by an internally consistent virtue. Indeed, in Riken's former, and probably preferred, interpretation, distance *does* in fact matter, as closeness produces only predictable boredom—a view that reinforced his own personal choice of an abstractly conceived "kingdom of dreams" to establish between himself and the social universe around him.

It is hardly startling, given the previous examples, that Riken's summation of the introductory section of the *Analects*, upon which Miyake based his lecture, should similarly be strikingly different. Miyake had used that section to undergird a related set of philosophical propositions regarding human nature, the study and practice of virtue, and the universality of the human essence, "being a sage fully this day and then thus instructing his students on the basis of these precepts of becoming one again the next." Riken's summary leaves little doubt that he did not believe that a comprehensive and internally consistent philosophy could be extracted from these early lines of the *Analects*. The terms were imprecise. While interpretations could be made of such concepts as "studying" and "learning," their meanings were hardly explicit and conclusive propositions could not be made. Most of all, however, ideas advanced by the Sung philosophers were drastically off the mark and should not be relied upon, among them being that deep human satisfaction results from strenuous scholarly and meditative effort—*kufū*; that the "prince" does not involve himself personally unless there is such deep satisfaction or joy; and that the realization of this highly special pleasure is a superior human achievement. Riken denounced all of these speculative insights in his summary, not simply because they were misinterpretations but because there was no logical relationship to the original language whatsoever, thus making it nothing more than foolhardy and drunken chatter.[68]

Riken's interpretive slant on the ancient sources can be seen in his reading of *The Book of Mencius* as well. Based on the opening lines of that classic, Miyake, again drawing on Sung commentaries, had advanced the

provocative idea that the concept of "advantage" or "profit" was not op-
probrious as long as it was in accord with the norm of "righteousness,"
this latter being, along with compassion, innate to the "basic spirit"—
honshin—of all human beings. While "profit" was arbitrary and shortsighted, Miyake had lectured, righteousness was accurate, fair, and just;
and then he continued to say that if one were "righteous," profit would
accrue without effort, shorn of the negative implications of passionate
greed. Each individual must therefore constantly and strenuously exert
himself to assure that righteousness reigns over passionate whim. Riken,
while not denying that judgments of external events could be fair or accurate, and while agreeing with the basic point to be found in *The Book
of Mencius* that human beings all possessed an intuitive capacity for goodness as expressed in compassion and righteousness, denied that this idea
suggested an essential coherency with the natural universe in its ultimate
sense and further objected to the use of these moral concepts to assimi-
late the human quest for "profit." "How embarrassing," Riken noted,
"that our previous moral teachers [sentetsu] should have expressed such
a view."[69]

Riken was not inclined to mask his impatience with Neo-Confucian
interpretations of ancient texts as he presented views reminiscent of Itō
Jinsai and Ogyū Sorai. Relying on a method of textual analysis similar
to these great scholars, he uncovered some of the same flaws in Neo-
Confucian philosophy that his predecessors had. Riken, however, steered
his scholarship on a course he defended as being an independent one,
distinguishing himself from Itō despite his sympathy with some of his ideas
and distancing himself especially from Ogyū. While Ogyū had turned his
historical theories to confirm the idea of the talented few governing the
land in accordance with the norm of the ancient kings that only that
elite could fully grasp, Riken held to the broad proposition that commoners possessed the capacity to know moral knowledge and that this
was not the privilege of the few, thus remaining firmly within the pedagogical tradition formulated at the Kaitokudō and, before that, by Itō
himself, who had shaped a general moral philosophy of goodness inclusive of commoners.

Riken agreed with Itō that *The Book of Mencius* was indeed a classic of
great importance in its affirmation of the human capacity toward realizing
goodness. Stripped of the metaphysical glosses which were imposed on it
by later Neo-Confucian scholars with ideas drawn mainly from Zen Buddhism in his view, it should be encountered as a moral resource by all
scholars. Minus the interpretive excesses of later metaphysicians, Riken
viewed the *Analects* in a similarly appreciative light as did Itō, indeed

agreeing with him on it being the greatest moral text in all of human history. Riken also agreed with Itō that the classic *Great Learning* offered little of intellectual merit, as evidenced in Riken's case by a slim volume of "miscellaneous" comments. However, he disagreed with Itō on the virtue of the *Doctrine of the Mean*, one of the "Four Books" along with the previous three mentioned here, which scholars traditionally claimed to be central to Confucian moral thought. Itō claimed for *The Book of Mencius* the fundamental perspective into the ultimate meaning of the *Analects* and determined the *Doctrine of the Mean* to be internally inconsistent and unreliable as a moral text. Of the thirty-two some odd sections, the second half in Itō's reading did not follow the first, and while portions in the earlier half seemed consistent, the authorship was suspect and probably not attributable to the sage Tzu Ssu alone.[70]

Undaunted by this judgment of the great scholar Itō Jinsai, Riken proceeded to claim that the *Doctrine of the Mean* offered perhaps the most central insight into the *Analects* and hence ought to be appreciated as fundamental to Confucian moral thought.[71] The inconsistencies in the arrangement of sections, he claimed, were errors made by later editors, thus conveying the sense of discrepancy between the earlier and later segments. By rearranging the sections, such as by placing the twenty-fourth immediately after the sixteenth, Riken claimed the text emerged as a consistent whole. In fact, however, neither the lack of symmetry in the overall sequence nor the probability of multiple authorship seemed to bother Riken very much at all. He focused instead on what he saw to be the internal underlying consistency in the text, which he identified as the epistemological concept of "truthfulness" with which human beings "chose" the "mean" as an exercise of "reason." He saw in that text the ultimate moral confirmation of his conviction that commoners possessed the capacity "to know" and hence also "to judge." While Mencius had shaped a key insight into the *Analects* by clarifying that human beings in general, regardless of class, could intuit goodness and act inevitably in ways that were compassionate, Riken was persuaded that the *Doctrine of the Mean* offered an alternative and, in his view, more powerful insight, namely judgmental reason as a universal human possession. Analogous to the human tendency to do good, the exercise of reason was also inevitable and spontaneous and it resulted in choices that could be judged in terms of their relative proximity to the "mean."

Now it would appear that in this emphasis on rational epistemology as a property of all human beings, Riken's main polemical target was not Itō but Ogyū Sorai and the scholarly tradition that stemmed from him. Ogyū had denied the subjective dimension of moral virtue, claiming the self to be passionate and incapable of generating general moral choice and that, this being the case, human beings had as their only recourse, if they did not wish to live in chaos, the reliance on totally external norms that must be identified with the social intent of the ancient kings when they first created history. It was from this basic premise that Ogyū proceeded to deemphasize the importance of the major Confucian texts. While conceding the *Analects* to be important, he detracted from it by denying Confucius was an original thinker as he had merely edited the received wisdom traceable ultimately to the ancient kings. His comments on *Mencius* were even less kind as may be recalled. And as for the *Doctrine of the Mean*, he had rejected it as simply a rhetorical and polemical defense of Confucius. As he outlined in the opening passages of his treatise of the "way"—*Bendō*—the *Doctrine of the Mean* was a critique directed against Taoists who had said that Confucianism was artificial and that Confucius himself was not an important sage. As it was used with *ad hominem* intent to defend Confucius, the idea of the "mean" could not serve Ogyū as a stable norm to rely on. Precisely because it lacked such stability, it was said to be "chosen"—*yue ni erabu to iu*. Being an unstable point between two equally unstable extremes, the "mean" is in effect arbitrarily set by subjective choice—by which Ogyū meant passionate preference. A norm, on the other hand, could not be something one chose but upon which one had no choice but to rely. The "mean" could not serve as such a norm since it was always relative to something else.[72]

Riken's response to this overall reading was measured and scholarly, as he scrupulously avoided turning his commentaries into an argumentative diatribe against Ogyū that would surely have diminished the value of his scholarly project. Thus, quite unlike Chikuzan's vehement outburst, Riken set out dispassionately to achieve a comparable aim of discrediting Ogyū's perception of human moral epistemology and proposing his particular interpretive slant into the *Doctrine of the Mean*. The textual bases from which Ogyū shaped his operating premise, "rites," "history," and "songs," Riken rejected out of hand as spurious and inauthentic and virtually devoid of moral ideas identified with Confucianism. But more importantly, Riken's position on the text on the "mean" was diametrically opposed to Ogyū's. The language in the text that says men "choose" an objective "mean" should not be taken to signify that the mean is therefore relative and unreliable. It points instead to the proposition that individual human beings are active and knowing moral agents. The contention that the individual self makes moral choices based on knowledge does not reduce moral acts from within as totally arbitrary. The idea that "norm" by definition must be externally fixed, unshakably permanent, and hence totally beyond the realm of the exercise of human choice is to misconstrue the fundamental importance of the individual quest for moral knowledge in ancient Confucian thought. Riken's interpretive grasp of the entire text was based on those presuppositions and, in particular, on the human capacity to acquire moral knowledge through the exercise of "choice." The "mean," Riken therefore argued, was to be understood as the conscious human selection of the "center"—*naka o toru.*[73] While this idea was present in Confucius's own thinking, it was so only in an implicit manner as Confucius himself focused most prominently on the ethic of "benevolence." It was only with the *Doctrine of the Mean* that the concept of active moral choice on the part of the individual was persuasively put into focus, constituting in this sense an innovative and creative insight into Confucius's moral thinking. Riken offered two related themes to reinforce his overall thesis: one was the inherent intellectual potential of all human beings; the second was the crucial significance of the moral guideline of "truthfulness" in unifying inner subjective intent and external forms of knowledge and action.

For the concept of the "mean" to be philosophically viable, the individual self must be an active, cognizing agent and not merely a passive recipient of external norm. Acutely aware of this problem, as was Chikuzan, Riken repeatedly affirmed the universal human capacity to know things in general and moral knowledge in particular. The source of that capacity he defined as a transnatural endowment from Heaven—*Tenmei*—a gift specific to human beings and not to be confused with the organizing principle—*ri*—of the natural order. How men organized knowledge was distinct from the way nature ran its course and was to be understood exclusively in terms of the human way—*jindō, jinri.* Riken repeatedly emphasized that Confucian moral thought from its inception was oriented toward virtues close to the human self. When Confucius spoke of "intelligence" or "benevolence" or "courage"—*chi, jin, yū*—he discussed them with reference to the concrete human way and not as they reflected the underlying forces of nature. Nor should that epistemological power be confused with individual characteristics—*katagi*—personal traits that one might inherit from parents and which are infinitely variable. That special gift Riken emphasized was the universal capacity of human beings to know from within—*ware kore o shiru*—through observation and, in his words, "mental discrimination"—*gakumon shiben.* It is this internal capacity to know that gives significance to the idea of a "mean" as an object, target, or norm, to "choose."

The real issue for Riken, then, was not so much whether the "mean" was always absolute as an external norm, or that the choices of men were

200

always perfect, but that they were never totally arbitrary. The very act of choice itself must include "mental discrimination." It is only when the individual surrenders this capacity that choices become arbitrary as they are not choices at all in the reasoned sense which would thus also render the philosophical idea of the "mean" to be untenable.[74]

Riken added to his theory of epistomology the moral guideline of "truthfulness"—*sei* or *makoto*. Here again Riken stressed the freshness of treatment of this concept in the *Doctrine of the Mean*, as it did not have a great deal of prominence in previous classical texts:

> In ancient times the term of truthfulness was not used at all. The principle underlying the Way was therefore rarely discussed. This is verified by examining the *Analects* or other classics such as on *Song*, *History*, and *Changes*. It became a substantial concept, however, with Tzu Ssu's *Doctrine of the Mean*. There is no other work as discriminating as this one. Those who wish not to distort the history of the ancients should take note that the idea was not handed down directly from Confucius' personal school.[75]

Riken's basic understanding of "truthfulness" is easy enough to extract from his commentaries. It meant accuracy, striking the mark without prejudice—*hen nashi*—and as the well-known phraseology had it, being neither excessive nor insufficient—*sugizaru wa oyobazaru ga gotoshi*. The underlying concept in these conventional phrases is discrimination. One does not simply act, but rather *chooses*. Discrimination, however, does not imply long and strenuous preparation, as in disciplined scholarship or meditation, but the exercise of one's inherent knowledge acquiring potential. "One who is truthful," he thus wrote, "strikes the mark without strenuous preparation, without deep reflection. One who is truthful simply chooses goodness and holds firmly to it"—*zen o erabite kataku kore o toru mono nari*.[76] There is the suggestion of an effortlessness in making moral choices, although quite assuredly Riken remained firmly attached to the idea that the "mark" or "center" was always in a field of verifiable facts and not intuitively derived or metaphysically determined.

Of vital significance to Riken, the idea of truthfulness served as a philosophical norm—*junsoku*—to integrate the *internal* acquisition and the *external* manifestation of knowledge. The relationship between knowledge and action, inner virtue and externally documented norm, and more generally, the entire range of issues related to the potential contradiction between subject and object posed Riken with a dilemma to which he was deeply sensitive. In his words, "A benevolent person is invariably courageous, but one who acts courageously is not necessarily benevolent";

and similarly, "One who is virtuous has words of advice to offer others but one who speaks is not necessarily virtuous."[77] Through the concept of truthfulness, Riken argued, the *Doctrine of the Mean* offered the philosophical resolution to this discrepancy that Confucius had warned about. In Riken's critique, Confucius had relied on two separate ideographs—*chū* and *shin*—which he linked in a compound to mean "sincerity within and trustworthiness without" to describe the relationship between inner and outer moral spheres. Because two separate ideographic concepts were utilized, a sense of separation between inner and outer was inevitable, as between inner faith, which might be a purely personal matter, and trust among men in an external set of relationships.

The sage Tzu Ssu, in Riken's evaluation, had located in this philosophical problem one of the key difficulties in Confucius's moral thought and introduced the *single* ideographic concept of "truthfulness"—*sei*—that would embrace both inner moral intent and reliable action without. With that concept, it had then become entirely inconsistent to separate inner and outer as distinct moral spheres, so that filial behavior that was not "truthful" could not be said to be filial at all. Inner intent and observable act must be consistent. Moral concepts such as "honesty" or "sincerity" that might be thought of philosophically as oriented inwardly must not, within Tzu Ssu's insight, inform all external actions within any human context. By bridging the gap between inner and outer within a single philosophical idea—*masa ni bunretsu haizoku sezu*—Tzu Ssu had provided the *Mean* with perhaps the most profound insight into the *Analects* and generally strengthened the moral foundations of Confucius's teachings. Thus, while it is accurate to say that the basic meaning of truthfulness was to be located in Confucius's moral concept of faith within and trust without, in Riken's eyes, Tzu Ssu had illuminated the problem in such a profound manner that it was distinctive with him. Unlike any other ancient sage, he had integrated into a moral whole such diverse actions as studying (*gaku*), questioning (*mon*), reflecting (*shi*), discriminating (*ben*), and acting (*gyō*).[78]

Of particular importance to Riken, all intentional acts willed from within—*mizukara*—as "to kill" or "to pass judgment" must be seen as inseparable from external fact. "There can be no division between within and without in human speech and action," a pronouncement he illustrated with metaphors drawn from ordinary life of the human dislike of foul odor or the attraction to exquisite things in which inner and outer were always in total accord—*sono naigai mukan o satoru nomi*. And since this realization of union between inner and outer is known to ordinary human beings from their daily experiences, it most assuredly ought not be thought of as a state of enlightenment that might be achieved out of the intensive self-identification with an abstract and absolute moral principle of the universe. It also further meant, therefore, that the act of relying on the self—*onore ni yoru*—to select moral ideas was a unified and cohesive act and not a bifurcated one as some thinkers, notably Ogyū Sorai, had theorized.[79]

As is evident, Riken had, to a large degree, reformulated the idea of "inner sincerity" to mean epistemological and judgmental capacity, as in knowing what is goodness as articulated by the ancient sages or in judging what is close to or wide of the mark. Although Riken used this conceptual strategy to repudiate the views of idealists in the tradition of the Ōyōmei school of thought that emphasized the comprehension of an abstract universal idea through introspection and found thinkers in this tradition as being involved in mere "verbal sophistry"—*moji mawashi*—it was more fundamentally the empiricist thinking of Ogyū Sorai that concerned him.[80] In Ogyū's scheme of thought, as previously noted, inner and outer realms of knowledge constituted a fault line that the idea of the "mean" could not mend, as the mean was simply a subjective and arbitrary determination. Riken's philosophical proposition that the human self possessed a capacity to know not simply one's own "little virtue" but to discriminate and choose among external things including documented moral concepts constitutes a direct rejection of Ogyū's position.

To deny the individual the inner capacity to know goodness and to judge reliable action, Riken argued consistently, as Goi and Chikuzan had also in their critique of Ogyū, was to demean ordinary human beings by denying them the intelligence to know moral knowledge and relegating them to a totally dependent relationship with externally formulated norms presumably grounded in a virtually unrecognizable historical past. While some of these norms may indeed be fundamental Riken rejected the view that human beings could not grasp their meaning in a universal sense. Men did possess such an intellectual capacity and hence made choices and abided by them, which is the force of meaning embedded in the phrase: *zen o erabite kataku kore o toru*. Seen in this perspective, the underlying "intent" in Riken's painstaking "encounter" with the textual sources can hardly be called an exercise in antiquarianism, but a systematic scholarly attempt at articulating the claims long held to be *sine qua non* to commoner education at the Kaitokudō, that ordinary human beings indeed possessed the intrinsic capability to acquire moral and secular knowledge and hence also to act in ways that could be judged as trustworthy and righteous.

That Riken took strong exception to the use of Confucianism to reinforce the supremacy of the aristocracy is readily apparent in certain key interpretations he chose to make. A well-known set of lines in the *Analects* suggest that those above the median line in society—*chūjin ijō*—should address themselves to those above while those below that line—*chūjin ika*—should refrain from doing so. The usual instruction drawn from this passage was that only those in the upper levels of society should involve themselves with advising those on high while commoners should not since, being lowly, they lacked the appropriate knowledge to do so. Riken challenged that interpretation on the ground that the verb "should not," as in commoners "should not" advise those on high, was an inappropriate reading and that it meant rather "cannot"—*fuka*—or even "forbidden from"—*kinji*. The line should more properly be understood to mean that those below the median line, referring to commoners in general, do have appropriate knowledge and do speak but "cannot" be heard or alternatively are "forbidden" from communicating with those on high. The emotive drive of that passage, Riken thus reasoned, was not that commoners are ignorant and should not speak, but *how lamentable it was* that their voices could not be heard. The interpretation rendered by Sung philosophers that Confucius had thus meant that commoners should study diligently and advance upward beyond the "median line" in order to be heard was to Riken, a completely fanciful misreading of the text. Riken's argument that commoners indeed possessed the capacity to know, judge, and speak, it should be emphasized, contained long-term political significance especially as it was rigorously consistent with the rest of Kaitokudō thinking that endorsed ordinary human beings acquiring moral knowledge without regard to questions of status and hierarchy.[81]

Riken's impatience with the elitist view of Confucianism can be discerned in the following example as well. He objected strenuously to the reading of the opening passages of the *Great Learning* to mean that the ordering of "self," "house," and "nation" would result from intense and disciplined scholarly effort, an effort, moreover, that was said to involve the prolonged observation of nature. After gaining deep insight into the self and the universe from these exercises, it was proposed, one then gained clear understanding of self, society, and government. Riken flatly denied any grounding in the text for such an abstract philosophy relating "nature" and "governance." On the contrary, the entire orientation of the *Great Learning* was its focus on the mundane and stress that "grand" knowledge was not in the distant and abstract cosmos but in the immediate and close at hand. The idea of "observing things" as set forth in that text, therefore, did not constitute a prescription for prolonged study, but the commonsensical idea of ordinary human beings relying on the natural characteristics of particular objects with which they happened to be working; and the suggestion that this engagement should be done intently is simply to emphasize the importance of care and accuracy involved in it. Thus, for example, a farmer works with nature by calculating its regularities, the time of day, the seasons. And similarly, through practical "observation" one learns that a bridle works with a horse but not a cow. Nature cannot be altered completely into something that it is not, however much human beings may wish it to be so. Now it is this simple idea that things cannot be bent and distorted by the human will beyond certain "natural" limits that, if properly understood, then serves as a lesson on governing the self and others: One ought not regulate the self in terms of what he is not; and similarly the king and those on high ought not govern according to what the people are incapable of achieving. The suggestion, however, that all human beings, commoners and aristocracy alike, must engage in exhaustive and disciplined study of nature and the universe to gain moral self awareness was a severe distortion of the textual source.[82]

We may interpret this tendency noted in Riken's criticism along with his denial of a philosophical separation between inner and outer—*naigai mukan*—as being strategies to affirm the capacity of commoners to acquire moral knowledge. Knowledge was not to be gained with prolonged, strenuous, and anxiety-ridden exercises in order to "overcome" the perceived discrepancy between subject and object, interior self and external things, as taught in Neo-Confucian philosophy. Nor was it valid for Ogyū Sorai to say that since the subjective self was infinite in variety it could not be a source of general moral knowledge and that the bulk of society therefore ought to rely on externally given norms and not be taught about their inner meaning—*shirashimubekarazu*. Riken saw these exclusivist interpretations of Confucian moral thought that denied commoners their active intelligence regarding general moral problems as intellectually repugnant. Thus, although hardly a "populist," Riken's philosophical position rested decidedly with the cause of the commoners in his society. Focusing on the issue of epistemology rather than on the idea of spontaneous compassion that Itō Jinsai had, Riken provided reinforcing scholarly endorsement to human beings universally possessing the intelligence to shape moral purpose from within and to choose a proper moral mark or center without. It was a vastly more sophisticated scholarly variant of the concept of accuracy or "righteousness" than had been taught at the Kaitokudō to merchant audiences at its inception.

Riken's thinking bore a coherent relationship with the historicist ideas of the merchant scholar Tominaga Nakamoto who had also concluded that ordinary human beings possessed a commonsense intelligence to know the "truthfulness" of human events. While it is of course true that Tominaga did not anchor his existential ethic in a classical text, as he thought them all to be unreliable, he too had advanced the idea that being reasonably true to the mark was the key to ethical existence, not trying to identify action with religious and philosophical abstractions. Despite Riken's positive reading of the ancient text, the *Doctrine of the Mean*, that Tominaga would not have accepted, both shared a related understanding of the concept of "truthfulness" as a universal human possession and from this point of view rejected the idea of prolonged scholarly training as a prerequisite to moral knowledge. They may be seen therefore as being in a discursive relationship with each other, as well as with Itō Jinsai, in orienting their scholarly ideas to the formulation of moral philosophies appropriate to commoners.

Riken's thinking differed from Itō and Tominaga, however, in one very important respect. His ideas contained in them an unmistakably "political" significance in a way that was not apparent in his predecessors. Riken's retreat into his "kingdom of dreams," after all, was an active choice, and it colored his scholarly findings in interesting ways. His accusation that scholars had erroneously separated inner and outer, and had created a needless sense of distance between high and low, carried political meaning. Confucian scholars, he believed, should not deal with an "outer" world that was inconsistent with "inner" moral knowledge. They should discard the mistaken, and ultimately immoral, idea that commoners below "ought not be taught" because of the futility of it and, instead, side with them as they could not be heard by those on "high." Riken's political concern, therefore, was quite distinct from Ogyū's focus on governance by those with exceptional talent who would bring peace and well-being to society. Whereas the critical thrust of Ogyū's thinking had been that much in the present should be changed so that the norm of benevolence of the ancient kings could become a reality in the present, Riken utilized the theory of rational epistemology and the disjunction between inner and outer to assess his own history, the distant as well as the recent past, as it continued through his own times. He utilized, in sum, the moral concept of "truthfulness" to shape a critical perspective into history and politics, giving full credence to the view that his historicism, far from being an antiquarian immersion in ancient philology to show textual authenticity was, in fact, part and parcel with an effort at understanding his own present. Indeed, following his own prescription that the inner capacity to gain knowledge involved the ability to judge,

Riken judged his own history, pointing to its failings; and, in his utopian kingdom where he was free to think the unthinkable, he dreamed, as Itō and Tominaga had not done, of the dissolution of the political world around him.

The accurate evaluation of history precluded for Riken the reliance on two widely utilized approaches: one being the beautification of the ancient origins of Japan by scholars of national studies; the other being the misrepresentation through idealization of more recent political history. Regarding the former, Riken criticized as totally untenable the efforts of scholars such as Motoori Norinaga of national studies to mystify in religious terms the birth of Japanese civilization. Their depiction of the ancient Japanese people living in harmony within the comforting embrace of nature all under the benevolent rule of the early emperors was entirely fallacious and deceptive in the extreme. Equally absurd is the assertion that the monarch ruled "naturally" without providing moral instruction to the people—*oshiezu shite kuni onozukara osamaru to iu*. That beginning, Riken argued, was anything but beautiful, being in fact primitive, uncivilized, devoid of written communications. Even after language and law were introduced from China in the sixth and seventh centuries, he went on, it was not humane Confucianism that was made to prevail but rather harsh governance based on "legalism." Far from being harmonious and natural, conditions under those so-called great ancient emperors were, in fact, quite wretched and filled with treacherous rebellions, assassinations, and ambitious coups. Where, he asked indignantly, are the historical evidences that say otherwise: *nani shōko to shite iu ni ya aran.* Thus Riken had nothing praiseworthy to say of the pivotal figure in the shaping of this romantic historicism: "Motoori is a deeply ambitious and deceptive person, as he seeks to create a religion with mystical arguments. To him everything foreign is bad and things of Japan good. . . . Now this is being dishonest."[83]

The failing could be traced, according to Riken, to a blindness to the fact that virtually every nation had a sacred myth about its beginning, invariably identified with a divine source in heaven. Whether the country in question was India or any of the lands of the "red beards" the same could be said. The conclusion to be drawn from this general truism, therefore, was not that Japan was unique in having a sacred myth about its beginning, but precisely the opposite—that such a myth had nothing to do actually with uniqueness or superiority since that myth was merely part of customary folklore and unrelated to objective happenings. Thus, although Riken, like his mentor Goi, retained a deep fondness for Japanese literature and often wrote essays in the native literary style, he took a dim view of romantic national studies as mythmaking and distractive of the goal of objectively evaluating history.[84]

Also to be avoided, along with the above, was the glorification of the more recent past. Here the issue was not so much the absence of reliable evidence but the self-conscious interpretations imposed on generally available facts to glorify certain well-known political happenings. Like most scholars of his day, Riken viewed the tenth through the fifteenth centuries to be politically crucial in shaping the comprehensive tradition of noncentralized governance, or *hōken*. It was during this era that the aristocracy of the sword came to maintain its irresistible control over the political fate of the country, and conversely, the imperial court underwent steady decline to a level of inconsequentiality in governing the land. Aside from an abortive attempt at restoring imperial authority in the fourteenth century, the history of the court over that period was bleak and inglorious. Although previous scholars, notably Arai Hakuseki and Dazai Shundai, had explained the rise of the samurai aristocracy and the decline of the imperial courts as an inexorable and inevitable movement in history without relation to the moral failings of one side or the other, therefore vindicating the rise of the samurai class and the founder of the existing order Tokugawa Ieyasu (1542–1616) along with it, Riken found this view, which prevailed among the aristocracy, to be superficial and unacceptable.

In his survey of that historical era called *Tsūgo* (written sometime in the 1760s and published later by his students in 1832 and 1843), Riken presented the rise of the military aristocracy in terms of repeated acts of treachery and disloyalty or the total disjunction between moral awareness and outward action. Underlying all of the major events surrounding the founding of the Kamakura Bakufu in the mid-twelfth century, for example, was the repeated flounting of legal and moral relationships, as between ruler and minister, in one treasonous act followed by another. The so-called heroic contestants for power, Taira Kiyomori (1118–81) and Minamoto Yoritomo (1147–99), were nothing more than ambitious traitors. They were not granted office through imperial grace—they took it through intimidation. The political history of these centuries, moreover, clearly demonstrates the inability of rulers to maintain the confidence of the people. Holding it momentarily, they all, without exception, failed to provide benevolent rule—*jinsei*—and thus lost the support of the populace at large.[85]

Although Riken did not take his account into the sixteenth century to examine the rise of Tokugawa Ieyasu, the interpretive implications of his historical overview made it plain that he saw Ieyasu as one in a line of military rebels who won in a contest of arms and established his legitimacy after the fact by threatening the use of superior military power. His purpose in seizing power, moreover, was not to provide "justice" or "benevolent rule" for the people. It would follow that, in time, his regime too would lose the spiritual support of the general populace. It already had lost Riken's as indicated in his declaration of not belonging to the present. This negative reading of recent political history placed him at odds with Chikuzan who, as noted earlier, had written a laudatory account of the rise of the Tokugawa House and about which he, Riken, had been deeply disturbed.

Riken's overview of history situated him much more closely with the interpretation advanced by loyalists of the 1760s, such as Takeuchi Shikibu (1713–67), who had taught court nobles in Kyoto on the virtue of an "imperial restoration," and Yamagata Daini (1725–67), who had sketched out, as a teacher in Edo, a regionally based strategy of rebellion against the Tokugawa center. Based on a view of history similar to Riken's, they argued the failure of political justice due to the illegitimate character of the Tokugawa regime. In what came to be known as the "Meiwa Incident," Yamagata Daini was tried and executed while Takeuchi was sent into exile where he died under torture. Quite aside from whether a discernible "influence" can actually be traced, it is worth noting that it was during these very same years that Riken penned his historical account from which he later taught within the confines of his secluded kingdom. It was also during these years that Riken had begun his reading of Mito's "Great History of Japan"—*Dai Nihon shi*—which was also a major source for "loyalist" ideas. When Riken's work was finally published, the interpretive view he had advanced had begun to gain wide currency among the politically articulate, mainly through Rai Sanyō's elegantly crafted "General Outline of Japanese History"—*Nihon gaishi*—perhaps the single most influential work offering a critical historical perspective in late Tokugawa. It was from Riken, however, that Rai, during his many visits to Osaka, is said to have extracted the basic thesis for his work.[86]

Although Riken did not turn his sense of dissonance between inner moral knowledge and external reality into radical activism of the sort advocated by Yamagata Daini or by loyalists during the last two decades of the Tokugawa era, he nonetheless shared with them a "loyalist" discontent with the course of events, which, in turn, he saw as integral with a larger piece of history covering some five hundred years. Aware of the discordance between inner moral conviction and political failings without, Riken severed all formal involvement with that external world and chose a life of seclusion over accommodation with it.

He refused all invitations to advise domainal lords on moral questions or the state of the economy. He also openly expressed his contempt for Chikuzan's friends who did such work regularly for lucrative pay: "At our home," he once sarcastically told Shibano Ritsuzan, "we get by just with what we need"—*waga kakei ni wa kore nite tareri*—after which Shibano is said to have left abruptly without comment. On another occasion he was reported to have conveyed this message to Bitō Nishū: "If I were in Edo, I'd tell Bitō 'scholarship gets better even after the age of eighty.' Tell him that!" This outburst late in his life was with reference to the pride he felt in his work yet to come and to the decline in imaginative scholarly work among Bitō and his friends who had ensconced themselves within the Bakufu. When these friends of Chikuzan held poetry gatherings in Osaka to discuss obscure ancient poetry at the Kontonsha, Riken, although invariably invited, always refused, calling those sessions intellectually foolish and naive. Then there was his much talked about refusal to meet with Matsudaira Sadanobu during the latter's visit to Osaka. Riken left Sadanobu's invitation unanswered, refused to appear at the appointed time, and when a personal aide was sent to accompany him to Sadanobu, Riken escaped through the back of his residence and went into hiding at a student's home. Although Riken later denied having any personal animosity toward Sadanobu—noting that he found his poetry to be quite excellent—it was nonetheless evident that he preferred not to interact with an official of the order from which he had already distanced himself. Hearing of this incident, Koga Seiri remarked that Riken was an "unusual person"—*ijin*—which could mean outstanding but more likely meant in this context bizarre or eccentric. In another related incident, a scholar employed by the Bakufu (one Kōbo Kiichi) requested an audience with Riken through the Osaka magistracy to discuss Riken's ideas on literature. Again the request went unanswered and when a personal messenger from the magistrate's office called on him, he had conveniently absented himself, leaving the messenger waiting in vain late into the evening.[87]

Riken's fierce defense of his world of seclusion was well known in Osaka. The sign at the entranceway of his apartment did not welcome the public but warned those without special purpose to refrain from entering. He lived in poverty and taught only a handful of dedicated students and took little by way of fees. Known to be kind and compassionate to those in pain and suffering, he was stridently intolerant to those who even unwittingly might disturb the peace in his kingdom. The famous historian Rai Sanyō, mentioned a few pages earlier, confirmed this in an anecdote he was fond of telling his friends. Desiring the chance, as a young student, to meet Riken, he once accompanied a scholar—one Koejie Kōshū—to Riken's hideaway. Not expecting Rai, Riken left him waiting in the front entranceway, only to have Rai interrupt the conversation asking if he might not join them. According to Rai, Riken turned white with fury. All conversation ceased. And Riken is said to have shouted to Koejie: "Take him home! Take him home!"—*Tsurete kaere, tsurete kaere.* Overwhelmed by Riken's rage, Rai admitted: "I felt like crawling into a hole"—*ana ni demo hairitaki kokochi shitari.*[88]

Refusing thus to accommodate his virtue—*toku*—with the "uncentered" political and social world around him, Riken, in the words of Nishimura Tenshū, lived as a "hermit"—*itsumin*—resembling something of an exile who had morally disengaged himself from his present, almost including Chikuzan himself due to his bureaucratic friends. Within the hustle and clatter of the Osaka urban context, he pursued, in seclusion, his scholarly mission. The impatient defense of his autonomy also involved his wishing to dream without interference, within his imaginary kingdom, of how things might perhaps someday be completely unlike what they were in his time.

He articulated this vision in a short allegorical fable that he entitled "A tale from a kingdom of dreams"—*Kashokoku monogatari.*[89] Only thinly veiled as a tale about a distant and mythical land, it was quite obviously about Tokugawa Japan, a tale spun out of his own secluded kingdom. It is about a dream in which benevolent imperial justice nourishes the people so that, to put it in Riken's frame of reference, moral purpose and political actuality are brought into accord as truthfulness. The aristocracy withers away and commoners are seen actually engaged in administering the land.

Written in elegant Japanese literary style, no doubt to conceal the politicality of the story, the opening lines set the tone of a dreamlike fable: "In a distant kingdom of dreams that some say resembles scenic places in Japan but whose actual whereabouts somewhere in the skies is impossible to determine—*kumoi no izuko to mo sadamegataki kokudo . . .*—as the roadways leading to and from it are not known except by someone in a state of perfect religious bliss, it is said that a wise sage prince brought nourishment and aid to the suffering populace"—the *tamikusa.* The details that follow, consistently set forth and presented in the same literary style, are about political economy in the present. In this kingdom, the political center is a city under an "administrative monarch"—*ōkan*—an allusion most certainly to the Bakufu and with the emphasis falling on the image of "bureaucratic" chief. Extending in all directions from that center are "provinces" each with a "head"—*gunshu*—the analogy here being with domainal lords. The aristocratic leadership of the provinces spend a good deal of the time away at the center, again the reference to the present system of regular attendance at Edo being clear. In one of these provinces, the fable goes on, a young prince who had been away at the capital for many years is sent back to his home to serve as the new head. Having lived in the capital for many years, he no longer recognizes the local scene that he had left. In particular, he is deeply grieved at the economic chaos that now pervades the province. The agricultural resources of the land have been depleted by costly trips on the part of the provincial aristocracy to the capital city and back. Extensive borrowing from merchant houses has been resorted to, burdening still more the populace who live like "the lowly grasses beneath the flowerless tree that simply dry away with each autumn season"—*hanasakanu ki no shimokusa wa akigoto ni kare yuku nomi ni nan.*

Moved by the suffering of the people, the young prince dedicates himself to rectifying the miserable situation. He discards his aristocratic luxuries and wears the garments of the peasantry, sleeps on rough mats, and eats mountain roots and fern shoots that the very poor, on the verge of starvation, eat. He reduces the taxes immediately by one-half the previous amount. And he drafts a lengthy appeal to the "administrative monarch" in the capital city describing the actuality on the local scene. The populace, he emphasizes, lives in such cruel and utter misery that they are being driven to the brink of total disorder—*midare no hashi.* He asks, therefore, to be relieved of all further formal obligations of being in attendance at the capital city in order to devote his entire energy to assist and save the people—*tami o sukui.* Despite knowledge of his official duties at the capital, the young prince pledges himself to spread the higher justice of imperial compassion and grace—*suberamikoto*—throughout the land without regard to existing laws and without fear of facing execution for disloyal action.

Faced by the absolute and unequivocal moral stand taken by the prince, the "administrative head," while reminding him firmly of his formal duties, is also persuaded by his moral fervor and accedes to the appeal, thus avoiding the possibility of an act of treason by a loyal servitor. He also arranges to have the emperor send a decree to the prince praising him for his devotion and encouraging him in his course of action. The prince is advised in this imperial decree not to rely on "law" to oppress the people and instead to find ways to bring relief and well-being among the populace.

Blessed by imperial grace, the prince thus sets out to reform the province in extensive ways. The principle of accuracy and calculation will supplant arbitrariness and corruption in the handling of actual domainal resources. Every effort will be made thereby to increase savings and to repay ruinous debts pegged to high interest rates. Luxury items will be sold with that same aim in mind or be kept in special storage as security for emergency situations. The entire aristocracy, including their relatives, must discard their luxurious style of living and adjust to a new life of austerity identical with the peasantry; they must work the land along with the commoners. A school system is established to educate all children regardless of status: the very talented, again without regard to previous background, will be selected to become teachers; the unusually gifted ones will be advanced to special academies in the cities for scholarly training; and Buddhist monks are retrained to teach in the new provincial schools. Economically, drastic reforms are executed: property is redistributed and a limit placed on the amount each household may possess; surplus lands in excess of these allotments are purchased out of domainal funds and distributed with a nominal fee to those without land. Through the policy of land redistribution, the main source of ignoble misery, the inequity in wealth is eradicated. To increase agricultural production, moreover, new technology is introduced. A powerful water wheel expands the area of irrigated land; a new water pump now draws water from the highlands and drains swamps. The newly reclaimed lands are worked by the previous aristocracy, which has been divided into work teams of 100 men with subsections of ten. Although the aristocracy continues to receive stipends, these will be terminated as reclaimed lands become productive. Along with stipends, all hereditary official duties in the provincial government are terminated. The administration of the province is assumed instead by the general populace itself. Each group of ten households selects from within itself two individuals who then serve for a limited period of time—between three to five years—and are rotated out and replaced by two new representatives. Besides selecting these rotating "officials," the basic group of ten households is also responsible for maintaining the administrative costs of these two individuals, constituting a self-imposed tax of roughly one portion in ten of agricultural production for this purpose.

Through these varied yet systematic reforms of the prince, the province once again flourishes. Debts have been paid for, and the granaries are full. The people are happy and adorn themselves with colorful pins and ribbons designating the kind of work they do. But the aristocracy of the sword is gone. The hereditary administrative class has been dissolved. There is no further mention of the capital city at the center. Everyone belongs to a comprehensive class of commoners who work the land, educate their young, and select their own administrative leaders on a rotation basis. With the aristocracy thus disempowered, and before the question can be raised of implementing similar reforms in other provinces throughout the land, the fable comes to a close with the piercing crow of a cock that ends the dream—*torigane ni yume wa same ni keri.*[90]

In related writings on political economy,[91] Riken stated concerns similar to those expressed in his fable. Bakufu and domainal governments had acted in the economical and political life of the country in ways they should not and had failed to adopt reforms where they should. For example, they acted in the manner of financial houses competing with commercial institutions of commoners by exacting heavy loans from the populace to cover emergency needs and to loan money back to commoners at high interest rates during periods of hardship. Due to the size of the aristocracy, which was extremely costly, governments were compelled to seek profit like a commercial house. Meanwhile, they have been negligent in areas where they should act to improve the conditions of the people. Left neglected, for example, were such obvious matters as dredging rivers to prevent floods or to improve irrigation and, equally as important, regulating the growing discrepancy in wealth in the countryside, as witnessed by the expanding wealth of a few living off of rents and the impoverishment of the multitude living under, at best, marginal conditions. As prescribed in his fable, Riken urged that governments establish a policy of land equalization through the use of official funds, with peasants working on public lands being paid wages. And finally, to maintain order, rulers had failed to use humane means to improve the actual conditions in the country but had relied instead on harsh punitive laws in which punishment was rarely in accord with the crime, being thus arbitrary rather than righteous and on the mark. Most of the penal codes that rulers continued to rely on were formulated under conditions of general warfare when the Tokugawa House rose to power and were largely inappropriate in times of "peace and tranquility." Unduly harsh and inhumane means of punishment such as crucifixion and boiling ought to be abolished, and prison conditions should be improved by increasing the internal spaces and separating convicted criminals from those awaiting trial.

These essays, along with his fable, would tend to place Riken squarely within the eighteenth-century discourse on political economy. The entire moral force behind Riken's fable and other essays on the topic that government must be truthful, meaning being "righteous" or accurate in attending to the needs of the people at large, was entirely appropriate within the scope of the existing framework of "providing order and saving the people"—*keisei saimin*—a concern that for Riken as for Chikuzan provided the final justification for all scholarship, including the analysis of ancient texts. It is also the case that beneath the elegant literary surfaces the themes Riken presented, especially in his fable, were drawn from that discourse and were not drastic departures from it. For example, the reliance on commoners to select administrators from among themselves was first advanced by Goi to underscore, quite aside from the economy of it, his conviction that commoners "below" possessed the intelligence to acquire knowledge and regulate their world. "Farmers should be selected here and there as leaders," Goi it will be recalled had taught, "and be made to take over official functions. Even if they serve well, they should be rotated out every three to five years . . ."[92]

Similarly, the related idea of returning the aristocracy to the land to work among the peasantry—*dochaku ron*—was a prescription that Ogyū Sorai was especially fond of advancing on the ground that the aristocracy did not have a monopoly on "talent" to govern, as this virtue was distributed at random by heaven. By failing to recognize this principle, Ogyū had reasoned, the aristocracy had turned into an unproductive class economically and politically. The proposal to provide general education to all young children with the very best talents advanced to higher levels of learning, moreover, was clearly a plan Riken shared with Chikuzan. The same can be said of terminating the system of alternative attendance to the capital city and abolishing samurai stipends. All of these are conspicuously present in Chikuzan's *Sōbō kigen.*

When the various parts of Riken's thinking, as found in his fable, are integrated within this more general intellectual context, they hardly appear to be startling or unusual departures from widely known ideas about political economy. Yet they do add up to a provocative whole, which the form of the fable itself contributes to by providing at once overall shape to the various ideas as well as conveying a sense of a hidden vision or secretive yet "true purpose"—or *shishi* as proponents of this ethic of action in the late Tokugawa period would term it. The reference to the Bakufu as "administrative monarchy," the emperor as the source of imperial blessing (*tennō no megumi*) that embodies the higher ideal of justice, and the juxtaposition of these with the abused and suffering populace (*tamikusa*) in such a manner that it is the administrative monarchy that appears insensitive and must be confronted with an absolute moral proposition all point to a framework of action that contained counterstructural potential. The prince, after all, is prepared to disregard existing "law" and face his own demise in the cause of justice, a position that would be widely utilized by *shishi* loyalists who would overthrow the Bakufu a generation after Riken's time.

Within the form of the fable, Riken also reveals the political implications of his own ideal of truthfulness that he found central among the moral ideas of the ancient sages. Inner moral conviction must be in uncompromising accord with the existence of justice and righteousness without, and when such did not prevail, the self possessed the capacity to know and to judge the reasons for the discrepancy. To Riken (as with Goi and Chikuzan) this was an epistemological prepossession of all human beings which justified entirely the dissolution of a special aristocracy, the promotion of education among all youngsters, and the entrustment of the administration of the land to commoners. It is clear that his textual scholarship which stressed the fundamental importance of truthfulness, joining inner and outer as a norm, and his critique of political economy as witnessed in his fable fall into place as a consistent structure of thought. His sense too of not belonging to his age and of seeking solitude therefore also emerge as integral to it.

*   *   *

A major philosophical issue remained unresolved in Riken's structure of thought, however. Having immersed himself in the classical sources, Riken also had come to emphasize the view, held by students of ancient studies, of the crucial importance of *ancient* texts as ultimate resources. He thus had altered a key emphasis in Goi's teachings. To Goi "text" had always been relative to "nature" as an ontological absolute, thus validating the insight of the Neo-Confucian scholars into the classics as to the moral significance of observing principle in natural things. Riken, however, rejected this interpretation as an implausible reading of the actual language in the texts, siding with the findings of historicist scholars in ancient studies. While it was unequivocally true that he took his scholarly findings to a conclusion opposite to that of Ogyū in affirming the universal capacity of human beings to grasp external moral knowledge, thus retaining his intimate connection with Goi, the philosophical question remained as to the actual place that "nature" might have had as a field of knowledge in Riken's thinking.

Human morality and natural principle remained in an ambivalent and unresolved state in Riken. To him the problem of the "mean" was an entirely human or social one, so that while politics could be judged in terms of "truthfulness," nature ought not. Ogyū had said similarly that the idea of truthfulness had nothing to do with nature as it was a polemical strategy on behalf of Confucius against his Taoist detractors. Nature, Ogyū had theorized, was so vast and complex that the human mind could never unravel its secrets and in light of this futility ought not try to.

Here again Riken's position is ambivalent. While sharing with Ogyū the general insight that the classics were all about human morals and not about nature, Riken did not conclude that nature was, therefore, incomprehensible and an inappropriate object for the human mind to study. Riken held to the view that although nature ought not be used to confirm moral insights found in the classical texts, it could still be observed and studied and that the "principle" specific to it could be cognized. That principle, moreover, was not arbitrary. Nature ran its course on it, as witnessed in natural time, the tides, the seasons, and those other dynamic elements that underlie the ceaseless flow of the universe. Thus while Riken did not believe this natural principle to be related to human morals, he nonetheless retained a lively interest in nature as a legitimate object of knowledge.[93]

It was without apology that Riken carried out experiments with the microscope with merchant colleagues such as Aburaya Kichiuemon and observed, documented with amazement, the details of insects and parasites. Riken also pursued his interest in nature through his association with the scholar Asada Goryū, a close friend and colleague of Miura Baien, who had taken refuge as an exile in Osaka near the Kaitokudō to continue his studies in astronomy and medicine. Aside from astronomy, Riken experimented with Asada in vivisection as taught in Dutch medical manuals. Riken documented his observations on human anatomy in a volume called *Esso rohitsu* (1773), meaning comments on a subject beyond the writer's scholarly capabilities. Praised for its accurate descriptions of human anatomy by historians of medical science in Japan, Riken's work appeared virtually simultaneously with Sugita Genpaku's more famous translation from the Dutch on human anatomy—*Kaitai shinshō* (1774).[94]

Riken's fundamental intellectual mission, however, was to study moral philosophy as it was grounded in history. It was from this perspective that he had come to conclude that while the ancient sages spoke of truthfulness among men, they did not speak of it as being in nature or of nature being moral in the human sense. Thus although he was an active participant in the comings and goings at Asada's school and while his friendship with him was a very close one indeed, Riken's involvement with the study of nature was a matter of free intellectual play and of unprejudiced curiosity; his discovery of moral dissonance between himself and the outer world had not come through the examination of "nature" but of ancient "text." His "Taoist" retreat into the kingdom of dreams was thus a moral and political act, not a scientific one to uncover the ultimate "principle" in nature. It was entirely consistent with this framework that Riken began to construct a new "scientific" calendar for his secluded kingdom, a new conception of "time" based on the heliocentric conception of the universe. Science was being marshalled to serve the needs, he felt, of having to "order" in more "accurate" manner his world of "dreams."[95]

Riken yearned for order and stability even as he defended his isolation in acerbic and eccentric ways. He explained some of these outbursts against intruders on the ground that human passion—*ninjo*—was inevitable to the human spirit and that Confucius and the other ancient sages allowed a wide range of emotive feelings ranging from gentle goodness to anger. It was foolish, he insisted, to suppress one's anger when anger was appropriate, for it was to deny one's humanity. Eradicating passion through meditation he believed to be the height of folly, especially when such practices were made to seem philosophically profound. To be a scholar or thinker in solitude it was more important, he was fond of telling students he had just agreed to teach, to first learn how to drink *sake*—*nanji mazu sake o nomu koto o manabe*—for without it one was sure to invite illness and perhaps even death—*byō o hasshite shi sen.*[96] The personal struggle involved in the life of the recluse, that is evident in this advice to students, reappears in more poignant fashion in his yearning for permanency and stability, wishing perhaps that his kingdom could remain in a fixed place but knowing all the while that this was impossible as his regal space was a "dream." About to leave one rented place for yet another Riken composed a poem whose imagery is of a pristinely beautiful and motionless object that he sees and embraces: "Although I know not what tomorrow will bring me, a single blossom now settles in my soul here in my rented lodging"—*Asu shiranu waga mi nagaramo kari no shuku ni kokoro zo tomaru hana no ippon.*[97] Reminiscent of Goi's aesthetic appreciation of literature, and of his daughter's sad presence at his deathbed, we see Riken affirming an aesthetic object in his impermanent rented surroundings and cherishing it within himself as "truthful."

·   ·   ·

It was to this complex and eccentric Riken, rationalist at times and tender at others, who had chided his bureaucratic colleagues for their greed and lack of imagination and who also wrote poems about his solitude, that Chikuzan turned to, just prior to his death, to plead that he assume the instructional headship of the Kaitokudō. Given his hermetical ways, Riken obviously could not assert the sort of vigorous leadership required by the academy. With his death in 1818, the Kaitokudō would not again display the intellectual vigor of the previous seventy-five years or so beginning with Goi. However, the Kaitokudō maintained itself as an important place to study mainly due to the lingering prestige of the Nakai brothers and their texts. Denigrating comments as to the "Osaka-style"—*Osaka ryū*—of scholarship taught to please merchants came to be heard with less frequency as Chikuzan and Riken emerged as formidable scholarly figures. Their differences in personality and intellectual orientations also came to be well known, and each gained widespread respect and admiration for their separate virtues. Chikuzan's *Sōbō kigen* had become a work read by all serious students of political economy. And Riken gained the reputation of being, along with Itō Jinsai and Ogyū Sorai, one of the three great textual critics of the Tokugawa era. Through the Nakai brothers the Kaitokudō had gained academic prestige as a key nodal point, known to all Tokugawa intellectuals, within a broader intellectual sphere spanning the various cities and regions especially in east, west-central, and west Japan.

In the sense that the reputation of the Kaitokudō had spread beyond the immediate merchant community in Osaka, Chikuzan may be said to have realized his vision of an expanded role for the academy. But in a more fundamental sense his vision remained unfulfilled, a provocative formulation containing a historical potential whose time had not yet arrived. Riken's vision, too, remained imaginary, a "dream." Both were acutely aware of the structural constraints posed by the existing Baku-han order. Chikuzan's *Sōbō kigen* provides ringing testimony as to the specific institutional arrangements that must be altered: revision of the system of alternate attendance, dissolution of aristocratic stipends, general education for the entire populace. These were far-reaching proposals indeed, and history would vindicate Chikuzan a generation later when these proposals would be realized in fact during the upheavals surrounding the Meiji Ishin of 1868. Toward the end of his life, however, Chikuzan knew that the system would not be tampered within his day, a point driven home to him painfully by the meager support provided by the Bakufu in rebuilding the Kaitokudō after it had been destroyed by fire in the early 1790s. Remaining totally devoted to the academy, Chikuzan rebuilt it with the support of Osaka merchants and refused to join his colleagues Bitō, Koga, and Satō as chief historian within the Bakufu, thus remaining at the Kaitokudō, the *public* school for commoners.

Equally aware as Chikuzan of the limitations presented by the political order, Riken tended to be far less optimistic about new institutional possibilities. His vision of commoner education, dissolution of the aristocracy, the actualization of righteousness for the people, were thus expressed not as political prescription but as a utopian dream. Knowing that these changes would not be realized in his day, Riken disengaged himself from institutional life and indeed from the unfolding of history in his time altogether. Convinced that he was not part of his day, Riken revealed himself to be more of an idealist than Chikuzan, refusing to compromise his conviction that "virtue" must be consistent within and without, a conviction he nourished within his kingdom and which he painstakingly reconfirmed through the philological examination of ancient texts.

While each worked out his vision in different ways, in their common defense of humankind being endowed with the epistemological power to know moral knowledge, both Chikuzan and Riken remained devoted protégés of Goi Ranju. That key concept remained for them the philosophical grounding for commoner education and each stubbornly protected it in their polemical scholarly writings. The consistent antipathy toward Ogyū Sorai reflected in their essays invariably revolved around this central issue, as evidenced in Chikuzan's diatribe against Ogyū in his *Hi-Chō* and Riken's exhaustive examination of the classical texts in his multivolume series on the classics. Although in these works, Chikuzan and Riken went beyond Goi in both scope and depth, their intellectual indebtedness to him was profound, and his rationalism in particular remained the guiding spirit to them all through their maturation into eminent scholars. Yet more so than Goi and Miyake Sekian and Nakai Shūan before them, Chikuzan and Riken shaped intellectual tools with which to address the state of political economy.

With critical conviction and without apology, they spoke of the desperate need for reform out of a sense of crisis in the course of events. To Chikuzan "dreams" were always somehow grounded in the everyday world of experience, function, and work; to Riken "dreams" were conscious fabrications such as his "kingdom" or about a future still to be. Chikuzan could speak more readily about "dreams" to youngsters than Riken could. Only few would be allowed by Riken into his self-styled dream-space. Chikuzan retained an optimism absent in Riken; yet, their assessments of the current state of affairs were virtually identical. Both projected the vision of new talent and leadership from below replacing the anachronistic aristocracy of the sword, and in this sense, they had seen beyond the eighteenth century to the era of reform and transformation that would come with Japan's modern revolution, the Meiji Ishin. It would remain for practicing merchant leaders, however, to take that vision and the conceptual language embedded in it and articulate a specific claim for the political place of merchants in the unfolding future. Two synthetic constructions bearing the unmistakable markings of Kaitokudō thought attract our attention in this regard. One of these is Kusama Naokata and his "Historical Outline of Money"—*Sanka zu'i*. The other, more ambitious and important, is Yamagata Bantō and his opus, "In Place of Dreams"—*Yume no shiro*.

SIX

☐ IN PLACE OF DREAMS: ☐
☐ MERCHANT EPISTEMOLOGY IN ☐
☐ LATE EIGHTEENTH-CENTURY ☐
☐ OSAKA ☐

OUR FINAL CHAPTER TAKES ITS TITLE "IN PLACE OF
DREAMS" FROM YAMAGATA BANTŌ'S *YUME NO SHIRO*.[1]
DRAFTED BETWEEN 1800 AND 1805, THE WORK REMAINS A PIVOTAL REFER-
ence for late eighteenth-century Tokugawa thought. The title itself was
phrased by Nakai Riken, as Yamagata himself reports in his preface (without the actual wording that the eccentric Riken might have used to convey his advice). Yamagata had entitled his work *Saiga no tsugunoi*, or
"Saiga's Redemption," referring to one of Confucius's students who often
dozed through the master's lectures but who later redeemed himself
through his scholarly work. Yamagata had intended to pay tribute to his
teachers Chikuzan and Riken from whose eyes he pictured himself as a
lazy and seemingly inattentive student. The Nakai brothers, on the contrary, knew him from early on to be a truly exceptional intellect, and
Riken's advice that he abandon the self-effacing title to the more assertive
and provocative one appropriate to the work itself clearly documents the
respect held for him.

Yet the title is more than an effective statement for the written work of
one of the best students at the Kaitokudō. It is, more importantly, a metaphor for a comprehensive vision that Riken detected in Yamagata's manuscript in which all previous discussions of "dreams" that had gone on at
the academy and in other parts of society as well would be displaced by
scientific reason, or "astronomy." A drastically new view of knowledge,
in short, would gain preeminence from Yamagata on into the future.
"Dreams" as expressed in religion, superstition, escapes into fantasy, including in this sense Riken's own hideaway "kingdom," would all no
longer occupy legitimate space within the human mind. In all likelihood,
Riken would not have admitted the further implication that Yamagata's

222

scientific theory of knowledge would have the added effect of displacing the ancient "classics" as the basic intellectual resource that the mind must continuously "reencounter" in the manner that Riken himself had done through much of his scholarly career. In Yamagata's treatise the emphasis was placed decidedly on how much more there is to know about nature and the present, and the inappropriateness, therefore, of lionizing the ancient sages.

The title that Riken advanced to Yamagata is far-reaching indeed in interpretive implication. It includes within it all of the criticisms that had gone into the teachings at the Kaitokudō about the intellectual failings of the aristocracy. In this regard, it should be assessed in tandem with Chikuzan's *Sōbō kigen* and Riken's *Kashokoku monogatari*, which have been reviewed in the previous chapter. And by this same token, it should also be evaluated simultaneously with the writings of Kusama Naokata, Yamagata's neighbor and colleague, and in particular his "Illustrated History of Money"—*Sanka zu'i*.[2] Although far less known than Yamagata's celebrated treatise, this history of money is also a statement against "dreams" and a ringing affirmation of merchant epistemology. These are mutually related texts that reinforce each other, even though the methodological approaches are distinguishable. Together they clarify a good deal about critical merchant articulation at the turn into the fateful nineteenth century.

Kusama's history of money does not fly under the kind of brilliant metaphoric banner as Yamagata's *Yume*. And in truth it does not have the synthetic grandness of Yamagata's work. It is, nonetheless, an outline of enormous importance for it reveals the mind of an economist that surely, along with Yamagata, must be seen as formulating the conceptual foundations of Japanese entrepreneurial wisdom and ideology in early modern times. A grand theory of knowledge is not to be found in Kusama. Yet there is no reference to religious or superstitious beliefs or divine nativism to shore his arguments about political economy. His treatise is thus anchored like Yamagata's to the Kaitokudō where mystifications of all kinds had consistently been rejected. Riken's brilliant metaphorical insight into Yamagata, therefore, may be taken to our advantage as students of history as extending beyond the framework of Yamagata's specific text to include Kusama's descriptive "history" of money. Like Yamagata's work, this history is grounded in a theory of "righteous" knowledge and, far from being innocent, is ideologically charged with critical merchant thinking. Both, indeed, were extensions of Kaitokudō syncretism in which the study of "astronomy" and "history" was encouraged to go on at the same time.

Even Nakai Riken's "encounter" with the "original classics" and his concentration on the philological approach reminiscent of ancient studies did not indicate the abandonment of the eclectic intellectual tradition of the Kaitokudō. His scholarly project, in fact, profoundly reinforced the epistemological presuppositions of his training at the academy. And although he denied both allegiance to and antagonism toward any particular scholarly school, claiming to be an independent "house" unto himself, his prodigious philological exercises nonetheless added up to the unequivocal reaffirmation of the conceptual understanding of knowledge taught by his mentors at the Kaitokudō. The consistent emphasis Riken placed on the epistemology of "accuracy" and of "trust" and "faith" as being in accord with the concept of the "mean" is of pivotal importance in this regard. As emphasized in the previous chapter, the *Doctrine of the Mean* was of more than symbolic importance to Riken. Thus, far from going through a "conversion" to "ancient studies" as taught, for example, in the tradition of Ogyū Sorai or Itō Jinsai, Riken, underscored the crucial importance of the "mean" in recognizing truthfulness in the present. Moreover, Riken did not disturb the view taught consistently at the Kaitokudō that history contained a "relativity" of insights in historical time regarding the universe of things and events, so that the narration of historical developments well after the ancient era was likewise not challenged. Riken himself, it will also be recalled, relied on the narrative mode to describe the steady decline of history that accompanied the emergence of the aristocracy as the dominant class in society. In Riken, therefore, the philological study of ancient texts to correct the findings of other scholars, remained comfortably intertwined with "history" and the natural ontology underlying it.

The fact that both "history" and "nature" remained available at the Kaitokudō as viable conceptual devices with which to frame knowledge was important to the production of Osaka merchant ideology. In the case of Kusama Naokata, as will be examined first in this chapter, it is the framework of "history" that is the preferred mode within which to articulate a sharp critique against the existing order and, at the same time, to assert a claim to knowledge specific to merchants. In the other prominent example of Yamagata Bantō, on whom greater emphasis will be placed since it was he who summarized most completely the intellectual transformation of the Kaitokudō in the eighteenth century, "natural ontology" provides the contours of his synthesis of knowledge and within which he encloses "history" as a critical perspective on the present and future.

In these related yet distinguishable approaches, we see clearly discernible evidences of merchant intellectuals utilizing concepts available to them to articulate, in exacting language, their views of poltical economy. Faced with having to order their assessment of ongoing history and find a consistent language with which to present their thinking, Kusama relied on the historical mode of exposition to outline the unfolding of economic history; Yamagata, on the other hand, proceeded from the theory of universal nature to achieve a similar end. Although both drew on certain key ideas and perspectives from the Kaitokudō, Nakai Chikuzan in particular with regard to structural reform and Goi Ranju to nature, the conceptual choices being made here are of considerable importance. By framing his entire presentation within universal nature as the ultimate field of knowledge, Yamagata was also persuaded that Western "astronomy" was the most advanced science in the study of that field. For Kusama, while nature also serves as a theoretical norm for economic relations, the broad ontological canvass is avoided as an initial statement and the focus is placed clearly on a reduced and concrete "object" of analysis—in this case "money." Rather than advancing from the most universal to the concrete as in Yamagata, Kusama starts with refined datum and locates it immediately within history. Both, in turn, relate their approach to the present world of political economy and the troublesome evidences provided by the Baku-han system. Yamagata drew heavily from Goi's theory of natural ontology, as will be spelled out later. Kusama's approach through historical narrative, on the other hand, falls squarely within the teachings of the Nakai brothers. History is a narrative of an unfolding experience that leads to a basic understanding of the present. Like his mentors, Kusama avoids the circular "leap" from the present into the world of the "ancients" and back again, as evidenced in the thinking of Itō Jinsai and Ogyū Sorai, and concentrates on the recent past as it relates to the present. Kusama's history deemphasizes the importance of the ancients with reference to the specific "object" of analysis, namely "money," or the three variants thereof—*sanka*—and devotes most of his narrative to the meaning and role of money in recent history.

Kusama drafted his "Outline History of Money"—*Sanka zu'i*—over the same years that Yamagata Bantō wrote his opus against "dreams" roughly around the turn of 1800. Although their conceptual language, especially as regards the characterization of political economy, clearly is drawn from a common intellectual pool, neither makes overt reference to the other. As men who frequented the Kaitokudō over the same period of time and as competitors in the world of banking, it is unlikely that they would have been unaware of each other. We are reminded of the silence between Goi and Tominaga in this regard. Unlike their predecessors, however, the intellectual agreement in the case of Yamagata and Kusama was quite extensive. Their assertive affirmation of merchant knowledge obviously stems from an intimately related intellectual experience. Their silence we may surmise was due to the very closeness of their competitive relationship as financiers. The Kōnoike that Kusama served was the largest and most influential banking house in Osaka; the Masuya that Yamagata was attached to was a notch below, ranking in the early 1800s in the lower third of the leading fifteen or so houses, all pegged relatively to the Kōnoike's preeminent position at the top. Yet in the listings of the leading dozen or so houses making substantial philanthropic contributions on a regular basis to the Kaitokudō, or similarly those showing proportionate payments to the Bakufu to fulfill forced levies, the names of both Kōnoike and Masuya were conspicuously present. Thus, although Masuya was significantly less powerful financially than Kōnoike, both were obviously eminent houses in the Osaka merchant community.[3]

Also worthy of note here is that both Kusama and Yamagata shared similar upbringings. Both were brought from outside the immediate merchant family and raised as "boy apprentices"—*detchi kozō*—beginning with menial work and then, in both cases, advancing mercurially through demonstration of intelligence and ability to become powerful financiers. For their proven worth, both would be formally adopted into the main houses: Kusama was known in the merchant community as Kōnoike Isuke; and Yamagata as Masuya Kouemon. Although unrelated by blood to the main house, both were men of established reputations and commanded enormous prestige. Kusama was especially known for his direction of the finances of domains that included Hizen, Higo, and Nanbu. He was rumored to be fearless among the barons, speaking his mind as if their equal. Yamagata similarly attracted widespread attention for his management of the finances of the powerful domain of Sendai of the northern region. It was often remarked, in fact, that whatever solvency Sendai managed to maintain was entirely due to Yamagata's policies. It was a subject that Kaiho Seiryō would praise without reservation in his lengthy comments on Yamagata or "Masuya the Lesser": *Masuko dan.*[4] It was indeed a widely circulated "secret" that the lord of Sendai would deal with no one other than Yamagata from Masuya, including the actual head Hyōemon himself. While anecdotal, these bits of evidences suggest a competitive arena in which great fame and reputations were made on the basis of knowledge about finances. Clearly, Kusama and Yamagata were two who had succeeded in that world. But more important, they both reveal through their thinking something of the ideology of their social universe.

As inheritors of the ideas taught at the Kaitokudō, Kusama and

Yamagata turned these ideas into a merchant critique of politics and the deeply troubled history before them. While Kusama would enter into this subject through the mediation of the concrete object of "money," Yamagata would single out "dreams" and superstitious thinking of all kinds as the ultimate source of the crisis of the present. It is furthermore clear to both that the epistemological failings were most severe in the aristocracy that claimed responsibility for governing the country. Out of this critique, they shaped an ideological vision that went beyond the failings of the structures immediately before them and prefigured an era they could hardly anticipate or concretely describe. Thus, while these two men did not address themselves directly to each other, they may be seen for our purposes as being involved in a dialogue that presents a mutually shared sense of unease toward their present, a sense that linked them directly to the concerns of the Nakai brothers and, more broadly, to the intellectual history of the Kaitokudō.

Indeed, just as Yamagata makes plain his indebtedness to Chikuzan and Riken in his preface, we find in Kusama's *Sanka zu'i* an introduction written by Chikuzan himself, dated 1795, when the work was still in early draft stage. In these introductory pages, too, there is reference to Kusama as "Naokata of our party"—*Waga tō no Naokata*—further documenting his close relationship to the Kaitokudō.[5]

·　　·　　·

KUSAMA NAOKATA
(1753–1831)

Kusama wrote his outline history of money in Japan (with illustrations)— *Sanka zu'i*—over a twenty-year period ending in 1815. Its final version fills two large volumes, each over 500 modern printed pages. Born into the poor merchant house of Masuya Tadaemon, Kusama was sent as an apprentice, at the age of ten, to the banking house of Kōnoike in Osaka, which, like the Kaitokudō was located in the district of Amagasaki. An enormously successful financier for Kōnoike, Kusama was formally adopted into the Kōnoike in 1804 as head of a branch house assigned special responsibility in managing the business of currency exchange and extending credit to baronial houses. It was as financial advisor to regional barons that Kusama developed his impatience regarding the aristocracy's limited knowledge about money and market. That a specialist in banking should write a history of money is, of course, hardly startling. And there is indeed much in the work itself that suggests a genuine fondness and attachment to the subject as a favorite personal pastime. This is certainly borne out by the enormous amount of intricate details that Kusama presented with illustrations. And there is corroborating evidence in his compilation, over the same years as his work on money, of a multivolume work on the subject of elegant paraphernalia accompanying the tea ceremony—*Chaki meibustu zu'i*.[6] The format was again historical with rich illustrations to grace the pages. Kusama's outline history of money, however, went beyond distractive entertainment. The *Sanka* is a historical treatment of money in Japan as it related to the general state of the economy in the world around him, so that while the primary data is "money," it is used as the basis for entering into the related subjects of market, supply, and price and, in turn, their relationship to governmental policies. Scattered throughout Kusama's "history" is the insistent advice that detailed knowledge of economics is central to the art of governance and his equally consistent warning that much of the historical record shows clearly the lack of control over such knowledge by the men who ruled the country, thereby causing enormous strains on the general populace.

To situate Kusama's "history" in its proper setting, it is important to underscore the point that the subject of "money" itself was not of his creation. It had been a crucial subject for many of the major political thinkers from the early eighteenth century on. This is understandable in light of the shaky unfolding of the Tokugawa economy over these years, as witnessed in the famines and riots of the Kyōhō and Tenmei eras in the 1730s and 1770s respectively and the sporadic efforts at reform during these years. Before Kusama had begun his "history," much ink had already been spilled on the subject of money, and Kusama's own articulations suggest a discursive relationship between his own views and what had already been said. Outstanding examples of this were, for example, Arai Hakuseki's work on monetary reform, *Kaika gi;* Ogyū Sorai's treatise on political economy, *Seidan;* and Dazai Shundai's work on the same subject, *Keizai roku.* Even before the crucial writings of these thinkers, Kumazawa Banzan and Yamaga Sokō commented in considerable detail on the important role that money had come to assume in the present and of the manipulative role that merchants played in the new context. Important to note here is that while these commentators saw the rise of money economy as falling squarely within the vision of the ancient sages, especially in the idea that cash was a necessary ingredient in the maintenance of social well-being, they also couched their views in such a way that the usurious handling of money by merchants was seen as a corruptive influence that undermined society. The exacting of interests by merchants was thus invariably presented in a prejudicial light. It was within this framework that the debate developed over the issue of what constituted proper policy as regards money and why, theoretically, apart from merchant abuses, one policy was preferable over another. Indeed, quite aside from enterpreneurial passion, the commercial revolution of Generoku (late seventeenth century) witnessed in process the inflationary minting of money relative to the short supply of cash which generated an economic confusion that the ruling regime never resolved.

Several related issues remained central to the eighteenth-century commentaries on money, and a brief summary may serve as background for the statements of Kusama.[7] One involved the question of whether money should be minted according to a stable metallic content, that is, with a predictable "value" in mind. A second focused on whether minting should be done according to the relative "volume" required by the economy. And a third stressed the importance of general social "utility" as the guiding principle in the minting of money. One of the more influential positions that addressed these various themes was identified with Arai Hakuseki. Directly involved in the shaping of Bakufu policy in the early eighteenth century, Arai, while finding "utility" to be an adequate principle as regards minting copper cash for the populace at large, tended to reduce his basic position to the theory of the "volume" of money being relative to the overall requirements as politically conceived. Arai identified this as the critical ingredient in determining monetary policy. Arguing that because money was a "commodity" like any other item being traded from day to day, its value was determined largely by its availability, which is to say its volume, rather than its precisely fixed metallic content. Prices of goods tended to increase, he reasoned, when money was inexpensive, a phenomenon again determined by the large supply of available money. The appropriate correction was to impose a policy to reduce the supply of money. The point being pressed here was that "price" was a function of political intervention, or the application of "law" as he put it. Alternatively he reasoned that if prices were to decline, this reflected the reality of money being valuable, which in turn was determined by a relatively low supply of cash. Therefore, if higher prices were desired, as presumably would be the case for the aristocracy for which Arai spoke—the price of rice determining the cash income for that class—then the supply of money should be increased. Again, such a result could be realized only through political action, the execution of monetary policy consciously formulated to achieve desired goals. The supply or volume of money and the price of goods could be said to be in a state of equilibrium when all segments of society were in a relative state of well-being. The nation may then be said to be "affluent"—*Tenka no zaiyo yutaka ni tsūji okonaware sōrō.*[8]

The implication of this line of reasoning was clear: while, ideally, "equilibrium" was desirable, to assist the aristocracy, the supply of money should, more importantly, be increased to keep prices at a high level. As to the inflationary impact that this might have, Arai tended to discount it by saying that the unusually steep climb in prices was the result of the declining "quality" in the metallic content of money and not of the excessive "volume" in and of itself. The possibility, of course, that the quality of money had declined precisely because of the rapid increase in the volume of money, thus together causing an extreme upward spiraling of prices ruinous even to the aristocracy, remained basically unresolved in Arai's thinking. In the final analysis, however, he tended to assess "volume" as being the more fundamental force in the formulation of monetary policy. While recommending a maintenance of high metallic standards, he placed heavier emphasis on the idea of money as a commodity subject to the rule of exchange governing trade in general. It need only be said in passing that Arai did not peg his position on money on the expansive production of goods and leaned instead toward seeing prices exclusively as a function of monetary policy and thus as a reflection of politics.

Ogyū Sorai took issue with his political rival Arai.[9] While he, too, denied the necessity of high metallic content in money, he placed the emphasis on general social "utility." While money may be of poor quality, he reasoned, if it was available in great abundance for general use by the populace it would then gain value because of its universal utility. Volume in the sense used by Arai, or the actual value of the money in terms of metal, were thus not fundamental. Gold and silver must assume its proper "value" relative to the basic principle of utility. Ogyū objected to the implication in Arai's theory that the reduction in the volume of money would lower prices and thus bring "relief" to the populace. To reduce the supply of cash in the face of persisting high prices, Ogyū countered, would only increase social misery. The source of escalating prices, he further reasoned, was in "consumption"—the passionate pursuit of luxuries large and small, for which the aristocracy was mostly to blame. Given the structure of consumption—aristocracy with stipends living in cities—two policy options were open to those who governed: one was to maintain a large volume of useful, inexpensive money throughout society to regulate the exchange involved in consumption and the other was to drastically reduce consumption by placing the aristocracy back on the land where, denied guaranteed cash stipends, it would involve itself in productive agriculture and thereby regain self-sufficiency. Consumption based on cash would thus decline and the necessary volume of money would also fall, as would prices. Ogyū made it plain in his "discussion of politics," *Seidan*, that he preferred this latter solution of relocating the aristocracy back on the land, a position reinforced by the theoretical view that political "talent" was not hereditary and exclusive to that class but that such talent, as with all other talents, was distributed randomly. Insofar as the "system" was to be maintained as it had been received, Ogyū did not believe the reduction in the supply of money would alleviate the plight of the people and that, on the contrary, the system dictated a continuously high level of inexpensive and useful money to facilitate the needs of passionate consumption.

For Ogyū, then, the principle of social utility was the basis for his thinking and was more important than the actual metallic quality of money or its volume as politically controllable solutions. It followed that Ogyū should prescribe to the Bakufu the minting of more money and in particular the most useful of monies, copper cash, to allow everyone in society to go about their daily business of realizing their "little virtues" even while prices were high. Money, in his eyes, was a social and "systemic" phenomenon, and returning to a high level of metallic content— Keichō gold and silver, this high level was called—would have no impact on prices. Money, while valuable, would also be scarce and only intensify the misery of practically everyone.

The theory of utility proposed by Ogyū found articulation in other quarters as well, as by Miura Baien, whose intellectual relationship with the Kaitokudō was a close one, in his conceptually provocative work on the "Origins of Value"—*Kagen*—of 1773.[10] Unlike Arai and Ogyū, who were living in the aristocratic city of Edo and seeking to influence the Bakufu, Miura addressed his prescriptions to the regional domainal lord and did so from the point of view of the suffering peasants among whom he lived in his country home in Kyūshū. In probing for the origins of economic value—*minamoto o saguru*—Miura articulated a good deal that Arai and Ogyū would agree with: the purpose of governance is nourishing the people, as the people are the foundation of society; and the art of political economy is then to make "righteousness" an "advantage" for all—*gi o motte ri to su*—meaning too that the "interest" of those who ruled and were ruled ought to be indistinguishable. Beyond these oft cited platitudes, Miura went on to offer several intriguing theoretical insights. While it was always true since time immemorial that passion was unlimited and resources limited, in the present, he observed that "money" in and of itself had vastly superseded "goods" in "value," making money independently more desirable and thus exaggerating the price of "things" actually needed for livelihood. The social consequence of money having an independent value over goods was to create drastic inequities in wealth. As wealth had increased in terms of the value of money, so too had poverty increased relative to it. From the point of view of the peasantry, Miura believed the consequences to be disastrous.

Money, Miura argued, must be articulated in terms of the ultimate meaning of economic value. Human beings produced goods close at hand for reasons of survival, and money was a functional medium that facilitated the *distribution* of relatively scarce goods from one area to another. The ultimate *value*, however, must be identified with the act of production itself. The further that goods needed to be transported, the more *expensive* would be the mediating cash. In short, the "translation" of production to "use" was most universal when expensive money was least needed. The most universal form of money, therefore, ought to be the most available and "useful" in the immediate sense, not the most "expensive," meaning scarce and unavailable. For the bulk of society, he therefore reasoned, gold, silver, and even copper were irrelevant as metallic norms for money, and all cash should be made of *cast iron*, the least expensive and the most available of durable metals. In ancient times, he observed with an acerbic philosophical wit, what nourished the people most universally was called a "treasure"—*takara*. Now, due to the change in "custom," what was once valuable is no longer held to be so, and the useless and scarce or the ritualistic and decorative—*ganbutsu*—had become the norm of economic value. Replacing social utility as "value" was scarce metal, when, Miura concluded, the most "valuable" metal ought to be iron, as it was close to the ultimate source of value itself, namely production and utility.[11]

Next to volume and utility, a third crucial position, and one that was especially pertinent to Kusama, insisted that "value," meaning the accurate and nonarbitrary measurement of the metallic content of cash, was critical given the fact that cash had become a universal medium of exchange. Dazai Shundai was the key articulator of this point.[12] Although a protégé of Ogyū who had focused his attention on matters of political economy (as against others who had studied mainly ancient poetry), Dazai disagreed with his mentor on the matter of money. While obviously important, he believed the factor of "utility" to be subordinate to consistent metallic value. He thus also disagreed with Arai on "volume" as being the crucial factor. Although sharing Ogyū and Arai's concern with governmental policy and the minting of money, Dazai focused on the devastating negative implications of the metallic "debasement" of money as not only politically dishonest but naive in the sense that those directing these schemes believed that the ordinary populace could not recognize what had been done to the actual value of money. The social dimension of utility as expressed by Ogyū (and by Miura) was, in Dazai, articulated as a matter of commoners actually having the intelligence to recognize what kinds of money were "useful" and which ones were "valuable" and that the most "valuable" were, in the final analysis, the most "useful." The metallic content of money, therefore, was not simply a matter of political dictation by "policy" from above according to needs perceived from that vantage point, but of social "cognition" and hence also of "manipulation" from below.

Dazai saw the political distortion of the supply of money through debasement as a fundamental source of systemic instability. The cause of that instability was not "passion." Nor was it consumption. Nor was money a relatively stable commodity moving simply to and fro in the manner that goods conventionally do. Money was a mediating metallic construct that people relied on with the expectation of its being consistent and reliable. Thus, consistency possessed a value apart from the daily or seasonal vicissitudes of nature. It was not in this sense a "commodity." It was a fabricated *political* instrument that was *useful* insofar as society found it to be *reliable*. When reliable, economic agreements might be mutually arrived at on an accurate basis. Fair exchange becomes possible. When the supply of money is increased or decreased through politically determined debasement, Dazai insisted, the ordinary individual in society soon becomes aware of it so that the actual social value of that money declines precipitously because of its lack of reliability, thus, in turn, driving prices upward. In Dazai's analysis, this meant a constant demand by the aristocracy for more cash having less value. The issue for Dazai, therefore, was not simply the "volume" of money as emphasized by Arai or "utility" in the sense that Ogyū and Miura would have had it. To the extent that he saw policy as having to relate to the actuality of society, he was, in this sense, close to these latter two. But Dazai stressed the general human ability at an ordinary level to recognize political deception. The social evaluation of monetary "value," Dazai insisted, was crucial to policy. Debasement, in his analysis, was actually not that difficult to detect, and the question at stake was not how to correct human "greed" but to construct a reasoned policy based on that appreciation of social knowledge.

However, as policy continues to be devoid of "reason," as evidenced by the debasing of the metallic value of money, ordinary marketmen will inevitably seek ways to respond to that actuality. An example was the Bakufu's policy of minting monies of extremely poor quality. At first called Genroku gold and Genroku silver, they soon came to be referred to derisively as "first" [minting], "second," "third," and "fourth"—*hitotsu, futatsu, mitsu, yotsu*—without regard to metallic reference. This was because society had come to despise what was being done to the money they used—*tami kore o iyashimu*. The end result of this recognition of governmental deceit was that money with actually good content went out of circulation and those with poor grade remained, keeping prices artificially high. Around 1720, in the so-called Kyōhō reforms, the Bakufu sought to rectify its mistakes by taking the poor cash out of circulation and sought to maintain a stable monetary economy.[13]

It was within this swirl of commentaries on money that Kusama situated his own perspective, and he did this, as already emphasized, in the format of a descriptive "history" rather than as a direct critique on the economic policies of the Tokugawa's. It was a convenient framework to use, as it was readily acceptable to the society around him. The compiling of "histories" of tea ceremonies or of fauna or pottery (which, as mentioned earlier, Kusama himself indulged in also) were in vogue then. Moreover, money could be shown to be as ancient as the beginning of historical time itself. Archaelogical illustrations could be marshalled to verify this fact and thus dignify the subject. Such a perspective, however, was quite deceptive. The real analytical point that Kusama had to make was that, despite its ancient history, money in his day was a totally new phenomenon in terms of magnitude and substance so that not much could be learned from that ancient past, however fascinating the subject might in fact be.

Kusama thus employed history to show that the economic problems traceable to money were rooted in the very recent past. Prior to the Keichō era (1596–1615), the years surrounding the establishment of the Tokugawa regime, there was hardly any minting of cash in Japan. Most of it was imported from China. From the Keichō period, however, minting began on a large scale, and this was, for Kusama, the substantive "history" of money in Japan. He then took great pains to show how this history was marked by disastrous inconsistencies in policy. It was a history, he insisted, which could not be grasped through references to ancient times, although many moral philosophers, out of a mistaken belief that money was plentiful in ancient times, believed that lessons could still be learned from that distant past. "They all fail," he thus commented, "to reflect on the actual conditions that existed in ancient times."[14]

Establishing that within the framework of history the problem of money was of recent origin, "modern" rather than "ancient," Kusama set forth his own perception of the subject. Conceptually, Kusama held to a

position closer to Dazai than to either Arai or Ogyū in emphasizing the
consistency of metallic content of money. Unlike these previous commentators, however, Kusama spoke from the standpoint of a merchant
with a sure grasp of practical economics. Dazai's observation that commoners knew almost immediately when money had been debased is articulated in Kusama as an epistemological claim from "below" and in particular by merchants like himself who dealt with money in terms of trade
on a daily basis. Presenting his case from the viewpoint of a merchant
"commoner," Kusama stressed the theme of "utility," that government
policy must be closely in tune with how money is used at the ground level
where the people were actually involved in the activity of buying and
selling. Miura, it will be recalled, took the theory of utility to the source
of economic production and concluded the most useful money to be the
most widely available, namely "iron." Kusama took that idea to the nodal
point of economic *transaction,* the marketplace itself, rather than to that
of *production* and emphasized the consistency of content regardless of the
metal involved. Miura envisaged an agricultural economy in which "exchange" would be held to a minimum, thus reducing the demand for expensive money. Kusama had no such illusions, being a financier engaged
in large-scale interregional transactions. Like Miura, however, he emphasized that monetary policy must be articulated in such a manner that
it would be in accord with the "interest" of the populace in general and
not with the short-term advantage of those with power. In presenting a
history of money from an ideological stance clearly identified with merchants and "city dwellers"—*shimin*—however, Kusama's position held a
distinctive place in the overall discourse on money. Whenever the oppor-
tunity arose, he unhesitatingly reaffirmed merchant knowledge of money
and market to be a *public* virtue and not a private passion and argued the
inevitability of large-scale trade relations.

As mentioned, Kusama based his theory of money on metallic value.
The accurate and predictable metallic content he argued repeatedly was
the absolute prerequisite for money to be socially useful. The transaction
of trade through money, he further reasoned, was not merely a "physical"
exchange but an emotive and "ethical" one as well because the consistent
content of money made "trust" between men based on a nonarbitrary,
fair, and objective norm possible. Utility, in the final analysis, must be
based on interhuman trust; and money, as an accurately gauged and fixed
standard, made this possible in the realm of trade. Earlier arguments,
therefore, that money must be "cheap" are not important; nor is the volume of money itself the crucial ingredient; nor should trade be circum-
scribed so that money would not become independently "expensive" and

"useless"—nor for this same reason should it be argued that goods ought not be traded over vast geographical distances or to foreign lands.

All of these views of previous commentators only confused matters for Kusama. If money as an externally controlled and fixed item of value could be relied on as a norm of constancy, then goods however voluminous could be traded in ways that were righteous and fair. If money is stable and serves as a basis of mutual economic trust, then goods could also be traded across political boundaries and over great distances. The factor of supply or volume of money, Kusama admitted, was important. Artificially imposed scarcity of money invariably causes unease among the populace, sometimes even triggering unrest—*tami no sōdō ni oyobi sōrō*.[15] However, to increase the supply of money through debasement of its value, for example, by increasing the amount of copper and tin relative to silver, as he claimed was done on several occasions most conspicuously in 1705, was only to compound the difficulty. The net effect would always be a rise in prices which is exactly the opposite of what was desired. When a major currency, as in this case silver, is arbitrarily debased, the effect on other available cash is also immediately inflationary. Gold coins already in scarce supply will increase dramatically vis-à-vis silver, and also copper cash, again achieving results opposite to political intention and creating enormous hardships especially on the general populace below. Moreover, when money is debased and its reliability and value decline, commoners will resort to chicanery and speculation based on the fluctuation of the value of money, with unsuspecting producers of agricultural goods and craftware suffering egregiously as a result. Quite predictably, the populace will hoard good quality cash and trade off the debased ones, driving up the prices of good cash even more and putting into general circulation a certain kind of cash not because it is "useful" but because it has been deemed relatively "useless" due to its debased value. The actual value of that money will then be driven down even further and the "price" of goods will in turn rise. In short, the maintenance of a constant metallic content in money is not simply a mechanical political act but involves the feelings of the populace at large since it impinges, in fact, on the ethical matter of *trust* as this value is expressed in terms of economic livelihood.

To not see this social truth was to Kusama to compromise, in the end, the culture of the nation itself. Surely, Kusama reasoned, it would inevitably become a national embarrassment—*honpō no haji*—that all, including traders from foreign lands, would come to see. Thus, while the "supply" of available cash is an important factor, Kusama denied it to be fundamental in the way that Arai had said. Holding unequivocally to the

236

theory that value determined utility, Kusama insisted that only after money had been established as a reliable basis of economic interchange did the matter of the relative "supply" of cash enter as an important item. Whether the controlled ingredient be gold, silver, or copper made absolutely no difference in his view, distancing himself in this regard from Ogyū and Miura Baien as well.[16]

Kusama relied throughout on historical narrative to substantiate his point of view. In the early 1600s gold and silver cash of high and consistent quality, known as Keichō gold and Keichō silver, were minted and set the standard of measurement for monetary value. Roughly between 1690 and 1710, those years overlapping with the Genroku and Hōei eras, however, cash of decidedly lower quality was minted—gold and silver being debased with copper and tin. The populace responded immediately and predictably as his theory would have it, by hoarding Keichō gold and silver and keeping the debased monies in circulation, converting these whenever possible to the stronger Keichō silver and in turn to Keichō gold. Among the populace, the new debased monies came to be accepted at a face value of twenty percent less of the Keichō norm, which had the effect not only of taking the earlier cash out of circulation but of driving prices upward according to the socially determined "value" of the new money. The new silver and gold, in fact, also declined in value relative to copper cash which had retained its consistent content. The cash most useful to the populace in their everyday lives, thus increased in value, making it relatively scarce rather than bountiful as it should be. Indeed, more than silver, it came to be used by merchants involved in trade as a predictable basis of calculating the price of goods exchanged, reducing its availability for daily use. In the light of this economic chaos, the populace freely abandoned the debased money and converted it to durable goods with a stable value such as large amounts of grain or fabric and works of art, explaining indirectly in this regard the economic basis for the active merchant investment in the field of aesthetics. As the complaints from below grew louder, the Bakufu in 1714 finally decided to establish a fixed value to the "new" gold and silver relative to the earlier ones to reestablish a modicum of order after some twenty-five years of complete mismanagement. All of this stemmed from the fact that those who ruled had failed to grasp the basic principle that monetary stability as a determinant of price was fundamental to the governance of the nation as a whole—*chikoku hei tenka no konpon*.[17]

Having established consistent metallic value as a *sine qua non* for the economic livelihood of society, Kusama shifted his attention to the problem of "price" and the politically caused fact of domainal "indebtedness," both of which were related to the subject of money, in his view often in a confused and misleading manner, without adequate analytical delineations. Stable money, while necessary, is not by itself a sufficient cause for economic well-being. While it is obviously essential for the maintenance of stable prices, prices are not determined exclusively by money. Thus, while social disturbances of the 1730s were triggered by wildly fluctuating prices, these fluctuations were not caused by bad money but unstable agricultural production, which is a force of nature beyond political control. The "behavior" of money as reflected in prices is responsive in particular to the natural supply of rice. In one instance (1728), a bumper production of rice flooded the markets, driving the price downward and thus reducing the incomes for the aristocracy and the peasantry and stirring peasant rebellions. In another instance (1732), a severe decline in production due to unfavorable weather conditions resulted in the inadequate supply of rice in the urban markets, conversely driving prices upward and causing starvation and riots in the cities. In this framework of analysis, Kusama explained, "money" as an indicator of market prices did not function automatically for the good of all, however stable the content of money might be. His main point, however, was that those who worked the marketplace do not determine supply and price, although they were often wrongly blamed for the extreme fluctuations in this relationship.

The most important theory to bear in mind was that, depending on the level of supply, the marketplace was advantageous to some and disadvantageous to others—*eki; fueki*. Economic misery, Kusama reasoned, was not distributed evenly throughout society, as evidenced by the benefits that high supply brought to city dwellers in the form of low prices and conversely the relatively low supply yielding high prices for the aristocracy. Given this volatile relationship between supply and price, governments committed to righteous rule must set a base and ceiling within which the market was allowed to fluctuate and must construct cushions— as through granaries—so that the market functioned with relative equity for all—*byōdō ni*. Grievous deprivations that caused famines and in turn rebellions might thus be avoided. Kusama doubted that those who governed could establish those guidelines because of their relative inexperience in matters concerning the actual conditions of money and price in the marketplace.[18]

To Kusama the basic analytical distinction that needed to be made was a simple one. The supply of rice, being grounded in nature, reduplicates itself in a cyclical fashion and in patterns of high and low yields that men could not regulate. Money, on the other hand, is not a natural but an artificial construction based on human choice and regulation. Its supply is not cyclical but politically determined. Its function is also to be distinguished from nature and designed by men to facilitate the transaction and circulation of goods in a more or less equitable fashion throughout society. However, because its supply is limited, money maintains a relatively high value on a consistent basis, unlike agricultural production which fluctuates in value more drastically according to conditions in nature. The marketplace thus conjoins money of limited quantity with agricultural goods whose supply fluctuates. And since the former is limited, the expression in terms of "price" oscillates relative to the latter, namely agricultural supply.

The main thrust of Kusama's argument here was that this fluctuating relationship was not arbitrary and, in fact, calculable in terms of accurate standards of measurement. The arbitrariness, he contended, came from human mismanagement of the actual metallic value of money, which gravely distorted the ratio between supply and price. The alternative policy pursued by Bakufu and domainal lords to seek ways to increase agricultural production was similarly misguided. Although the means here were not "arbitrary," they revealed a lack of understanding regarding the function of the marketplace. Thus, these rulers chose the policy of increasing rice production through land reclamation and improved irrigation. While laudable in the conventional moral sense, this policy proved to be disastrous as it glutted an already amply supplied market. The calculated target of producing more cash through increased grain production to aid indebted samurai did not materialize at all, since the price of rice declined accordingly with the increase in supply; conversely, when production suddenly dropped due to cyclical natural conditions, the chaos that ensued was equally extreme for large amounts of rice had to be gathered from a diminished supply.[19]

Kusama based his theory on production and price on data he accumulated on the long-term pattern of the price of rice. Compiled for a hundred-year period (1715–1814), this data, in the form of a handbook and known as *Kusama Isuke hikki*, served as a basic reference for Kōnoike financiers.[20] In his evaluation of this data, the crucial factor in the continuing economic crises afflicting the land was not inadequate "production" but much more fundamentally that of "circulation" and "distribution" of available goods. A large supply of reliable money, Kusama insisted, was essential for adequate distribution of goods. The Bakufu and regional lords, however, were confused by the fluctuation in the price of rice and the popular riots that sometimes accompanied this pattern and assessed it to indicate lack of production. More often than not the main factor for price fluctuation was nothing other than seasonal factors that could have been ameliorated with improved means of distribution and stable money.

The fundamental point that was being missed, Kusama observed, was that despite the extreme fluctuation in the price of rice, the average price of rice over the long haul had actually *declined* steadily and continuously all through the eighteenth century. Calculating the market value of rice on gold and silver in the areas of Higo, Chikuzen, Hiroshima, and Chūgoku, all client areas for his house, Kusama documented the point that, despite gaps here and there, the averages—*heikin*—and broad percentages—*dairitsu*—clearly revealed this downward pattern. Caused by the steady increase in production, the inevitable decline in price created an annual shortfall in the supply of cash for domainal lords and the Bakufu. This led them either to sell more grain, which produced famine conditions during unfavorable weather conditions, or to invest valuable cash resources in the production of more rice, a faulty solution in Kusama's eyes.[21]

Above all, under these conditions of declining fiscal income, the aristocratic leaders of the land resorted to political solutions that were simply arbitrary and unsatisfactory, causing even more turmoil in the economy. One of these was the unilateral cancellation of debts—"refusing to honor contracts already signed and sealed."

While commoners may be excused for withdrawing good money from circulation due to the justifiable "fear"—*osore*—of debasement, the breaking of contracts by domainal lords was not only capricious but counterproductive to their very own interests. Aside from the fact that these cancellations of debt made it difficult for delinquent lords to secure favorable loans in the future, even more important, they had the effect of causing a net decline in the available supply of money in the economy to carry out the large-scale transactions that the aristocracy needed to maintain itself.

Equally as damaging to the economy was the Bakufu's policy of imposing extraordinary levies—*goyōkin*—on the merchants of Osaka to cover emergency administrative expenses. A direct consequence of poor management, of spending more than could be afforded, this policy reflected the Bakufu's lack of knowledge regarding the crucial role that capital played in the movement of goods throughout the country. The issue for Kusama was not that Osaka merchant houses were incapable of meeting these demands. As he described it, these houses deliberated in the various town councils and established a distribution scheme based on annual profitability. In one of these levies in 1761 that Kusama cites, the enormous sum of 1.7 million *ryō* of gold was demanded in three installments at the end of the year. Three Kōnoike houses were conspicuously present at the top of the list of some 200 houses—their contributions totalling 125,000 *ryō* of gold. That this and similar requests tended to come at the end of the year, when Bakufu expenses were highest and when much of Japanese society rested to enjoy the traditional religious holidays, created much resentment among Osaka merchants for easily understandable reasons. To Kusama, however, the arbitrary levies were evidence not of caprice alone on the part of the Bakufu but also of ignorance regarding economic matters. As with the cancellation of debts, these levies deflected capital from its proper economic use to unproductive administrative projects.[22]

Both schemes took large volumes of capital suddenly out of economic circulation, thereby reducing the social function of money in distributing goods needed in various parts of the country. As capital was withdrawn from large-scale trade, requests for additional emergency loans by domainal lords could not be met. Goods previously ordered had to be cancelled. In some cases, Kusama observed, goods already enroute to Osaka had to be intercepted by the various guilds and returned to the domains due to lack of transportation funds: *sho ton'ya unsō no shinajina kotowari sono kuni e okuri modoshi.* The losses brought on by the chain of events following the contributions were enormous—*sono sonshitsu hanahada ōku.* While none doubted that the Bakufu had the authority to impose such levies through a fiat, Kusama also concluded that the economic consequences were so extensive that such a policy must be deemed a total failure. It revealed clearly the Bakufu's inability to grasp the principle that the unilateral withdrawal of sound money from the economy had rendered that money "dead" and had totally sidetracked it from its primary social function of facilitating the flow of large amounts of goods over great distances. Uninformed by sound economic reasoning, the leaders of the country had turned to arbitrary political interventions that proved to be detrimental to society as a whole.[23]

Kusama's prescription called for a bold and decisive policy to activate lifeless capital and recirculate it in the economy to finance the transportation and distribution of goods in great abundance as required throughout the country. Since a return to an "ancient" form of pure and simple agrarianism was impossible, it was now imperative that a predictable supply of basic capital—*genkin*—circulate continuously throughout the economy. He summed up his thinking in the following manner:

> Since indebtedness creates an impact on the flow of money throughout the economy, enormous loans should not be transacted.

In Place of Dreams

> The proper way for the economy now is to choose between reactivating those large debts that are outstanding so that they contribute to the recovery of the nation, or alternatively treating them as lifeless objects. The choice between life and death in this case involves intelligent thinking by those who govern. Unless there is some sort of grand scheme through which to make active use of debts, it is unlikely that significant results will be realized.[24]

Kusama's language leaves little doubt that he did not foresee a bold plan forthcoming from those who ruled. Minimally, however, Kusama believed that all domains must first make "public" the precise extent of their indebtedness to merchants so that specific policies could be shaped with reference to that fact. Moreover, the amounts of capital used for nonproductive purposes should in turn be severely curtailed with an eye to minimizing debts and restoring credibility in the economy. He was convinced, however, that Bakufu and domainal lords would continue to drain the economy of large sums of money and, in benighted fashion, do exactly the opposite of what the economy needed.

Scattered throughout Kusama's outline history are warnings that the failure of the aristocracy in economic matters carried long-term structural and moral consequences. Repeated consistently over the previous 100 years, the policies of debasement, cancellation of debts, forced levies, and erroneous investment in rice production, unless corrected, would contribute inevitably to the further decline of the polity and generate popular disturbances from below. Being passionate, the general populace was capable of being "extremely noisy"—*hanahada yakamashi*—toward bad political policies. It would be dangerous, he warned, to underestimate the knowledge that merchants and "city dwellers" possessed. Yet, the errors repeated over time left no room but to doubt the ability of the leaders to correct them. The conditions in political economy will continue to decline, and the point will be reached where the idea of rebellion will be generated—*hangyaku no i kore yori shōzu.*[25]

The issue for Kusama was a moral one. Possessing basic knowledge of the marketplace, city dwellers would steadily lose faith—*fushin*—in those who governed. While the aristocracy mouthed the ethic of "trust" and "loyalty," they contradicted this when, for example, they cancelled debts. All the exhortative decrees from above about curbing passion and greed among the people could not counteract that one act of faithlessness. Drawing on teachings repeated at the Kaitokudō, namely that knowledge and moral trustworthiness must always be in accord, Kusama made plain the social consequences that would ensue from their misguided acts. When a domainal lord failed to honor a loan agreement,

Kusama noted, the implications went well beyond the mistreatment of a single merchant house, for in truth, what was being violated was the fundamental principle of "trust"—*shingi*—that made politics and social life possible. Insofar as the men who ruled continued to violate that basic morality, the possibility of social disturbance would constantly be present.

Among marketmen, the ethic of trust welded together an agreement between trading parties and served as the *sine qua non* of their social existence. For them, the ethic of trust and of practical "interest" were one, internal virtue and external compact unified, as all of the teachers at the Kaitokudō had consistently lectured. This unity, moreover, was embodied in an instrument known as a contractual agreement, which Kusama referred to often with such terms as *yakusoku, keiyaku, keiken no shinyaku, keiken no shinyō*—terms that survive in modern Japanese economic and legal vocabulary with their meaning intact. Beyond the calculation of "righteous" profit, these contracts affirmed the communal ethic of "trust" that bound merchant society in Tokugawa city life. To Kusama, as true undoubtedly of his community in general, an economic transaction was one and the same time a moral one. And, in its essence, this morality should be coherent with that of all other segments of society, including men entrusted with power. When rulers contradicted this morality with arbitrary action, they weakened the political order itself. To speak of "saving the people from their sufferings"—*kyūmin o sukuu*—as the justification for their claim to governance, and at the same time, to directly violate the "interests" of the people is indeed to transgress the basic moral code underlying social order. Confucianism, Kusama underscored, was a moral philosophy about the sustenance of human life throughout society, and this must mean the respect of rulers for society's natural "interests"— expressed here with the ideograph "profit."[26]

The ideological implications of Kusama's narrative are readily apparent. Hardly an innocent "history," Kusama accused Bakufu and domainal leaders of failing to understand the patterns associated with the market and of continuing to remain distant and aloof from that crucial nexus. This criticism, in turn, was an affirmation of merchants like himself at the ground level of the economy who continuously strived in systematic and nonarbitrary ways to maintain an orderly relationship between supply, money, and price. While merchants were not entrusted with public authority, they in fact contributed in a vital manner to the polity. Indeed, the extent that the economy functioned as well as it did was due not to public planning but to the "private acts of commerce"—*shōbai no shi*. His thinking along these lines is remarkably undisguised. It was unavoidable that those who govern should locate themselves at the upper reaches of the hierarchic scale. And he admitted that those "below" should be supportive of them in their righteous exercise of public law. This is also in accordance with natural principle that determines scarce items to be valuable and the ordinary or common to be inexpensive, as in the relative value in ascending order of iron, copper, silver, and gold.

It is also within this norm of nature that each possesses a "virtue" and hence a value specific to itself, the social value of each being, in fact, essential to the well-being of the whole. The analogy here with the social world around him was clear enough. The aristocracy was relatively scarce and occupied a more valuable position relative to the rest of society and received guaranteed stipends for this. Commoners living in the cities on the other hand did not have such an economic guarantee to sustain their lives and thus engaged themselves in the occupation of trade. As history evolved into the present, however, the virtue of commoners as market-men had now come to assume a vital significance for the public order to a degree that was unprecedented in Japanese history. Indeed, their execution of fair exchange was absolutely essential to the governance of the nation, as merchants and those in Osaka especially had developed a system of large-scale trade based on contractual trust. "By relying on a single contractual note—immense amounts of money were expended in the exchange of goods . . ." The nation, he concluded, could not be governed without these enormous transactions that merchants managed. Kusama likened merchants to "copper" in the hierarchy of "value," abundant and hence less "valuable," but turned the argument around and praised merchants in terms of broad social and political "utility," reminiscent in this regard to the argument advanced by Ogyū Sorai and Miura Baien that inexpensive money was "valuable" because it was "useful" to society as a whole. But most importantly, Kusama had invested a *political* virtue to what merchants did that Ogyū and Miura had not done in their theorizing about economic value.[27]

This ideological articulation, moreover, was entirely consistent with the ethical teaching of "truthfulness" espoused at the Kaitokudō throughout the eighteenth century. From Miyake Sekian on, the ethic of accurate judgment according to a natural norm was affirmed, and virtue within human beings was proclaimed to be consistent with the epistemology of systematic calculation. In this unity of inner and outer spheres, "trust" was deemed to be possible among human beings in community. The conception of market that we find in Kusama is in accord with this Kaitokudō ethic. The marketplace, in other words, was a moral arena at the ground level of human existence, and "profit" was calculated in terms of a contractual relationship of "trust." As Kusama would note, profit like trust was natural, analogous with the growth and transformation of plants and creatures, springing up from the soil—or from below among commoners: *ri wa shimo yori shōzu*—in ways that were calculable and not arbitrary. The well-being of society within this formulation is generated from below and not from authority exercised from above. As in nature, where all things produce an "advantage" or "profit" specific to themselves, so too in society the people possess an analogous interest and they should be allowed to pursue this without competition or violation through political interventions.[28]

       *   *   *

Kusama's "outline history" marks an important place in the intellectual history of Tokugawa merchants. Within the continuing debates over the meaning of "money," Kusama staked a position unmistakably identified with the leadership of his class: he disagreed with the theories identified with Arai Hakuseki on volume of money as well as with Ogyū Sorai on social utility as being high priority issues. He emphasized "trust" as to consistent metallic value over both volume and inexpensive and broadly useful cash; and, while he did not comment directly on Miura Baien, his disagreement on this issue was obvious for similar reasons. To Kusama, large-scale trade involving money, which Miura wished to avoid, was inevitable to the world at hand. In situating himself in this manner, he stressed the importance of the *political* determination of money as a consistent, unwavering and fixed "value." He furthermore defended this position on the grounds that *commoners* who actually carried out trade "know" what is consistent monetary value and cannot be deceived by the manipulation of metallic content, as through debasement. Here, his view dovetailed with that of Dazai's, who also emphasized the knowledge of traders. Unlike Dazai, however, Kusama pinned his view in the end to the ethic of "trust" upon which he believed all human history and society rested. Thus, despite the resonance between his thinking and that of Dazai, Kusama linked his entire theory of money and market to the educational principles of the Kaitokudō, namely the capacity of commoners to know moral and practical knowledge. The reliability of money and the fluctuating supply of goods were items that ordinary men knew as part of their daily work. They also were aware that while "nature" could not be controlled in terms of "supply" the content of money could indeed be regulated through political action. Most marketmen believed that while politics could not "fix" nature, it could and should do so for monetary value.

That which is "natural" and "artificial" is thus of considerable importance in Kusama's overall thinking. It was in the calculation of the relationship between fluctuating natural supply and politically fixed monetary value that price was determined. This determination among merchants yielded their relative level of livelihood. Fluctuating "nature" is somehow inevitably "principled"; money, while artificially and humanly determined must also be, like nature, "principled." The relationship between nature and politics, therefore, is intellectually consistent. However, insofar as the value of money is determined by human policy, "money," by definition, is part of "history" and, more specifically, of "political history." It is a past that can be reconstructed: the pattern of debasement can be traced just as the swings in the price of rice can. In all of this, Kusama is arguing that "politics," while principled like nature, is not a simple extension of the natural order and that, rather, as a construction based on intelligent choice, it can, unlike nature, be altered to assure a stable point of reference for trustworthy human relationships.

Kusama's thinking tended toward a "mercantilist" line of reasoning. Through the exercise of authority, money is stabilized and "limits" placed on the recurring problem of famine. While governments cannot alter the basic principles that regulate the marketplace, especially as regards "price," they have a vital responsibility in establishing a basic condition for trade and that is the consistent determination of monetary value. Kusama, while adhering to the theory of "principle" in nature, does not admit to the *laissez-faire* notion of economics. Politics has a crucial place, and merchants should be allowed entrance into it. Indeed, if "nature" and "money" could be brought into a coherent relationship, trade was possible among all human societies. As he emphasized, even men from foreign lands could understand the meaning of "trust" in this crucial sense. Kusama's theory of political economy was expansive, and this derived quite naturally from his general approach to knowledge.

It need also be reemphasized here, because it is vitally important to our account, that Kusama presented his overall view from the stance of "city dwellers" and, more concretely, of financiers like himself. Excluded from power, urban commoners possessed knowledge valuable to the polity. Indeed, they possessed a "virtue" that the aristocracy did not have, as his "history" of money clearly documented. In this sense, Kusama's work is a defense of merchant epistemology and of the general theory of knowledge espoused at the Kaitokudō by Goi and the Nakai brothers. Yet, with Kusama, that general theory is presented much more explicitly than before from the point of view of a practicing financier. Thus, while Nakai Chikuzan articulated it to promote the idea of a national educational system in which commoners like himself would command responsible and leading positions, Kusama turned the same idea to argue the case that commoners with "proven" economic knowledge be called upon to directly counsel men who governed the nation.

Reflecting his education at the Kaitokudō, Kusama made the above claim from a position of skepticism identified with Goi. Human knowledge was always incomplete. The conclusion to be drawn, however, was not that politics may thus be arbitrary but that some knew more about certain kinds of phenomena than others. Goi had taught from this point of reference that the Dutch knew more about "nature" than Asian sages. Kusama relied on this very same theory of relative knowledge in framing his assertive ideas. It is not to be taken as "shameful," he advised, to have to admit lack of knowledge of what is known—*shirite shirazaru to mōshi sōrō wa haji ni arazu. . . .*[29] But this admission that ignorance was not shameful must also mean that some know more than others and will thus deal with the market, for example, in better terms. The same theory that knowledge is not absolute and that therefore losses and gains were also relative informed Kusama's argument that merchants, in general, possessed greater knowledge about the working of the economy than men who held and gained stipends merely from being in positions of power.

It is amply obvious that while Kusama spoke for commoners in general, he in fact was an advocate for the stratum of financiers of which he was an outstanding member. While his argument that merchants in general knew the marketplace better than the aristocracy, the ideological perspective he had to offer was the place that the "great merchants"— *daishō*—should occupy in determining the future of political economy. They were, as he would put it, "embellishments of the nation"—*kuni no kazari*—because of what they knew and in fact did. While living under conditions of uncertainty, without guaranteed stipends, and building houses on systematic calculation alone, they in fact should be entrusted with the future of the nation's economy—*kokka no keizai*—since the aristocracy would remain at great distance from the world of trade. "No doubt it would be embarrassing for the samurai to seek the advice of lowly commoners," Kusama thus wrote, "but they are in truth inferior to what merchants know about price, money, and trade and should, therefore, consult them." Not having done so, they have neither "nourished" nor "saved" the people, as they claim in order to justify their possession of power, and instead have inflicted enormous harm on society—*sono gai mata ōi nari.*[30]

Historical hindsight clearly shows the future to have been on Kusama's side. Mastery of economic knowledge, he had insisted, and not the maintenance of aristocratic pomp and display would be the crucial determinant of effective governance. This general vision would not come to pass in his day, and Kusama did not expect it to. It was entirely appropriate, however, that his history of money would serve as a basic reference to the Ministry of Finance in its effort, in the early Meiji era, to radically redesign the basic economic structures of the country in order to generate an industrial revolution.[31]

*   *   *

The obvious need only be mentioned in passing here in concluding this section. Kusama's "history" exposes the contradictory nature of his own role as a financier. Pointing out the counterproductive action of the lords in cancelling debts and demanding forced contributions, Kusama at the same time cultivated close interpersonal ties with these very same individuals to secure their favor. That he was on intimate terms with some of them is suggested in a reference to him by the domainal lord of Hizen, one Matsuura Ichiki, whom Kusama advised. Referring in his diary to Kusama as one possessing remarkable perceptivity about basic human concerns, Matsuura noted also that he was lacking in "scholarly accomplishment"—*gakubun nakarishiga.* The emotional closeness on the one hand and the discrepancy regarding the appreciation of Kusama's knowledge is readily evident. Although fragmentary, there is here a reference to a relationship that relates to Kusama's own harsh indictment of the lack of knowledge on the part of his clients.[32]

YAMAGATA BANTŌ
(1748–1821)

Born into a relatively prosperous peasant family of Hasegawa in the village of Kazume, to the west of Osaka, Yamagata grew up in the interstices of the lower classes where the lines between peasant and merchant were ambiguous and blurred. Engaged in sericulture, the Hasegawa's traded with Osaka merchants. In the course of time, they established an especially close economic relationship with the house of Masuya, whose main family was Yamagata and whose leaders studied at and provided support for the Kaitokudō. At the age of thirteen, Yamagata was adopted into one of the branch houses of the Masuya enterprise which had come under the management of his uncle, Masuya Kyūbei. Following a spectacularly successful career as a financier, Yamagata was formally given the name Masuya Kouemon in 1804. Kouemon meant "the lesser" Masuya, but second only to the very head himself and thus the name carried enormous prestige. In the following year, he was further adopted into the main Yamagata household itself, formally establishing him as a "relative"—*shinrui nami*—of that family. His formal name was Yamagata Yoshihide, but he would favor the assumed business name of Bantō, a homonym for "branch manager." Born a Hasegawa, and known more familiarly in the Osaka world of trade and finance as Masuya Kouemon, he would be remembered in history as the author of *Yume no shiro*, Yamagata Bantō, a name he had taken on late in life and did not wish to pass on to his descendents.[33]

Yamagata's achievements were formally celebrated at the time of his adoption into the main household. Credited with restoring the financial fortunes of the Masuya enterprise through his management of the finances of regional domains, he was also honored for his scholarly accomplishments in moral philosophy, history, and the new sciences of astronomy and geography. Gratitude was extended to him for encouraging and teaching the methods of mathematical calculation—*sangaku*—to members of the Masuya enterprise. And, finally, he was praised for bringing esteem to the Masuya house because of the special recognition given to him by the great teachers Chikuzan and Riken.[34]

Worthy of note in connection with this event is that it was precipitated by a request from the lord of Sendai that Yamagata be given the status of a deputy head—*shujin nami*—of Masuya and not simply a representative or assistant of that house. While the laudatory praise extended him at the formal ceremony was irrefutably true and justifiable, Yamagata was aware of the adoption being primarily a matter of convenience. Agreeing to the adoption, therefore, he also made it known that after his death his descendents would relinquish the name of "Yamagata" and would revert to the "Hasegawa" family. Yamagata himself was buried in the Hasegawa family plot, not in that of Yamagata, although, as noted earlier, he would be remembered in history by his adopted name.[35]

The previous occasion underscores the important relationship that Masuya had with the domain of Sendai. Indeed, its emergence as a prominent banking house is linked to this, with Yamagata serving as the key advisor to Sendai during the 1790s. Among the dozen or so domains that Masuya helped to manage, such as Echizen, Owari, and Shirakawa, Sendai was the largest and most difficult case, as it had a populous samurai class and an unpredictable rice production due to the cold north-central climate. As a vassal domain to the Tokugawa's, moreover, it was often called upon to fulfill special duties, such as the maintenance of the regime's ancestral shrines at Nikko. Faced with a situation that led Sendai to a history of chronic indebtedness, Yamagata constructed an economic policy for which he gained widespread attention and that was also often emulated in late Tokugawa times.

The policy rested on a triangular relationship between domainal rice production, the Edo market, and the Masuya banking house in Osaka. The aristocracy's rice stipend as well as all surplus rice available in the domain would be sold through Masuya's agents in Edo for the most favorable price possible. The cash profit as well as all available bullion reserves in Sendai would be deposited in an account at the Masuya and this capital would be invested on behalf of Sendai. Masuya would guarantee a five percent interest income. Thus capitalized in Osaka, Sendai would then issue a standard paper currency within the domain, called variously as domainal currency—*hansatsu*—or just as often in Sendai's case, as "Masuya" currency. The value and credibility of the paper currency were pegged directly to the stability of the investment policies pursued by Yamagata Bantō within Masuya. Within the domain all financial transactions, as well as repayment of debts, would be made with paper currency. Indeed, with the domain's entire metallic cash supply in the hands of Masuya, a modicum of economic credibility was regained, although it was now widely known that the economic fate of the domain was entirely outside the domain and located in a merchant banking house in Osaka.

Whether or not even such a policy could have sustained Sendai's economic viability over the long haul is a controversial matter that need not be addressed here, although the picture remained clouded at best in the waning years of the Tokugawa era. The main point is that both Yamagata and the house of Masuya gained much praise for the bold plan they had devised. Yamagata had provided a mercantile intelligence for one of the regime's pivotal domains when it was afflicted with a faltering economy, and he had done so without fear or apology as a financier of commoner status from Osaka. Among the many stories that circulated about Yamagata's prowess one of the best known is told by his admirer, Kaiho Seiryō, in his treatise on Yamagata Bantō—*Masuko dan*. Yamagata requested that the lord of Sendai pay him for his services not with cash but with the spillage of the handful of rice caused by a bamboo shaft at each checkpoint enroute to the marketplace in Edo. Known as *sashigome*, this spillage was put to speculative use by Yamagata in the rice market and an impressive profit was said to have been reaped for Masuya. This anecdote coincided with Yamagata's view of the aristocracy as being inattentive to the mathematical calculation of the "margin" that determined the well-being of the whole. "Frugality" to the samurai was simply a matter of moral posture and was devoid of the scientific concept of precision. And indeed, Kaiho would extract this theory of calculation from Yamagata's policies and argue that it should be the new epistemology for determining the course of future history.[36]

Through Yamagata's efforts at Sendai, in any event, Masuya's fortunes rose rapidly as a banking house. In 1806, Masuya (along with the Osaka branch of Mitsui) was to be ranked for the first time among the top dozen or so merchant houses, making substantial contributions to meet the Bakufu's forced levies. Reflecting the expansive attitude of a house that had just risen to great prominence (as compared with the Kōnoike where Kusama served which had been a leading house for well over a century), Yamagata thought it entirely appropriate that merchant enterprises support the public order. Kusama, it may be recalled, denounced these demands for contributions as entirely arbitrary and negative in their economic effect, as they forced the withdrawal of "live" capital from circulation and undermined prices and the circulation of goods. Yamagata's view was quite different. Involved in an "untaxed occupation" that included taking profits from loans made to domainal lords, Yamagata reasoned, merchants ought to contribute to the well-being of the polity in lieu of a fixed tax. "It is entirely proper," Yamagata noted, "for merchants engaged as they are in an untaxed occupation [nengu korenaki shōbai] from which much profit is realized . . . to expect requests for fiscal contributions."[37] In short, financial advisors involved in the management of domainal economies are in fact involved in "public" acts from which they exact profits that are not taxed. Insofar as this is the case, Yamagata argued, merchants ought regularly to support the functioning of the overall system and, therefore, rather than being shocked by exactions from above, ought to set funds aside in anticipation of them. Like Kusama, Yamagata did not approve of the use of these exactions in economically unproductive projects. But Yamagata believed that a percent of merchant profits should support the polity and that in the absence of formal taxation, this was entirely justifiable.

After Yamagata had restored the finances of Sendai to a modicum of stability, he began to turn his attention (sometime in 1802) to the task of pulling together the notes he had compiled over the previous two decades at the Kaitokudō. The result would be his Yume no shiro. In 1804, Yamagata presented Chikuzan with a manuscript to criticize. Weakened with age, Chikuzan would praise the work and also make note of certain parts he found difficult to understand. Riken, as already noted, also critiqued the draft, making extensive comments and advising that the treatise be retitled. The final and much expanded version was completed between 1805 and 1807. Aside from the brief epilogue of miscellaneous comments—*batsubun*—that he inserted shortly before his death in 1821, the work remained in the form completed in 1807. Yamagata's eyesight failed rapidly after that time until he lost it almost entirely around 1814. Indeed, he seems to have compiled his final synthesis over a relatively short period of time with his failing eyesight very much in mind, as he noted in a passage in his brief postscript written shortly before his death:

> I bequeath to my young descendants the foregoing *Yume no shiro* that I have compiled. Since the years of Bunka [beginning 1804] I have been afflicted with an eye ailment and about eight years ago I lost my eyesight completely. I was thus unable to put the finishing touches to the work. As I have been very ill since last year, it seems unlikely that I will live through spring . . . And so I write this final addendum in spite of my illness.[38]

Yamagata's preface sets the tone for the entire treatise. Referring here and there to the Kaitokudō as "our school"—*waga mon*—Yamagata confessed his sense of responsibility to synthesize the entire corpus of teachings at the academy and to convey his frankly critical views about conditions in the nation. While admitting it to be inappropriate for one without the proper status, he went on to say he would dare to do so anyway since he was writing for his descendants only. This was a formulaic disclaimer since many of the critical views were openly expressed elsewhere by the Nakai brothers. The opening lines unfold in the following manner and convey a sense of what was to follow:

> Drowsy from the long summer days, I rested on my pillow seeking sleep, but I suddenly thought to myself 'how embarrassing it is to be as I am, past fifty and lazily nestled against a pillow enjoying grain and fine cloth.' Although it is not properly the task for someone like myself to be involved in teaching society and talking about governing the country, I felt compelled at least to pursue my main goal of setting down in an orderly form all that I have learned from my two teachers Chikuzan and Riken, so that this might then serve as instructions for my descendants. As these thoughts came to mind, I decided to face the inkstone and to write, and even when drowsiness set in I simply would take the brush from the desk and keep on writing.
>
> Now contained within are observations that relate to matters concerning the national polity. But these need not be worrisome as they are intended for the benefit of our house only and not for others to read.
>
> In the beginning, I had entitled the volume 'Saiga no tsugunoi' suggesting that I had written it having just come out of a lazy nap. In

response to Riken Sensei's advice, however, I changed the title to
Yume no shiro.[39]

Judging from Yamagata's introductory comments, his primary instructor
at the Kaitokudō was Chikuzan. Since most of the ideas are traceable to
his teaching, Yamagata noted that he did not make special references to
him by name. However, Riken commented extensively on the draft
as well, so that Yamagata indicated he would refer specifically to him
as 'Riken Sensei said' to specify his contributions as compared with
Chikuzan's more generally. While paying tribute to the Nakai brothers in
this manner, Yamagata claimed as his original contribution the use of the
Copernican or heliocentric theory of the universe to organize the parts
within a whole. This, indeed, is the distinctive feature of Yamagata's
Yume. Through this intellectual procedure Yamagata took Kaitokudō
moral epistemology and thinking on political economy to a new level of
theoretical meaning. Yamagata also observed that his denunciation of religious and superstitious ideas—*muki ron*—was also original. But this was
somewhat of an overstatement insofar as the attack on superstition and
religious ideas had a long instructional tradition at the Kaitokudō going
back to Goi and continued by Chikuzan. What is fresh about Yamagata's
presentation, however, is the sustained and uncompromising manner in
which he presented his broadside attack on mystifications of all sorts, including nationalistic teachings about Japan's spiritual uniqueness.[40]

.   .   .

Unlike Kusama's "history" that located concrete data in human time as
the initial step, Yamagata proceeded through an alternative procedure of
first articulating knowledge in its most expansive and universalistic possibility so as to include all known and unknown phenomena. Yamagata in
this regard was overtly sympathetic to Goi's epistemology based on natural ontology. In Goi's syncretism, it will be recalled, universal nature
served as the ultimate reference for making intellectual choices, in particular for selecting relatively insightful philosophical and aesthetic statements regarding nature. Yet while nature was universal, Goi wished to
first and foremost observe visible things close at hand. To Yamagata, on
the other hand, phenomena close at hand, inclusive of natural and social
objects, must first be located in relation to a prior universal "center" that
could not be grasped through commonsense "observation." Plants, animals, creatures, the physical landscape, history, social classes, all must
first be reinterpreted or recentered in accordance with an ultimate first
principle of the universe. The planet earth itself, along with other bodies

in space, must be viewed in relation to the sun. In this manner, all natural things and received wisdom must be "decentered" from one's immediate objective presence and denied dogmatic certitude. Thus, while for Goi natural ontology served as a theoretical premise from which to make reasoned choices as to texts, it was transformed in Yamagata's hands into a radical device with which to shape a critical skepticism toward received history and the claims made by men in power of controlling the course of political economy.

In the context of the intellectual history of the Kaitokudō, Yamagata Bantō's *Yume* raises the question about knowledge that had been asked all through the eighteenth century: How does the human mind know what is "accurate," or "righteous"? Throughout this history the intellectual concern remained at a deep level, focused on this issue of the "center," an ideograph that was read as a noun *chū* and as a predicate *ataru*, meaning to strike the mark as an accurate decision and not as a result of an arbitrary and random act. Miyake's lecture on "righteousness," as a general human capacity, Goi and Chikuzan's teachings on the rationality of acquiring knowledge and acting accordingly, and Riken's laborious scholarly efforts to authenticate the theory of the "mean" all confirm this general point. It was crucial in this history, moreover, that the coherence between "inner" knowledge and "outer" action or "language" and "action" be consistently affirmed, a theme that expressed itself in the polemics against Ogyū Sorai's historicism that theorized the disruption between inner virtue and external norms. The men at the Kaitokudō remained adamant in their view that the human interior and external fields of action were mutually linked, and it was in maintaining the "truthfulness" or "righteousness" of that relationship that human beings in general, and merchant commoners in particular, could see themselves as men of virtue. Yamagata remained true to this ethical tradition and no doubt saw himself as a practitioner of it as a financier of Masuya. Yet, he also departed drastically from that tradition as well.

By constructing an epistemology that said that the "righteousness" of anything must first be decentered in terms of an ultimate universal, Yamagata insisted that the observing eye must first remove things from the concrete present and the immediate world of identifiable objects and relate them to a heliocentric "center" that was distant, ultimate, infinite, and scientific. In other words, he transformed the concept of the accurate "center" in the external world in terms of a scientific principle grounded in the methodology of heliocentric *astronomy*. By thus decentering and relativizing all things far and near, by denying special privilege to any one place or location or status on the earthly globe in relation to the sun,

Yamagata could then readdress critically the meaning of the "relative" yet immediate world of human cognition, which was his little universe of Tokugawa political economy and the tenacious traditions of superstition and mysticism that in his eyes still permeated Japanese culture.[41]

Yamagata's thinking, it must be emphasized, did not simply confirm merchants in their status as men of virtue. Nor did he wish that they see themselves in an autonomous sphere as in a secure "kingdom" detached from the flow of events. It was rather an affirmation that all human beings, including commoners like himself, could articulate their views on matters of science, history, and the polity—that is, on critical knowledge in general. The *Yume*, is, therefore, a treatise on epistemology, on how to know, how to organize general knowledge in an orderly and controlled manner, and how to apply that knowledge to the proper assessment of the human condition in the present. Perhaps most important is the sweeping endorsement of the fundamental pedagogical philosophy assumed at the Kaitokudō that commoners possessed the capacity to acquire sure knowledge and to make this knowledge manifest in action as there were no theoretical moral limits on the human capacity to know and to act. Herein lies the significance of Yamagata's references in the preface and the introduction of his delving into political subjects which commoners conventionally should not indulge in. In that preface, Yamagata expresses his unwillingness to impose artificial limits as to what human beings in general should know.

Yamagata proceeded from the view that human knowledge must rest ultimately on the proposition that the universe is an infinite absolute preceding all human and historical experiences. What men know, therefore, must be tested with reference to the best-known science of studying the universe, this being in his view "astronomy." As Riken would comment to him, therefore, all forms of superstitious and irrational knowledge must be evaluated as being "prior to astronomy." Yamagata summed up his basic epistemology in the following language:

> The reason astronomy is said to be an immense subject is this: the universe exists prior to all else. The earth follows, and after that comes human beings and moral norms. Compassion, righteousness, propriety, filiality and loyalty are all parts of the way men order society and do not exist prior to the universe. Thus it is said that the ultimate source of all things is the universe.[42]

This vast assumption obviously undergirded Yamagata's decision to organize his *Yume* within the premise of an infinite cosmos within which all things on earth derived meaning. The opening chapter, therefore, centers on the subject of astronomy—*Tenmon daiichi*. It is true that Nishikawa had taught astronomy, and Goi had also been fascinated with astronomy as it reinforced his general theory of moral knowledge. Riken, too, was attracted to the subject after studying closely with Asada Goryū at the latter's Senjikan. And among Yamagata's merchant colleagues, Hashimoto Sōkichi (1763–1836) and Hazama Shigetomi (1756–1816) also accepted this new knowledge and studied together with Asada. These were men of considerable ability and expertise who would go on to distinguish themselves as teachers of astronomy and Dutch studies. The Bakufu would rely on Hashimoto and Hazama to revise the Japanese calendar in line with the Western one in the 1820s. Yamagata Bantō's distinction came from his attempt to include all of the known fields of knowledge within the theoretical framework provided by astronomy. The universe thus precedes human morality; and knowledge of that universe—or "heaven"—cannot be derived through the analysis of moral historical texts.[43]

Yamagata thus introduced his synthesis of Kaitokudō thought with a celebration of astronomy as articulated in the West. It was a science based on the precise and objective measurement of the universe. This was achieved, moreover, by developing a technology appropriate to this effort. The telescope was developed to observe the celestial bodies; and colored tinting on lenses—*songarasu*—was further devised to view the sun directly. Through this new science, the theory of gravity was further formulated; just as profoundly in terms of philosophical reasoning, the central place of the earth in terms of heliocentricity was denied, placing, for the first time, the human earth as a planet revolving around the sun. In all of this, Yamagata claimed, Western scientists (Copernicus, Keppler, and Newton are a few he mentions) built their studies on a theory of knowledge that tested and validated new findings and discarded the errors and false assumptions of the past. In general, they avoided the acceptance of ancient wisdom as scientifically truthful. This same critical tradition, he urged, should also be incorporated into Asia. Echoing Goi's overall epistemology, Yamagata used more radical language identified with science:

> Westerners have accumulated discovery upon discovery. And as the Japanese and Chinese too have begun to adopt their approaches, the errors of the ancients can now be shown through actual experimentation. Moreover, as knowledge not yet known is gradually uncovered in the future, the errors of today will be made clear. And people beyond that will in turn do likewise of the errors they receive. What then can be the advantage of extolling the ancients?—*inishie o ronjite nan'no eki zo ya.*[44]

Knowledge of the universe, however, will always be incomplete even as more things are uncovered about it. There may indeed be other helio-systems besides the one governed by the sun. In any case, there is neither beginning nor end to the universe. It was not created by a divine being, and its past and future are infinite.

In contrast to the universe, the earth is limited and measurable and describable according to a science of geography—*chiri gaku*—which is the chapter that follows on "astronomy." While it does not precede the universe, it provides the actual physical context within which human be-ings live, and it is knowledge of the workings of the universe that deter-mine the accuracy with which that physical, geographical, space is quali-tatively comprehended. Thus, for example, by situating the world in relation to the sun, geographers can show that there is no "center" or "east" or "west" to the globe, a point Yamagata demonstrates in a simple drawing of the earth from the perspective of the south pole with Japan appropriately placed alongside identifiable land areas. Geographical loca-tion and climatic conditions are all "relative," and in a comparative rela-tionship. No place can be absolutely unique or privileged. It is on the basis of this knowledge, Yamagata argued, that Western navigators pro-ceeded to circle the globe, claim geographical "discoveries," explore un-charted waters, measure vast land masses, and quite "embarrassingly" for East Asians—*hazubeki ni arazu ya*—to supply "names" to land areas with-out regard to existing indigenous appellations. Thus, while indigenous names are used locally, only names given by Western discoverers are uti-lized by other nations. Asia, Africa, America, and Australia are cases in point, as are "Indeya," "Shina," and "Yapan."

In outlining geographical conditions around the world, comparing ter-rain and weather in the various land masses and islands, Yamagata betrays an obvious ambivalence of admiration and resentment toward Western explorative expansionism. His admiration is, of course, directed toward Western science, its discarding of the useless, and the persistent orienta-tion toward breaking new ground. He is also impressed to the extent that language has been adapted to that task. Language is simplified to an al-phabet of "twenty-six letters" so that by the age of ten all youngsters are thoroughly familiar with the "national language" and are capable of uti-lizing it in ways that are devoid of mysticism. However, Yamagata goes on to reflect on the exploitative dimension of Westerners: "The way in which they seize precious goods and force the various countries to capitu-late must be said to be excessive." In most societies, as in Japan, the people are so involved in their daily lives that they are unaware and hence unprepared for such an imposition of national "disgrace"—*chijoku*.

Moreover, these daily activities are usually "useless," habitual, repetition of custom—*muyō no keiko*—or irrelevant religious practices. This is to be "lamented"—*kanashimubeki kana*—and ought to be drastically altered so that the nation "will not be insulted and trampled on by a foreign country." To Yamagata, the most potent approach was to teach empirical science to the entire populace, high and low alike—*jōge banmin*. Fortunately, Yamagata went on to conclude, Japan, like England, was militarily prepared so that there were no threatening enemies that might suddenly seize Japan's substantial supply of "bullion." Believing that no national area was specially blessed, so that no country was totally at a disadvantage, Yamagata concluded nonetheless that Western expansion was based on economic need, the lack of self-sufficiency and hence of weakness, while Japan, as an island nation was relatively secure and, on the whole, wealthy and self-sufficient.[45]

Having used astronomy to decenter the globe and then comparative geography to relativize physical spaces on earth, Yamagata then turned his epistemological perspective to specific pieces of national history, beginning with the problem of historical genesis in the so-called "age of the gods"—*jindai*. Here his thinking closely follows the teachings of Goi, Chikuzan, and Riken in refusing to mystify historical origins. Goi had appreciated ancient literary texts for their truthful insights into nature but did not go beyond that. Chikuzan was hostile to the entire approach called "ancient studies" that had led to the beautification of undocumentable "origins," which is what he believed Ogyū Sorai was guilty of having done. And Riken was loud and candid about his impatience with scholars in national studies such as Motoori for their utopian views about national genesis and also with Riken's own colleague in Osaka, Ueda Akinari, for writing novels about popular superstition. Yamagata followed on this intellectual tradition, except that he placed the subject of historical genesis as being superseded by the prior existence of the universe and the physical planet; its emergence therefore must be seen in that relative light. It was a perspective that allowed Yamagata to discuss national origins in comparative perspective and to focus especially on the written language as the key ingredient in the formation of a coherent historical beginning.

Prior to the possession of a written language, Yamagata argued, there was only an oral tradition which is unreliable as evidence for later times. To romanticize ancient myths is the height of absurdity and should be discarded out of hand. These myths about origins, whether they relate to China or India or Japan or wherever, are all later "fabrications"—*mina mina koshiraetaru mono*.[46] It is the written language that separates the world of divine mythology and that of history—*jindai/rekidai*. And while it is not unusual or embarrassing to lack such a language, as is the case in many societies, it is nonetheless the crucial factor in establishing historical consciousness.

His commentary goes as follows:

> The origin of a nation is to be found in the possession of a written language. Without such a language, a country persists as though not existing . . . When things are written down there is clarity for the first time. Without documentation, there is darkness. Even if a country has a written language, if events are not written down for posterity, it is as though that society did not possess language. There is no other way of knowing about our ancestors. Even with language, knowing the past is difficult. This would be even more so for an ancient society without a written language.[47]

Yamagata's theoretical point was that historical genesis was a self-conscious act of documentation. Even after history had begun in this sense, however, a good deal was "forgotten" because events were not written down and preserved—*nokosazareba shirukoto nashi*. The same can be said of recent history. The genealogical background of Hideyoshi, for example, was not known. And while the chronicles of the twelfth century document the main happenings in the contest for power, there is no way of knowing what went on in the distant coastlines and hinterlands because there are no records. The conclusion to be drawn from this relative knowledge of history is that the origin of the Japanese nation is to be located in the use of the written language sometime in the fifth century some 1,400 years ago, not 6,000 years ago as in Judea or 4,000 as in China. In short, history is about language and "books."[48]

The thrust of Yamagata's reasoning was to debunk in no uncertain terms romantic myths about Japan's sacred origin and, along with this, the idea of divine imperial descent. Everything in the "age of gods" are later fabrications—inauthentic attempts at seeking a semblance of parity with imported religions such as Buddhism. Indeed, Yamagata rejected the identification of national genesis regarding the Sun Goddess Amaterasu as a myth, a lie. The idea and imagery of the founding divinity as "female" was, Yamagata was convinced, a fabricated attempt at establishing a divine counterpart to the goddess of mercy in Buddhism. The original myths about the imperial founding of Japan Yamagata believed centered on a "male" figure. Whether his view of the sexuality of the original imperial image was justified or not, his real iconoclasm was pointed elsewhere.

If the myth of divine imperial descent is indeed just that, a myth, as he was convinced, and if "heaven" does not yield such gifts to national societies and is best "looked at" through the science of "astronomy," how then do kingships and hierarchy more generally come into existence? In Japan and in all other societies as well, Yamagata theorized, kings and emperors did not exist in some kind of divine form prior to the formation of the land or the coming into existence of the people. Land preceded the people and, to him quite logically and totally opposite from Ogyū, *the people came before the monarchy*. Kings are thus functional and symbolic extensions of a people, not divine manifestations of heaven. "There is first a people," he thus wrote, "and then later a king is created to govern them. There is national land and then people produce things. The people come first." He went on in the following manner:

> Everywhere there is first the national land and then later the people; the people come into existence followed by the king. This is the proper sequence. To have a king first and then later the people, the people and then the land is as farfetched as having children without parents. All this is in reverse order.[49]

Shinto myths that began the story of the nation with divine creation and emperors traceable to divine descent are "all lies"—*mina uso*—as there is no credible documentation for those assertions at all. Reconstructions of the establishment of the first emperor Jimmu were made 1,000 years after he presumably established his kingdom, when the Japanese people had acquired a written language; thus they are factually unreliable.[50]

The conceptual progression followed easily from the age of gods to history. While the former was preideographic, mute, and unverifiable, the latter, however incomplete, was part of Japan's documented past. And quite consistent with his theory as to how kingships and hierarchy came into existence, Yamagata focused on the construction of a "political system"—*seido*—as the essential theme underlying the rise and fall of fortunes in *recorded* history. The particular form of hierarchy formulated in Japanese history was not divinely ordained nor simply chosen whimsically by a single person, but shaped persistently, in a long historical process by human beings. The present is thus not an accident thrown forward by the past. It is an *inevitable* outgrowth of it. It was from making this explicit conceptual distinction between the mythic past and the recorded historical one and from the added notion that the people preceded monarchy and hence helped determine the character of politics that Yamagata proceeded to present his ideas on history. In its generally positive orientation toward the more recent past, his history reflected the interpretation of Arai Hakuseki in his *Tokushi yoron*. However, in turning that perspective into a critical reading of the state of political economy in the present, his ideas were decidedly closer to the teachings of Chikuzan and Riken, especially of Chikuzan's *Isshi*.

Following the outline provided earlier by Arai and more directly by Chikuzan, Yamagata sketched out a history in terms of nine critical turning points—*hen*—which are fairly standard ones and need not be repeated here. Suffice it to say that the weight of the summary fell on the period from the "third turning point" onward, namely with the decline of the Fujiwara rule and the inexorable rise from the eleventh century onward of the noncentralized form of governance—termed *hōken*, which, as noted elsewhere, came to be used as a translation for "feudal" in modern times. What was created during these years was not pure kingship or centralized imperial rule. Indeed, during this history, the imperial court declined as in the waning "spring and autumn" years of the ancient Chou dynasty. After power shifted to the Kamakura regime, it remained with the new aristocracy of the sword. Yamagata added several related points: the aristocracy never wavered in its reverence for the diminished monarchy; the tradition came also to be entrenched from then on that political succession would not be determined by prescriptive moral norms or by blood genealogy or by legally tested and screened ministers, but by "power" and "strategem." This political tradition culminated in the establishment of the "glorious" Tokugawa regime.

More than any other government in the past, the Tokugawa Bakufu combined power and legitimacy and thus earned the righteous prerogative to distribute legal authority. Yamagata thus accepted the legitimacy of the Tokugawa Baku-han system and denied the validity of rebellion against it. Discussing this subject with reference to the forty-seven lords who transgressed Bakufu law and thus were ordered to commit suicide, Yamagata argued that these lords had not challenged the Bakufu's legitimacy as the source of law, as Ogyū and Dazai claimed they did and thus called for their execution. To Yamagata (as with his predecessors at the Kaitokudō), the lords had carried out in the objective world their "inner purpose" to rectify the image of their lord's discredited dignity and so were acting as men of "virtue" and not as rebels against the Tokugawa regime. Yamagata's point of view was consistent with his endorsement of the recent past of noncentralized rule that had produced the existing order and which was entirely justified in managing the legal affairs of the country. As in the case of Arai, history had a confirmatory force as regards the events of the recent past. Chikuzan had likewise taken this approach to justify his own expansive vision for a rightful "place" for his academy in the Tokugawa order.[51]

For Yamagata, however, a broader issue was involved as well. The previous 1,000 years revealed to him that within "history" the Japanese had shaped a particular form of governance and, in doing so, had *excluded* other possibilities, most notably granting absolute power to a single monarch. What had been created instead was a system where hierarchy was determined by a relative distribution of authority, an authority which as a political form embraced all of society and which rebellion could not undo as Dazai had recklessly set forth. The fact that power was not totally in the hands of a single emperor as in China, Yamagata reasoned, was central to the creative agony in the history of Japan and it ought to be appreciated in positive fashion. With "language" introduced from China, "history" began and replaced centuries of ambiguous and undifferentiated political relationships with explicit distinctions regarding the distribution of authority. The historical product, however, was not the centralized model of imperial rule practiced in China, where the "language" of documentation had been derived, but something quite different. His views are worth quoting here at some length, as they clarify a strong "feudal" antipathy for monarchical absolutism:

> As already noted, the system of noncentralized rule, *hōken*, in this country developed in an inevitable manner and was not determined on the basis of weighing one way of ruling as against another as though there were two comparable models to begin with. Noncentralized rule came to be the way of governing this country. The centralized system began with the first emperor of the Chin dynasty [third century B.C.] and is founded on the norm of personal rule. In the noncentralized system, unless the emperor governs by virtue the various lords will not submit to him. Should his rule be contrary to the Way, the fear is always present that the lords will rise in rebellion. Thus, he cannot afford to be selfish, nor to indulge in excessive luxury. In the centralized system, the emperor controls all military power as a personal possession so that he is not concerned about lords who might not submit to his authority or rise in regicidal rebellion. He rules entirely selfishly and his indulgence in luxury knows no bounds. . . . In a noncentralized system, wealth is parcelled out among the lords. In the centralized one, the emperor alone is wealthy. When a noncentralized system falls into disrepair, however, it breaks apart into myriads of pieces. Such occurs when the influence of the monarch wanes. When centralized imperial rule deteriorates, the result is total collapse.[52]

As the previous passage makes clear, Yamagata's view of national history was confirmatory. As an island nation, a political tradition was formed that was congenial to its geographical conditions. Yamagata believed that a true form of noncentralized government—*shin no hōken*—had been established with the founding of the Kamakura Bakufu under Yoritomo in 1185, and the tradition of distributing wealth, land, and power in manageable and *relative* proportions had been established. It was a mode of governance closer to the natural actualities of most kingdoms and which contrasted with centralized rule under a personal despot—*hasha*—such as on the Asian continent which was given to arbitrary and artificial governance. Thus, while in China noncentralized rule gave way in ancient times to centralized governance under emperors, in Japan the system of noncentralized rule came to be erected over some one thousand years as its way of organizing society, which, as he put it, "ought to be thought of as beautiful"—*bi to iubeshi . . . aa hōken no hoka wa arubekarazu.*[53]

This confirmation of received history, however, did not lead Yamagata to simply endorse the continuing present unfolding before him. Indeed, as had been the case with Dazai Shundai who had used a similar historical scheme, and with his own teacher Chikuzan, Yamagata turned his reading of history into a critical perspective on the present. Noncentralized rule, though vastly preferable to the despotic imperial rule in China, was still subject to deterioration if not managed intelligently. The history he extolled provided ample evidences of such decline and fragmentation. Any political system, he argued with ideas drawn from Riken, could be eroded beyond recognition by certain practices that became stagnant "custom" in a relatively short time by the guise of being "ancient" and this produced disastrous consequences. As Riken had taught Yamagata, inside of fifty or one hundred years an evil "custom" could erode a political order far beyond what could be imagined. This was the force behind Riken's comment to Yamagata, "We cannot now tell to what end the customs of the land will lead us."[54] Both Yamagata and Riken had uppermost in mind the "custom" of conspicuous spending by the aristocracy, which the ruling regime had not dealt with in fundamental terms and which affected the entire political system in a negative manner.

Yamagata located the crux of the problem in the intellectual failings of the aristocracy. The samurai seemed incapable of accepting the basic proposition that "everything in the nation being under heaven belonged to the whole"—*Tenka wa tenka no tenka nari.* Yamagata's preference for "noncentralized" rule did not preclude him from arguing the overriding importance of the "whole." Ultimately, the land, its produce, and the transactions generated therefrom were not, in his eyes, possessions of individuals. Only when this principle was accepted could the source of long-term imbalances then be met head-on without flinching. The source of political deterioration, he went on, was due to the relationship between limited land or productive capacity and the evergrowing need for cash for aristocratic stipends. Insofar as agricultural production was basically "fixed" by geographical conditions and did not possess the capacity for unlimited expansion, the aristocracy must devise ways to allow for a natural attrition in the demand for cash stipends. The self-conscious curbing of consumption was one obvious means. In addition, if a house did not have a natural male heir, that house should be allowed to come to an end naturally as an act of heaven and not be maintained artificially through adoption. Arguing thus as Dazai Shundai had a generation earlier as well, Yamagata defied the conventional dedication to house immortality by asserting that the termination of a house should not be regretted—*danzetsu wa oshimubekarazu.*[55]

The practice of adoption to assure house immortality and the natural increase through reproduction in the size of the aristocracy had inevitably placed an enormous burden on agricultural production, the base of national well-being itself, as Yamagata and most political economists in the East and West alike agreed. While it was entirely justifiable to reward large stipends to faithful servitors when the Tokugawa regime was first founded, Yamagata reasoned, the granting of such stipends without the demonstration of ability was a mistaken policy. As cash needs for stipends rose, the burden on the peasantry increased accordingly, forcing that class either to revolt—*sōran, sōdō*—or to abscond into the cities as vagrant people—*yūmin.* Yamagata believed the severe imbalance between agricultural production and aristocratic need to be ruinous, generating the sort of "custom" that would lead in fifty years or so to unimaginable results. All sense of relative proportion in the original distribution had thus been dissipated. A domainal lord with 10,000 *koku* of rice seeks to emulate—*mane*—a lord with 100,000 and the latter a lord with one million *koku.* Relying on Riken's comments as to the ideal ratio between land productivity to population—eighty percent of the rice distributed to the peasantry and the remainder to the other classes—Yamagata went on in this vein:

> When we look at the situation today, a domain with one-hundred thousand *koku* of rice pays out ninety-thousand of it as stipend to the aristocracy. Although faithful retainers of the current regime received large stipends at the beginning, servitors under today's condi-

tion of order should not be granted huge stipends however outstanding their achievements. As lords maintaining the order, they ought not refer back to the princes at the creative beginning and aimlessly grant large stipends. Since this is done, however, stipends have steadily increased among the aristocracy, causing agony among high and low alike.[56]

Most serious of all, the Bakufu and domainal governments had not only promoted this cruel imbalance but had failed to grasp with any kind of precision the economic ramifications that stemmed from it in matters of money and price. Yamagata thus drew his basic epistemological perspective from the heliocentric universe and applied it to the conditions of political economy in his day, assessing those conditions in terms of a deep crisis. As he proceeded to discuss these problems of money and price, his concepts now intersected with those of his colleague Kusama Naokata.

•   •   •

As with Kusama, Yamagata discussed the problem of money in recent times as being unprecedented in all of previous history. Unlike any other past epoch, the Tokugawa era had produced an economy totally dependent on money. The life and death of individuals and the rise and fall of houses were all bound to the relative acquisition of money. The movement of aristocratic retinues from regional domains to and from Edo and the payment of cash stipends to retainers had been instrumental in this. The Bakufu, however, had failed to deal effectively with the economic demand for money that it had generated within its system. It relied repeatedly on the deceptive policy of monetary debasement, increasing the content of cheap copper relative to gold and silver with the unwarranted assumption that the surface value would retain the same strengths as the previous cash. Covering much the same ground as Kusama, with comparable detail, Yamagata presented the facts of debasement: beginning in the 1690s, and continuing into the early 1710s, the Bakufu repeatedly debased money by approximately twenty percent per minting, so that Genroku gold and silver stood at that debased level vis-à-vis the previous standard known as Keichō gold and silver. By the end of four successive debasements between 1705 and 1710, the cash from each being referred to derisively among the public as "one," "two," "three," and "four"— hitotsu, futatsu, etc.—gold and silver stood at only one-fourth the value of the Keichō pieces used through the better part of the seventeenth century. As the actual value of money declined, prices increased dramatically, especially of staple goods such as rice, causing much agitation and open disturbances among the people—banmin no sōjō. It was only after much confusion and pain that the Bakufu finally in 1718 established a public rate of exchange between its "new gold" and "new silver" and the silver and gold of the various previous mintings.[57]

Having outlined the fiascos of the Bakufu in minting debased money and tending to affirm the desirability of metallic consistency, Yamagata believed, at the same time, that a monetary policy could no longer bring about a rectification of the economy. It was in his view much too late to rely on stable money alone, as the ultimate source of disturbance in the economy was systemic. Thus while the metallic content of money might be stable, prices would not decline because, he reasoned, the demand for money by the aristocracy would continue to remain high, which would prevent prices from declining. Within the political arrangements of the noncentralized system, then, other means would be needed. Ogyū Sorai, it will be recalled, had reached a similar conclusion as to the relative in-effectiveness of metallic content as a stabilizer of the economy and pre-scribed that money be made universally "cheap" and that the aristocracy, the source of the demand for money, return to working the soil as farmers. Kusama had also observed the persistence of high prices and pointed to the uncertain "natural" production and ineffective distribution of goods as determinants of such prices. Being familiar with the ideas taught by Riken, Yamagata would have agreed with the egalitarian ideal of dissolv-ing the aristocracy. He would also not disagree with the views of Kusama that "supply" and "distribution" were key elements in the overall picture and that price affects society in uneven ways.

However, Yamagata saw little reason to believe that the political sys-tem would not persist into the foreseeable future. That baneful "customs" of the present might well destroy it at some indeterminable point in the future, as Riken tended to think, he would not dispute. It nonetheless followed logically for Yamagata that the maintenance of a high price level would be beneficial to the order, a view at odds with that of most moral philosophers at this time. To Yamagata, the significance of the consistent metallic content of money was not that it drove prices down, but that it would enhance the possibility of maintaining a steady price level, which he argued should be kept high. Those responsible for the well-being of the nation, however, continued to deceive themselves with ancient mo-rality in which it was said that since men by nature despise poverty, the price of goods ought to be kept low to maintain tranquility among the populace. This ancient view was no longer valid according to Yamagata because society is organized in such a manner that the price of goods as determined in the marketplace did not affect all parts equitably. A high price is relatively favorable to the aristocracy and the agricultural sector and less so for city dwellers. But since the city population is only twenty percent in proportion to eighty percent of aristocracy and peasantry, a high price level is, overall, socially preferable, contrary to the views of those in power:

> However, those who govern quite carelessly believe that when the price of rice increases the populace in general will suffer . . . and simply seek to reduce the price. This is shallow benevolence and half-hearted love as it lacks a basic understanding of how to govern. When the price of rice is high those who suffer are urban dwellers. It is the generally accepted norm from ancient to recent times that maintaining a low price of rice under conditions of peace and tranquility is to be called righteous rule. In today's context, however, when there is so much consumption throughout the land that has driven the prices of goods in general upward, the aristocracy and peasantry would be at a loss as to what to do if the price of rice should be kept low. Only city dwellers would welcome this latter.[58]

What we have here is an analysis saying that insofar as an economically unproductive class, the samurai, continues to demand cash to maintain itself, the prices of goods in general will remain high and that, therefore, the price of rice should be kept high by artificial means if necessary to sustain the overall system. Social utility here is articulated in terms of the overall balance of the political order as it is influenced by the price of goods and in particular of rice, the principal source from which the aristocracy and the peasantry derived their income. To achieve this end, Yamagata, much more explicitly than Kusama, urged the Bakufu and regional domainal governments to exercise "emergency" authority—kendō—and not stubbornly cling to old customary ways—kabu o mamoru bekarazu. As the purpose of government is "to save the people," conventional policies—keidō—must on occasion be abandoned when there is an obvious systemic crisis. In the end, the responsibility to enhance the well-being of society is in the hands of those with authority, and it simply will not do to place the blame of economic deterioration on merchants and commoners and, in a vindictive manner, drive the prices downward erroneously expecting to inflict harm on rice merchants on behalf of the people. Yamagata's defense of his class was unmistakable:

> How can [the Bakufu] act in that manner? To compete for advantage is the merchants' way of life. It is intrinsic to their occupation to buy and sell according to a calculation of the harvest. Why should they be despised for this?[59]

While it may be excusable that those without education should put the blame for the declining economy on merchants, "Why," he complained angrily, "should men who govern society accept such a view?" By seeking to keep the price of rice low believing thereby to have reduced the profits of merchants, those who rule in fact have done a terrible disservice to the aristocracy and peasantry. They actually should pursue the opposite policy of keeping the price of rice high so that less rice in the city markets would produce the same or higher levels of cash income and thus also allow for a larger bulk of rice to remain in the countryside to stave off famines. To achieve this balance between cash income and humane food distribution, merchants ought to be allowed to mediate in the process by systematically buying a percentage of the annual rice produce—*kaimochi*—at a high level. The usual view of merchants is that they buy to "hoard"—*kaitori*—rice for profiteering purposes, but Yamagata insisted this practice itself should be incorporated into the heart of the "emergency" policy of the Bakufu to promote social well-being. Rather than being "unprepared" and "recklessly" seeking petty goals, political leaders ought to incorporate the buying practices of merchants as an essential part of governmental policy. "That large merchant houses throughout the country buy large portions of the supply of rice," Yamagata thus observed, "is a blessing for the nation and should not be condemned out of hand." This activity could produce the net effect of keeping prices high and allowing the storage of rice for emergencies. Should merchants in the domains not be able to buy large portions of rice, the governments themselves ought to follow such a policy (which of course Yamagata had already prescribed for Sendai) to ensure the adequate cash intake of the aristocracy and provide a necessary supply of rice that would stave off famine. The Bakufu and domainal governments throughout the nation were to blame for the unfortunate state of the economy. The "weather," "merchants," and "markets," then, were not at fault for the crisis in the order. The source of the problem was political leadership: "It is the political leaders who are to blame for the deaths by famine, not the natural harvest. High prices result from the level of the annual harvest, not the actions of merchants. Based on a careful distinction of these matters, emergency policies must be set in motion to save the people."[60]

Two additional themes were embedded in Yamagata's critique on politics. One was the responsibility of those who ruled to establish a reasonably equitable distribution of goods. The other was that these rulers ought not tamper with the way merchants worked the marketplace. It is considered righteous for kings "out of compassion for the downtrodden to take a portion from those with wealth and redistribute it so as to realize equity"—*heijun.* "This calls for a plan to be carried out over months and years." Building granaries was a case in point. Domainal lords, however, lacked the resources to build them, as the bulk of their rice was traded for cash to meet ongoing stipendiary expenses. Indeed, those in power tended only to respond to needs as they arose, blaming the general woes afflicting the land on merchants because they pursued their strategies of buying and selling. As the real cause for these complaints is the frustration over the aristocracy's lack of cash stipends, political authority is not being used to redistribute wealth to save people but, on the contrary, to add wealth to wealth—"like piling soil on high ground." Many among the aristocracy who are nourished by this policy, in Yamagata's words, "should not be saved at all."[61]

Given the plight of the people throughout the country, Yamagata contended that the rulers of the land must be held responsible for adopting consistent measures to counteract the imbalanced use of agricultural products. This meant, as already observed, maintaining a high price for rice, which, aside from the positive social impacts noted, would also encourage the diversification of the diet among the populace, resulting in a boon for agricultural production in general. Equally as important, if this general policy were to be combined with the reliance on merchant mediations in systematically redistributing large volumes of food materials to meet famine crises as they occurred, then the wealth of merchants would be applied toward humanitarian ends. In this regard, the wealth of merchants certainly ought not be confiscated from above simply to meet the immediate needs of the aristocracy. Since it was the agreed upon moral philosophy that it was the populace at large that must be "saved" and not the samurai, the wealth of the "great city" of Osaka, where the financial wealth of the nation converges, ought to be directed so as to achieve the well-being of society as a whole.[62]

Yamagata added the following thought: when merchants are called upon in this manner to serve the public good, they should not, as individual merchants, manipulate the situation for the acquisition of great profit. The norm should be what is acceptable—righteous—in terms of the workings of the market. The crucial ingredient, Yamagata therefore argued, was the agreement to rely on the "principle" of the marketplace without tampering with the central work of merchants. The marketplace, Yamagata insisted, was determined by elemental norms that did not interest men in power. In what may seem to be a theoretical ambivalence on his part, Yamagata argued that "emergency" governmental intervention could be entirely detrimental unless informed with proper economic knowledge. Thus, while governments should take bold measures to maintain a relatively high price level that would be conducive to the maintenance of the overall social order, Yamagata also insisted that such a level tended to be determined in large measure by social "demand," as in the case of the samurai for cash. The Bakufu and domainal lords, under such circumstances, should not interfere politically to establish a price level that was artificially low and based on faulty moral reasoning.

The language that he advanced to substantiate his general argument illustrates the point of our analysis. The problem ostensibly at hand is that of "price," but the central issue to him was the relationship between political authority and his own world of trade. His description is grounded in the imagery of practical trade, as this passage illustrates:

> Let us take the case of firewood. Cut and transported from the various mountains of Tosa, Hyūga and elsewhere, it is purchased by special guilds and distributed to small retailers . . . When a political order was issued to lower the price of firewood, the remaining supply was simply returned to the producers. The flow of further supplies from the mountains stopped. Firewood in the city was depleted. Woodcutters refused out of distrust to provide new supplies though encouraged to do so. The price of firewood suddenly increased two-fold. The bureaucracy was helpless about this. From this one example, the general point can be drawn that whether the items are oil, sake, paper, silk, wool, cotton, thread or what have you, the attention given to price alone leads to miscalculation that causes much ensuing damage. When addressing the matter of price, cheap level should not be thoughtlessly set. When items are too expensive men choose not to buy them. The matter of price quite simply put should be left in the hands of merchants. When prices are too high and buyers decline, they will be lowered. . . . All this is based on general principle.[63]

The analogy, as it relates to the key factor of rice, is clear enough. Although price is obviously a function of natural supply, the Bakufu still held merchant retailers at fault and sought through political intervention to have it *lowered*. It is the "natural principle," however, that the response to high prices is a reduction of demand. If demand relative to supply is high, the "basic price"—*genka*—will be accordingly high, and retail prices in the cities will be similarly high. While commoners are familiar with this principle, those who rule act in ways that are contrary to it, thus further undermining a feeling of "trust" among the people. In short, to govern in an effective and ethical manner, precise knowledge of the workings of the market, and of the rice market especially, was imperative. And it was in Osaka, he concluded, that such knowledge is understood best and where through constant buying and selling with bills of credit and other written agreements—*kogitte*—the "natural" level of price was realized.[64]

If the systemic imbalance generated by the aristocracy's demand for cash is not rectified, Yamagata warned, the result would be rapid deterioration of the sort envisaged by Riken in his fable from the kingdom of dreams, *Kashokoku monogatari*. Noting that Riken had written this piece to discuss "conditions under the governance of domainal lords," Yamagata outlined the main themes in Riken's piece in some detail and then offered this advice to those who ruled:

> Although merely a fable, it contains useful ideas and is worthy of close attention and . . . leaves out nothing in matters of political economy. I thus outline it here with the added advice to the ruling domains in the country: avail yourselves of this work for additional details and read it very carefully.[65]

As the foregoing suggests, Yamagata owed much of his general perspective on political economy to Chikuzan and Riken. The expansive vision he held for Osaka merchants contributing to the well-being of the nation through the control of the marketplace paralleled the view Chikuzan had for the Kaitokudō within a national educational system. The assertive ideological claim that merchants with their superior knowledge of market and price ought to be called on to play a dynamic role in governance also certainly overlapped with Kusama Naokata who had urged rulers similarly in his history of money. While sharing the broad visions of these men on behalf of Osaka financiers, Yamagata also was deeply aware of the long-term corrosive impact of "custom" on the polity that Riken had taught and written about. As a financier, Yamagata could not "exile" himself and enter the reclusive world of dreams in which Riken had sought refuge. But that he comprehended Riken's pessimistic vision of the future there can be little doubt.

· · ·

Along with his assessment of the economy, Yamagata's moral philosophy was also drawn from his mentors Chikuzan and Riken and, before them, Miyake Sekian and Goi Ranju. Compassion, or the human capacity to feel deeply the sufferings of others—*hito no itami*—was combined with the mental power to cognize things and to organize knowledge in ways that were truthful and to the mark. In particular, the concept of "righteousness" as articulated in *Mencius* was stressed along with the idea of knowing the "center," as found in the classic of the *Mean*. Following the teachings of Riken, Yamagata also subscribed to the view that this latter text was a coherent whole, in contrast to the interpretation offered by Itō Jinsai, that the section on the human spirit—*kishin*—had been misplaced by later editors, and that it should be relocated to introduce the final sections on "truthfulness." But most of all it was the affirmation that all human beings possessed the epistemological power to know and acquire knowledge that Yamagata valued. "The *Doctrine of the Mean*," he thus noted, "prizes intelligence above all else. While the *Analects* held compassion to be primary and intelligence to be next to it, comparing thereby the relative merit of one virtue to another, in the *Doctrine of the Mean* compassion is said to be essential to the sagely self, but that broad knowledge is crucial, for without it action will be unreliable. Intelligence was thus cherished."[66] From this defense of general human capacity to know, Yamagata, like his mentors, also took a stern oppositional stance against Ogyū Sorai: "With the two refutations of Goi Sensei in his *Hi-Butsu hen* and Chikuzan Sensei in *Hi-Chō*, Sorai's erroneous views were at last made plain."[67]

Despite his endorsement of the scholarly interpretations of the classics espoused by Kaitokudō teachers, Yamagata, it must be emphasized, also revealed a strong skepticism regarding a good deal of sinological studies. Much of it he observed was "useless"—*mueki no koto*—including even the textual studies of the classics—*keisho ni mo*. It would be enormously beneficial, he ventured further, if Japan abolished the use of Chinese ideographs and adopted the phonetic system entirely, especially since expressive precedents could easily be identified, as in the *Tale of Genji* and the *Tale of Ise*—*mina iroha nomi*. Just as in the West there is "a, b, c up to twenty-six letters only," on the basis of which all their books are written, Japan too should rely exclusively on its phonetic syllabary. Yamagata's section on the "classics," therefore, ends with a critique of Chinese culture and of sinological studies in his own cultural universe, with language interestingly reminiscent of Tominaga Nakamoto:

> The intellectual attitude of the Chinese is that everything began with written words, even before the ten-thousand things of nature came into existence. They do not seem to realize that humankind and human events postdate the existence of things and that events precede the written word. . . . Men in China today seem to be blinded by their possession of written ideographs, thinking it to be somehow completely true and pure. It is certainly the case as noted in an earlier section on "the age of gods" that a nation unfolds when it acquires a written language. Without it several tens of thousands of years could pass by without much awakening. Without denying

its value, language is something to be used and not for men to be used by it.[68]

Decidedly of greater significance for Yamagata than the skills attached to sinology was the judgmental epistemology taught at the Kaitokudō. In this intellectual tradition, it was repeatedly emphasized that knowledge was not mysterious, that even "dreams" were not outside the realm of human experience and hence comprehension, and that ordinary human beings, commoners without power or status, could know external things and norms and judge them according to standards of accuracy and fairness. The ultimate value of the *Doctrine of the Mean* and of *The Book of Mencius* was in this affirmation of general human epistemology. Just as Goi had idealized the image of Mencius embracing the light of day after a night of dreams, Yamagata, too, was adamant in his view that human reality, in its inner and outer dimensions, as well as the natural order, visible and invisible, were comprehensible in some accurate and reasonable manner and that all mystifications that played on human fantasies and fears were false. This proposition, which is present throughout the entire treatise from the beginning, builds up to the interrelated sections directed against "heresies" and "spirits"—*itan; muki*. In a phrase, all religions and speculative schemes about superstitious forces are "heresies" insofar as they distract human beings from their most essential search for virtue, which was to study and grasp the way of governing self and society. All else was heretical and, as Riken had pronounced, was also "pre-astronomy." Key ancient texts that articulate the truthfulness of the "mean" and modern ones that outline the science of "astronomy" serve as valid reference points of human knowledge against the claims of saints, shamans, and the everyday believer in the occult and mysterious. This theme that we saw present in Goi, Chikuzan, and Riken culminates in Yamagata's sustained attack of over one hundred pages on religious beliefs and irrational thought.[69]

Yamagata identified one of the key sources of irrational beliefs to be in the misinterpretation of the classics themselves. The reference to "heaven," for example, was often combined with the term meaning "spirit"—*kishin*—which prompted later scholars to speak of a spiritual realm transcendent of or detached from physical reality. In Yamagata's view, however, these references were always made in connection with secular human moral problems and not as a category apart from human life. "Thus when Confucius was asked about spirits," Yamagata commented, "he discussed human affairs in response; and when asked about death, he talked about life." In another example, "spirit" or "life spirit"

273

was used with reference to the intangible force in "things." It was used in this manner in the *Doctrine of the Mean*. But, Yamagata insisted, this language simply referred to nature—*Tennen shizen no i*—much in the manner that Sung philosophers theorized on the "principle" of "heaven."

In the case of the *Doctrine of the Mean*, the language of spirit, or life in things, was a metaphor to mean the "truthfulness" of any given object including the human self. The moral teaching there was to insist on the importance of being "respectful" of truthfulness. Thus the text spoke of hearing the "voiceless" and seeing the "shapeless," and it rendered life and death as being "godlike"—*kami no gotoshi*. These were references to the human perception of truthfulness in the world within and without, the visible and the invisible, life and death. More often than not, "spirit" referred to an individual's "power" to govern self and polity and had no bearing on immortality or magic. Nowhere does the text say that "spirits" actually exist disembodied from the universe of natural phenomena. In the ancient world of the Chou Dynasty, Yamagata explained, paper images—*katashiro*—were erected to stand in place of the deceased. This practice provides conclusive evidence that the ancients did not believe in spirits and thus created a paper image "in place"—*shiro*—as in the title of his opus—of the spiritual life of the deceased. The images of parents are similarly preserved to remember the departed spirit and thus, these paper emblems stand in place of the actual spirit that once was.

It was this perception of ritual as rational and knowable by the cognizing mind, much in the manner that Chikuzan had sought to ground "dreams" in actual human experience, that informed Yamagata's "replacing" of spirits and dreams with rational metaphoric image. The creation of paper images of the departed individual had nothing to do with the existence of that individual's spirit but with the "truthfulness" of the inner feelings of "respect" that one had for that deceased person. It was this perception that closely dovetailed with Riken's thinking; Yamagata believed he must "replace dreams" and this idea remains, captured at the very heading of his work.[70]

When this intellectual insight is substituted for dreams and illusions and other superstitious excuses, one is then left with the lasting legacy bequeathed by Mencius: "Heaven does not speak. It expresses itself only through actions and deeds." Thus while the great Confucian scholars from the Han Dynasty on, including Chu Hsi and his colleagues of the Sung, Arai Hakuseki, Yamazaki Ansai, Ogyū Sorai and others in more recent times in Japan, have all dealt with "spirit," attributing to it a non-rational force, their teachings on this matter are entirely misleading and deceptive and should be rejected. Men should accept the truth that social rituals may reveal the truthfulness in individuals, but they do not contain a spiritual force that can help men rule themselves or the people. At the individual level, one ought to be filial by extending affection and respect to parents while they are alive but not believe that ceremonies after their death sustains in actuality a spiritual communion. And at the national level, rituals dealing with filiality and other customary practices count for precious little:

> Though rites may be diligently practiced, a nation that should flourish flourishes, a nation that should decline declines. Let it be observed that this has nothing to do with spirits, but completely with the virtue of men who govern.[71]

We need not catalogue in great detail here Yamagata's invectives against all forms of religious thinking and superstitions which he consistently labeled and debunked as foolish—*mina gu nari*—the Sun Goddess in Shinto, the Buddhist pantheon of gods and the fantastic imagery of infinite paradisium, Christian theological preachings about salvation in heaven, as well as popular folk beliefs about the magical powers of beasts, mountain goblins, and unusual creatures. Suffice it to say that in presenting his case against spirits, he drew on the thinking of his predecessors, as he readily admitted. His impatience with the superstitious fascination among commoners about foxes and badgers turning into or possessing human beings is clearly reminiscent of the teachings of Goi and Chikuzan, as the following passage suggests:

> Human beings are said to possess a superior spirit among the ten-thousand things. If they do not examine things, however, they do not possess knowledge; without hearing sounds they cannot speak; without special training, they cannot write; without studying medicine they cannot heal; without acquiring things they have nothing to give others. . . . Foxes and badgers do not know about such matters. They cannot speak, write, read, cure . . . Human beings alone give names to things. Although it is true that names differ among the various nations, the birds and beasts do not assign names to things.[72]

And similarly, his critique on Buddhism as being largely fabrications and mystifications well after Shakamuni's time bear the markings of Goi and also of Tominaga Nakamoto's iconoclastic treatise against Buddhism. He broadens Tominaga's comparative perspective, however, into a global one, reflecting the new knowledge of geography that was within his intellectual grasp but was not available to Tominaga. After recounting the spread of Buddhism from South India to cover the better part of Asia, Yamagata went on in this vein:

> Those who know Buddhism are limited to this area of the world only. This being the case, it is not known in five of the other great continents. If only a portion of one continent knows about heaven and hell as taught in Buddhism, these should not be understood as global norms. Furthermore, most of the nations from Europe up to India believe in Christianity . . . And then there are the American continents about which details are altogether unclear, though surely the ideas of heaven and hell such as believed in Asia are not to be found there. When considered in this manner, Buddhism obviously cannot be taken to be the universal moral law of all the lands.[73]

In the place of believing in such unwarranted religious claims, Yamagata reaffirmed the scientific approach to knowledge and the application of this for the social good. Through science, he emphasized again toward the end of the treatise, the ravaging effects of epidemics such as measles and small pox would be kept in control and infant mortality reduced. Having perused with conscientious interest Udagawa Genzui's translation of the eighteen volume Dutch work on internal medicine by Johannes de Gorter—rendered as *Naika sen'yō* (1793)—Yamagata identified the basis of Western science as the precise search for primary causes.

> Western works on medicine all have as their primary concern the search for the cause of an illness. Experiments are carried out by the individual alone. Yet if he is not intellectually satisfied he seeks the advice of others. And when he finally has established the cause and sets out to treat it at its root, he is in control of all the little details. The Western approach to knowledge is almost entirely in-fused by precise calculation [*menoko zanyō*]. In astronomy, medicine, craftsmanship, the Japanese and Chinese do not come close to it.[74]

This passage contains the critical vision informing the entirety of the *Yume*. In organizing knowledge one begins with the general truth, the underlying cause, ultimately the universe as ontological premise, rather than the aimless tampering with details. When the root cause is established, as he noted, the parts fall into place. It may appear at a glance that Yamagata had proposed this approach as "replacement" not only of "dreams" but all East Asian modes of objective inquiry. Although this was not the case, clearly he, and merchant colleagues around him studying Dutch medicine, had reached a conceptual accommodation with Western science as a coherent approach to knowledge about the universe and human life. Yamagata did not intend to replace the intellectual tradition that he had received from the Kaitokudō, but he had dramatically shifted the terms of the concepts he had received, a theme that will be addressed again in the epilogue. His synthesis, it should be emphasized here, was of the main ideas he had been taught. It is undeniable, for example, that in his attack on superstition and on assertions about "spirit" that went beyond the verifiable, Yamagata had taken to task the great Confucian thinkers of the past, including Chu Hsi, Ogyū Sorai, and Arai Hakuseki, by identifying himself with the teachings of the Kaitokudō:

> When I speak in this manner, I do not mean to denounce the great Confucian scholars as though I had come to this view on my own. I also was given instruction on it. The school of Miyake and Nakai never muddied its teachings with ideas about the spirit. So quite the contrary, how can this view be mine alone after having been taught in close personal manner by great scholars of the stature of Chikuzan and Riken.[75]

Thus, while noting at the end of his opus that nature was universal and devoid of moral preferences and social schemes of reward and punishment, he also affirmed that among the various systems of moral thought in the human world, Confucianism was superior to all of them. This was so because of its clarity in discussing human relations in society and, more generally, because of the insights it provided for understanding political economy in the present, or history as an ongoing reality, without the glossings of mystifications and fantasies of previous ages. It taught compassion and righteousness, grasping the emotive truthfulness in others and in things and innocent creatures, and knowing the accuracy of external events. It taught, in short, the theory of action that led men of virtue to act on behalf of others in society—ultimately the people as a whole. This he believed to be the way of all virtuous men, regardless of status.

Yamagata makes this point in a conversation with Riken about the allegedly indecisive character of Hayashi Razan, one of the key exponents of Confucianism in the early Tokugawa period. When asked by the shogun as to how "the way of the sages" might be realized in the present, Hayashi is claimed to have said that this was not possible. In Yamagata's eyes, Hayashi had failed by not prescribing at that juncture precisely how the shogun ought to act to make compassion and righteousness a reality for all in the land. Riken's comment to Yamagata is also worth reporting: "Like a cook without the skills to prepare a dinner, when ordered unexpectedly to prepare a splendid feast with the appropriate utensils provided, Razan shrunk from the task. Though knowledgeable and eloquent, scholars are not capable of preparing such a meal." Yamagata left no doubt about his own annoyance at the timidity of one of the founders of Tokugawa Confucianism.[76]

To him, Confucianism contained within itself the intellectual power to transcend the mystifications and irrational thinking of the past and address in direct fashion the problem of widespread human agony in the present. In providing the analysis as to what was systemically wrong in the present and in offering prescriptions as to how to solve it, Kaitokudō thought seemed to provide him with a moral philosophy entirely in accord with the approach to knowledge he had distilled from Western science. His vision of replacing dreams thus contained within it a central place for a "moral science" based on the critical Confucian orientation to political economy. It was from this premise that he encouraged merchants to contribute willingly, as an act of "righteousness," a portion of their income as a fiscal contribution to the well-being of the general populace.

Yamagata's consistent emphasis on "righteousness" and "truthfulness"—makoto—clearly establishes his Yume within the genealogy of Kaitokudō moral epistemology. Riken had also placed himself within this same lineage by affirming the basic concept of accuracy located in the Doctrine of the Mean; and, as with Goi before him, this epistemology had taken them to the recognition of the importance of Western scientific thought. Yamagata received this legacy of "righteousness" and "science" and rearticulated the entire corpus of Kaitokudō thought within a vision of universalistic science. The line between "dreams" and "reason" would not be drawn with reference to the classics, as Goi and Chikuzan had done, but to astronomy. In formulating this broad synthesis Yamagata, while being utterly loyal to the Kaitokudō, had taken ideas familiar at that academy to a level that went beyond what even Riken had achieved. His "text" in this respect may indeed be taken as a decisive "act" appropriate to the crisis at hand, an act that Riken had said Razan earlier had not lived up to. As a financier immersed in the actualities of trade, moreover, Yamagata did not indulge in retreating into an isolated world of "play" and "dreams"; and his characterization of political economy is not done within the framework of a "fable."

Yamagata's vision is of a future devoid of all dreams and mystifications, and it is expressed in terms that extended well beyond the intellectual universe of his mentors to the broad philosophical discussion of science of the late eighteenth century. The most provocative thinker in this development was Miura Baien, and therefore Yamagata must be viewed in relation to the ideas of Miura. In him, too, is to be found a radical epistemology that, like Yamagata's, sought to clarify the basis of "righteous" or objective knowledge through the identification with ultimate and universal premises. Indeed, the two men share a closely related place in eighteenth-century thought that represented the most clearly refined statement of objective science and the rejection of "dreams" and "superstitions." Since the dialogical relationship between them is sufficiently intimate (especially as it also connects with modern intellectual leaders such as Fukuzawa Yukichi, about whom more will be said in the Epilogue) a brief comment is relevant here before concluding this chapter.

.   .   .

A few key social relationships help to clarify the intellectual connection between Yamagata and Miura. Yamagata studied with Miura's students at the Kaitokudō, the best known among them being Waki Guzan and Hoashi Banri, leading teachers of science in late Tokugawa (and to whom the intellectual legacy of Fukuzawa is to be traced). These men especially came under the influence of Nakai Chikuzan and his philosophy of general education for commoners. Yamagata, moreover, studied astronomy with Asada Goryū, a lifelong friend and colleague of Miura. Asada's father (Isobe Dōsai) was the principal teacher of both Asada and Miura, and even after Asada exiled himself to Osaka to assume a new name and teach medicine and science, these two scholars continued to exchange ideas through letters. And, as noted in the prologue, Miura admired enormously the teachings of the Nakai brothers and hoped that one or the other would write the epithet on his gravestone. These evidences suggest a set of close social and intellectual relationships, especially through Asada, Waki and Hoashi, that help to clarify the closeness of thinking in Miura and Yamagata.

There is indeed a striking degree of conceptual sympathy in the thinking of these men. Like Yamagata, Miura based his overall epistemology on the theory of natural ontology: men ought continuously to seek to know more about infinite nature. Similarly, he took great pains to show the limitations of proceeding to nature through historicism, or more specifically through received custom, which he believed to be filled with superstitious beliefs or "dreams." Miura did not deny the relevance of moral philosophies for society and accepted the fact that these philosophies were shaped within social history. But, like Yamagata, history was relative, useful in the practical and functional sense, and not fundamental to basic epistemology. Each also affirmed the capacity of commoners to control knowledge in concrete ways and manage their lives. The peasantry, Miura believed, could and should organize themselves in self-help cooperatives—*mujin kō*—and consciously agree through "contract"— *yakusoku*—to work toward communal causes. Miura in fact organized such a cooperative in his village and drafted the contractual agreement himself, to which every member of the village affixed his or her signature.[77] Both appreciated the importance of politics, Yamagata perhaps more emphatically, and offered prescriptions based on consistent intellectual premises regarding the economy, but they were, at the same time, pessimistic of the capabilities of those who ruled.

Comparable to Yamagata's investigations as recorded in his *Yume*, Miura too sought knowledge rooted to a universalistic theory and concentrated on astronomy and comparative geography—*tenmon chiri*. As with Yamagata, Miura addressed the problem of language as the bearer of useless custom. Yamagata was especially concerned with the inappropriateness of Chinese ideographs for Japan, while Miura turned to the general problem of language as conceptual expression, which he outlined best in his celebrated work on knowledge, "Basic Propositions"—*Gengo* (written over the years 1755–75).[78] The search for sure knowledge must begin with intellectual skepticism—*utagai*—regarding all received custom and conventional claims to truth.

Articulated first by Kaibara Ekken a century earlier, Miura's skepticism proposed that everything must first be conceptualized with reference to a prior universal. This theme, as emphasized, was also crucial to the entire organization of the *Yume*. While thus remaining close to the empiricist mode of thought formulated by Kaibara and his agronomist colleagues (that truthful knowledge could be acquired through the consistent and systematic observation of objective things and deducing from that method deeper insights into the workings of nature), both Miura and Yamagata took that method a long step forward by emphasizing that the cognizing mind observing things was also a social mind filled with conventional reasoning that was superstitious, irrational, and prejudicial. Miura observed, for example, that men believe that things in nature are arranged in terms of superior and inferior categories, thus obviously approving of them in human society as well. They believe that their functional physical parts are superior to those of other creatures. Insects and fishes without arms and legs are seen to be "handicapped"—*fujiyū*—relative to humans. *Nature*, however, has no limbs, but the days run their course and flowers bloom. Yet because men impute subjective feelings, some moralistic, others purely superstitious, into natural objects such as creatures, flowers, the landscape, their view of reality is like the depiction of nature in children's cartoon books—*kodomo asobi no ehon*.[79]

To Miura and Yamagata, the main obstacle to understanding nature is the way men acquire knowledge in general. While the mind is said to gain information through sensate observation, which through repetition and acquired familiarity is then claimed to be categorical truth, much of this is simply social convention and has little to do with the workings of nature. To both Miura and Yamagata, therefore, the commonsense procedure of "observation" proposed in a good deal of Neo-Confucian thinking was simply inadequate. The observation of repetition did not warrant the normative conclusions about "categories" that were often drawn. To Yamagata "observation" required the telescope and the miscroscope, since much about nature could not be observed with the naked eye. By claiming to know the norm through sight, Miura argued, the human mind tended to react to the abnormal as "strange" or "mysterious"—*fushigi*. Men thus view with wonder flowers blooming on a dying tree. But they do not ask why flowers bloom at all, because it is assumed to be known through commonsense observation. Similarly Miura observed, men are attracted to thunder and lightning as mysterious and miraculous happenings, but they do not ask what principle governs weather conditions in general, including days that are "normal" and thus "known."[80]

To break this fallacious tendency, the human mind must doubt what is conventionally believed to be beyond doubt—*heizei narete tsune to suru koto o utagai*—and then asking "why"—*nani yue*—general phenomena occurred the way they did in nature. As the great sages were human and flawed, the critical mind in the present must first turn his gaze *away* from received history, place another more forceful principle prior to it, and seek the meaning of things in terms of principles that do not meet the eye. To achieve this, Miura speculated, one must rely on a consistent set of conceptual "methods"—*jutsu*. Confronted with this same intellectual issue, Yamagata, it will be recalled, turned to the heliocentric theory of the universe and astronomy. To both men, in other words, what can be seen directly must always be displaced in relation to what could not be viewed in the conventional sense, as for example, the earth's movement in space could not be observed as both their theories emphasized.[81]

Although too complex to go into here in any kind of detail, this thrust is especially pronounced in Miura's thinking and is worth summarizing. Miura based his entire epistemology on an oppositional or binary theory of natural phenomena. Since the governing dynamic of things is beyond the visual powers of men, he theorized, there must be a "hidden" dimension involving oppositional and interactive forces that men must abstractly envision. Just as the sun appeared to move westward while moving constantly, in fact, toward the east, the critical mind must first perceive the outwardly observable as a "sign"—*chō*—of a deeper dynamic. All phenomena, he thus hypothesized, were manifestations of unseen counteractive processes and outward signs. Referring to this as a continuous process of confrontations and syntheses—*hankan gōitsu*— resembling what might be termed a dialectical process, Miura also theorized this process to be mathematically consistent as an infinite sequence. In his language, "one" is always "two," and "two" always unfolds as "one," as a mathematical principle without beginning or end. Beyond the dialectic and theory of infinity, Miura suggested other possible hypotheses inherent in nature. All phenomena, Miura proposed, possessed the oppositional dimensions of form and nonform; contained within them a gridded construction along horizontal and vertical lines or longitudinal and latitudinal ones; and moved in ways that were simultaneously rotative and linear—*katachi aru/katachi naki; tate/yoko; en/choku.*[82]

In seeking to go beyond the conventional language with which "names" were ascribed to "things," Miura offered a philosophy certainly as comprehensive as Yamagata's synthesis of knowledge. Both saw the human mind as always being relative to universal and infinite nature, so that things and events beforehand must also be seen in relative and hence critical light. In Yamagata's theoretical scheme, the earth was relative to the sun around which it revolved. From this perspective of skeptical relativism both thinkers endorsed the ability of commoners to acquire and use knowledge in relative yet effective ways. To Miura, indeed, all men in pursuit of the study of nature were to be taken as colleagues in a common effort—*dōmon no hōyū*—without regard to status, geographical location, or name of school.[83]

It was Yamagata more than Miura who would take that same egalitarian concept of knowledge to make a special argument on behalf of marketmen like himself. Yamagata's *Yume* may be seen, therefore, as containing a purpose from the outset to proceed from a distant and comprehensive universal to the concrete and decentered reality of received history as it presented itself to him. Because his knowledge of the universe is relative and the concrete flow of events before him also relative, he could similarly claim for himself "relative" yet critical insights into the probable course of events and the place of human intelligence in it. Unlike Miura's "basic propositions," which do not lead directly to an analytic rendering of the present, Yamagata's *Yume* is aimed, finally, at the world of political economy. Thus, while Miura's "Basic Propositions" is a separate treatise from his "Origins of Value" that dealt with the economy, in Yamagata, the discussion of "astronomy" proceeds without hesitation to "economics"— *keizai.* In combining basic epistemology with a critique of the present within a single "text," Yamagata had forged a synthesis that in its completeness constitutes a major conceptual achievement that has withstood the test of time.

.　　　.　　　.

The greatness of Yamagata Bantō's *Yume*, then, was in its comprehensive synthesis of ideas taught and discussed at the Kaitokudō and its intellectual environs. More specifically, it may be seen as having synthesized the dual themes of "nature" as the universal source of knowledge and hence also of virtue and the ethic of trust and righteousness drawn from "history," as from the texts of *Mencius* and the *Doctrine of the Mean*. This latter theme had been present at the inception of the Kaitokudō in the 1720s, when it was still known as the Tashōdō, and was incorporated into the opening lecture offered by Miyake Sekian in 1726. The explicit endorsement that commoners possessed the virtue to know external norms of goodness and fairness, while articulated within the legal confines of a public academy, was entirely sympathetic in purpose with Itō Jinsai's use of Mencius to confirm compassion and the capacity to act out goodness as a universal human endowment and not a superior form of knowledge known only to the educated or to the aristocracy. The conviction that human beings of ordinary status, hence in Osaka, mainly merchants, possessed this universal virtue, was repeated throughout the eighteenth century at the Kaitokudō, receiving especially strong and polemical articulation in the hands of Goi, Chikuzan, and Riken. While directed against Ogyū Sorai in good measure because of this thinker's theoretical tendency to disengage "inner" from "outer," imputing in the former a limited range of what could be known and in the latter the legacy of the ancient kings as an externally given norm, the central purpose throughout was to affirm the capacity of ordinary human beings to organize knowledge beyond the immediate self in some social and political field and to make cogent judgments as to the "righteousness" of events as they unfolded. In the narrower sense, this meant the instruction to merchants that their calculation of accuracy—the mean—was not only fair and virtuous in the practical and moral senses, but it also constituted a cognizing method through which to analyze political economy and make prescriptions accordingly to those who governed the land.

Chikuzan's *Sōbō kigen* serves as a crucial testimony in this line of thinking. It was repeated forcefully, without hesitation or embarrassment, by Kusama and Yamagata as practical financiers. The relationship between "virtue" and "accuracy"—*toku* and *gi*—as being potentially coherent served to join human interiority and the analysis of the flow of external events. Riken's reflective thinking on the moral and political crises of his times reappears in more concrete statements in Kusama and Yamagata on politics and money. Both emphasized the absolute importance of keeping capital "alive" and flowing so as to transact the necessary distribution of goods. Wealth, they emphasized, was dynamic and distributed in relative ways throughout society. Economic knowledge, they asserted, was fundamental to politics, the art of "ordering and saving the people"; for this reason, merchants, and other commoners as in Riken's utopian fable, ought to take part in the process of governance itself. These claims were being made with the conviction that the knowledge they controlled was consistent with "virtue," that this knowledge was trustworthy, and above all, it was totally devoid of superstitions, myths, and "dreams."

The lines with which Yamagata ended his grand synthesis, therefore, may be taken here in conclusion as including his own approach to knowledge through astronomy as well as Kusama's through "history," for both stood on common ground in demanding that the world of political economy be seen without the lenses of deception:

> After death there is neither hell nor heaven nor self; There is only humankind and the ten-thousand things. In a universe without gods, buddhas and demons, there are surely no mysterious and miraculous happenings. [84]

SEVEN

Epilogue

IT MAY BE APPROPRIATE HERE IN THE EPILOGUE TO RE-
ADDRESS SOME OF THE INTERPRETIVE PREMISES WHICH
WERE SET OUT IN THE BEGINNING. THE METAMORPHOSIS OF THOUGHT
within the Kaitokudō illustrates the general point that Tokugawa thinking
on political economy—*keisei saimin*—contained the dynamic capacity to
cross class lines and travel outside of the ruling aristocracy to assume an
ideological significance among Osaka merchants. In much the same
manner that religious and cultural ideas are often known to spill over
stylized barriers, the ideas of political economy in Tokugawa times were
also expansive and came, in the course of the eighteenth century, to interact with new theories of knowledge that were absent at the outset.
Yamagata Bantō's engagement with Western astronomy is a dramatic case
in point. The overall record suggests this engagement was part of a broad
pattern beginning with an initial query regarding the relevance of "virtue"
to commoners. It led to larger issues of knowledge, such as representing
the political history of the previous 1,000 years in a comprehensive and
synthetic manner; defending the proper approach to an understanding of
ethics with reference to nature or to first articulations in ancient history
and explaining why general education for all commoners was morally, legally, and practically valid. In all of these themes there is the recurring
epistemological question: How do human beings verify what they openly
profess to know, and what are the ultimate underpinnings to such claims
as in the fields of nature and history just noted? And how does knowledge, properly acquired, in turn, directly instruct human action in everyday life or in the public realm?

At the Kaitokudō this last issue was informed by a skepticism, based on natural ontology, that said that knowledge was always incomplete, constantly expanding. Knowledgeable "action," therefore, must also be relative and was most certainly not a monopoly of the ruling class nor totally determined by customary practices. Echoing the view of Miura Baien that the past was a repository of misleading "habits," men at the Kaitokudō such as Nakai Chikuzan and Yamagata Bantō emphasized the need to question the validity of received structures and suggest "emergency" measures that departed from previous ways of doing things. This theme, as with many others as well, is traceable to the teachings of Goi Ranju; but it was the later teachers who expanded this theme to include such matters as comprehensive educational reform.

The intellectual history of the Kaitokudō also suggests the sustained interaction between the academy in Osaka with individuals and groups within a "network" that extended to other cities, domains, and academies. The movement of ideas along well-traveled roads over the Tokugawa landscape, such as the Tokaidō, does not appear from this history to have been a vague and abstract process at all but, as with the transference of commercial things, was attached to specific carriers traversing concrete routes and converging in certain pivotal locations such as academies like the Kaitokudō. Miura's students from Kyushu and established academics from Edo visiting the Kaitokudō enjoyed the relative absence of constraints by domainal and social boundaries. Edo and Osaka, Bungo, Hiroshima and Osaka, city and country, center and region, all begin to lose their stereotypical "place" within presumably fixed constructions.

The often used demarcation between those with power and those without it, likewise appears, from our analysis of this intellectual history, to be provisionally unstable. Miura and his students, as well as the Nakai brothers and theirs, were outside of the ruling class and, at best, members of that ambiguous stratum known as "Confucianists"—*jusha*—a mixture of physicians, lesser samurai, merchants, and peasants. Yet, the fact that the conceptual and philosophical vocabulary they relied on was consistent with the aristocracy's as a whole seems more than reasonably certain. Miura's prescriptive treatise on political economy in terms of the theory of social utility was easily within the grasp of the local domainal lord to whom it was addressed. That his advice was not carried out because of its radical implications is somewhat moot from the viewpoint of our assessment. The same overall comment is appropriate to Chikuzan and his outline of general education for commoners and, for that matter, to Kusama and Yamagata and their economic view of politics. It would be erroneous to see the consciousness of these merchant intellectuals as being anything but political. What we see, in fact, is the formation of an ideological perspective informed by several generations of critical intellectual efforts that sought to explain the failings of the political order and was articulated specifically from the viewpoint of those who had knowledge but not power. This knowledge was expressed without apology for the politically articulate to examine in books or listen to in lectures.

It is of crucial significance that this knowledge not be seen as simply mimetic of the aristocracy. Kusama and Yamagata saw themselves as financiers who, because of their work, controlled a certain kind of knowledge in a superior manner to the class that held power. Rather than seeking the status of the latter, they offered the knowledge specific to their daily work as being of central importance to the management of the overall course of history itself. The ideological proximity between "wealth" and "power"—*fu-kyō*—being generated here within the interstices of Tokugawa classes is plainly evident. It suggests conceptual "gradations" that might facilitate "alliances" across class lines such as those that combined to construct the modern industrial order.

As we reflect on our account within this broad history, we are struck by the conceptual transformation that took place between Miyake Sekian's initial lecture at the Kaitokudō in 1726 and the treatises produced at the end of the century by Kusama Naokata and, especially, Yamagata Bantō. Relying on moral assertions supported by specific aphorisms drawn from the classical texts attributed to Confucius and Mencius, Miyake had argued that virtue was universal and thus inclusive of the marketmen in the audience. Neither Kusama nor Yamagata relied on this approach. Their authoritative "texts" were not the classics: in the case of Kusama, the documents relate to the minting of money and the format of the presentation is historical; with Yamagata, data from different fields of knowledge are all rearranged within a scientific theory of the universe. These designs are not present in Miyake. Yet, there is at the same time a shared ideological purpose from the beginning that is of crucial significance to our overall interpretation.

If Miyake taught that moral knowledge was entirely within the intellectual grasp of merchants, Yamagata and Kusama pointed their epistemologies to say that merchants could analyze the structure and content of political economy with greater accuracy and insight than the ruling aristocracy. They insisted, in short, that the polity itself was a field of knowledge appropriately within the systematic purview of merchants. The idea of "interest"—*ri*—as a righteous "virtue"—*toku*—was transformed into the righteousness of merchants being a *public* virtue. Thus, however extraordinary Yamagata's *Yume* in particular may still appear to be, it was, in all of its various dimensions, a creative conceptual extension of this long Kaitokudō tradition. It was not an isolated phenomenon in a world of hedonistic merchants who were unaware of the deepening political crisis in the ongoing present. Indeed, Yamagata's work takes on its deepest significance when taken as a profoundly self-conscious effort at making sense out of the troubled reality in which he lived. Viewed in this light, Yamagata's ideas appear as a critical insight into his surroundings that also strains toward being optimistic with reference to the new science of astronomy. In this sense, they are deeply embedded in the historicity of late eighteenth-century debates about the probable course of political economy and are not simply "ahead of the times" as unique and embryonic of modernity.

Interpretive monographs on Yamagata have tended to see him as *sui generis* and as a solitary genius who had shattered the limits of feudal thought. It is undeniable that his thinking did anticipate many of the ideas that would resurface within the Meiji Enlightenment of the 1870s; and his *Yume* did serve as an important resource for intellectuals opposed to the irrational and often militant pulls toward expansive political goals generated in the twentieth century. Without denying the importance of these later appropriations, this analysis also suggests an additional perspective in Yamagata's thinking that is oriented directly toward Tokugawa political and social structures, especially Yamagata's own "relativized" critical stance toward them as an Osaka financier. This perspective was an essential part of the dramatic metamorphosis of Kaitokudō thought.

It is moreover intriguing to see within this history the continuous discussion about the relationship between "reason" and "dreams." Goi and Chikuzan commented in their sessions with students about dreams that confused the mind at night in contrast to the light and reason of day. Riken took the metaphor of the "dream" and redefined it to mean defiant and eccentric autonomy against the political world that had lost its sense of the "mean." And Yamagata "replaced" all dreams, including Riken's "kingdom," with radical scientific reason. As everything in Yamagata's epistemology was said to share in relative degree the light of the universal sun, no geographical place, no sanctuary, could claim privilege. It is also apparent, upon reflection, that this discussion of "dreams" reveals a radical alteration in the terms with which "virtue" was to be understood. What had begun as a search for a concrete moral center for merchants had been transformed by Yamagata, following on ideas advanced by Goi before him, into a conception of infinite nature as being prior to conventional definitions of "virtue," or, for that matter, of "language" and "history." In Yamagata one discovers an epistemological reordering and re-framing of received knowledge within a scientific worldview. And in this sense, it is worth emphasizing again that Yamagata marked the decisive culmination of some one hundred years of Kaitokudō intellectual history in which ideological claim and the epistemological displacement of the "dream" are collapsed into an ordered whole.

The very completeness with which Yamagata summarized Kaitokudō thought allows us to see his *Yume*, therefore, as something of a "closure" to the most creative period in the history of the academy—and indeed, of the rationalistic optimism that characterized much of eighteenth-century thought. Coming as it did at the beginning of the fateful nine-teenth century, midway into which Japan would transform itself into an industrial society, Yamagata's synthesis clearly did anticipate the future—as in an "epilogue." Facing the challenges of this turbulent future, the later teachers at the Kaitokudō would not make new conceptual advances and achieve the kinds of intellectual breakthroughs that had been real-ized from Goi on through Yamagata. The likelihood of decline, in fact, was predicted by critics during the latter days of Chikuzan and Riken.

Writing from the viewpoint of national studies that detested Chinese moral philosophy, the famous novelist Ueda Akinari (1734–1809) had little praise for the Kaitokudō. Whatever "virtue" that might once have been identified with the academy, as with Goi whom Ueda admired, had been completely fulfilled in his view with the Nakai brothers. After them there was only decline. No worthwhile students, he harped, had been produced there—*roku na deshi wa dekinu;* and although outwardly still an "official academy"—*gakumonjo*—it had come to resemble, more appro-priately, the "gates of hell"—*gokumonjo.*[1]

Ueda, it might be mentioned here briefly, was far less critical of the neighboring school of the eccentric merchant intellectual, Kimura Sonsai (1736–1802), who became known simply as Kenkadō after the name of his school.[2] The Kenkadō actually resembled more a "museum" as it housed an extraordinary collection of exotic fauna, herbs, and gadgets from Asian and Western sources. Upwards of four thousand individuals from throughout the country are known to have visited the Kenkadō ac-cording to Kimura's own diary, which he kept assiduously between 1780 and 1802.[3] Quite interestingly, Kimura himself received his early educa-tion at a school that drew its inspiration from Ogyū Sorai's ancient his-toricism. Founded in 1765 by one Katayama Hokkai, and known as the Kontonsha, this school emphasized ancient poetics rather than political theory. The seminars were noted for discussions in which participants puzzled over ancient ideographs (which is the sense of the term *konton*) late into the night with food and drink and in which Nakai Chikuzan actively took part and Riken sarcastically did not. Kimura also developed an early dislike for ancient poetics and turned the empirical concerns with "language" to the study and documentation of natural history, a branch of knowledge known as *honzōgaku*. Besides writing such histories, he also collected material objects and displayed them in a systematic manner. It was this Kimura Kenkadō that Ueda admired, for he had collected objects for their intrinsic significance and not because they could be sold for profit. Yet Ueda was fascinated, most of all, by the fact that Kimura Kenkadō invented a new meaning for an ancient Japanese term.

Read in Sinic manner, "Kenkadō" referred to the Japanese term for "read" or "rush"—*ashi*—which was no doubt expressive of the setting of the "museum" in the marshes along one of the Osaka waterways. From Kimura Kenkadō's day, the term for "reed" in its predicative form took on the meaning of the systematic observation, collection, and documentation of things as of natural and scientific objects—*ashikabi*. A nativist interested in Japanese literary imagination, Ueda wrote a poetic song of praise to Kenkadō—*Kenkadō o tataeyoru uta*.[4] Given this interest of his, Ueda did not refer to the "scientific" dimension of Kenkadō's museum project and how, intellectually, this was in fact close to the scholarly concerns of the men at the Kaitokudō. He seems to have been unaware of Kusama and Yamagata, and makes no mention of other merchants such as Hashimoto Sōkichi who pioneered the development of Dutch studies in Osaka. Nakai Chikuzan and Riken also visited Kenkadō often, as documented in the previously mentioned diary. Having little interest in the new sciences that used the telescope and microscope, (and thus quite unlike Yamagata, Riken, and Kimura Kenkadō in this regard), Ueda offered a view distinctive to his personal intellectual interest. His acerbic comment about the Kaitokudō being "the gates of hell" should for this reason be taken with a generous sprinkling of salt. Yet, even with these allowances, it is incontestable that Ueda had seen through to the declining future of the academy.

The difficulty at the Kaitokudō was due in some measure to the lack of strong intellectual leadership after Chikuzan. The principle enunciated when the academy was first founded that "blood" lineage would not determine the head of the academy could not, in fact, be sustained in practice. Local notables in late Tokugawa, relying on the Katitokudō as a model for their own school, would refer to it as the academy headed by the Nakai family "from one generation to the next"—*Nakai ke dai-dai*. However, after Chikuzan and Riken, no one of outstanding intellectual strength came from that family. Chikuzan's son Sekka (1772–1840) and

Riken's Yūen (1796–1831) were men who could do the formal lectures and administer the academy from day to day, but they were not innovative thinkers. The library, it is said, continued to improve under them. The same was true of their successors who ran the academy over the last years—1840–1869—Namikawa Kansen (1796–1879), Sekka's adopted son, and descendant of Namikawa Seisho, who had assisted Miyake Sekian when the academy was founded and who now served as head professor, and Riken's grandson Tōen (1822–81), who oversaw the academy's administration. Under them, the academy would continue to teach merchant students in comparable numbers as in the past, but the intellectual vibrancy was no longer as it had been. The firm intellectual "place" the academy held as part of a "network" was no longer secure; and the productive and expressive scholars that had linked themselves with the Kaitokudō as part of an articulate grouping were also not replaced because those capable of doing so turned their sights to other ventures.[5]

The passing away of Chikuzan in 1804, Riken in 1818, and Yamagata in 1820 coincided with the deaths of the outstanding and visible scholars who had frequented the Kaitokudō. Between 1800 and 1820, the years known as Bunka and Bunsei or simply Ka-Sei, these men who had dominated much of late eighteenth-century scholarship left the scene along with the leaders of the Kaitokudō: Asada Goryū in 1799 at the age of 65; Hosoi Heishū in 1801 at 74; Minakawa Kien in 1808 at 74; Shibano Ritsuzan in 1808 at 75; Bitō Nishū in 1814 at 69; Waki Guzan in 1814 at 50; Rai Shunsui in 1817 at 71; and Kaiho Seiryō who had lived in the environs of the Kaitokudō, studying Yamagata and other merchants, in 1817 at 62.

Yamagata Bantō belonged to this generation of intellectuals. More importantly, his *Yume* appears at the extreme outer edge of the rational approach to knowledge to which they all subscribed. By deemphasizing classical texts as the primary source of knowledge and imposing a scheme of knowledge arranged from the most universal to the particular, cognizing mind, and redefining thereby the basis of "righteousness," Yamagata had shaped out of eighteenth-century thought a radical position beyond which there could only lie further extreme acts in scientific study or political management. An extension of his intellectual heritage, Yamagata's dynamic vision, however, could not be sustained by the academy where he had acquired his knowledge.

The conceptual position staked by Yamagata was, in this respect, as "eccentric" as that of his predecessor of two generations earlier, Tominaga Nakamoto, and it thus makes eminent sense that modern historians should anthologize them together. Just as Tominaga's iconoclastic historicism could not be promoted within the academy, Yamagata's new science based on "astronomy" could not be dealt with there in a systematic way. The matter of "expulsion," however, was not an issue in the case of Yamagata, and he would not be sent into exile. But just as Tominaga's radical position could not be comfortably housed within the "official academy," so too, Yamagata's grand reorganization of knowledge could not be effectively integrated within the curriculum. Asada Goryū taught, in the shadows of the Kaitokudō in his small private school, the Senjikan, the study of astronomy along with the reading of texts, more or less in harmony. But Yamagata's division of knowledge into pre- and post-astronomy, was a new conception of knowledge as to what was "righteous" and "truthful" that the Kaitokudō could not absorb within its original "chartered" aim. As a public academy, the Kaitokudō could not now declare itself a center to study the meaning of "virtue" through Western science, just as earlier it could not admit to being a school of "ancient studies" to show classical sources to be polemical tracts inappropriate to the present. Despite the enormous expansion in intellectual fields, as exemplified in Yamagata's own thinking, the Kaitokudō remained, finally, a "public" academy chartered by the existing source of law, the Tokugawa Bakufu. Although interested in some aspects of Western science (as in making calendars), the Bakufu was distrustful of this knowledge and had begun, in the early 1800s, to systematically hunt down and imprison outspoken advocates of it.

Yamagata's synthesis, in sum, had created intellectual demands that had outgrown the instructional capacities of the Kaitokudō. In reintegrating within a scientific worldview the intellectual legacy of the Kaitokudō to which he was self-consciously and reverentially indebted, Yamagata ironically had also rendered its teachings obsolete. It is therefore doubtful that the Kaitokudō could have adapted and expanded the range of the curriculum any more than it had.

Indeed, standing at the outer edge in the metamorphosis of Kaitokudō thought, Yamagata's ideas may better be seen as now melding with a broader flow of conceptual events cutting across social strata and class lines that eighteenth-century academies such as the Kaitokudō could no longer effectively mediate. As we see the Kaitokudō in a pattern of decline in late Tokugawa history, it is important, therefore, that we also juxtapose that development in relation to two events in Osaka of momentous importance. One of these was the devastating rebellion led by Ōshio Heihachirō in 1837. The other was the construction, a year after Ōshio's rebellion, of the Tekijuku, a major school of Dutch Studies by Ogata Kōan, to which the intellectual vitality anticipated in Yamagata's *Yume* would in fact shift. While these two events are not causally tied to each other, nor for that matter, extensive of the internal history of the Kaitokudō, they resonate with that history and deserve brief elaboration here in closing out our account of the academy in the waning decades of the *ancien regime*.

•   •   •

Soon after Yamagata's death and especially with the Tenpō era (1830–44), Osaka and much of west-central Japan surrounding the city was in a state of siege.[6] Famines and peasant rebellions rocked the countryside during these years. As Yamagata had suspected would happen, much of the blame for the general economic crisis would be placed before the gates of the merchant houses of Osaka. While commoners could be pardoned for this one-sided view, Yamagata had pointed out, such should not be tolerated of educated men in power who ought to know better. The Bakufu's decree in the 1840 Tenpō Reforms dissolving the monopolistic guilds, however, confirmed the view anticipated by Yamagata that merchants would be called to task for the ailing economy. And, just as he and Kusama had feared, the Bakufu and domainal lords resorted to authoritative exactions of monetary contributions that would damage, in their view, the circulation of much needed capital. At the house of Sumitomo, for example, some thirteen such exactions were made between the crisis ridden years of 1837 and 1841; and over the next decade up to the eve of Perry's decisive entrance into Edo harbor in 1853, another ten or so were levied.[7]

But by far the event that severely shocked Osaka and brought it and the Kaitokudō to a standstill was Ōshio Heihachirō's rebellion of 1837.[8] Convinced that the dissonance between moral "ideal" and "law" was too great to be breached, Ōshio, a former servitor of the Bakufu, sold his library to purchase guns and launch an attack from within Osaka. Made up of only twenty or so students from his "school to cleanse the inner spirit"—*Senshindō*—the rebellion set fires in Osaka in order to summon the peasantry in the countryside to join in a general populist revolt against the existing order. Although this did not happen, word of the revolt spread and sporadic uprisings were launched in Ōshio's name by peasants believing that the rebel leader had not died as reported and that his followers had scattered into the countryside to lead further revolts. The fires of rebellion ravaged more than one-fourth of Osaka. The areas singled out for attack, moreover, were those populated by the leading merchant houses, many of which were patrons of the Kaitokudō. The distinguished houses of Kōnoike, Mitsui, Sumitomo, Hiranoya, Tennōjiya and many others all suffered extensive damage. And for more than a decade or so after that, it was expected that rebellions would again bring fire and destruction to Osaka, an expectation that reflected the initial unreadiness for Ōshio's revolt.

The next "attack," interestingly, would not come from another Ōshio but from the Western naval powers in the early 1850s. Within the Osaka merchant community, more importantly, Ōshio's revolt triggered introspective concerns about organizational discipline in the face of internal unrest. Laxity and not being prepared were to be rectified through the careful scrutiny of house rules along with the assignment of more explicit definitions of duties to the various key administrative positions in the overall enterprise. These houses, it appears, went into a carefully articulated "defensive" posture that resulted, in retrospect, in more disciplined organizations. Indeed, historians theorize that the early foundations of Japan's modern corporate system are to be traced to this Tenpō period and specifically to the responses to the disturbances generated by Ōshio.⁹ As it took Osaka the better part of the decade to rebuild itself, there can be little doubt but that Osaka never did recover its former stature before the transformational events of the 1850s and 1860s would set a totally new historical course for the country. Although students at the Kaitokudō were forced to flee as the flames drew near, the academy itself was spared any damage. It is clear from the notes of students, however, that there was much soul searching that went on at the Kaitokudō about the events of the day, more so certainly than of the specific classical texts scheduled for discussion. In the language of one entry, "The entire discussion [by Nakai Sekka] was about Ōshio. Nor was there any casual conversation"— Ōshio no ohanashi nomi, zatsuwa mo nashi.¹⁰

As a youngster raised in the Bakufu's district office in Osaka, Ōshio had studied the classics at the Kaitokudō under Sekka, Chikuzan's son who was still head instructor at the time of the rebellion. He was remembered for his stubborn and defiant temperament that was often manifested in his impatience over grammatical nuances in Chinese sentences. To the well-known passage from the Great Learning, "A minister who levies unreasonable taxes is not a minister but a common thief," Ōshio was known to emphatically slap the "matting"—goza—on which he sat, to mean "indeed"—also pronounced goza—nothing but a common thief.¹¹ Once beyond his early education, Ōshio would go on to formulate a philosophical position that would diametrically contradict the basic propositions advanced at the Kaitokudō and other established academies throughout the country.

He would single out Satō Issai, the professorial head of the Bakufu's

college in Edo, for especially harsh criticism. After studying at the Kaitokudō for a year with Chikuzan, around 1792, Satō had gone on to establish a distinguished academic career in Edo. To Ōshio, Satō personi-
fied hypocritical scholarship, for he lectured in public about reason and
observation while believing personally in moral idealism and teaching
about it in his private seminars. Such a bifurcation was untenable, a critique that Ōshio could have leveled at Riken as well, as he insisted that
the only choice was the primacy of universal moral ideal. Beyond reason,
even of the most radical kind, there was for him only one possibility that
remained, which was the fusion of ideal in action. Idealism in this sense
was not a "dream" but objective "righteousness" itself, given solid shape
by human action.[12]

What was especially disturbing about Ōshio for the men at the Kaitokudō, however, was not his critique of Satō. Most disturbing to them
was the philosophical thrust of his ideas: he denied that the public order
could serve as the basis of a privileged space relative to moral truth; he
himself had once sworn "loyalty" to the Bakufu as one of its retainers.
That Ōshio should attack the Tokugawa order which would include, by
definition, the academy itself was undoubtedly threatening and intellectually perplexing. The Kaitokudō, after all, possessed a public charter
that established itself as a legal "sanctuary"; and this very conception was
directly challenged in Ōshio's philosophy. For Ōshio the "guarantee" of
the academy meant very little in light of the "thieves" who enforced the
laws of the land. Such a space was a deception or, to use Yamagata's phraseology, a "dream." Ōshio would displace this "dream" with idealistic
"action."

Ōshio exemplifies a distancing from the political order that was shared
by a wide variety of scholars, artists, and migrant intellectuals who no
longer had faith in the existing order of knowledge and power. Riken and
Kaiho Seiryō are examples of these men who we have referred to often.
Despite the extreme form of action taken by him, Ōshio may be counted
among these other alienated eccentrics. He did not, however, wander
about in a world of "play" like Kaiho; and unlike Riken he did not retreat
into a "kingdom of dreams." His rebellion thus marked a deep and indelible point in this history of seeking objective "righteousness" detached
from existing politics.

Fully versed on the entire range of ideas about ordering knowledge,
Ōshio was convinced that the source of misery in the real world was
nothing other than the epistemology of the regime that claimed to know
"distinctions" among things by observing nature. To be sure, dissatisfac-
tions with this epistemology had been voiced before from a number of

different perspectives. Ogyū, for example, had said that the approach was unreliable since nature as an object was not knowable. Kaibara, on the other hand, had insisted that nature must remain the ultimate object of knowledge, but had gone on to criticize the dualistic structure in that form of thought that led to philosophical confusion regarding the procedure of acquiring knowledge. Others such as Yamazaki Ansai and Ishida Baigan had also turned away from the proposition of "observation" as an unmediated approach to knowledge, emphasizing instead the spiritual interior as the basis of knowing the meaning of ultimate essence in beings and things. Nature was not to be seen as an object to be intellectually ordered.

Ōshio's own theory of action derived from that previous discussion on knowledge. Like Kaibara, he rejected dualism as conceptually unreliable. However, unlike Kaibara and reminiscent of the idealists, he emphasized the unity of spiritual interiority with an absolute moral ideal. Thus, in his lectures on "cleansing the spirit"—*Senshindō sakki*[13]—he repeated that the approach to knowledge through observation of things led to the making of prejudicial distinctions among things, resulting in faulty dualistic contrasts—idea-matter; metaphysical-physical; self-object; inner-outer; thought-action; past-present; and high-low or hierarchical arrangements more generally. While Kaibara, Goi, Miura, and Yamagata had argued that unifying all these apparent binary contrasts was ultimately a universal principle of nature, Ōshio concluded in diametrically opposite manner and claimed unity in an absolute moral ideal of universal goodness which was one with nature in the ultimate sense. He thus identified himself with previous idealists especially of the Ōyōmei tradition such as Nakae Tōju and Kumazawa Banzan who had denied the intermediate virtues of bureaucratic hierarchy and sought to solve the problems of human suffering and misery totally apart from it.

Once having identified false hierarchy based on empirical distinctions as being the source of social misery, Ōshio assumed a radical idealism to intersect and level structural reality. And since dualistic distinctions between thought and action, self and object, and past and present were equally suspect, there remained only truthful "righteous" action in the universal moral present. Thus, while his predecessors Nakae and Kumazawa took their idealism to agrarian work among the peasantry, Yamazaki Ansai to committed action within bureaucratic form, and Ishida Baigan to education among commoners as to their "spiritual" worth, Ōshio pointed his to a theory of revolt. Introspection and objectification, he concluded, must be joined apart from, and against, hierarchical form.

For Ōshio this meant rebellion in the name of the moral worth of the people against the very Bakufu that he had served.

Finally, then, Ōshio had come not only to distrust profoundly the approach to knowledge through "observation" but to reject it totally. What he saw was not an orderly and principled actuality that contained general moral meaning but rather pervasive suffering and oppression. Ogyū Sorai and Itō Jinsai a hundred years or so earlier had also come to suspect "observation" as it similarly did not yield orderly norm but rather a chaotic commercial reality that the existing political order and its moral ideas could not explain or cope with in a nonarbitrary manner. Yet, while Itō and Ogyū had turned to find norm in creative "ancient" origins to explain and critique the present, Ōshio rejected such scholastic solutions, emphasizing the urgency of action in the present against the illusion of structured certainties. The creative moment was not in an ancient beginning but in the obliteration of past and present in the universal present. In short, if Yamagata had "replaced" dreams with radical reason, Ōshio set out to destroy the rational "dream" about the present being morally rectifiable. Ōshio, it may be said, had launched his critique against the claims of rational epistemology espoused in Tokugawa Confucianism in general, including the more scientific and analytical offshoots of it, of which a conspicuous center was the Kaitokudō itself. And in this respect, while Ōshio articulated his ideas vis-à-vis the rationalistic intellectual universe as a whole, his critique may also be placed within the smaller frame of Osaka as being a counterphilosophy to Kaitokudō thought and, more pointedly, to the most complete synthesis of its intellectual tradition, namely Yamagata's *Yume*.

On the other side of Yamagata's radical reordering of eighteenth-century "reason" we thus see his younger contemporary, Ōshio, speaking out angrily against "reason" for it could not reveal how one ought to act against perceived injustices. The claim to objectivity itself, he argued, served to reinforce human prejudices about high and low. Only when these distinctions were erased, so that the cognizing self, other human beings, and the natural order were one and undifferentiated in terms of moral principle could this contradiction of knowledge and action be resolved. Ōshio had, therefore, greatly expanded the meaning of "truthfulness" as it had been articulated previously, as for example by Tominaga Nakamoto. To the idea that the past was unreliable as a textual guide to action in the present, Ōshio infused the radical prescription that action in the present must be the attack against received history embodied in a corrupt present. Yamagata Bantō's exclusive faith in "reason" and Ōshio's in "ideal" set dramatic alternative terms for political action in the last two decades of the Tokugawa order. Beyond them, the discursive space relating to critical action in the present would be decisively broadened; and even though the intellectual syncretism involving the reassembling of conceptual fragments from recent intellectual history would persist, it would now be readdressed to the imminent possibility of acquiring new forms of scientific knowledge or to dismantling the political system. While "loyalty" might have meant vendetta against a wicked lord in the case of the forty-seven *rōnin* at about the time the Kaitokudō had been founded, it now could mean, within Ōshio's framework, "revenge" to be acted out in the *public* arena against the Bakufu on behalf of the suffering populace.

Yamagata's vision of action would similarly unfold in energetic manner. The egalitarianism, as regards the acquisition of knowledge, and the capacity, therefore, of human beings to control knowledge and history would be played out in the 1860s and beyond in the establishment of a tradition of enlightened reason. If to Ōshio and activists after him, the ultimate sacrifice of the moral sage was realized in "death," no such emotive significance was attached to it by Yamagata. Death was simply an intrinsic part of universal nature that the human mind would continuously gain more knowledge about but never exhaust. Nothing in the universe, including "death," was to be treated as being beyond the realm of reason. In the end there would always be "humankind and the ten-thousand things" continuing into the infinite future, and the search for "knowledge" as a basis of "action" accordingly must be realized in relative terms in the structured arena of political economy and in light of that broad principle of nature.

Yamagata and Ōshio may be seen as representing polar positions on a broad yet continuous epistemological axis. Whether one gains knowledge through universal reason or idealistic intuition, these extreme positions are linked by a common emphasis on the theory of unity between inner virtue and external action—*naigai itchi* or *naigai mukan*. Throughout the history of the Kaitokudō the idea had been advanced that all human beings could, from within themselves, know what was accurate and hence also moral in the world around them. Riken's retreat into his private world was precisely to secure a space where this unity could be realized without the interference of external bureaucracy. Knowing the system was destined to fail, he chose "to do nothing," as suggested in Taoist philosophy, and to let the faltering order continue in that course of inevitable decline. Ōshio denied that alternative and insisted, as already noted, that the appropriate "space" where interior and exterior might be made one and consistent was the "public" realm itself. But in both senses of utopian space, whether writ small or public and large, the unity of inner and outer was held firm, and in this sense Riken's "retreat" and Ōshio's "revolt," while obviously distinct, are also conceptually related.

Similarly, Yamagata also emphasized that the inner human capacity to acquire knowledge about the universe ought to be connected directly to how men acted in the objective world. Properly ordered knowledge should produce accurate prescriptions as to the kinds of "emergency" action that should be taken. Drawn directly from Chikuzan's teachings, especially as set forth in his *Sōbō kigen*, Yamagata incorporated this idea within his scientific framework and pointed it in the direction of critical action. The sections on political economy in *Yume* that impinge on matters of the nation are thoroughly informed by this theory of action. It may be worth mentioning again in this connection that among Yamagata's colleagues at the Kaitokudō in the 1770s were men from the domain of Tatsuno who would take a similar set of ideas based on "reason" to challenge domainal politics and establish policies designed to support the people. Warned firmly by Chikuzan at the academy of the reckless implications of dogmatic idealism, which he told them was ultimately "poisonous"—*doku*—these men nonetheless took Kaitokudō ideas and engaged themselves in political protest against the lack of a famine relief program. This would cost them dearly, as the leader among them (one Kunieda Shiken) would be executed in 1782 and the others imprisoned and scattered into exile.[14] Quite aside from the details of this incident, the main point to be underscored here is the activist implications of the ideas organized around the principle of both "reason" and "ideal." Each contained within its epistemology, an action theory oriented to saving the people.

A related linkage is to be found in historical perception. As already outlined, two views were deliberated at the Kaitokudō. Chikuzan's represented political history, in positive terms, as producing a form of noncentralized governance or *hōken* within which the Kaitokudō had acquired its legitimate "place." Relying on this interpretive scheme, Chikuzan then went on to prescribe far-reaching structural reforms, especially as regards education. Yamagata Bantō subscribed to this view as well and utilized the framework to assert a critical place for merchants in determining the fate of the nation. In the alternative view advanced by Riken, recorded history over the previous 1,000 years was one of deception, treachery, and decline. Justice as political "righteousness" was no longer possible in the light of this history. Much influenced by this view of Riken, the historian Rai Sanyō similarly viewed the past in these terms; Sanyō's reading of history coincided with Ōshio's perception of the past as a basis for radicalism in the present. Sanyō was greatly attracted to Ōshio's idealistic philosophy; Ōshio admired Sanyō's historicism and claimed that among all the scholars in the country only Sanyō understood his moral philosophy. Yet it is crucial to note that while Sanyō undoubtedly understood Ōshio's idealism, he was at the same time closer in intellectual temperament to the teachings of the Kaitokudō, a sympathy he had acquired during the many visits he and his father, Rai Shunsui, made to the academy. Sanyō, therefore, expressed his deep concern with the sacrificial and self-destructive implications of Ōshio's view that, beyond reason, there was only idealistic and moral "action" against the present. In one of his last visits with Ōshio, therefore, he left behind a poem advising him to always remember to sheath his sword after polishing it, advice that echoed Chikuzan's warning to his students from Tatsuno.[15]

Sanyō's intellectual friendship with Ōshio and his close interaction at the same time with the Kaitokudō underscore our general point that despite the polar positions represented by radical rationalism and idealism, they belong to a related conceptual universe. Although previous studies tend not to juxtapose these two positions as they appear too dissimilar, they may be seen as falling within a common frame, albeit at opposite ends of it. The warnings of political failing found in Chikuzan, Riken, and Yamagata interact profoundly with Ōshio and Sanyō. It is fair to surmise that at the Kaitokudō such a connection with Ōshio was not stressed; as his rebellious fires raged, the message was as Chikuzan had taught—radical idealism was "poisonous." But at a deeper level perceived in retrospect, there is a mutual reference to the realization that the world of political economy was in a state of disarray, and drastic measures needed to be taken to restore order. In this respect, Yamagata's radical affirmation of science and Ōshio's of moral idealism may be seen as anticipating a new era beyond their eighteenth century. They serve to identify for historians the extreme reference points in the conceptual "contradiction" informing the thought and action that went into the dismantling of the old order and the building of the new.

•   •   •

Adding yet another complex dimension to the previous pattern of development was the establishment of the Tekijuku by Ogata Kōan.[16] Founded in 1838, only a year after Ōshio's rebellion, when the epidemics from the aftermath of the fires still cast a pall over Osaka, the Tekijuku set out on the bold path of teaching medical science through the prior study of the Dutch language. It was located only a few walking minutes away from the Kaitokudō and situated strategically in relation to the ships from Nagasaki that docked in Osaka to unload valuable supplies of medicine, instruments, and books from China, Korea, and the Western world. Scholars and Dutch envoys traveling from Nagasaki to Edo and back invariably stopped over at this point in Osaka. Although dedicated mainly to medicine and not astronomy, it was this Tekijuku that would come to house the commitment to science and reason that Yamagata had prized from within the Kaitokudō.

Ogata Kōan was the son of a lowly domainal samurai of the lord of Ashimori of Bichū (within present-day Okayama) assigned to manage the granary of Osaka. While in Osaka, Ogata studied Dutch science among merchant students like Naka Tenyū (1783–1835) and Hashimoto Sōkichi (1763–1836). Close colleagues of Yamagata Bantō, these men, like Yamagata, were also protégés of Asada Goryū. Choosing not to return to serve the domain, Ogata pursued his study of the Dutch language and science as his calling. Interestingly, he drew on Taoistic philosophy, akin to Riken and Kaiho in this regard, to articulate his quest for objectivity. The school is sometimes said, therefore, to have taken its name from the Taoist philosopher Chuang-tzu's insight into tolerance and objectivity regarding human nature. What is appropriate to another, he had theorized, should not be tampered with by others, and by the same token, one should not seek to emulate what seems essential to others. It explained Ogata's decision not to return to serve the domainal lord in ways others might think dutiful of him, but rather to establish a school of Dutch studies in Osaka for the good of society. One should not be concerned with the "function" of others or what seems appropriate to them, he reasoned, and seek instead to know the objective condition of things without imposing his own personal feelings—*Hito no eki o eki to shite, hito no teki o teki to shite, mizukara sono teki o teki to sezaru mono nari.*[17]

Of equal importance is the ideal shared by Ogata with the teachers of the Kaitokudō. Another reading of Tekijuku traces the ideographs to lines commonly used in the introduction to Neo-Confucian ethics. The ideographs emphasize the unity of the inner human spirit, or virtue, and knowledge acquired through direct sensate perceptions. This was a premise that was entirely in accord with the Kaitokudō philosophy of the unity of inner "compassion" and empirical "righteousness." It also reinforced the idea that accurate knowledge was accessible to human beings and that such knowledge should serve the cause of nourishing and "saving the people" totally without regard to their prescriptive status. Ogata wrote down his moral philosophy in one of his instructional handbooks with the following words:

> The work of the physician is purely to help others. It is fundamental to the aim of this profession not to promote the self. One does not seek idle rest or dream of personal fame, but simply seeks without regard to the self to save other human lives. No other purpose should be held to other than maintaining life, curing the ill, relieving those in pain.[18]

And among the basic propositions to which he expected his students to adhere, he included the following:

> View the patient simply as a patient. Never distinguish between the high and the low, the poor from the rich. Be clear as to what you stand to gain within yourself in choosing between the handful of money extended by the rich and the tears of gratitude in the eyes of the poor.[19]

This scientific humanitarianism dovetailed with ideas found in Yamagata Bantō. All superstitious reliance on gods and buddhas would be discarded—*mushin mubutsu*. Knowledge would be sought in terms of basic scientific propositions that were presumed to be universal. Science was not the exclusive possession of nations located in any area on the globe. Diagnosis and prescription are also seen to be universal. To secure scientific knowledge, moreover, Ogata, while remaining within the mainstream of Tokugawa ethical thought, believed language ought to be simplified. As had been the case with Yamagata, Ogata revealed a decided impatience with sinology, with its heavy concentration on ideography. Yamagata, it will be recalled, marveled at how the Dutch wrote complex scientific treatises with an alphabet of only twenty-six letters. Unlike Yamagata, however, Ogata actually immersed himself in the study of the Dutch language itself, first with Naka and then with a trading officer in Nagasaki named Nieman.

In the early years, the financial burden of operating such a school was heavy, and the Tekijuku relied on the philanthropic support of Osaka merchants, most significantly the wealthy financial house of Tennōjiya with its complex of some thirteen or so related houses. A key supporter is said to have been a manager of a successful branch house—a *bantō*—one Tennōjiya Chūbei.[20] Tennōjiya here parallels the kind of support the houses of Kōnoike and Masuya had provided to the Kaitokudō and also to Asada Goryū's private school. From a somewhat shakey beginning the

Tekijuku would develop into the major center of Dutch studies in west-central Japan. It would gain great prominence from Ogata's success in helping to bring cholera under control through preventive hygiene and successfully experimenting, again with active merchant support, with the small pox vaccine during the epidemics of the 1840s. Ogata also produced a number of well-known works on medicine, the most celebrated of these being a taxonomy of human illness—Byōgaku tsūron (ca. 1844). Recognizing the importance of the Tekijuku, the Bakufu would summon Ogata in 1860 to head the bureau of Western medicine in the Edo government. Of frail health throughout much of his life and deeply dedicated to his own Tekijuku, Ogata would agree to the invitation only with much misgiving, although his contributions would survive him in more elaborate form in the modern era via the medical college of Tokyo University.[21]

But above all, it was Ogata's success as a teacher for which he was best known. Between 1838 and 1863 when he passed away, the number of registered students from the various domains who had studied at the Tekijuku had mounted to an impressive 633. Unregistered students from nearby have been estimated at about 2,000. From the area of Yamaguchi alone, where the domain of Chōshū was located, fifty-three students studied at the Tekijuku; and Ishikawa, Okayama, Hyōgo, Hiroshima, Fukuoka, and Saga all sent thirty or more students. Having to study intensive Dutch, these students would leave behind graphic testimonies of their frustrations with angry sword slashes on the central upright beam in the boarding area of the academy.[22]

Although known primarily as a school of Dutch language and medicine, the Tekijuku in fact taught Western science in a broader sense. Students were thus expected to read from texts on engineering, chemistry, and mathematics besides those in medicine. There is in this history the broadening of the meaning of "science" to mean Western civilization in its diverse meanings. The implications of this trend can be detected in the efforts of Tekijuku scholars to establish a new "great school" in Osaka in 1869, shortly after the demise of the Tokugawa order. The proposed draft called for the establishment of a center of general science to be called the institute of seimi, this term being homophonous with "chemie" or chemistry. Besides seimi, however, other subjects in the curriculum were to include: English, French, medicine, mathematics, and law. This latter category may here be interpreted broadly to mean constitutional theory, political history, and social thought. No mention is made of Mencius or the other classics. The overall plan, it may still be said, fell within the grand vision of educational reforms shaped by Nakai Chikuzan and Hoashi Banri a generation or two earlier, and it certainly related to the commitment to scientific learning espoused by Yamagata Bantō. The articulation of subject matter, however, was a good deal more specialized and referred to such items as Western languages and law that were indicative of the educational experience fostered at the Tekijuku and which prefigured the creation of the Osaka University in modern times.[23]

The breadth of instruction, it might further be added, manifested itself in the subsequent careers of some of the better known students. Although many of them were sons of domainal physicians, their future lives reveal interesting variety. Hashimoto Sanai (1834–59), for example, became an intellectual leader advocating industrialization and opening the country to the West. He would be executed for his involvement in radical politics against the Bakufu. Ōmura Masujirō (1824–70) would emerge as an instrumental figure in organizing and arming the multiclass army in Chōshū that would defeat in battle the forces of the Tokugawa Bakufu. Still others such as Ōtori Keisuke (1832–1911), Hanabusa Yoshimoto (1842–1917), Takamatsu Ryōun (1836–1916) and Sanō Tsunetami (1822–1902) would serve variously as medical advisors and specialists of Western knowledge in the military and foreign ministries of the Meiji government. Similarly, Nagayo Sensai (1838–1902) would head the new public health system; Sugita Kyōji (1826–1917) would introduce the study of statistical methods in determining policy in the new government; and Mitsukuri Shūhei (1825–86) would become an advocate of educational reform as a member of the reformist group of intellectuals known as the Meiji Six Society.[24]

By far the most distinguished alumnus of the Tekijuku was Fukuzawa Yukichi (1834–1902). A giant among intellectual leaders responsible for introducing Western positivism and liberal ideas to early modern Japan, Fukuzawa wrote best-selling books such as "Conditions in the West"—*Seiyō jijō* (1867); "An Advancement of Learning"—*Gakumon no susume* (1872); and "An Outline of the Theory of Civilization"—*Bunmeiron no gairyaku* (1875). He also published an important newspaper, *Jiji shinpō*. And he founded an academy Keio that combined the virtues of the Tekijuku and the Kaitokudō and which remains today as a distinguished private university. This Fukuzawa, who readily admitted in his autobiography his indebtedness to the education he received at the hands of Ogata Kōan at the Tekijuku,[25] serves to illustrate two interrelated themes pertinent to this epilogue, namely the declining intellectual status of the Kaitokudō in relation to the Tekijuku and the continuing discursive links that nonetheless joined these two neighboring academies together in late Tokugawa history.

While in the late eighteenth century the students of Miura Baien trav-eled from their region of Bungo in Kyūshū to study at the Kaitokudō, by Fukuzawa's time a generation later, this pattern had shifted to the Tekijuku. Fukuzawa's predecessors studied at the Kaitokudō and inter-acted on intimate terms with the likes of Yamagata Bantō and Asada Goryū. By Fukuzawa's day, the choice was clearly Ogata and the Tekijuku. When Fukuzawa openly ridiculed Chinese studies in general, the im-plications of this with regard to the Kaitokudō was readily evident even though the latter was not specifically named. Fukuzawa and his colleagues oriented their study toward the acquisition of Western language and sci-entific knowledge, not toward the classical moral philosophy taught at the Kaitokudō and academies like it. It was the new curriculum of West-ern studies that presented itself as the adventurous alternative to choose. However, had Fukuzawa traveled to Osaka in the late eighteenth century with Miura's students, such as Waki Guzan or Hoashi Banri, he too would have undoubtedly boarded and studied with them at the Kaitokudō.

The choice of Dutch studies over the offerings of moral philosophy at the Kaitokudō that Fukuzawa represented as being new to himself and his generation, while dependable in good measure, can also be misleading. Despite Fukuzawa's mocking attitude toward sinological studies, the con-ceptual themes that run through his own overall thinking clearly place him within an intellectual history through which the Kaitokudō had evolved and produced a scholar such as Yamagata Bantō a generation be-fore him. It happens that through his elder brother, Fukuzawa was made aware early in his life of the intellectual legacy handed down by Hoashi Banri. The unusual aspect of Hoashi, Fukuzawa noted in his *Autobiog-raphy*, was that he taught mathematics and the importance of the "aba-cus" in matters involving political economy.[26] Hoashi, it will also be re-called, was a disciple of Miura Baien's teachings and had also studied at the Kaitokudō when Yamagata was assiduously organizing the ideas he had learned there. It is in any event quite certain that some of the basic ideas that Fukuzawa came to champion and became justly famous for as a leader of the Meiji Enlightenment were those that were also firmly em-braced by scholars such as Hoashi and the Nakai brothers and their pro-tégé Yamagata Bantō.

These concepts may be summarized here in the following terms: Nature is ordered in accordance with an "infinite principle"—*kyūri*—that is not of human design yet upon which all humankind must rely; nature does not create unequal status among human beings and, indeed among all creatures; virtue is a universal possession of humankind; knowledge is relative and accessible to all men regardless of social and political status; knowledge is inexhaustible and hence always incomplete, never absolute, and constantly undergoes revision as new knowledge is uncovered; the human mind must never rely on superstitions and religious beliefs handed down through custom—the life of thought and action must be without gods and buddhas; and knowledge systematically acquired should be applied critically to conditions of political economy.

Whether Yamagata Bantō directly "influenced" Fukuzawa, such as with the idea of human history devoid of gods and buddhas—*mushin-mubutsu* —which is central to Yamagata's treatise against dreams and also clearly articulated by Fukuzawa, is largely of secondary interest.[27] Of greater pertinence is the historical context in which the intellectual universes of Fukuzawa's mentors in Kyūshū, the Tekijuku in Osaka, and the scholarly tradition at the Kaitokudō were in fact compatible and closely entwined. The theory of relativity to which Fukuzawa subscribed was regularly repeated by Goi in his daily teachings in the 1730s and remained an underlying premise in Yamagata Bantō's *Yume*. Although separated by chronological lines, these men quite clearly shared a related discourse on knowledge that Fukuzawa's claims of radical newness for himself and his endorsement of modern Enlightenment should not obscure.

Viewed within this flow of intellectual history, the Kaitokudō appears to us, in the new history of the revolutionary upheavals of the late Tokugawa era, as obviously diminished in lustre from the dynamic academy that it once was. By the same token, it was also part and parcel of that broader, complex, unfolding of conceptual events represented by leaders such as Fukuzawa and, for that matter, Sakuma Shōzan (1811– 64), the samurai intellectual who brought together men such as Fukuzawa to translate Western works on scientific knowledge for the Bakufu. Like Yamagata earlier, Sakuma saw science as universal and thus accessible to all human beings regardless of the particularity of geographical "place" and cultural "history." Besides Fukuzawa, many of the leaders of the time, including activists such as Yoshida Shōin (1830–59) and intellectuals of the highest stature, Katō Hiroyuki (1836–1916) and Nishi Amane (1829–97), came under the influence and patronage of Sakuma in a dramatic moment in late Tokugawa history but that need not detain the present account.[28]

The point that deserves emphasis is that, beyond the academic environs of Osaka, we see the convergence of thinking in Yamagata Bantō and Fukuzawa and Sakuma a generation later. Although Sakuma was a servitor of the Bakufu and Yamagata a financier in Osaka, the shared vision relative to universal science is unmistakable. Sakuma identified this science as "mathematics" and Yamagata as "astronomy"—although inter-estingly, Kaiho, the observer of Yamagata, also had seen "mathematics" as the central scientific method in Yamagata. Sakuma, drawing together men of like mind to translate Western works on science, and Yamagata, articulating a future beyond "dreams," share an interrelated intellectual history that extends well beyond the Kaitokudō—an academy swept along by political events in a downward pattern of decline.

It is also well to note in this connection that even as the intellectual energies of Osaka and the nation at large turned unequivocally from moral philosophy to the new fields of science, the Kaitokudō as an "offi-cial" academy did not resist and speak out against this trend. As already emphasized, the Kaitokudō was intellectually sympathetic to the Teki-juku rather than contestual, as one might expect an institution thor-oughly committed to tradition to be vis-à-vis the rapidly changing tide of history. Goi's theory of knowledge remained central to the Kaitokudō's teachings, and this dovetailed with the vision of the new sciences that now captured the imagination of intellectual leaders. Thus, although constrained by its own legal status from becoming a center of scientific study, its philosophical foundations did not lead it to dispute the emerg-ing new history. Limited by its source of legitimation, the Tokugawa "superstructure," the Kaitokudō, nonetheless remained within the intel-lectual framework of the changing times, as evidenced especially by the close intellectual relationship between Yamagata Bantō and those of Fukuzawa and his peers.

In the late Tokugawa history of dramatic political deterioration, then, the Kaitokudō would continue to function loyally in terms of its charter. Founded to confirm a moral center for merchants at a time when pro-found economic concerns still did not entail the expectation of political dysfunction, the Kaitokudō was hedged in by that initial quest for institu-tional certitude to articulate a persuasive *new* place for itself in the con-text of systemic crisis. To disavow its legal position, however unstable the conditions of the time, would have been tantamount to committing an act of treason, which, in retrospect, does not present itself as a likely option in the wake of Ōshio's destructive uprising. As the problematic of "virtue" that had occupied the center of intellectual attention in the eighteenth century gave way to that of "science" and "action," the Kaitokudō did not emerge as a visible participant in the deep interplay between these polar forces.

Yet, as suggested in these final pages, Kaitokudō epistemology can be located in bits and fragments which would come to be appropriated and combined within new visions being shaped in an era undergoing revolutionary transformation. The expansive view of general education that Chikuzan championed would acquire new significance within a vastly reordered context in which "science" would be a crucial intellectual object and serve as an organizing pedagogical concept. Along with this, the aristocratic principle of social organization would be dissipated, as late eighteenth-century critical intellectuals, including the Nakai brothers, had envisioned. Mathematics combined with political economy, as articulated by Kusama and Yamagata, and found broad elaboration in the study of Western science and social science. The economic perception of politics that these men repeatedly emphasized would undergo transformation into the new science of "economics"—keizai—and this knowledge would be built into the structures of the modern industrial order. In time, even the virtues prized at the academy—compassion, righteousness, accuracy, and trust—would be recombined to give moral purpose and legitimation to centralized industrialization.

Reminiscent, in this regard of the teachings at the Kaitokudō, Shibuzawa Eiichi (1840–1931), one of the principal architects of the modern industrial order, would "reencounter" Confucius's Analects in his lengthy Jikken Rongo toward the end of his illustrious career and ponder through this work the meaning of the history through which he had come.[29] Strikingly evident throughout is the theme of "righteousness" and "trust" as the basis of "ordering and saving the people." Raised in the interstices of agriculture and commerce in late Tokugawa, Shibuzawa emerged in the modern era to contribute mightily to the designing of the national banking system and to the private sector by fostering allegedly some five hundred different enterprises. His reflective opus states at the outset his conviction that economics is the basis of politics, and it is to this theme, clearly set forth earlier by Kusama and Yamagata, that he dedicated his career. That he would contribute his support toward the end of his life to establish an institute to study the "abiding" common people— Jōmin kenkyujo—is not inconsistent with the path of his career, as it was rooted in the social ethics of his Tokugawa upbringing. All of these, however, belong to a history that is squarely set in the context of rapid industrialization—a history that is radically distinct from the one that the Kaitokudō had experienced in the Tokugawa era.

A prominent academy in the intellectual history of the eighteenth century, the Kaitokudō in the waning decades of the Tokugawa Bakufu could no longer sustain itself as an active center of learning in the context of political disarray. Having lost patrons to widespread bankruptcy, the Kaitokudō would turn as a last resort in 1867 to the Bakufu's magistracy in Osaka for emergency financial aid. Fatally attacked from within, the Bakufu would be unresponsive; and the Kaitokudō, in turn, would quietly end its life in the spring of 1868, shortly after the defeat of the Tokugawa forces. Pinned to the front gate of the once proud merchant academy was a poetic note penned by Namikawa Kansen, the last head instructor, that conveyed the sense of resignation and finality at the academy's end:

> After some one hundred and forty-four years, this home for the study of literary culture covering all the ages, as of today, glances at its past and leaves the world—*Hyaku amari yosoji shi [144 years] tose no fumi no shuku, kyō o kagiri to mikaerite izu.* [30]

. . .

Yamagata's House of Masuya, along with dozens of other leading merchant houses in Osaka, would fall at the same time. Aside from the handful of Mitsui's and Sumitomo's that would survive the upheavals of the 1860s, most of the other houses would go bankrupt, dragged down by the collapse of the feudal system. In Masuya's case, the domain of Sendai, whose finances it had managed from Yamagata's days in the latter half of the eighteenth century, would be defeated in the civil war as a stalwart supporter of the Tokugawa Bakufu. The Masuyas would not accept bankruptcy with poetic resignation and would rally the faltering merchant houses in Osaka, facing comparable conditions of insolvency, to appeal to the new Meiji government to have it honor the outstanding loans of the feudal domains. Houses such as Masuya could then contribute in decisive economic ways to the creation of the new nation. But this plea fell on deaf ears. The Bakufu's debts to foreign nations would be honored; but not those of domains to Osaka merchant houses.

What is most intriguing about this painful moment is not that the new government, hard-pressed for capital itself, should take this adamant position, nor that Masuya and houses like it lost in their appeal, but rather that Masuya, in one of its last acts before bankruptcy, would invest the residual resources it had at its disposal to help establish a small elementary school near the Kaitokudō. Still located in a little corridor in downtown Osaka and incorporated within the public school system, it was named by the Masuyas as "the school that loves the light of day"—*Aijitsu shōgakkō.* The name echoes the language of the Englightenment movement in early Meiji Japan that intellectuals such as Fukuzawa Yukichi led and in which human "reason" and "light," as developed in Western civilization, were pitted against the superstitious darkness and "dreams" of the feudal past. Viewed from the perspective of our study of the Kaitokudō, however, the idea of celebrating the light of day was taught at the academy for over 100 years. After a night of inexplicable dreams and unhappy nightmares that played tricks on the human mind, youngsters were taught that the human sage welcomed and enjoyed the light of dawn and did not speculate in a superstitious manner what reason could not unravel. As noted in the discussion on Goi, this instruction was drawn initially from Mencius and interpreted to say that not even the ancient sages knew what "dreams" were about, and had they known, they would not have kept it a secret. The sages, as it ought to be with men in all times, admitted what they did not know. Acknowledging ignorance, these sages simply welcomed the universe of light that came with dawn when once again reason could govern. The little school that loves the light of day, in short, is a restatement of Yamagata's more provocative expression about displacing dreams with the "light" of science that had been suggested to him by Riken.

As mentioned at the beginning, the Kaitokudō would be renovated in the 1910s after the industrial revolution was firmly underway. It would be destroyed during the Pacific War and its library was relocated in the postwar era as an important archive at Osaka University. It is absolutely consistent with the history of the Kaitokudō, however, that Yamagata's own personal library still remains housed in the little elementary school near the Masuya household. Despite the absurdity of this situation at first glance, since young students in Japan are no longer trained to read the complex books that Yamagata had used as references to write his treatise against *dreams*, this library, located specifically where it is, in a school dedicated to young minds embracing the light of dawn, serves as a quiet metaphoric reminder of the link between the intellectual world of Yamagata's Kaitokudō and the continuing discourse on reason in modern Japanese history.

NOTES

One

1. Nishimura's lecture "Goi Ranju" referred to here was republished in *Kaitoku* 37 (1966): 18–37, and its main idea is incorporated in his elegant and concise history of the Kaitokudō: *Kaitokudō kō* (Osaka: Kaitokudō kinenkai, 1923). Naitō Kōnan's reflective series of essays on Tokugawa thinkers "Sentetsu no gakumon" are in his collected works, *Naitō Kōnan zenshū*, 14 vols. (Tokyo: Chikuma shobō, 1970) 9: 319–519; Kōda Rohan's best known work on Osaka is his historical novel of 1910, *Ōshio Heihachirō*. For important essays on themes related to Osaka intellectual history, see Takeuchi Yoshio's collected works, *Takeuchi Yoshio zenshū*, 10 vols. (Tokyo: Kadokawa shoten, 1978–79), especially vol. 10. Of interest is the special issue on Osaka intellectual history in *Nihon shisō shi* 20 (1983), which contains essays by well-known Osaka scholars: Miyamoto Mataji, the eminent doyen of Osaka social and cultural studies; Sakudo Yotaro; Wakita Osamu; Umetani Noboru; and Tokinoya Masaru. A good example of recent interest in Osaka is the set of lectures, by some of the scholars just noted, presented on the Kinki radio station and published by Osaka University as *Osaka no gakumon* (Osaka, 1980). Essays of interest are included in Miyamoto Mataji and Nakagawa Keiichiro, eds., *Nihon keiei shi kōza, v. 1: Edo jidai no kigyōsha katsudō* (Tokyo: Nihon keizai shinbun sha, 1977). I have written "Kaitokudō ninshikiron to jūhasseiki ni okeru hihanteki buijyon no sōzo," *Kaitoku* 53 (1984): 38–51. Other more journalistic examples of essays on the Kaitokudo are in: *Tōyō Keizai* 11–21 (1980), and *Senba* 5 (1983). In Western language, an informative analysis of the economic history of Osaka as seen through the cotton industry is William B. Hauser, *Economic Institutional Change in Tokugawa Japan* (London: Cambridge University Press, 1974).

2. Especially informative on the subject of the Kaitokudō within the Osaka context is Miyamoto Mataji, *Chōnin shakai no gakugei to Kaitokudō* (Tokyo: Bunken shuppan, 1982); and *Osaka keizai bunka shi dangi* (Tokyo: Bunken shuppan, 1980). Beginning with such well-known works as *Kinsei shōnin ishiki no kenkyū* (Tokyo: Yūhikaku, 1941), Miyamoto has written steadily and extensively on merchant consciousness and culture and his collected works add up to ten

volumes. Also see Nakazawa Morito and Mori Kazuo, *Nihon no kaimei shisō* (Tokyo: Kinokuniya shinsho, 1970).

3. On regional academies, with a special emphasis on the Gansuidō, see Tsuda Hideo, *Kinsei minshu kyōiku undō no tenkai* (Tokyo: Ochanomizu shobō, 1978).

4. Ogata Tomio, *Ogata Kōan den* (Tokyo: Iwanami shoten, 1963); and Ban Tadayasu, *Tekijuku o meguru hitobito—Rangaku no nagare* (Osaka: Sōgen sha, 1978).

5. Miyamoto, *Chōnin shakai*, 209–15; the most detailed source for the social interactions of the Kaitokudō with the wider intellectual world is the official history of Osaka, Osaka shi sanjikai, ed., *Osaka shi shi*, 7 vols. (Osaka: Seibundō, 1978; first published 1911–15). Also informative are Fujii Sadayoshi, *Kaitokudō to keizai shisō* (Osaka: Osaka furitsu daigaku keizai kenkyū sōsho, 1975) and Oya Shinichi, *Nihon keizaigaku shi no tabi* (Tokyo: Kōwa shuppan, 1980) in which Kaitokudō scholars are included.

6. Theoretically suggestive is Michel Foucault, *The Archaeology of Knowledge* (New York: Pantheon, 1972), 166–77.

7. I have found suggestive the essay by Stanislaw Ossowski, *Class Structure in the Social Consciousness* (New York: Free Press, 1963); and also, Colin Summer, *Reading Ideologies* (New York: Academic Press, 1979). Among Japanese historians, the writings of Nishikawa Shunsaku point to complex intermixing across class lines: *Edo jidai no poritikaru ekonomii* (Tokyo: Kōhoku shuppan, 1979).

8. J. G. A. Pocock, *Politics, Language and Time* (New York: Atheneum, 1971), 3–41. The arguments for "social capitalism" in preindustrial Japan—*saimin-ron*—provide interesting comparisons with Albert O. Hirschman's *The Passions and the Interests* (Princeton: Princeton University Press, 1977).

Two

1. Amino Yoshihiko, *Muen, kugai, raku* (Tokyo: Heibonsha, 1978).

2. The structural foundations of this system are analyzed in Wakita Osamu, *Kinsei hōkensei seiritsu shi ron* (Tokyo: Tokyo daigaku shuppan kai, 1977).

3. The *Chōnin kōken roku* is included in Nakamura Yukihiko, ed., *Nihon shisō taikei, 59: Kinsei chōnin shisō* (Tokyo: Iwanami shoten, 1975), 175–233.

4. Ihara Saikaku's *Nippon eitaigura* has been translated by G. W. Sargent, *The Japanese Family Storehouse* (Cambridge: Cambridge University Press, 1959).

5. The *Shison kagami* is in Nakamura, *Nihon shisō taikei, Kinsei chōnin*, 17–84.

6. Ibid., 34–35 passim.

7. I have relied primarily in my analysis on Yoshikawa Kojiro and Shimizu Shigeru, eds., *Nihon shisō taikei, 33: Itō Jinsai–Itō Tōgai* (Tokyo: Iwanami shoten, 1971). Also useful are: Yoshikawa Kojiro, *Jinsai-Sorai-Norinaga* (Tokyo: Iwanami shoten, 1975) and the English translation with that title (Tōhō gakkai, 1983); the biographical essay by Ishida Ichiro, *Jinbutsu sōsho, 39: Itō Jinsai* (Tokyo: Yoshikawa kōbunkan, 1980); and the stimulating recent work by Koyasu Nobukuni, *Itō Jinsai—Jinrinteki sekai no shisō* (Tokyo: Tokyo daigaku shuppan, 1982).

8. Quentin Skinner, "Meaning and Understanding in the History of Ideas," *History and Theory* 8 (1969): 3–53.

9. Itō's key statements are *Gomō jigi*, his textual critique of Confucius and Mencius (in Yoshikawa and Shimizu, *Itō Jinsai–Itō Tōgai*, 11–113; and his "lec-

tures" for beginners, *Dōjimon*, in Ienaga Saburo, Shimizu Shigeru et al., *Nihon koten bungaku taikei, 97: Kinsei shisōka bunshū* (Tokyo: Iwanami shoten, 1966), 49–200.

10. See Yoshikawa, *Jinsai, Sorai, Norinaga*, 1–63; or his analysis in *Itō Jinsai– Itō Tōgai*, 565–621; and also Takeuchi Yoshio, "Jinsai no keigaku," *Takeuchi zenshū* 10:301–17.

11. The classic study on these intellectuals is Maruyama Masao, *Nihon seiji shisōshi kenkyū* (Tokyo: Tokyo daigaku shuppan kai, 1952) and translated by Mikiso Hane, *Studies in the Intellectual History of Tokugawa Japan* (Princeton: Princeton University Press, 1974). Also, the pioneering study by Honjo Eijiro, *Kinsei no keizai shisō* (Tokyo: Nihon hyōron sha, 1931) and his essays in the English version, *Economic Theory and History of Japan in the Tokugawa Period* (New York: Russell and Russell, Inc., 1965). The theme of rationalistic thought, which much of my study is about, is treated in a broad and synthetic manner by Minamoto Ryoen, *Tokugawa gōrishisō no keifu* (Tokyo: Chūō kōron sha, 1972). On Tokugawa "historicism," see Noguchi Takehiko, *Edo no rekishika* (Tokyo: Chikuma shobō, 1979). Also informative is Matsumoto Sannosuke's collection of essays, *Kinsei Nihon no shisōzō* (Tokyo: Kenbun shuppan, 1984); and the special issue on "ancient" and "national" studies, *Nihon shiso shi* 8 (1978).

12. Tahara Tsuguo and Morimoto Junichiro, eds., *Nihon shiso taikei 32: Yamaga Sokō* (Tokyo: Iwanami shoten, 1970). A key essay is "Seikyō yōgo," 7–28.

13. The analysis of Ogyū here is based mainly on his pivotal text, *Bendō*, available in Yoshikawa Kojiro, Maruyama et al., eds., *Nihon shisō taikei, 36: Ogyū Sorai* (Tokyo: Iwanami shoten, 1973). See also Bito Masahide, ed., *Nihon no meichō, 16: Ogyū Sorai* (Tokyo: Chūō kōron sha, 1974). The same themes presented here can also be gleaned from Ogyū's *Benmei*, found in these same anthologies.

14. Ogyū, *Bendō*, section 20.

15. Ibid., section 7.

16. Ibid., section 14.

17. Ibid., sections 1 and 6.

18. Nakae Chōmin, *Ichinen yūhan* (Tokyo: Hakubun kan, 1901), 26–30.

19. This is a theme scattered throughout Itō's *Gomō jigi*, (Yoshikawa and Shimizu, eds., *Nihon shisō taikei 33: Itō Jinsai–Itō Tōgai*) as well as *Dōjimon* (Ienaga and Shimizu, eds., *Nihon koten bungaku taikei, 97: kinsei shisōka bunshū*).

20. Itō's views on the *Great Learning* are in *Gomō jigi*, 98–106; and on the *Doctrine of the Mean*, in his "Chūyō haiki," in *Nihon no shisō 11: Itō Jinsai bunshū*, edited by Kimura Eiichi (Tokyo: Chikuma shobō, 253–311).

21. Itō, *Gomō jigi*, 19; 73–77.

22. Itō, *Gomō jigi*, 54–58, 74–75; and *Dōjimon*, 138–42.

23. Itō, *Dōjimon*, 73, 80–95.

24. Itō, *Gomō jigi*, 15–19, 56–59; and *Dōjimon*, 73–75, 143–44.

25. Itō, *Dōjimon*, 108–9; and *Gomō jigi*, 73–81.

26. Itō, *Dōjimon*, 84–85, 89, 93.

27. Itō, *Dōjimon*, 94; *Gomō jigi*, 64–65, 69–78.

28. Itō, *Dōjimon*, 81; *Gomō jigi*, 104–5.

29. Araki Kengo and Inoue Tadashi, eds., *Nihon shisō taikei 34: Kaibara*

Ekken—Muro Kyūsō (Tokyo: Iwanami shoten, 1970). I have written on Kaibara in "Intellectual Change in Early Eighteenth-Century Tokugawa Confucianism," *The Journal of Asian Studies* 34 (1975): 931–44.

30. The *Taigi roku* may be found in: Araki, *Nihon shisō taikei 34* : 9–64.

31. Nishikawa's *Chōnin bukuro* is in Nakamura's *Nihon shisō taikei 59: Kinsei chōnin shisō*, 85–174; and the *Hyakushō bukuro*, Takimoto Seiichi, ed., *Nihon keizai taiten*, v. 4 (Tokyo: Meiji bunken, 1967).

32. Nishikawa, *Chōnin bukuro*, 105.

33. Ibid., 138.

34. Ibid., 101.

35. Ibid., 88–89, 95–98, 101–5, 116.

36. For both quotes in the paragraph: Ibid., 133–34.

37. Ibid., 143, 168; and also, *Hyakushō bukuro*, 3–6.

38. *Chōnin bukuro*, 153, 161.

39. Ibid., 160–65; and *Hyakushō bukuro*, 2–4.

40. *Chōnin bukuro*, 147; and *Hyakushō bukuro*, 5–10 passim.

41. *Chōnin bukuro*, 143 passim.

42. Ibid., 115.

43. Dazai's *Keizairoku shūi* is contained in Rai Tsutomu, ed., *Nihon shisō taikei, 37: Sorai gakuha* (Tokyo: Iwanami shoten, 1972), 45–47. I have written on Dazai in "Political Economism in the Thought of Dazai Shundai (1680–1740)," *The Journal of Asian Studies* 31(1972):821–39.

Three

1. Tsuda Sōkichi, *Shina shisō to Nihon* (Tokyo: Iwanami shoten, 1938); and *Bungaku ni arawaretaru kokumin shisō* (Tokyo: Iwanami shoten, 1969).

2. I have edited with Irwin Scheiner essays on this general subject in *Japanese Thought in the Tokugawa Period* (Chicago: University of Chicago Press, 1978). See also Peter Nosco, ed., *Confucianism and Tokugawa Culture* (Princeton: Princeton University Press, 1984).

3. Hirose Tansō's piece "Jurin hyō" is in *Kinsei juka shiryō*, 3 vols. (Tokyo: Hanchō shobō, 1942), 1:1–22.

4. Tsuda Hideo, *Kinsei minshu kyōiku undō no tenkai* (Tokyo: Ochanomizu shobō, 1978), 77–92. The most complete reference to the Gansuidō is Umetani Noboru and Wakita Osamu, eds., *Gansuidō Tsuchihashi bunkō mokuroku* (Osaka: Osaka daigaku toshōkan, 1971); and they have compiled key documents in *Hirano Gansuidō shiryō* (Osaka: Seibundō, 1973).

5. Umetani and Wakita, *Hirano Gansuidō shiryō*, 322. Tsuchihashi's general account of the founding of the Gansuidō is his *Gansuidō ki* (Ibid., 260–63), which is sometimes credited to Miwa Shissai.

6. Ibid., 323.

7. Ibid., 325.

8. Ibid., 260–63.

9. Ibid., 329.

10. Of particular significance is Munenobu's (Tsuchihashi's son) discussion of the *Great Learning* which clarifies the differences with Itō: "Daigaku shigi," written around 1747, (Ibid., 328–30).

11. Tsuda, *Kinsei minshu kyōiku undō no tenkai*, 233.

12. Ibid., 225–70.

13. Umetani and Wakita, *Hirano Gansuidō shiryō*, 229–30.

14. Tsuda, *Kinsei minshu kyōiku undō no tenkai*, 187–90.

15. Umetani and Wakita, *Hirano Gansuidō shiryō*, 260; and Tsuda, *Kinsei minshu kyōiku undō no tenkai*, 98–138, 175–84, 202.

16. Miwa's generous views on the Kaitokudō are documented in Umetani and Wakita, *Hirano Gansuidō shiryō*, 260. See also Miyamoto Mataji, "Miwa Shissai no gakufū to Kaitokudō," *Nihon shisō shi* 20:3–19.

17. Nishimura Tenshū, *Kaitokudō kō* (Osaka: Kaitokudō kinenkai, 1923), 22–23. An account by a scholar intimate with the history of the Kaitokudō and its environs is Suenaka Tetsuo's "Kaitokudō gakuha no hito-bito," in *Edo no shisōka tachi*, 2 vols., edited by Sagara Tōru, Matsumoto Sannosuke, and Minamoto Ryōen (Tokyo: Kenkyūsha shuppan, 1979), 2:73–96. Also very informative are lectures published by Osaka University: Umetani Noboru, Wakita Osamu, Sakudo Yotaro et. al., *Osaka no gakumon* (Osaka, 1980). One of the best recent collaborative studies of the Kaitokudō by scholars close to Osaka historical scholarship is Kobori Kazumasa, Yamanaka Hiroyuki, Kaji Nobuyuki, and Inoue Akihiro, *Nihon no shisōka 24: Nakai Chikuzan–Nakai Riken* (Tokyo: Meitoku shuppan sha, 1980), especially 114–40. A suggestive essay is Wakita Osamu, "Chōnin gakumonjo to shite no 'kō,'" *Nihon shisō shi* 20:20–31. Important materials as well as essays are in journals and in pamphlets published by the Kaitokudō Association as in special issues such as *Kaitokudō yōran* (1942); and Kaitokudō Kinenkai, ed., *Kaitokudō no kako to genzai* (Osaki Kaitokudō Kinenkai, 1979).

18. All of the accounts of the Kaitokudō invariably refer to the five merchant comrades who played a crucial role in founding the Kaitokudō. See especially, Osaka shi sanjikai, ed., *Osaka shi shi*, 7 vols. (Osaka: Seibundō, 1978), 5:1077–78; Kobori, Yamanaka et al, *Nakai Chikuzan–Nakai Riken*, 12–30; and Nishimura, *Kaitokudō kō*, passim; Miyamoto Mataji, "Kaitokudō to Osaka no chōnin tachi," *Kaitokudō no kako to genzai*, ed. and published by Kaitokudō Kinenkai, 31–40.

19. The *Naijiki* and *Gaijiki*, internal and external affairs respectively of the Kaitokudō and known jointly as "Gakumonjo konryūki," are reproduced in Osaka shi sanjikai, ed., *Osaka shi shi*, vol. 5 and *Kaitoku* 12 (1934). Most of the basic documents, including these, were reissued in original form by Nishimura Tenshū and others in the commemorative collection known as *Kaitokudō ishō* (Osaka: Matsumura bunkaidō, 1911). I have relied heavily on this collection at the Kaitokudō archive in Osaka University. The details are also in "Kaitokudō kyūki shūi" reproduced in *Kaitoku* 14(1936):15–16.

20. The details are in "Kaitokudō kyūki shūi," ibid.

21. Osaka shi sanjikai, ed., *Osaka shi shi*, 1:795–96 and 5:1076–79; and *Naijiki*.

22. *Gaijiki*.

23. "Kaitokudō kyūki shūi," *Kaitoku* 14:11; and also Kobori, Yamanaka et al, *Nakai Chikuzan and Riken*, 52–55.

24. The letter is dated "sixth month, third day," probably of 1725; in ibid., 13–14.

25. Ibid., 9–12.

26. Ibid., 11.
27. Ibid.; and *Naijiki.*
28. A great deal has been written on the religious and communal form of the *kō*. Its relationship to the intellectual history of political economy remains to be analyzed. A good collection of essays is Sakurai Tokutaro, ed., *Sankaku shinkō kō no kenkyū* (Tokyo: Meichō shuppan, 1976); a standard work, also by Sakurai Tokutaro, *Kō shudan seiritsu katei no kenkyū* (Tokyo: Kōbunkan, 1962); also useful: Suzuki Eitaro, *Nihon nōson shakaigaku genri* (Tokyo: Jikōsha, 1940).
29. Tsuda, *Kinsei minshu kyōiku undō*, 3–48; Ishikawa Ken, *Nihon shomin kyōiku shi* (Tokyo: Tōkō shoin, 1929); and Shibata Minoru, *Baigan to sono monryū* (Kyoto: Mineruba shobō, 1977).
30. "Kaitokudō teiyaku" and "fuki," *Kaitokudō isho* and Osaka shi sanjikai, ed., *Osaka shi shi* 5:1083–90. Some of these documents as well as discussions are in pamphlets published by the Kaitokudō Association, *Kaitokudō yōran* (1942); and also Wakita Osamu, "Kaitokudō no seiritsu to sono keiei," *Kaitokudō no kako to genzai* (1979), 19–30.
31. "Kaitokudō teiyaku," *Kaitokudō isho* (see note 19 above).
32. Kobori, Yamanaka et al., *Nakai Chikuzan–Riken*, 52–55, 150–58.
33. The addendum to the basic rules, "Kaitokudō teiyaku fuki," is in *Kaitokudō isho.*
34. Ibid.
35. "Kaitokudō teiyaku," in *Kaitokudō isho* and *Osaka shi* 5:1083.
36. "Kaitokudō teiyaku fuki," in *Kaitokudō isho* and *Osaka shi* 5:1088.
37. Ibid.
38. Kobori, Yamanaka, *Nakai Chikuzan–Riken*, 39–42.
39. Miyake's "Ron-Mō Shushō kōgi" is included in *Kaitokudō isho*, 12 pp.
40. Ibid., "Ron-Mō," 2–4.
41. Ibid., 5.
42. Ibid., 7.
43. Ibid., 8.
44. Ibid., 9–10.
45. This is Nakai Shūan's "Towazu katari," included in Hayakawa Junzaburo et al., eds., *Nihon zuihitsu taisei*, 3d segment, vol. 3 (Tokyo: Nihon zuihitsu taisei kankōkai, 1933), 443–70.
46. Ibid., 460–61.
47. Nakai Chikuzan's "Kayōhen" is included in *Kaitokudō isho.*
48. See Kobori, Yamanaka, *Nakai Chikuzan–Riken*, 150–58.
49. See Nakazawa Morito and Mori Kazuo, *Nihon no kaimei shisō* (Tokyo: Kinokuniya shinshō, 1970), p. 61.
50. Ishida's *Tohi mondo* has been anthologized in numerous places. A good reference is in Ienaga et al., *Nihon koten bungaku taikei 97: Kinsei shisōka bunshū* (Tokyo: Iwanami shoten, 1966), 370–499, especially 399–434. The landmark analysis of Ishida's religious ideas is Robert N. Bellah, *Tokugawa Religion* (Glencoe: Free Press, 1957).

Four

1. See Ishihama Juntaro's discussion of Tominaga and his writings in Ienaga et al., *Nihon koten bungaku taikei 97: Kinsei shisōka bunshū* (Tokyo: Iwanami

shoten, 1966), 519–36; and also his earlier *Tominaga Nakamoto* (Osaka: Sōgen sha, 1940). Generous words of praise for Tominaga were written by the eminent scholar of Chinese history Naitō Kōnan in his essays on Tokugawa thinkers, "Sentetsu no gakumon," *Naitō Kōnan zenshū*, 14 vols. (Tokyo: Chikuma shobō, 1970), 9:315–519, especially on Tominaga, 370–93; and also by Takeuchi Yoshio, "Tominaga Nakamoto ni tsuite," *Takeuchi Yoshio zenshū*, 10 vols. (Tokyo: Kadokawa shoten, 1978–79), 10:318–37.

2. The *Okina no fumi* is in Ienaga et al., *Nihon bungaku taikei 97, Kinsei shisōka bunshū*, 539–61; and the *Shutsujō gogo* is in Mizuta Norihisa and Arisaka Takamichi, *Nihon shisō taikei 43: Tominaga Nakamoto–Yamagata Bantō* (Tokyo: Iwanami shoten, 1973), 11–138. See also Nakamura Hajime, *Kinsei Nihon no hihanteki seishin* (Tokyo: Shunjūsha, 1965), 171–240.

3. Tominaga, *Okina*, section 9, 554.

4. Tominaga, *Shutsujo*, section 1, 14–20.

5. Tominaga's original language on Ogyū is reproduced in Yoshida Toshio, "Tominaga Nakamoto no Rongochō bassetsu," *Kaitoku* 11(1933): 86–95.

6. Tominaga, *Okina*, section 11, 556–57.

7. Ibid., section 12, 557–58.

8. Tominaga, *Shutsujō*, section 11, 51.

9. Ibid., 51–53.

10. Ibid., 52.

11. Ibid.

12. Ibid.

13. Ibid., 104.

14. Tominaga *Okina*, sections 3 and 4, 548–50; and Tominaga, *Shutsujō*, sections 8 and 24, 38–42 and 88–92.

15. Ibid., 38–40.

16. Tominaga, *Okina*, section 14, 558–59.

17. Ibid., 559–60.

18. Ibid., 560–61.

19. Ibid., section 6, 551–52.

20. Ibid., 551.

21. Ibid., 552–53.

22. For Tominaga's views on Itō and Ogyū, Tominaga, *Okina*, section 6, 556–57 and Tominaga, *Shutsujō*, 88–92.

23. See my "Political Economism in the Thought of Dazai Shundai," *Journal of Asian Studies* 31(1972):821–39.

24. Quoted in Mizuta Norihisa, "Shutsujō gogo to Tominaga Nakamoto no shisōshi kenkyūhō," in *Nihon shisō taikei 43: Tominaga*, edited by Mizuta and Arisaka, 653–84, esp. 679.

25. Ibid. For Musō's piece, see Shirao Junkei, ed., *Nihon shisō tōsō shiryō* (Tokyo: Tōhō shoin, 1930), 3:239–66.

26. Mizutani, "Shutsujō gogo to Tominaga Nakamoto no shisōshi kenkyūhō," *Nihon shisō taikei 43: Tominaga Nakamoto*, edited by Mizuta and Arisaka, p. 680; Hirata Atsutane, *Shutsujō shōgo* in *Hirata Atsutane zenshū*, 14 vols. (Tokyo: Meichō shuppan, 1977), vol. 10; and *Nihon shisō tōsō shiryō*, 8:1–299, especially 1–2.

27. Umetani Fumio, "Shutsujō gogo no hanpon," *Nihon shisō taikei 43: Tominaga*, edited by Mizuta and Arisaka, 685–92.

28. Nishimura Tenshū, *Kaitokudō kō*, 37–45 and also his "Goi Ranju" *Kaitoku*, 37(1966):18–37. The high evaluation of Goi can be seen also in commentaries by his contemporaries: *Sentetsu sōdan*, 2 vols. (Tokyo: Shoseidō, 1892), 2:83–85. See also Haga Yoshichiro, "Goi Ranju to Yamazaki Ranshū," *Nihon rekishi* 166, 4(1962):87–100; and Kobori, Yamanaka, *Nihon no shisōka 24: Nakai Chikuzan-Riken*, 49–52.

29. Nakai's letter is the addendum of documents "Kaitokudō kyūki shui," *Kaitoku* 14(1936):9–12.

30. Nishimura, *Kaitokudō kō*, 31–32.

31. Ibid., 37–45.

32. Goi's *Meiwa* is included among the basic texts in the collection of documents, *Kaitokudō isho*. These texts are reproduced in the original Tokugawa print form and not published in modern form.

33. Goi, *Meiwa*, bk. 1, 28.

34. Ibid., 11 and also bk. 2, 24.

35. Ibid., bk. 2, 18.

36. Ibid., 9 and also bk 1, 12, 25–26.

37. Ibid., bk. 2, 15.

38. Ibid., bk. 1, 27; bk. 2, 15.

39. Ibid., bk. 9, 1–5.

40. Ibid., bk. 1, 4 passim.

41. Goi's *Hi-Butsu hen* unfortunately has not been transcribed and reprinted in modern type, and the only edition available is the 1766 version, a set of which is in the Kaitokudō archive at Osaka University.

42. Goi, *Hi-Butsu hen*, bk. 1, 13–14; bk. 6, 14–17.

43. Ibid., bk. 6, 23–24.

44. Ibid., bk. 1, 8; bk. 3, 28–29; and bk. 5, 4–5, 14.

45. Ibid., bk. 6, 33, passim.

46. Ibid., bk. 6, 16; bk. 5, 2–5.

47. Goi's view on nature is scattered throughout the *Hi-Butsu hen*: bk. 1, 14; bk. 2, 18; bk. 4, 4–8; bk. 6, 27–28.

48. Ibid., bk. 6, 27; bk. 4, 4–7; and bk. 5, 2–5.

49. From Ogyū's *Bendō*, section 17.

50. Goi, *Meiwa*, bk. 2, 19 and 36–37.

51. Ishida Baigan, *Tohi mondō* in *Nihon koten bungaku taikei 97: Kinsei shisōka bunshū*, edited by Ienaga et al., eds., 373–500, especially 435–62. Also, Iwahashi Junsei, *Dai Nihon rinri shisō hattatsu shi*, 2 vols. (Tokyo: Meguro shoten, 1915), 1:781–828; and Ishikawa Ken, *Ishida Baigan to "Tohi mondō"* (Tokyo: Iwanami shoten, 1968).

52. "Kaitokudō teiyaku fuki", Osaka shi sanjikai, ed., *Osaka shi* 5, 1083–90.

53. Goi, *Meiwa*, bk. 1, 16 passim. A few of the literary texts with Goi's critical annotations, texts used in his seminars, are included in the *Kaitokudō isho*.

54. Goi, *Meiwa*, bk. 1, 1–2; Nishimura, *Kaitokudō kō*, 38.

55. Goi, *Meiwa*, bk. 2, 28.

56. Ibid., bk. 1, 4 and bk. 2, 37.

57. Ibid., bk. 2, 22.

58. Ibid., bk. 2, 27–28.

59. Ibid.
60. Ibid., bk. 1, 28.

Five

1. Nishimura Tenshū, *Kaitokudō kō* (Osaka: Kaitokudō kinenkai, 1923), 43; Kobori Kazumasa, Yamanaka Hiroyuki et al., *Nihon no shisōka 24: Nakai Chikuzan–Nakai Riken* (Tokyo: Meitoku shuppansha, 1980), 46–52.
2. Nishimura, *Kaitokudō kō*, 55.
3. Kobori, Yamanaka, *Nakai Chikuzan–Riken*, 46–147, 179–278.
4. Nishimura, *Kaitokudō kō*, 54–55.
5. See "Kaitokudō kyūki shūi," *Kaitoku* 14 (1936), addendum, 9–12.
6. Ibid., 10.
7. Kobori, Yamanaka, *Nakai Chikuzan–Riken*, 55–78.
8. Ibid., 64–79; Nishimura, *Kaitokudō kō*, 58–59.
9. Nakai Chikuzan's account of the founding of the Kaitokudō, "Gakumonjo konryū ki," is in the commemorative collection of original documents, *Kaitokudō isho* (Matsumura bunkaidō, 1911). See also, Kobori, Yamanaka, *Nakai Chikuzan–Nakai Riken*, 89–94.
10. "Teiyaku fuki" in *Kaitokudō isho;* and Osaka shi sanjikai, ed., *Osaka shi* 5: 1083; and also Nishimura, *Kaitokudō kō* 59, 73–74.
11. Nakai Chikuzan, "Keizai yōgo," Takimoto Seiichi, ed., *Nihon keizai taiten*, 60 vols. (Tokyo: Meiji bunken, 1966) 23: 585–94, especially 585. This basic theme runs through Chikuzan's "textbook" for teaching youngsters, Nakai Chikuzan, *Chikuzan kokujidoku* (publication date not known), in *Kaitokudō isho*.
12. Nakai Chikuzan, *Chikuzan kokujidoku*, bk. 1, 3–4.
13. Ibid., bk. 1, 17.
14. Ibid., 18.
15. Hino Tatsuo, *Edojin to yūtopia* (Tokyo, Asahi shinbun sha, 1977).
16. Nakai Chikuzan, *Chikuzan kokujidoku*, bk. 1, 19–20.
17. Ibid., 10.
18. Ibid., 10.
19. Chikuzan's introduction to his *Hi-Chō*, in which he states his major arguments, is included in Nakamura Yukihiko and Okada Takehiko, eds., *Nihon shisō taikei 47; Kinsei kōki juka shū* (Tokyo: Iwanami shoten, 1972), 43–62. See also, Kobori, Yamanaka, *Nakai Chikuzan–Riken*, 132–47.
20. Nakai Chikuzan, *Chikuzan kokujidoku*, bk. 1, 11–12, 29.
21. Ibid., 21.
22. Ibid., 31.
23. Ibid., 32.
24. See Chikuzan's *Hi-Chō* in Nakamura and Okada, *Nihon shisō taikei* 47: 50, 45–58 passim.
25. Nakai Chikuzan, *Chikuzan kokujidoku*, bk. 1, 26–28.
26. Nakai Chikuzan, *Hi-Chō*, in Nakamura and Okada, *Nihon shisō taikei* 47: 55–56.
27. Nakai Chikuzan, *Chikuzan kokujidoku*, bk. 2, 22; Kobori, Yamanaka, *Nakai Chikuzan–Nakai Riken*, 301–9.
28. Nakai Chikuzan, *Chikuzan kokujidoku*, bk. 1, 28. This view is also stated

in Nakai's "Kankyō yohitsu," Seki Giichiro, ed., *Nihon jurin sōsho,* 14 vols. (Tokyo: Hō shuppan, 1927–38), 4:18 pp.

29. Nakai Chikuzan, "Kankyō yohitsu", Ibid., 4–6, 14.

30. Nakai Chikuzan, *Chikuzan kokujidoku,* bk. 1, 7–8 and bk. 2, 12–13.

31. Ibid., bk. 2, 15 passim.

32. Ibid., bk. 1, 7–8.

33. Ibid., bk. 2, 33.

34. Ibid., bk. 2, 33.

35. See Chikuzan's "Keizai yōgo," in *Nihon Keizai taiten,* 60 vols., edited by Takimoto Seiichi, 23:585–94, especially 587, (Tokyo: Meiji bunken, 1966).

36. Nakai Chikuzan, *Chikuzan kokujidoku,* bk. 1, 22–23.

37. A well-known piece, the *Sōbō kigen* has been anthologized in numerous collections. I have relied on Takizawa Seiichi, ed., *Nihon keizai taiten* 23: 315–543.

38. Ibid., 343–46 and 356–63.

39. The discussions here and below on the economy are mainly from Chikuzan's *Sōbō,* 444–55, 449–55, 458–64, and 465–68.

40. Ibid., 412–15.

41. Nakai Chikuzan, *Chikuzan kokujidoku,* bk. 2, 24.

42. Ibid., bk. 2, 37–43, especially 38.

43. Ibid., 37.

44. Ibid.

45. Nakai Chikuzan, *Sōbō,* 405–12; also, Takeiwa Hiroshi, *Nihon shomin kyōiku shi,* 2 vols. (Tokyo: Rinsen shoten, 1970), 1:403–14.

46. Nakai Chikuzan, *Sōbō,* 410–12.

47. Ibid., 413–15.

48. For various ideas on schools and educational reform, Nakaizumi Tetsuya, *Nihon kinsei gakkōron no kenkyū* (Tokyo: Kazama shobō, 1976), especially 283–301 on the Kaitokudō, and also, 471–81 on Shōji and 510–20 on Hoashi; Ishikawa ken, *Nihon shomin kyōiku shi* (Tokyo: Tōkō shoin, 1929), 67–75, 98–100, 260–67; and Takeiwa Hiroshi, *Nihon shomin kyōiku shi,* 2 vols. (Tokyo: Rinsen shoten, 1970), 1:403–14. Also for Hoashi, "Nyūgaku shinron" in Nakamura Yukihiko and Okada Takehiko, ed., *Nihon shisō taikei* 47: Kinsei kōki juka shū (Tokyo: Iwanami shoten, 1972), 163–220; and his biography by Hoashi Tonaji, *Hoashi Banri–Waki Guzan* (Tokyo: Meitoku shuppan sha, 1978). Waki Guzan's respectful comments about the Kaitokudō based on his study there at about age 24 are in his "Mishi yo no hito no ki," in *Zoku Nihon zuihitsu taisei,* edited by Mori Senzo and Kitakawa Hirokuni, 41 vols. (Tokyo: Yoshikawa kōbun kan, 1927–31), 3:3–29, especially 12–16.

49. Hoashi's ideas on education are included within a lengthy treatise on many subjects, including the coming of Western science, *Tōsenpu ron,* in *Nihon keizai taiten* 38, edited by Takimoto Seiichi. See also Nakamura, ed., *Nihon shisō taikei* 47:163–220.

50. Nishimura, *Kaitokudō kō,* 74–77. A much abbreviated version of Chikuzan's *Isshi* is in *Nihon keizai taiten,* edited by Takimoto 51:417–18. See also Tokinoya Masaru, "Kaitokudō no rekishi kan," *Nihon shisō shi* 20(1983):32–57.

51. Kobori, Yamanaka, *Nakai Chikuzan–Riken* 140–44; and Nishimura, *Kaitokudō kō,* 77.

52. Nishimura, *Kaitokudō kō,* 65–75, 88–89; and also Kobori, Yamanaka, *Nakai Chikuzan–Riken,* 114–47 passim.

53. Nishimura, *Kaitokudō kō,* 101.

54. Kobori, Yamanaka, *Nakai Chikuzan–Riken,* 203; and Naitō's "Riken gaku no eikyō" in his collected works, *Naitō Kōnan zenshū,* 9:434–46, especially 446.

55. Nishimura, *Kaitokudō kō,* 104.

56. The sense of restless "discontent" and "curiosity" that all of the late eighteenth-century eccentrics shared is a subject that deserves close historical analysis. Interpretive beginnings have been made by Haga Toru, *Watanabe Kazan* (Tokyo: Tankō sha, 1974) and, edited by the same author, *Nihon no meichō 22: Sugita Genpaku, Hiraga Gennai, Shiba Kōkan* (Tokyo: Chūō kōron sha, 1971). Also of interest is "The Western World and Japan in the Eighteenth Century" in *Hikaku bungaku kenkyū* 16(1978):1–27, in which he suggests an approach to the poet Yosano Buson. An excellent essay that discusses the concept of "play" in Kaiho is Hiraishi Naoaki, "Kaiho Seiryō no shisōzō," *Shisō* 11(1980):47–65. Yasumaru Yoshio has written "Kaiho Seiryō no rekishiteki itchi," *Meijō daigaku jinbun kiyō* 1(1963):1–23; and I have discussed Kaiho in "Method and Analysis in the Conceptual Portrayal of Tokugawa Intellectual History," in *Japanese Thought in the Tokugawa Period,* edited by Tetsuo Najita and Irwin Scheiner (Chicago: University of Chicago Press, 1978), 3–38.

57. Nishimura, *Kaitokudō kō,* 111; and Kobori, Yamanaka, *Nakai Chikuzan–Riken,* 196–221.

58. Nishimura, *Kaitokudō kō,* 105

59. Hino Tatsuo, *Edojin no yūtopia* (Tokyo: Asahi shimbun sha, 1977).

60. These are Riken's *Nanakei hōgen* and companion *Nanakei chōdai,* multi-volumed textual studies of the "seven" ancient classics. I have relied on the key studies such as on the *Great Learning,* the *Doctrine of the Mean, Mencius,* and the *Analects* that are included in Seki Giichiro, ed., *Nihon meika shisho chūshaku zensho,* 3 vols. entitled *Rongo-bu; Moshi-bu,* Gaku-Yō bu (Tokyo: Tōyō tosho kankō kai, 1923–26).

61. Takeuchi Yoshio, "Kaitokudō to Osaka no jugaku," *Takeuchi zenshū* 10: 338–60. See also Sagara Toru, *Kinsei no jukyō shisō* (Tokyo: Kōshobō, 1966), 200–207; and Naitō Kōnan on Riken in his "Sentetsu no gakumon," *Naitō Kōnan, Naitō Kōnan zenshū,* 14 vols. (Tokyo: Chikuma shobō, 1970), 9:434–47.

62. For example, his study of the *Analects, Rongo hōgen,* Seki, ed., *Nihon meika shisho chūshaku zensho: Rongo-bu* 22, 30–31, 58, 99, 107, 129, 139, 179, 226; and the same pattern can be discerned in his work on the "Mean," *Chūyō hōgen,* Seki, ed., *Nihon Meika shishō chūshaku zensho: Gaku-Yō bu,* 19–25.

63. Nakai Riken, Ibid. *Chūyō hōgen,* 71.

64. Ibid., 72.

65. Ibid., 74–75, 78.

66. On "study" as compared with "learning," Nakai Riken, Seki, ed., *Nihon meika: Rongo-bu, Rongo hōgen,* 10–22.

67. Ibid., 197.

68. Ibid., 2–11.

69. Nakai Riken, *Mōshi hōgen,* in Seki, ed., *Nihon meika shisho chūshaku zensho: Mōshi-bu,* 13–14.

70. Takeuchi Yoshio, "Kaitokudō to Osaka," in his collected works, *Takeuchi*

zenshū 10:338–60, especially 345–47; and "Eki to Chūyō no kenkyū", 323–335. Also pertinent is Sagara Toru, *Kinsei no jukyō shisō*, 200–206.

71. Nakai Riken, *Chūyō hōgen*, in Seki, ed., *Nihon meika shisho chūshaku zensho: Gaku-Yō bu*, 105 pp.

72. Ogyū's thinking on this is best stated in section 3 of his *Bendō*, available in Yoshikawa Kojiro, Maruyama et al., eds., *Nihon shisō taikei, 36: Ogyū Sorai* (Tokyo: Iwanami shoten, 1973).

73. Nakai Riken, *Chūyō hōgen*, 4–5.

74. Nakai Riken, *Chūyō hōgen*, 4–5, 18–19, 24, 61; and *Rongo hōgen*, 179, 225.

75. This passage is translated from Sagara's citation in *Kinsei no jukyō shisō*, 201.

76. Nakai Riken, *Chūyō hōgen*, 62; and also his brief analysis of the *Great Learning, Daigaku zatsugi* in Seki, ed., *Nihon meika: Gaku-Yō bu*, 1–24, especially 13–17.

77. Nakai Riken, *Rongo hōgen*, 272.

78. Nakai Riken, *Chūyō hōgen*, 62–63.

79. Nakai Riken, *Daigaku zatsugi*, Seki, ed., *Nihon meika: Gaku-Yō bu*, p. 18 and Nakai Riken, *Rongo hōgen*, Seki, ed., *ibid: Rongo-bu*, p. 225.

80. Nishimura, *Kaitokudō kō*, 109.

81. Nakai Riken, *Rongo hōgen*, 107, 179.

82. Nakai Riken, *Daigaku zatsugi*, 16–17.

83. Kobori, Yamanaka, *Nakai Chikuzan–Riken*, 271.

84. Ibid., 268–70.

85. Ibid., 217, 265–71; and Tokinoya, "Kaitokudō no rekishikan," *Nihon shisō shi* 20(1983):39–44.

86. Nishimura, *Kaitokudō kō*, 118–21, 268–70. I have touched on the Meiwa Incident in "Restorationism in the Political Thought of Yamagata Daini (1725–1767)," *The Journal of Asian Studies* 21(1971):17–29.

87. The various incidents are described by Nishimura, *Kaitokudō kō*, 119–23.

88. Nishimura, *Kaitokudō kō*, 124; and Kobori, Yamanaka, *Nakai Chikuzan–Riken*, 243.

89. Nakai Riken, *Kashokoku monogatari*, in Takimoto Seiichi, ed., *Nihon keizai taiten* 23:735–45.

90. Ibid., 743–45 passim. Also of interest is Naitō Kōnan, *Naitō kōnan zenshū* 9:434–46.

91. Summarized here are: "Nensei roku," "Kinden bōgi," "Yodogawa bōgi," and "Jukkei bōgi," all of which are in Takimoto, ed., *Nihon keizai taiten* 23:597–714.

92. Goi's *Meiwa*, bk. 1, 28 and bk. 2, 8–9, (in collection of documents, *Kaitokudō isho*; and cited in chap. 4 above).

93. Nakai Riken, *Chūyō hōgen*, 19–25; Kobori, Yamanaka, *Nakai Chikuzan–Nakai Riken*, 247–49.

94. Kobori, Yamanaka, *Nakai Chikuzan–Nakai Riken*, 214–17.

95. Ibid., 214.

96. Nishimura, *Kaitokudō kō*, 127–29.

97. Ibid., 106.

Six

1. The most detailed study of the various editions of this work is by Suenaka Tetsuo, *Yamagata Bantō no kenkyū*, 2 vols.: *Yume no shiro hen* and *Chosaku hen* (Osaka: Seibundō, 1971 and 1978). It is also anthologized in Takimoto Seiichi, ed., *Nihon keizai taiten* v. 37 (Tokyo: Meiji bunken, 1969); Mizuta Norihisa and Arisaka Takamichi, eds., *Nihon shisō taikei 43: Tominaga Nakamoto–Yamagata Bantō* (Tokyo: Iwanami shoten, 1973), already used with reference to Tominaga, and from which the citations on Yamagata will also be drawn; and in somewhat abridged form in Minamoto Ryoen ed., *Nihon no meichō 23: Yamagata Bantō—Kaiho Seiryō* (Tokyo: Chūō kōron sha, 1971). Interest in Yamagata Bantō in the modern era was generated via the writings of Naitō Kōnan and Kōda Rohan for the *Osaka Asahi* in 1910. As journalists, they were also involved in the compilation of the history of Osaka in which materials about the Kaitokudō were conspicuous. In Western language there is Albert Craig's "Science and Confucianism in Tokugawa Japan" in *Changing Japanese Attitudes Toward Modernization*, edited by Marius Jansen (Princeton: Princeton University Press, 1965), 133–60. A full bibliographical survey of works on Yamagata is in Suenaka, *Yamagata Bantō no kenkyū—chosaku hen.*

2. Kusama's *Sankà zu'i* is in Takimoto Seiichi, ed., *Nihon keizai taiten*, vols. 39 and 40.

3. Osaka shi sanji kai, ed., *Osaka shi shi*, vol. 5 (Osaka: Seibundō, 1978), 973–1027 passim.

4. Kaiho's *Masuko dan* is in the Takimoto Seiichi, ed., *Nihon keizai sōsho*, 36 vols. (Tokyo: Nihon keizai sōsho kankōkai, 1914–17), vol. 18, and summarized in his larger synthesis, *Keiko dan*, Tsukutani Akihiro and Kuranami Seiji, eds., *Nihon shisō taikei*, vol. 44.

5. See the introduction to *Sanka zu'i* in, *Nihon keizai taiten*, vol. 39. Also, Nishimura, *Kaitokudō kō*, 53–60 and 90.

6. Compiled at about the same time as his *Sanka*, this work remains unpublished in modern form.

7. The best coverage is Nakamura Kōya, *Genroku oyobi Kyōhō ni okeru keizai shisō no kenkyū* (Tokyo: Kokumin bunka kenkyūkai, 1927). The classic study on this general subject is Honjo Eijiro, *Kinsei no keizai shisō* (Tokyo: Nihon hyōron sha, 1931). See also Takao Shimazaki, "Kinsei kaibutsu shisō no ichi kōsatsu," *Mita gakkai zasshi* 71, no. 5 (1978): 20–42; and also "Introduction to the Economic Thought of Japan," *Keio Economic Studies* 5(1968): 11–34.

8. Nakamura, *Genroku oyobi Kyōhō*, 460; also Honjo, *Kinsei no keizai shisō*, 1–42.

9. Nakamura, *Genroku oyobi Kyōhō*, 498–512; Honjo, *Kinsei no keizai shisō* 43–62. Ogyū Sorai's economic prescriptions are in his *Seidan*, Yoshikawa, Maruyama et al., *Nihon shisō taikei* 36: 260–445.

10. Saigusa Hiroto, ed., *Miura Baien shū* (Tokyo: Iwanami shoten, 1953), 37–82; and Nakamura, *Genroku oyobi Kyōhō*, 545–52.

11. Miura Baien, *Kagen*, Saigusa, ed., *Miura Baien shū*, 40–42 passim.

12. Nakamura, *Genroku oyobi Kyōhō*, 513–21, 556–79. I have written, "Political Economism in the Thought of Dazai Shundai (1680–1747)," *The Journal of Asian Studies* 31(1972): 821–39.

13. See selections of Dazai's writings in Rai Tsutomu, ed., *Nihon shisō taikei 37: Sorai gakuha* (Tokyo: Iwanami shoten, 1972), 18–56.

14. Kusama, *Sanka zu'i*, Takimoto, ed., *Nihon keizai taiten* 39:326.

15. Ibid., 39:259.

16. Ibid., 39:170–72 passim.

17. Ibid., 39:262–63.

18. Ibid., 39:281–86.

19. Ibid., 40:3–17.

20. Osaka shi sanji kai, ed., *Osaka shi*, 5:789–971. Also, Kusama, *Sanka zu'i*, 40:156–57, 184–202, 223.

21. Kusama, *Sanka zu'i*, 39:145–50; 40:156–57, 184–202.

22. Kusama Naokata, "Kusama Isuke hikki," in Osaka shi sanji kai, ed., *Osaka shi*, 5:842.

23. Kusama, *Sanka zu'i*, 40:183–202.

24. Ibid., 40:12–13.

25. Ibid., 40:10–12, 437–48.

26. Ibid., 40:1–12, 437.

27. Ibid., 40:5–6.

28. Ibid., 40:1–2.

29. Ibid., 40:1–2.

30. Ibid., 39:285; 40:53, 146.

31. Ibid., 39:"Introduction."

32. Ibid., 39:1–14.

33. The details of Yamagata's biography are in Suenaka Tetsuo's *Yamagata Bantō no kenkyū, Chosaku hen*. Also valuable are Kamata Jiro's pioneering study, *Yamagata Bantō* (Osaka: Zenkoku shobō, 1943) and Naitō Kōnan on Yamagata in "Sentetsu no gakumon," in his collected works, *Naitō kōnan zenshū*, 9:448–64.

34. Arisaka Takamichi, "Yamagata Bantō to 'Yume no shiro,'" in *Nihon shisō taikei* 43:693–728, especially 707.

35. Ibid., 707–10.

36. My essay, "Method and Analysis in the Conceptual Portrayal of Tokugawa Intellectual History," in *Japanese Thought in the Tokugawa Period*, 3–37, especially 23–36, outlines Kaiho's description of Yamagata. Yamagata's straightforward advice and prescriptions to the leaders of Sendai are in his "Itchi kyōwa taisaku ben," with accompanying letter, in *Kinsei shakai keizai sōsho*, 12 vols. edited by Honjo Eijiro (Tokyo: Kaizō sha, 1926–27), 5:295–324. The ideas set forth in these are incorporated in his *Yume*.

37. Arisaka, "Yamagata Bantō to 'Yume no shiro,'" 43:711.

38. Yamagata, *Yume no shiro*, in *Nihon shisō taikei*, vol. 43, edited by Mizuta and Arisaka, 141–616, especially 616. All subsequent citations of *Yume* are from this collection.

39. Ibid., 142.

40. Ibid., 146.

41. Suenaka, *Yamagata Bantō, Yume no shiro hen*, 354–490 and his afterword in English, 1–22.

42. Yamagata, *Yume*, 216.

43. Ibid., 149 passim; and also for the genealogy of scholars of Dutch Studies in Osaka, inclusive of Yamagata, see Fujino Tsunezaburo, ed., *Ogata Kōan to*

Tekijuku (Osaka: Tekijuku kinen kai, 1980), 6–13; and Miyamoto Mataji and Sakudo Yotaro, "Tekijuku to Osaka chōnin," *Osaka no gakumon* (Osaka: Osaka daigaku, 1980), 149–70. A technical study that looks at "science" rather than "ideology" is Shigeru Nakayama's *A History of Japanese Astronomy, Chinese Background and Western Impact* (Cambridge: Harvard University Press, 1969).

44. Yamagata, *Yume*, 213; and also 153–57, 171, 187–88, 193–99.
45. Ibid., 245, 253–54, 263–69.
46. Ibid., 286.
47. Ibid., 293.
48. Ibid., 270–98.
49. Ibid., 297–98.
50. Ibid., 298.
51. Ibid., 304–9, 323–24.
52. Ibid., 333.
53. Ibid., 334.
54. Ibid., 340.
55. Ibid., 335–36; and also Dazai's "Keizairoku shūi," in Rai, ed., *Nihon shisō taikei* 37:45–56.
56. Yamagata, *Yume*, 364.
57. Ibid., 353–57.
58. Ibid., 367.
59. Ibid., 370.
60. Ibid., 372–73.
61. Ibid., 375–76.
62. Ibid., 378–85.
63. Ibid., 378–79.
64. Ibid., 383, 397–400.
65. Ibid., 389.
66. Ibid., 410.
67. Ibid., 424.
68. Ibid., 427; and also 425–26.
69. Ibid., 448–583.
70. Ibid., 487–99, 506 passim.
71. Ibid., 509.
72. Ibid., 571; also 520–40 and 550–51.
73. Ibid., 582–83.
74. Ibid., 594.
75. Ibid., 507.
76. Ibid., 432.
77. The text of Miura's agreement for his village cooperative, "Jihi mujin" is in Shinozaki Tokuzo, *Jihi mujin no sōshisha, Miura Baien* (Tokyo: Chūō shakaijigyō kyōkai shakai jigyō kenkyūjo, 1936), 53–57.
78. A fine presentation of Miura's basic ideas, as well as texts, is Yamada Keiji, ed., *Nihon no meichō 20: Miura Baien* (Tokyo: Chūō kōron sha, 1982), especially his thorough introduction, 3–295. See also Taguchi Masaharu, *Miura Baien no kenkyū* (Tokyo: Sōbun sha, 1978); and Saigusa Hiroto, *Miura Baien no tetsugaku* (Tokyo: Dai ichi shobō, 1941). I have relied here on Miura's own explanation of his basic thesis in *Gengo,* as written to one of his students in 1776, that has been

compiled as "Taka Bokkyō kun ni kotauru sho," in *Miura Baien shū*, edited by Saigusa, 9–31.

79. Miura, "Taka Bokkyō kun," 12.

80. Ibid., 13–14.

81. Ibid., 15.

82. Ibid., 15–25, passim.

83. Ibid., 27.

84. Yamagata, *Yume*, 616.

Seven

1. From Ueda Akinari's memoirs, *Kandai shōshin roku* as quoted in Kobori Kazumasa, Yamanaka Hiryoyuki et al., *Nakai Chikuzan–Nakai Riken* (Tokyo: Meitoku shuppan sha, 1980), 149.

2. Ueda's views are documented in Shikada Seishichi, *Kenkadō shi* (Osaka: Shōundō, 1901), 10–21. See also Takahashi Mitsuji, *Kenkadō shoden* (Tokyo: Kenkadō kinen kai, 1926); and Osaka shi sanji kai, ed., *Osaka shi shi*, 7 vols. (Osaka: Seibundō, 1978), 1:1158–60 and 2:139 passim.

3. Kimura's diary is *Kenkadō nikki* (Osaka: Kenkadō kinen kai, 1970).

4. Shikada, *Kenkadō shi*, 12.

5. Nishimura Tenshū, *Kaitokudō kō* (Osaka: Kaitokudō kinenkai, 1923), 133–44.

6. The monographic literature on the Tenpō period is extensive and deserves systematic attention among Western historians. Most social and economic histories of the Meiji Restoration by Japanese historians, quite correctly it seems to me, begin with this Tenpō reference. A suggestive collection of essays in this regard is Nishikawa Shunsaku, *Edo jidai no poritikaru economee* (Tokyo: Nihon hyōron sha, 1979), 114–38. The subject retains its importance in general historical accounts, as for example: Tsuda Hideo, *Nihon no rekishi 22: Tenpō kaikaku* (Tokyo: Shōgakkan, 1975); Aoki Michio and Yamada Tadao, eds., *Tenpō ki no seiji to shakai* (Tokyo: Yūhikaku, 1981); and Aoki Michio, *Tenpō sōdō ki* (Tokyo: Sanseidō, 1979). Informative scholarly essays, especially with regard to social responses in Kyoto, are in Hayashiya Tatsusaburo, ed., *Bakumatsu bunka no kenkyū* (Tokyo: Iwanami shoten, 1978); and also Hongo Yakamori and Fukaya Katsumi, eds., *Kinsei shisō ron* (Tokyo: Yūhikaku, 1981). Apropos these various works are many of the essays by Ichii Saburo on "tradition" and "transformation" in his *Kinsei kakushin shisō no keifu* (Tokyo: Nihon hōsō shuppan kyōkai, 1980). An extensive and detailed eyewitness account of some of the events of this period is *Ukiyo no arisama*, compiled by an anonymous author, probably a physician in Osaka (*Nihon shomin seikatsu shiryō shūsei*, 20 vols., Tokyo: Sanichi shobō, 1970, 11:1068).

7. See for example Nakase Juichi, "Ōshio jiken to Izumiya Sumitomo no 'kaji kaikaku'—Tenpō kaikaku zenya o chūshin ni—," *Ōshio kenkyū* 9(1980):1–14.

8. Discussions of Ōshio's rebellion are in the citations in the previous two notes. A fine discussion of Ōshio and his ideas is in Miyagi Kimiko, ed., *Nihon no meichō 27: Ōshio Chūsai* (Tokyo: Chūō kōron sha, 1978). I have written "Ōshio Heihachirō (1793–1837)" in *Personality in Japanese History*, edited by Albert Craig (Berkeley: University of California Press, 1970), 155–79. There has been a revival of interest in Ōshio in recent years in the Osaka area as wit-

nessed in the periodic publication of a journal devoted to that subject: *Ōshio kenkyū*.

9. Nakase, "Ōshio jiken to Izumiya Sumitomo," *Ōshio kenkyū* 9:1–14.

10. "Kaitokudō yawa," *Kaitoku* 15 (1937): addendum, 19.

11. Nishimura, *Kaitokudō kō*, 137.

12. Najita, "Ōshio," 158–70.

13. Miyagi, *Nihon no meichō* 27:73–273.

14. Kobori, Yamanaka, *Nakai Chikuzan–Riken*, 171–78.

15. Najita, "Ōshio," 175.

16. Ogata Tomio, *Ogata Kōan den* (Tokyo: Iwanami shoten, 1963); Ban Tadayasu, *Tekijuku o meguru hito bito—Rangaku no nagare* (Osaka: Sōgen sha, 1978); and Tekijuku kinen kai, ed., *Ogata Kōan to Tekijuku* (Osaka: Tekijuku kinenkai, 1980); and Naramoto Tatsuya, ed., *Nihon no shijuku* (Tokyo: Tankō sha, 1969), 232–48. A stimulating work on Dutch Studies, including about Ogata Kōan, is Akagi Akio, *Rangaku no jidai* (Tokyo: Chūō kōron sha, 1980).

17. Ogata, *Ogata Kōan den*, 81.

18. Ban Tadayasu, "Tekijuku no enkaku," *Osaka no chōnin gakumon* (Osaka: Osaka University, 1980), 77–92, especially 82. Especially insightful is Kurauchi Kazuta, "'Teki tekisai juku' to 'Kaitokudō,'" *Tekijuku* (Tekijuku kinen kai, 16, 1980), pp. 3–11.

19. Ogata, *Ogata Kōan den*, 146.

20. Miyamoto Mataji and Sakudo Yotaro, "Tekijuku to Osaka chōnin," *Osaka no gakumon*, 149–70, especially 150–53.

21. Ogata, *Ogata Kōan den*, 16–19.

22. Tekijuku kinenkai, ed., *Ogata Kōan to Tekijuku*, 15, 55–57; and also Ban Tadayasu and Umetani Noboru, "Tekijuku no hito bito," *Osaka no gakumon*, 127–44.

23. Shiba Tetsuo and Matsuda Takeshi, "Nihon no kindaika to Osaka no gakumon—Seimikyoku—Osaka igakkō nado—," *Osaka no gakumon*, 171–88.

24. Ban, *Tekijuku o meguru hito bito*, 88–116.

26. *The Autobiography of Yukichi Fukuzawa*, translated by Eiichi Kiyooka (New York: Columbia University Press, 1960), 58–92.

26. Ibid., 13.

27. Ibid., 68–71, for Fukuzawa's language against superstitions and dreams. Also of interest is Nishikawa Shunsaku's "Fukuzawa Yukichi," *Keizai seminaa* 19(1983):72–79.

28. See Harry D. Harootunian's excellent discussion of Sakuma in his *Toward Restoration* (Berkeley: University of California Press, 1970), 129–83; and also directly pertinent is the chapter on Yokoi Shōnan, 321–79.

29. The entire second volume of Shibuzawa's collected works, *Shibuzawa Eiichi zenshū*, 6 vols. (Tokyo: Heibon sha, 1930) is his *Jikken Rongo*. Written toward the end of his career it is a complex statement that deserves close analysis. Also suggestive for this theme is Cho Yukio, ed., *Gendai Nihon shisō taikei 11: Jitsugyō no shisō* (Tokyo: Chikuma shobō, 1964).

30. Cited in Tokinoya Masaru, "Kaitokudō no enkaku," *Kaitokudō no kako to genzai* (Osaka: Kaitokudō kinenkai, 1979), 6–18, especially 18. Also, Kimura Hideichi, "Kaitokudō to wa nanika," *Kaitokudō no kako to genzai* (Osaka: Kaitokudō kinenkai, 1953), 1–18, especially 12.

INDEX

Index

www.ingramcontent.com/pod-product-compliance
Lightning Source LLC
Chambersburg PA
CBHW020334270326
41926CB00007B/182